TOY STORY

Animation: Key Films/Filmmakers

Series Editor: Chris Pallant

Titles in the Series:

Toy Story: How Pixar Reinvented the Animated Feature edited by Susan Smith, Noel Brown and Sam Summers

Princess Mononoke: Understanding Studio Ghibli's Monster Princess edited by Rayna Denison

Norman McLaren: Between the Frames by Nichola Dobson

TOY STORY

How Pixar Reinvented the Animated Feature

Edited by

Susan Smith, Noel Brown and Sam Summers

Bloomsbury Academic
An imprint of Bloomsbury Publishing Inc

B L O O M S B U R Y

NEW YORK • LONDON • OXFORD • NEW DELHI • SYDNEY

Bloomsbury Academic
An imprint of Bloomsbury Publishing Inc

1385 Broadway
New York
NY 10018
USA

50 Bedford Square
London
WC1B 3DP
UK

www.bloomsbury.com

BLOOMSBURY and the Diana logo are trademarks of Bloomsbury Publishing Plc

First published 2018

Library of Congress Cataloging-in-Publication Data
A catalog record for this book is available from the Library of Congress.

ISBN: HB: 978-1-5013-2491-8
ePDF: 978-1-5013-2492-5
eBook: 978-1-5013-2493-2

Cover design by Louise Dugdale
Cover image © Jesse Grant/Stringer/Getty images

Series: Animation: Key Films/Filmmakers

Typeset by Newgen KnowledgeWorks Pvt. Ltd., Chennai, India

CONTENTS

INTRODUCTION

Noel Brown, Susan Smith and Sam Summers

Toy Story (John Lasseter, 1995) is a cinematic landmark, a commercial phenomenon and an icon of contemporary popular culture. Very few films have been so popularly and critically celebrated or so influential. As Hollywood's first wholly computer-generated feature, and the first full-length film to be produced by Pixar Animation Studios, *Toy Story*'s significance was apparent well before its initial theatrical release in November 1995. An immediate box office hit, it went on to become the highest-grossing film of the year in North America, and eventually earned over $300 million internationally. The film's success can also be gauged by the numerous awards it has received, the glowing testimonials and its consistently high ranking in surveys of the best films ever made.[1] Indeed, *Toy Story* has become a hugely lucrative multimedia franchise that encompasses three theatrical sequels (at the time of writing) and numerous books, games, theme park rides and merchandise and licensing tie-ins. All of these have extended the parameters of the text into different media, each with their own storytelling possibilities. At the centre of the franchise, of course, is the original *Toy Story* film. It is, in our view, one of only a handful of Hollywood animated films that can legitimately be said to have redefined the medium.

As the chapters in this book demonstrate, there is a great deal that can be said about the *Toy Story* phenomenon. While many responses to the film have centred on its technical accomplishments, critics have also noted its particular appeal to adults as well as children, its 'hipness', its modern sensibilities, its indebtedness to postmodern literary and artistic movements and its engagement with tropes and conventions of Hollywood cinema (and of consumer culture more broadly). Almost single-handedly, *Toy Story* established computer-generated imagery (CGI) animation as a central pillar of the contemporary Hollywood cinema, and announced Pixar as a major creative force. The post-*Toy Story* generation has come to think of animation primarily as a computer-generated form. Computer animation had widely been used to augment cel-animated films in Hollywood during the 1980s, and director John Lasseter's acclaimed CGI short films for Pixar, *Luxo, Jr.* (1986) and *Tin*

Toy (1988), demonstrated its aesthetic potential. But *Toy Story* was the critical intervention, proving that it could sustain an entire feature-length production; every subsequent computer-generated animated film has followed in its path. Although CGI animation draws on many of the conventions of cel animation dating back to the 1920s, *Toy Story* introduced new aesthetic styles and production methods that later films have built upon.

Toy Story is a relative rarity in being a mainstream animation that has attracted a good deal of scholarly attention. It is the subject of a recent volume in the British Film Institute's 'Film Classics' series, and of the international conference (*Toy Story at 20*, hosted in November 2015 by the University of Sunderland) that is the precursor of this book; it is also, as one chapter in this volume explicitly argues, a work of 'art'. Prior to the release of *Toy Story*, popular perceptions of animation were of a traditionally hand-drawn form in the classical Disney mould, despite the long history of other styles, such as three-dimensional puppet and stop-motion animation. The seriousness with which *Toy Story* was received by film critics undoubtedly contributed to the subsequent growth of animation studies as an academic discipline, as well as to the upsurge in scholarly literature on children's films and family films. Like the *Toy Story* films themselves, these areas of enquiry are now global in reach (a fact reflected in the international calibre of contributors to this book).

This volume builds on such prior research, but explores *Toy Story* with greater breadth and depth. It examines the film's industrial and cultural contexts, production history, aesthetic innovations and reception and legacy. In pursuing these themes, we have aimed for a comprehensive but wide-ranging selection of chapters that encompass a variety of critical, theoretical and methodological approaches. The collection begins with Peter Krämer's chapter, '*Toy Story*, Pixar and Contemporary Hollywood'. Krämer here contextualizes *Toy Story* within broader developments in post-1970s Hollywood cinema, particularly concentrating on the mainstream trend towards adaptations and sequels, and Pixar's incongruity as a successful developer of 'new stories': those that are neither adapted from other sources nor sequels to previous films. Krämer goes on to identify other areas in which Pixar has differentiated itself from its competitors. He notes the unprecedented commercial success of its films both domestically and internationally, pointing out that the critical responses to Pixar releases, similarly, are far more favourable than is typical for animated features. Finally, he situates the themes of the *Toy Story* films – especially their engagement with everyday concerns – in relation to those of Hollywood family-orientated blockbusters more broadly.

Noel Brown's chapter, '*Toy Story* and the Hollywood Family Film', also situates the film within broader histories of mainstream Hollywood cinema. Brown points out that while *Toy Story* has often been discussed in terms of its technological innovations, it is also a key text in its engagement with the inherited conventions of the family film genre. More specifically, the film embodies a dialectic between consolidation and innovation. Brown argues that the film's basic narrative framework can be linked to classical-era Hollywood family films, with its use of spectacle, adult stars, nostalgia for childhood, moral overtones and 'happy ending' all being recurrent characteristics of the genre. Conversely, the film's modes of comedy are seen as innovative in several key regards: in their self-avowed 'hipness'; in their self-reflexivity and allusions to other films and to contemporary pop culture; and in their doubly coded visual and verbal gags. Brown, like Krämer, suggests that part of *Toy Story*'s appeal lies in its engagement with contemporary social norms, thus differentiating it from the displaced temporality of Disney's fairy-tale films. He concludes by comparing *Toy Story* to post-1990s live-action Hollywood family films, noting several areas where its influence – and that of other computer-animated features – is strongly apparent.

In his chapter, 'The Cowboy, the Spaceman and the Guru: Character and Convention in the Screenwriting of *Toy Story*', Andrew Gay considers the role the film played in developing Pixar's reputation for strong and effective storytelling. Asking how a team of animators inexperienced in feature film writing learnt this craft to such effect, Gay pinpoints two shaping influences over the development of *Toy Story*'s screenplay: the storywriting principles of Robert McKee and the genre conventions of the buddy picture. By exploring how each of these find their way into the specifics of *Toy Story*'s script, Gay then poses the question: how can Pixar's reputation for inventiveness be reconciled with this adherence to convention? He finds that the answer lies (as for Brown) in an interaction between innovation and convention in *Toy Story*. In particular, he points to the film's ability to avoid cliché by reworking storytelling conventions in new, imaginative ways as central to *Toy Story*'s success, establishing an approach that would be adopted elsewhere in Pixar works.

Heather L. Holian's chapter, 'New and Inherited Aesthetics: Designing for the *Toy Story* Trilogy One Film at a Time', explores the visual aesthetic that characterizes the entire film series. With particular reference to the design work of Pixar's art director, Ralph Eggleston, Holian outlines some of the key creative decisions that led to the 'look' of *Toy Story*. She describes the design process as collaborative, with Eggleston and his team working with creative input from John Lasseter. Drawing on personal interviews with many of the design team, Holian argues that the film's aesthetic was dictated, to some degree, by technical limitations at the time of production. She notes the influence of the painter Grant Wood and the illustrator and painter Maxfield Parrish on the film's often saturated colour palette and bright lighting. However, the design work also contains pertinent allusions to other films; the upstairs carpet in Sid's house, for instance, resembles the hotel carpet in Stanley Kubrick's horror film *The Shining* (1980), reflecting the darker mood of these sequences. Holian then moves on to discuss the design work in *Toy Story 2* and *Toy Story 3*, noting that these sequels retained a high degree of fidelity to the visual aesthetic established in the first film, despite the technical advances made in the intervening years.

In 'Rough and Smooth: The Everyday Textures of *Toy Story*', Lucy Donaldson also considers the film's visual aesthetic but does so in relation to debates about the dramatic limitations or possibilities of CGI. Considering critiques of the film in terms of whether digital filmmaking promotes merely a surface sheen and hence lacks depth or offers possibilities for achieving materiality, substance and sensory engagement, Donaldson finds significance in *Toy Story*'s ability to create a fictional world that is expressively textured according to a counterpoising of rough and smooth surfaces. Analysing key elements of the film, Donaldson demonstrates the ways in which surfaces are distinctly rendered, layered and their scale manipulated. Acknowledging the collaborative contributions of *Toy Story*'s visual effects artists, she reveals the importance of texture in materializing *Toy Story*'s universe in ways that are deeply imbricated with the dramatic concerns of the film, have the capacity to connect with the everyday nature of our own lives and are fundamental to shaping the kinds of feelings that certain spaces and characters evoke.

Christopher Holliday's chapter, 'Toying with Performance: *Toy Story*, Virtual Puppetry and Computer-Animated Film Acting', argues for computer animation in general, and *Toy Story* in particular, as a site of digital puppetry. Animated characters, as Holliday observes, are 'virtual marionettes' controlled by the animator. *Toy Story*'s various instances of on-screen puppetry – in which Andy is seen manipulating his toys in various ways – serve as a creative analogue of how computer-animated film performance is engineered through a similar encounter between an invisible performer (the animator) and the visible performing object. Holliday also emphasizes the collaborative nature of film performance. On-screen characters like Woody and Buzz, while inflected with the vocal performances of actors Tom Hanks and Tim Allen, also bear the imprint of creative and technical personnel such as artists, animators, designers, painters and sculptors. *Toy Story*'s visions of puppet manipulation, Holliday argues, are thus inherently self-reflexive, acknowledging the techniques of puppetry that are fundamental to the illusionism of the medium itself. Holliday's analysis of *Toy Story* through this lens adds to an ever-expanding body of scholarship on performance in digital cinema.

In her chapter 'Toy Stories through Song: Pixar, Randy Newman and the Sublimated Film Musical', Susan Smith focuses on musical performance, an aspect central to the appeal of *Toy Story* and its sequels yet all too often marginalized by scholars writing in this area. Arguing that such neglect manifests itself even in places where one might expect the *Toy Story* songs to receive fuller attention, Smith considers Randy Newman's contribution in terms of his role as collaborator rather than *auteur* and interrogates the idea that Pixar's innovative approach to music and sound arises from a rejection of the Disney animated musical format. Using close analysis of the three songs in *Toy Story* and the various reworkings of 'You've Got a Friend in Me' in *Toy Story 2* and *3*, she explores the ways in which these are sensitively attuned to the conditions of the toys' existence. This leads her to contemplate that *Toy Story* may actually enjoy an expectedly subtle relationship with the musical, the sublimated elements of which emerge more strongly (almost like a return of the repressed) in the sequels.

An integral part of the landscape of *Toy Story* is, of course, the toys themselves, many of which are drawn directly or indirectly from actual, ownable playthings. In 'From Shelf to Screen: Toys as a Site of Intertextuality', Sam Summers looks at how the filmmakers bring to life familiar real-world products, as well as original characters inspired by common toy archetypes, in order to root the action of the film in a setting recognizable as contemporary North America. By manipulating intertextual fields, including tapping into the uniquely intimate and nostalgic feelings associated with childhood toys, the film compounds the emotional affectivity of its settings and characters, whether this be the comforting familiarity and innocence of Andy's room or the visceral body-horror and uncanny anxiety of Sid's house.

In her chapter on 'Fear, Guilt and the Future of Play in *Toy Story*', Karen Cross takes a psychoanalytical approach which shifts focus from the typically Oedipal, father-centric readings of the film to look at the narratives of play which are enacted through its story. Moving on from the extra-textual understanding of nostalgia and familiarity introduced in Sam Summers's chapter, Cross examines the relationship between toy and fictional child, and how this evolves over the course of a trilogy which spans Andy's childhood. This discussion acts as a platform to address the Toy Story series' articulation of the maternal bond, as well as anxieties surrounding consumption and even its own mode of production.

In 'Mirrors and Shadows: Duality, Illusion and the Divided Self in *Toy Story*', Jane Batkin confronts the reflection in *Toy Story*'s many sheen surfaces, providing a Lacanian psychoanalytical account of the binary oppositions established in the film. Drawing on the symbolism of the mirror, the shadow and the doppelganger, and the history of these concepts in psychoanalytical theory, Batkin shines a light on the duality of the film's characters, illuminating the ways in which Woody and Buzz, Sid and Andy reflect one another and the dualities that they reveal within themselves.

In 'Woody, Buzz and the Koons Corollary. . . Or Why *Toy Story* Is Art', Paul Wells provocatively enquires how the film (and the trilogy) is allied to the cultures of 'Art'. Noting some of the issues arising from discursive use of this term and its application to a work of mainstream animation and popular entertainment, Wells considers *Toy Story*'s eligibility for such status within several contexts and with regard to the film's (and series') ongoing cultural relevance and significance. Ranging far beyond Hollywood, animation and cinema, he situates *Toy Story*'s emergence in relation to North American arts culture and the film's eligibility as (pop) art, arguing that artist Jeff Koons offers a compelling point of comparison with Pixar, especially where this film and trilogy are concerned. Through detailed scrutiny of their creative rationales, Wells finds parallels in Pixar and Koons's shared interest in speaking directly to adults while at the same time rooting their approach, among other things, in an association with children and childhood and a belief in the power of their work to provoke emotional and imaginative engagement.

With a view to the film's legacy, Helen Haswell takes a retrospective look at the film and its sequels in 'Story Is King: Understanding the *Toy Story* Franchise as an Allegory for the Studio Narrative of Pixar Animation'. The focus here is on Pixar's creative culture and the emphasis the studio places on narrative when developing its films. Using this as a basis for a reading of the trilogy as a metaphor for Pixar's complex relationship with Disney, casting the high-tech Buzz as the innovative CGI studio and the antiquated Woody as the older corporation, the chapter also serves as a definitive history of the often-fraught creative collaboration between the two entities.

In the book's final chapter, 'An Interview with Steve Segal', the *Toy Story* animator provides a valuable insight into the production process of the film, and on the challenges and motivations for an independent animator during the 1970s and 1980s prior to being employed at Pixar. Segal begins by recalling his childhood making flip-books and the prize-winning series of short films he made as a student at Virginia Commonwealth University. He discusses his subsequent career making commercials and educational films, as well as the film he spent almost ten years animating with co-director Phil Trumbo, the cult success *Futuropolis* (1984). Segal moves on to talk about his friendships with John Lasseter and screenwriter Joe Ranft, and how this eventually led to his employment as an animator on *Toy Story*. Finally, Segal gives some revealing insights into what a 'typical day' working on the film was like, the creative process during production, his thoughts on Lasseter as an 'auteur' and the feeling of anticipation at the studio shortly before the film's release.

Note

1 The film's accolades are too many to fully enumerate here, but they include its addition to the US Library of Congress's National Film Registry; its three Academy Award nominations and eight Annie Awards; and its placing of #44 in *The Hollywood Reporter*'s 'Hollywood's 100 Favorite Films' poll, #99 in *Empire Magazine*'s survey of the 500 greatest movies, #101 in the IMDb's user-generated list of the best films ever made, and #95 in Rotten Tomatoes' list of the best-reviewed films ever made.

Chapter 1

TOY STORY, PIXAR AND CONTEMPORARY HOLLYWOOD

Peter Krämer

In 1995, the press book for *Toy Story* (John Lasseter, 1995) announced it as 'the first full-length animated feature to be created entirely by artists using computer tools and technology': 'Four years in the making, this delightfully irreverent new comedy-adventure combines an imaginative story and great characters with the visual excitement of 3D computer-generated animation.'[1] The film was thus presented as the coming together of a long tradition of high-quality storytelling and recent technological innovations, the former embodied in the output of the Walt Disney Company and the latter the specialty of Pixar, which the press book introduced as 'a Northern California-based pioneer in computer graphics'.[2]

Disney and Pixar were said to have 'join[ed] creative forces' on this film project,[3] their relationship 'dat[ing] back to 1987, when the two companies embarked on a joint technical development effort' (known as CAPS) for which they received the 1992 Academy Award for Scientific and Technical Achievement.[4] In 1991, said the press book, 'Disney and Pixar entered a three-picture deal . . . with *Toy Story* being the first film to be green-lighted.'[5] It was 'conceived and directed by John Lasseter', Pixar's 'vice president of creative development' who was 'a former Disney animator'.[6] Indeed, following on from an early interest in animated movies, Lasseter had been one of the first students on an animation course that Disney had set up at the California Institute of the Arts (CalArts). According to the press book, he had 'apprenticed at Disney' during summer breaks, and worked for five years in the company's 'feature animation department' after his graduation in 1979: 'Inspired by Disney's ambitious and innovative film *Tron* [Steven Lisberger, 1982], which used computer animation to create its visual effects', Lasseter produced an experimental short film and eventually left Disney for 'the Computer Division of Lucasfilm, Ltd.'[7]

When Steve Jobs acquired the division, the press book continued, 'it was incorporated as an independent company' under the name Pixar.[8] Lasseter, who had won Student Academy Awards for animated shorts made at CalArts, wrote and directed Pixar's first computer-animated short, *Luxo Jr.* (1986), which was nominated for the Best Animated Short Film Oscar, an award won by Lasseter's third Pixar short, *Tin Toy* (1988), in 1989.[9] Already at Lucasfilm, the later Pixar team had been responsible, said the press book, for 'computer animation sequences' in major blockbusters such as *Star Trek II: The Wrath of Khan* (Nicholas Meyer, 1982) and *Return of the Jedi* (Richard Marquand, 1983), while their software had also been used in all of Disney's animated features from *The Little Mermaid* (Ron Clements and John Musker, 1989) onwards, and for special effects sequences in blockbusters such as *Terminator 2: Judgment Day* (James Cameron, 1991) and *Jurassic Park* (Steven Spielberg, 1993).[10]

The press book summarized Pixar's unique status as follows: 'Pixar has been responsible for almost every major breakthrough in the application of computer graphics to filmmaking', in both animated and live-action films; and 'in recognition of its pioneering work in computer animation, the company and its employees have to date been awarded 12 Academy Awards'.[11] In this way, the press book positioned Pixar at the centre of three important developments in Hollywood cinema: the digital enhancement of special effects in live-action movies (especially in the science fiction genre); the digital enhancement of traditional cel animation (initially at Disney); and the production of computer-animated features, starting with *Toy Story*.[12]

The first two developments concerned genres which had come to be very prominent in box office charts both in the United States and in the rest of the world by the mid-1990s. The reign of science fiction – previously, with very few exceptions, a marginal genre at the box office – had started with *Star Wars* (George Lucas, 1977) and had recently included the success of *Terminator 2: Judgment Day* and *Jurassic Park*.[13] Disney's animated features had, after several decades in which the company mostly relied on the success of re-releases, returned to the top of the charts, somewhat tentatively with *The Little Mermaid* in 1989, and then triumphantly with *Beauty and the Beast* (Gary Trousdale and Kirk Wise, 1991), *Aladdin* (Clements and Musker, 1992) and *The Lion King* (Roger Allers and Rob Minkoff, 1994), all of them digitally enhanced.[14]

As is well known, *Toy Story* and Pixar's subsequent features, as well as computer-animated films by other companies, were able (more or less) to match the box office success of Disney's hits of the early 1990s, and traditional cel animation disappeared from the charts.[15] At the same time, the digital enhancement of live-action films proceeded to the point where some, including several of Hollywood's biggest hits, most notably *Avatar* (Cameron, 2009), consisted to a considerable degree of computer generated imagery, and thus could be categorized as live-action/computer-animation hybrids.[16] The implied promise of the *Toy Story* press book that Pixar and its technologies would transform Hollywood has thus come to pass, but only, it has to be noted, because two of Hollywood's leading companies – Lucasfilm and Disney – provided necessary support along the way (all three companies now, of course, belong to the same corporate entity).

I have discussed the ways in which George Lucas and Disney have shaped contemporary Hollywood cinema in various previous publications, in which I have also begun to explore the role of Pixar.[17] In this chapter I extend my earlier work by situating the *Toy Story* films in the context of Pixar's overall output, and also within hit patterns at the US box office and in Hollywood's export markets. I pay particular attention to the increasing box office dominance of adaptations and sequels, and highlight Pixar's role as one of the few hugely successful generators of *new* stories (i.e. stories that are neither adapted from other sources nor sequels to previous films) in contemporary Hollywood. I then examine both the first *Toy Story* film and its two sequels in terms of the rather complex and very peculiar stories they tell.

I should explain that I use the shorthand 'films based on original scripts' for films that are neither adaptations nor sequels; this is in line with the Academy Award categories which consider scripts for sequels under 'Best Adapted Screenplay' rather than as original screenplays. It is worth pointing out that the question whether a film is an adaptation is not always easy to answer, because one might want to consider whether a source text is acknowledged in the film's credits, or how close a film is to a particular source text. This is a difficult issue especially with regard to films featuring superheroes from comic books. For the purposes of this chapter, I count all of them as adaptations, and I also count both reboots of superhero franchises, and all but the first film in a series (such as the James Bond series) as sequels.[18]

Hits, Original Scripts and Animation

It is an easily overlooked fact that until 1976, the vast majority of the biggest box office hits in the United States were adaptations of books (including the Bible) and Broadway shows.[19] In most cases, the source book or show had been very successful in its own right before being adapted into a hit movie. However, *Star Wars* and *E.T. The Extra-Terrestrial* (Spielberg, 1982), which were the biggest breakaway hits of the late 1970s and early 1980s, were based on original scripts, and the majority of the other big hits of this period were also based on original scripts, or they were sequels to such originals.[20] While sequels had occasionally been very successful before 1977, they became much more prominent in the charts from the late 1970s onwards. Nevertheless, for about two decades after 1977, films that were neither adaptations nor sequels were much more successful at the US box office than they had ever been before. While it is difficult to gather sufficient evidence for the decades before the 1970s, it would seem that the same applies to Hollywood's export markets, although, as we will see, the shift after 1977 towards hit films based on original scripts was less pronounced outside the United States.

In previous publications, I have compiled charts which allow us to compare Hollywood's biggest domestic hits since 1977 with its biggest export hits; I have done so by listing the ten biggest hits from the Internet Movie Database's all-time domestic and foreign charts for each five-year period from 1977 onwards.[21] The resulting domestic top ten for the period 1977–81 contained three adaptations – *Grease* (Randal Kleiser, 1978), which was based on a hugely successful Broadway show, as well as *Superman* (Richard Donner, 1978) and *Superman II* (Richard Lester, 1980), featuring a classic comic book character. Apart from *Superman II*, the only other sequel in the top ten was *The Empire Strikes Back* (Irvin Kershner, 1980). The foreign top ten for these five years contained four sequels (including three films in the James Bond series), and altogether six adaptations: the three Bond films, *Grease*, *Superman* and *Saturday Night Fever* (John Badham, 1977), which was based on a long magazine article. Only three of the top ten films were based on original scripts, as compared to five in the domestic top ten.

For the periods 1982–86, 1987–91, 1992–96 and 1997–2001, the number of films based on original scripts in the foreign top ten increased slightly so that by and large it matched the number of such films in the domestic top ten, which went down a little bit. However, starting with the period 2002–6, films based on original scripts almost disappeared from both charts. During those five years, the only film which was neither an adaptation nor a sequel in either chart was Pixar's *Finding Nemo* (Andrew Stanton and Lee Unkrich, 2003), and the only film based on an original script in the top tens for 2007–11 was *Avatar*.

In the preliminary charts (as of 29 June 2016) for the most recent period (since 2012), both top tens are made up entirely of sequels and adaptations, and the only films based on original scripts which come close to the top tens are Pixar's *Inside Out* (Pete Docter and Ronnie del Carmen, 2015) and Walt Disney Animation Studios' *Zootopia* (Byron Howard and Rich Moore, 2016).[22] Interestingly, already during the periods 1992–96 and 1997–2001, half of the films based on original scripts in the domestic top ten were animated features: the Pixar movies *Toy Story* and *Monsters, Inc.* (Pete Docter and David Silverman, 2001) as well as Disney's *The Lion King*. In other words: while for many decades the vast majority of Hollywood's animated features had been adapted from fairy tales and classic children's books, since the mid-1990s animation has become the area most likely to generate original scripts which become the basis for films able to compete, at least at the US box office, with otherwise completely dominant adaptations and sequels. And the most successful generator of such scripts is, of course, Pixar.

Pixar's Commercial and Critical Success

From 1995 to June 2015 (the month *Inside Out* came out), Pixar released fifteen animated features, presenting a new film in almost every year since 1998 (the exceptions being 2000, 2002, 2005 and 2014, which means that in the last decade Pixar has only missed out on a single year). All of these fifteen films made it into the top ten of the *annual* US box office charts.[23] The highest ranked Pixar films in the United States were *Toy Story* (no. 1 in 1995), *Toy Story 2* (no. 3 in 1999), *Finding Nemo* (no. 2 in 2003), *Cars* (no. 3 in 2006) and *Toy Story 3* (no. 1 in 2010). Only in three of the fifteen years with a Pixar release was that film beaten at the domestic box office by an animated movie from another company – namely by the first three *Shrek* films in 2001, 2004 and 2007. Thus, Pixar did not only clearly dominate the field of animation in the domestic market, but was able to deliver an unbroken string of hits over a period of twenty years, which is an achievement without historical precedent. The fact that *The Good Dinosaur* (Peter Sohn), released in November 2015 (2015 thus becoming the first year with two Pixar releases), was regarded as a huge box office disappointment, despite its domestic gross of $123 million (which placed the film at no. 26 in the annual chart), only confirms that the company's overall track record has been utterly exceptional.

Pixar's performance in foreign markets has been similarly unprecedented, but ever so slightly less impressive. All but two of Pixar's first fifteen releases made it into the top ten of the *annual* export charts, and the remaining two only missed the top ten very narrowly, being placed at numbers 11 and 12, respectively.[24] Once again, *The Good Dinosaur* fell short (with a foreign gross of $209 million, it is nowhere near the top ten).[25] The highest ranked Pixar films abroad were *Monsters, Inc.* (no. 3 in 2001), *Finding Nemo* (no. 2 in 2003) and *Toy Story 3* (no. 3 in 2010). While these three films were the top-grossing animated films in foreign markets during their year of release, the other Pixar releases were beaten in the export charts by animated features from other companies (in some years by more than one). The more successful competitors included three *Ice Age* sequels (from Blue Sky), all three films in the *Despicable Me* franchise (from Illumination), three films in the *Shrek* franchise, two *Kung Fu Panda* movies and three *Madagascar* sequels (all from DreamWorks) as well as Disney's *Pocahontas* (Mike Gabriel and Eric Goldberg, 1995), *Tarzan* (Kevin Lima and Chris Buck, 1999) and *Frozen* (Chris Buck and Jennifer Lee, 2013).

While the consistently high level of success of Pixar films in foreign markets was thus almost as daunting as it was in the domestic market, abroad the company did not dominate the field of animation to anywhere near the same degree. It is worth noting at this point that the number of commercially successful animated features has increased dramatically since the mid-1990s, not only because more studios have become involved in the production of hits based on original screenplays but also because they released a large number of highly successful sequels to such hits.

Over the years, there have been some concerns about Pixar's move towards the production of sequels, because it could be seen as a kind of sell-out.[26] The company's first sequel, *Toy Story 2* (Lasseter), came out in 1999, and three of its six releases between 2010 and 2015 were sequels (or prequels): *Toy Story 3* (Lee Unkrich), *Cars 2* (Lasseter, 2011) and *Monsters University* (Dan Scanlon, 2013). To some extent, concerns about sequels have been alleviated by the perceived quality of *Toy Story 2* and *Toy Story 3* (although the same cannot be said about the other two films). More fundamentally, however, I want to highlight Pixar's remarkable *restraint* when compared with the rampant sequelization of hit movies elsewhere in the field of animation and also in the live-action sector.[27] As previously hinted, the main reason for the spread of sequelization is that, commercially, it works remarkably well. During the periods 2002–6, 2007–11 and 2012–16, the top tens for both the domestic and the foreign markets were dominated by sequels, usually accounting for seven or eight of the top ten hits. Thus, Pixar stands out from the rest of Hollywood not only because it is consistently successful at the box office, but also because it achieves such success with a comparatively small proportion of sequels (only 25 per cent of its overall output up to this point; however, starting with the release of *Finding Dory* [dir. Andrew Stanton] in June 2016, it seems that Pixar also is going to focus on sequels).[28]

In addition, most Pixar releases were, rather unusually for Hollywood's biggest hits, highly acclaimed by critics,[29] and also by industry peers. Most notably, Pixar films were nominated ten times for the Best Animated Feature Oscar (introduced in 2001); that is, ten out of thirteen films that *could have been* nominated *were* nominated (the exceptions being *Cars 2*, *Monsters University* and *The Good Dinosaur*). Pixar *won* the award eight times – for *Finding Nemo*, *The Incredibles* (Brad Bird, 2004), *Ratatouille* (Bird, 2007), *WALL-E* (Stanton, 2008), *Up* (Docter, 2009), *Toy Story 3*, *Brave* (Mark Andrews and Brenda Chapman, 2012) and *Inside Out*. What is more, *Up* and *Toy Story 3* were nominated for Best Picture Oscars, becoming only the second and third animated films in history – after *Beauty and the Beast* – to be honoured in this fashion.

Perhaps most significantly, *Toy Story*, *Finding Nemo*, *The Incredibles*, *Ratatouille*, *WALL-E*, *Up* and *Inside Out* were all nominated for Best Original Screenplay, and *Toy Story 3* for Best Adapted Screenplay. Indeed, rather than focusing primarily on technological innovation, both statements by Lasseter and other Pixar representatives, and reviews of Pixar films have, from the outset, highlighted the importance of scripts – of stories, characters and themes. The press book for *Toy Story 2*, for example, introduced the film as follows: 'Buzz Lightyear, Woody and a colorful cast of toys are joined by a delightful group of new characters for an incredible action-filled comedy-adventure that is loaded with laughs, emotion and surprises.'[30] It goes on to refer to 'storytelling magic', mentions that *Toy Story* had been 'the first animated feature ever to be nominated' for the Best Original Screenplay Oscar and quotes co-director Lee Unkrich: 'The film taps into a lot of themes and a lot of primal human emotions – being afraid of growing up and getting older, being afraid of your kids moving away from home, etc.'[31]

Richard Schickel's review of *Toy Story 2* in *Time* magazine observed that 'Woody . . . confronts toy mortality, the temptations of celebrity and, yes, the possibilities of sexual adventure.'[32] And in his *Newsweek* review, David Ansen agreed that Woody was now facing existential problems, and he declared the sequel's storytelling to be 'tight, urgent and inventive', before asking: 'Why can't scripts this clever be written for human beings' (i.e. for live-action movies)?[33] The trade press tended to agree. Thus, Kirk Honeycutt wrote in the *Hollywood Reporter* that *Toy Story 2* 'does what few sequels ever do: Instead of essentially remaking an earlier film . . . [it] delves deeper into its characters while retaining the fun spirit of the original film . . . As with the original film, *Toy Story 2* is a meditation on friendship and fears of abandonment.'[34]

While it would, of course, be of great interest to study all of Pixar's films with regard to their stories, characters and themes, in the context of a book on *Toy Story* it is appropriate for me to restrict myself to the three *Toy Story* movies. Continuing with the approach of this chapter so far, I relate the stories told in these three to those told in Hollywood's other big hits.

The World of the Toy Story *Movies*

At the most basic level, we might say that the *Toy Story* films are set in contemporary America. This rather banal observation gains significance against the backdrop of the ever-increasing prominence in US box office charts since 1977 of films set in the past, the future, an alternative universe and/or outside the United States. This tendency is *more* pronounced in export charts. Even when considering hit movies set *in* contemporary America, we can note that in these films the everyday world is often completely transformed by the intrusion of supernatural forces, encounters with aliens or new technologies.

Hence, the ten top US hits for the years 1992–96 include, in addition to *Toy Story* (at no. 8), four films set (largely or exclusively) in a recognizable version of contemporary (or perhaps near-future) America, whereby the everyday world is disrupted by an alien invasion in one of these four films (*Independence Day* [Roland Emmerich, 1996]). Thus, only three films are set in a version of contemporary America that *remains* recognizable by the end of the film. For the years 1997–2001, the US top ten include, apart from *Toy Story 2* (at no. 10), only two films set in contemporary America, in one of which ghosts intrude upon the everyday world (*The Sixth Sense* [M. Night Shyamalan, 1999]), while in the other it is aliens and a secret, high-tech organization (*Men in Black* [Barry Sonnenfeld, 1997]). Finally, the US top ten for 2007–11 include, in addition to *Toy Story 3* (at no. 3), four films set in a more or less recognizable version of contemporary America, in three of which alien robots transform everyday existence (the first three *Transformers* films) while in the fourth this is done by radioactively induced superpowers and destructive futuristic technologies (*Spider-Man 3* [Sam Raimi, 2007]). Thus, among Hollywood's biggest domestic hits, films set in contemporary America, without this world being transformed by fantastic or science fiction elements, have become very rare indeed (and this applies even more to Hollywood's biggest export hits), the *Toy Story* films standing out as such rare exceptions.

Of course, there is more to the *Toy Story* films than a straightforward depiction of contemporary America. In fact, we can identify at least two different narrative realms in the films: the realistic, contemporary American realm of the humans and the otherworldly, magical realm of living toys. Obviously, the focus of all three films is on the toy world. Perhaps not so obviously, its relationship to the human world is rather complicated.

The realm of toys is often directly influenced by the human realm. For starters, whenever a human appears, the toys know that they have to play dead – whereby it is not altogether clear how this works with delusional toys who do not even realize that they are the playthings of humans (this applies in particular to Buzz Lightyear for most of the first film). By playing with the toys, humans give them a sense of a meaningful existence (as their self-defined purpose in life is to be played with), and also much joy and the feeling of being loved. What is more, humans can damage toys, accidentally or on purpose; they can lose interest in them, steal them, sell them, put them into storage or give them away. Indeed, in all three films the main storyline is set in motion, and often given further dramatic turns, by such human acts, which shake up the previously well-ordered world of Andy's toys.

At the same time, the toys in their true form as thinking and feeling, goal-oriented agents have very little influence on the realm of humans – partly because one of the basic rules of their lives is that humans must never become aware of their existence as independent beings, but also because they largely avoid manipulating humans, which they *could* do without revealing themselves. Thus, in the human realm, which remains largely unaffected by the agency of toys, these toys exist as lifeless objects that are only given life by human imagination during play.

There are several occasions in which the toys *do* interfere with the human realm, most of them very minor, but some not so trivial. In *Toy Story* the toys reveal themselves to Sid so as to save Buzz from being blown up, and also to teach Sid a lesson about how to treat his toys. Later on they cause a series of car crashes. *Toy Story 2* features many more accidents in the human world which are caused by the toys, and this time they have an impact on the life of the toyshop owner Al by ruining his best ever sales deal. At the end of *Toy Story 3*, they do not reveal themselves but secretly manipulate Andy so that he gives his toys to Bonnie rather than storing them away (perhaps for his own future children) in the attic.

In some ways, then, the structure of the *Toy Story* films is similar to that of the majority of Hollywood's top hits set in contemporary America in recent years, insofar as they reveal the existence of another layer of reality next to, or within, the everyday world. Indeed, the first *Toy Story* film references the (adjusted for ticket-price inflation)[35] most successful of these Hollywood blockbusters – *E.T. The Extra-Terrestrial*, which tells the story of an alien stranded on Earth and of the boy who befriends him. In one scene of *E.T.*, Elliott's sister Gertie dresses the alien in women's clothes, just as Sid's sister does with Buzz in *Toy Story* (while in *Toy Story 2* a girl at the airport announces that Stinky Pete will get a makeover). The difference between the *Toy Story* films and hit movies like *E.T.* is that the second layer of reality does *not* serve to transform the everyday world. In *E.T.* the alien helps to bring first the siblings and then the whole family (as well as other people) closer together, thus healing wounds the family had previously suffered. But, as already stated, in the *Toy Story* films the toys have minimal influence on Andy and his family (although they do have an impact on the bad guys).

In *E.T.* (as well as many other Hollywood hit movies since 1977), the reason why the family needs healing in the first place is a deeply problematic father – in the case of *E.T.* a man who has left his wife and children.[36] Interestingly, the very same configuration is constantly hinted at in all three *Toy Story* films, because Andy's father is never seen and thus likely to have left his wife and two children, just like Elliott's father did (Sid's father, who is seen for a few seconds sleeping in front of the television set, does not appear to be a very constructive presence either). This suggests a particular reason for the complete dedication of Andy's toys to their owner, for their perception that they have to be there for him at all times, that the joy and meaning in their lives derive from being with him (especially during play): in a sense, the toys have to stand in for the absent father. Their dedication to Andy is that of a truly committed, loving parent. (*E.T.* also serves, albeit only temporarily, as such an ideal parental figure.) Once Andy leaves his home, starting a life separate from his parent(s), it therefore makes sense that, in *Toy Story 3*, his toys are given to Bonnie whose father also appears to have left (although there is a background figure appearing for a few seconds at the end of the film who could be Bonnie's father).

In fact, if we do not understand the toys' dedication to children in parental terms, it becomes a very uncomfortable kind of social relationship to deal with. The frequent reference to the fact that the toy characters are owned by someone evokes the institution of slavery (a connection the evil bear in *Toy Story 3* makes quite explicit), whereas the unthinking, almost automatic way in which many of the toys want to serve human beings, evokes the idea of entities that are programmed to serve, such as brainwashed people or robotic machines. If one were indeed to understand the toy characters as slaves – and what is more, as slaves who by and large embrace their enslavement wholeheartedly – or as beings who have been thoroughly brainwashed, or as robots, the films would perhaps become even more interesting than they are already, but they would also, I think, become much less enjoyable. The latter does not apply if the toys are, implicitly, understood as parental, and especially as paternal substitutes.

As already indicated, I have tried to show in previous publications that problematic fathers or father figures – problematic because they are absent, weak, abusive or just plain evil – constitute a central issue in the stories of many of Hollywood's biggest hits since 1977.[37] The archetype of such a father in contemporary Hollywood is Darth Vader, who was first introduced in *Star Wars*. In this film, it is not yet revealed that Luke Skywalker is his son, although we do find out that Luke has lost his biological father, and in the course of the film also loses his adoptive father and his fatherly mentor. It is, I believe, no coincidence that, before Buzz is enlightened about his status as a toy in *Toy Story*, he inhabits a *Star Wars*-like universe, complete with an evil emperor, an ultimate weapon and crucial knowledge about its only weakness. And in *Toy Story 2*, another unenlightened Buzz finally confronts his nemesis and learns that it is in fact his father (just like Luke learns at the end of *The Empire Strikes Back* that Darth Vader is his father).

Thus, the *Toy Story* films playfully address what is arguably the key problematic of contemporary Hollywood's biggest hits, with specific reference to the very film which has come to define the contemporary period in American (and world) film history. *Toy Story 2* also presents a quick and happy solution: the unenlightened Buzz plays catch with his father – whereas in *Return of the Jedi*, Darth Vader has to sacrifice himself so as to save his son and thus redeem himself. In a way, in *Toy Story 2* fatherhood and child's play become identified with each other, which echoes the argument I made earlier that Andy's toys can be understood as stand-ins for his absent father. I do *not* want to claim that the absent father is the key issue of the *Toy Story* films. On the contrary, it seems to me that contemporary Hollywood's tendency to focus on problematic father figures is made fun of here, or, at the very least, the father problematic is treated very lightly. In fact, the single women and their fatherless children seem to be coping just fine, and the only kid who is rather disturbed is Sid, whose father is still around.

Similarly, the division in many of Hollywood's biggest hits in recent decades between the everyday world of contemporary America and a fantastic or science fiction layer, whereby the latter brings about a transformation of the former, is not so much replicated in the *Toy Story* films as it is playfully referenced. The story of the toys in these films is *not* focused upon a transformation of the human world. And therefore, by implication, the films which carry the title 'Toy Story' are not going to transform the audience's everyday world. By contrast, the story of *E.T.* is about the character E.T. transforming the world of Elliott's family as well as that of various bystanders, which is clearly meant to suggest that the film *E.T.* will do the same for its audience.[38] This also applies to many other Hollywood hits, in which the relationship between the everyday world of contemporary America and a second realm of fantasy and science fiction models the relationship between the everyday world of the audience and the movie: in the same way that the realm of fantasy and science fiction transforms the everyday world within the film, the film itself is meant to be understood by the audience as an opportunity to transform their own everyday world. Once again, I should clarify: I do *not* want to claim that the *Toy Story* films critique the operations of other Hollywood blockbusters, only that they playfully reference them, which, following the logic of their stories, is a worthwhile thing to do. After all, the idea that play is a joyful and meaningful activity in its own right – both for humans and for toys – is at the very heart of the *Toy Story* films.

Conclusion

In this chapter I have discussed the *Toy Story* films with reference to Pixar's overall output and to important trends among Hollywood's biggest (domestic and export) hits of recent decades. I have tried to show that the *Toy Story* films stand out from, but also how they engage with, dominant narrative and thematic patterns. In doing so, I have only just begun to discuss the films' narrative complexity and thematic richness. Among many other things, there is so much more to be said about the ways in which the films explore the role of storytelling as well as various forms of non-narrative play and make-believe in our lives.

Across the three films, we observe Andy and other kids (notably Sid, his sister and Bonnie) playing with their toys, imagining simple scenes or complex stories. We also encounter commercials, a television puppet show and a computer game featuring versions of the toys Andy and other kids own. Occasionally we enter the world imagined by kids or constructed by a computer game, experiencing it from the inside, as it were. And we encounter toys, like Buzz Lightyear (for parts of all three films) and the aliens, who mistake the world of the imagination for reality, as well as other toys who watch commercials or television drama with emotions ranging from utter dismay to complete absorption. What, then, do the films tell us about the function of the make-believe situations and stories we create and consume?

More specifically, the *Toy Story* films do, of course, have a lot to say about the place of actual toys in contemporary culture. Focusing on this could lead us to address questions such as the following: To what extent are changing toy fashions and the changing toy preferences of children who are growing up, a rehearsal for a culture of consumption? Can the 'love' for individual toys serve to counteract a commodity culture based on the principle of built-in obsolescence? To what extent can various forms of reuse (via yard or, more likely, online sales, storage for the next generation, donations to other people or institutions) alleviate the wastefulness of commodity culture? Is children's interaction with toys and other commodities replacing their interaction with people (in the *Toy Story* films, children rarely, if ever, play with each other or their parents)? And what is the implication of all this for the sale of the toys featured in the movies to the movies' audiences?

Obviously, the *Toy Story* films also use the magical realm of living toys to examine the complexities of human existence, with regard to both children and adults. From this analytical perspective, we could deal with some of the following issues: sibling rivalry; social hierarchies in groups of friends and work organizations as well as their strategies of inclusion and exclusion; fears of abandonment and death; the search for purpose and meaning in life as well as the anxiety to lose the purpose and meaning one's life once had. Our engagement as viewers and scholars with the *Toy Story* films thus allows, indeed encourages, us to contemplate the very foundations of our existence.

Notes

1 Press book for *Toy Story*, p. 13; in the press clippings collection of the Deutsche Filminstitut, housed at the Deutsche Nationalbibliothek, Frankfurt am Main, Germany.
2 Ibid., p. 13.
3 Ibid.
4 Ibid., p. 41.
5 Ibid.
6 Ibid., pp. 13, 47.
7 Ibid., pp. 40, 47–48.
8 Ibid., p. 40.
9 Ibid., p. 47.
10 Ibid., pp. 40–41.
11 Furthermore, 'Pixar has twice received the advertising industry's highest award' for its TV commercials; ibid., p. 40.
12 For detailed histories of computer graphics and Pixar, see, for example, David A. Price, *The Pixar Touch: The Making of a Company* (New York: Vintage, 2009); Charles Solomon, *The Toy Story Films: An Animated Journey* (New York: Disney Editions, 2012); Stephen Prince, *Digital Visual Effects in Cinema: The Seduction of Reality* (New Brunswick: Rutgers University Press, 2012); Richard McCulloch, *Towards Infinity and Beyond: Branding, Reputation, and the Critical Reception of Pixar Animation Studios*, unpublished PhD dissertation (University of East Anglia, 2013); and Ed Catmull with Amy Wallace, *Creativity, Inc.: Overcoming the Unseen Forces that Stand in the Way of True Inspiration* (London: Bantam, 2014).
13 Peter Krämer, 'Hollywood and Its Global Audiences: A Comparative Study of the Biggest Box Office Hits in the United States and Outside the United States since the 1970s', in Richard Maltby, Daniel Biltereyst and Philippe Meers (eds), *Explorations in New Cinema History: Approaches and Case Studies* (Oxford: Wiley-Blackwell, 2011), pp. 171–84, esp. pp. 175–76.
14 Ibid., pp. 175–76. It is also worth noting the success of the live action/cel animation hybrid *Who Framed Roger Rabbit* (Robert Zemeckis, 1988).
15 The exceptions have been several of Studio Ghibli's productions which earned so much money at the Japanese box office that they also rank quite highly in worldwide box office charts; cp. http://www.boxofficemojo.com/alltime/world/ (accessed 24 March 2016).

16 Cp. the films included in this hybrid category by the website 'The Numbers', http://www.the-numbers.com/market/ProductionMethods/AnimationLiveAction.php (accessed 24 March 16).

17 See especially Peter Krämer, 'Disney, George Lucas und Pixar: Animation und die US-amerikanische Filmindustrie seit den 1970er Jahren', *Film-Konzepte*, no. 33 (February 2014): 6–21, and Peter Krämer, 'The Rise of Animation', *Pure Movies*, 7 October 2014. http://www.puremovies.co.uk/columns/the-rise-of-animation/.

18 One could also classify a reboot as a remake, and a remake as a particular form of adaptation, namely an adaptation of an earlier film, rather than of a non-filmic source text.

19 Peter Krämer, *The New Hollywood: From Bonnie and Clyde to Star Wars* (London: Wallflower Press, 2005), ch. 1. I should point out here that the American film industry trade press from which I derive box office figures and charts counts Canada as part of the domestic market. It would be too cumbersome always to refer to the US/Canada chart, which is why I use 'American' or 'US' as a shorthand for the domestic market. Hollywood's export or foreign market excludes both the United States and Canada, but once again I am using 'non-American' or 'non-US' as a shorthand.

20 Krämer, *The New Hollywood*, Conclusion.

21 Krämer, 'Hollywood and Its Global Audiences', pp. 175–76; cp. Peter Krämer, 'Welterfolg und Apokalypse: Überlegungen zur Transnationalität des zeitgenössischen Hollywood', in Ricarda Strobel and Andreas Jahn-Sudmann (eds), *Film transnational und transkulturell. Europäische und amerikanische Perspektiven* (Paderborn: Wilhelm Fink Verlag, 2009), pp. 171–84. For these publications, and in the research for this essay, I used the following two Internet Movie Database charts: http://www.imdb.com/boxoffice/alltimegross (accessed 20 October 2015), and http://www.imdb.com/boxoffice/alltimegross?region-non-us (accessed 20 October 2015). Unfortunately, since the beginning of 2016, the IMDb no longer hosts these websites, and with regard to the top grossing films of all time outside the United States and Canada, I have not been able to find a satisfactory substitute. The equivalent chart on The Numbers only covers the top 100 films; http://www.the-numbers.com/movie/records/All-Time-International-Box-Office (accessed 24 March 2016).

22 See http://www.boxofficemojo.com/alltime/domestic.htm and http://www.the-numbers.com/movie/records/All-Time-International-Box-Office (accessed 24 March 2016).

23 Annual US box office charts can be accessed via http://www.boxofficemojo.com/yearly/ (accessed 24 March 2016).

24 I compiled the annual export charts from the now defunct http://www.imdb.com/boxoffice/alltimegross?region-non-us.

25 According to the all-time top 100 on http://www.the-numbers.com/movie/records/All-Time-International-Box-Office the ninth biggest export hit of 2015 was *The Martian* (Ridley Scott, 2015) with $412 million; as mentioned before, unfortunately, this chart does not go beyond the top 100 and hence does not include information about 2015 releases grossing less than *The Martian*.

26 Cp. McCulloch, *Towards Infinity and Beyond*, pp. 183–87.

27 Such restraint is characteristic of Disney's overall theatrical output of animated features; most of the company's sequels have been straight-to-video releases.

28 Cp. http://www.pixar.com/about/Upcoming (accessed 24 March 2016).
29 McCulloch, *Towards Infinity and Beyond*, ch. 6.
30 Press book for *Toy Story 2*, pp. 2, 11; in clippings file for *Toy Story 2*, Margaret Herrick Library, Academy of Motion Picture Arts and Sciences, Beverly Hills, California.
31 Ibid., pp. 11, 16.
32 Richard Schickel, review of *Toy Story 2*, *Time*, 29 November 1999, unpaginated clipping, clippings file on *Toy Story 2*, Performing Arts Research Center (PARC), New York Public Library at Lincoln Center, New York.
33 David Ansen, 'Further Proof: Toys "R" Us', *Newsweek*, 29 November 1999, unpaginated clipping, clippings file on *Toy Story 2*, PARC.
34 Kirk Honeycutt, review of *Toy Story 2*, *Hollywood Reporter*, 18 November 1999, pp. 7, 21.
35 See http://bosofficemojo/alltime/adjusted.htm.
36 Peter Krämer, 'Would You Take Your Child to See This Film? The Cultural and Social Work of the Family-Adventure Movie', in Steve Neale and Murray Smith (eds), *Contemporary Hollywood Cinema* (London: Routledge, 1998), pp. 294–311.
37 See, for example, Krämer, 'Would You Take Your Child to See This Film?'; and Peter Krämer, 'Steven Spielberg', in Yvonne Tasker (ed.), *Fifty Contemporary Film Directors*, 2nd edn (London: Routledge, 2011), pp. 372–80.
38 Cp. Peter Krämer, '"I'll Be Right Here!" Dealing with Emotional Trauma in and through *E.T. The Extra-Terrestrial*', in Adrian Schober and Debbie Olson (eds), *Children in the Films of Steven Spielberg* (Lanham: Lexington Books, 2016), pp. 91–121.

Chapter 2

TOY STORY AND THE HOLLYWOOD FAMILY FILM

Noel Brown

Not unreasonably, much of the scholarship on *Toy Story* (John Lasseter, 1995) has focused on its technical innovations as Hollywood's first computer-generated (CG) animated feature. But *Toy Story* is also a keynote of the contemporary Hollywood family film. Like the majority of Hollywood animated features, it explicitly targets so-called family audiences, utilizing a range of textual strategies to mobilize consumers of different ages and backgrounds. Its cross-demographic, 'family' appeal was widely observed by domestic and international critics upon initial release. The *New York Times* called it 'a parent-tickling delight . . . a work of incredible cleverness in the best two-tiered Disney tradition. Children will enjoy a new take on the irresistible idea of toys coming to life. Adults will marvel at a witty script and utterly brilliant anthropomorphism.'[1] *Newsweek* thought it had 'something for everyone on the age spectrum'.[2] The *Washington Post* called it 'an amazing animated feature that will captivate everyone from age 4 on up'.[3] The *Toronto Star* advised parents to 'Take your child, your grandmother, your great-uncle' and, 'above all, give yourself the gift of *Toy Story*'.[4] The *St. Petersburg Times* lauded its 'age-spanning wit'.[5] The *Philadelphia Enquirer* called it 'a triumph of storytelling, a thrilling comic-adventure with a theme of friendship and community that speaks to children and adults alike'.[6] *Variety* called it 'a clever mix of simplicity and sophistication that cuts across all age barriers with essential themes'.[7] *The Age* called it 'a classic example of "two-tier" entertainment'.[8] The *Daily Mirror* highlighted its appeal to 'the child in everyone'.[9] Finally, the *Independent* deemed it 'utterly assured in its flicking back and forth between the modes of adult and childish pleasure'.[10]

Toy Story's dialectical relationship with earlier Hollywood family films – both live-action and animated – was also highlighted. In its review, the *Washington Post* wrote:

> More powerful than all the Power Rangers combined, 'Toy Story' flies higher than anything starring Aladdin or Batman and is at least as far-out as 'E.T.' In

> fact, to find a movie worthy of comparison you have to reach all the way back to 1939, when the world went gaga over Oz.[11]

Its technical innovations were also situated against its 'family' sensibilities. According to Bruce Stockler, editor of *Millimeter* magazine, 'Up until now, computer animation has been cold and "high-tech" looking. This is a warm family movie.'[12] For Stockler, as a 'family movie' *Toy Story* possesses an appealing intimacy lacking in earlier 'computer animation'. Lasseter himself has repeatedly spoken of his desire to appeal to audiences of all ages. Before the release of *Toy Story 2* (1999), he admitted: 'We aim to make a great family film that's great for kids but that's even better for their parents and young adults that don't have kids.'[13]

The point is that to fully understand *Toy Story* we need to appreciate its placement within broader traditions of family entertainment. This chapter aims to do two things. First, it situates *Toy Story* within the industrial context of post-1970s Hollywood cinema, a period in which family films (and multimedia family entertainment more broadly) have become central to Hollywood's industrial infrastructure and creative identity. Second, it considers some key areas of continuity and innovation in relation to the wider generic context of the Hollywood family film. In so doing, it explores *Toy Story*'s inherent 'doubleness', analysing the strategies through which it engages with mixed audiences of children and adults.

Hollywood and the 'Family Audience'

Hollywood's interest in tapping the so-called family audience dates back to the 1900s, a period of increasing formalization in the US film industry.[14] The prototypical definition of the 'family audience' was parents and children watching together, but routinely the term has been used to describe mass audiences in the larger sense. Most silent-era Hollywood films were constructed for 'everyone', with little distinction between films for children and for adults. This changed decisively after the coming of sound, when a cycle of adult-orientated films – including crime thrillers, courtroom dramas and sex comedies – overtook movie theatres between 1930 and 1934. While vastly popular, these films aroused a huge backlash against the cinema concerning its potential ability to corrupt young minds. What we now refer to as the 'family film' – a production *explicitly* designed for the dual consumption of children and adults, and marketed and received as such – emerged in the mid-1930s. Initially, most major studio family films were child-star vehicles for performers like Shirley Temple or Jane Withers, or adaptations of child-friendly literary classics, such as *Little Women* (George Cukor, 1933), *David Copperfield* (George Cuko, 1935), *The Little Princess* (Walter Lang, 1939) and *The Wizard of Oz* (Victor Fleming, 1939).[15]

The Walt Disney Company's first animated feature, *Snow White and the Seven Dwarfs* (David Hand et al., 1937), was the second highest-grossing film of the decade at the North American box office. Disney was Hollywood's only major studio that geared all of its productions to the 'family audience', and between the 1940s and the 1970s it was the dominant force in the family film arena. However, the latter-day structural centrality of the family film in Hollywood, and that of family entertainment more broadly, can be traced to George Lucas's and Steven Spielberg's late-1970s blockbusters. Lucas's *Star Wars* (1977) and Spielberg's *Close Encounters of the Third Kind* (1977), alongside Warner Bros.' *Superman* (Richard Donner, 1978), represented a new type of family film. As Peter Krämer puts it, 'most of Hollywood's superhits since 1977 are basically, like *Star Wars*, children's films; more precisely, they are children's films for the whole family and for teenagers, too.'[16] *Star Wars* and *E.T. The Extra-Terrestrial* (Steven Spielberg, 1982), in particular, mobilized the now-vital teenage and young adult demographics. They repackaged the unpretentious action-adventure of Hollywood's 'poverty row' serials of the 1930s and 1940s within a blockbuster aesthetic that drew on new technological potentialities while retaining the emotive and didactic qualities of classical-era family films such as *The Wizard of Oz*. Equally important was these films' scope for 'ancillary' revenues, specifically licensing, merchandizing, pay-TV sales, and, slightly later, home video.

Family Entertainment and Contemporary Hollywood

The structural centrality of family entertainment in Hollywood is closely related to the wave of multimedia conglomeration during the 1980s and 1990s. In this period, all of the major Hollywood studios – except Disney – were either acquired by larger multinational corporations or merged with other media companies. In 1985, Turner Broadcasting purchased MGM and News Corporation acquired Twentieth Century Fox. In 1982, Columbia was bought by Coca-Cola, which then resold it to Sony in 1989. The same year, Warner Bros. merged with Time Life to form Time Warner. In 1990, Universal was acquired by Matsushita Electric, and then sold to Seagram, which in turn sold to Vivendi; since 2004, the firm has been owned by General Electric. In 1993, Viacom acquired Paramount. This list is cursory, but it is sufficient to say that the industrial process of sales, acquisitions and mergers began in earnest in the mid-1980s and continues to this day. Among the 'classical' Hollywood majors, only Disney has resisted takeover. This is due, in part, to the fact that its expansion and diversification has usually been based on the 'family' entertainment model, a fact demonstrated in recent years by its acquisition of Pixar in 2006, Marvel in 2009 and Lucasfilm in 2012. It is no coincidence that these media mergers coincided with an upsurge in the production of films possessing purportedly 'universal' appeal, with franchise potential, that could be realized across multiple media platforms. Contemporary 'family' entertainment, as I have argued elsewhere,[17] can be understood at least as much in terms of corporate infrastructure as consumer products. It is the *material* manifestation of a broader universalistic agenda; international conglomeration, expansionism and synergy are the equivalent *corporate* manifestations. They are two sides of the same coin.

Time Warner was the first of the major Hollywood studios to announce plans to create a 'family film' production division. This announcement (in December 1991) aroused very little surprise in the trade press: *Variety* observed that it reflected 'industry-wide awareness that survival in the 1990s may be a matter of creating wholesome, family-oriented entertainment', and that similar discussions regarding 'increasing production of family films, if not creating family film divisions' were ongoing at Universal, Paramount, TriStar and Columbia.[18] An April 1993 article in *Entertainment Weekly* cited a recent report by entertainment research firm Paul Kagan Associates that advocated greater production of family films, having noted that almost half of the 46 movies that grossed in excess of $100 million between 1984 and 1991 were rated 'PG'.[19] In May 1993, Warner Bros. confirmed the formation of its 'Family Entertainment' banner. During the 1990s, Twentieth Century-Fox (Fox Family Films), Miramax (Miramax Family Films), MGM (MGM/UA Family Entertainment), Universal (Universal Family & Home Entertainment), Viacom (Nickelodeon Movies) and Sony (Sony Pictures Family Entertainment Group) followed suit, creating specialized 'family' divisions orientated to the production and multimedia exploitation of live-action and animated films.

Disney, however, still held a substantial competitive advantage in the family animation market. Indeed, until the 1980s, its animated films had virtually no direct competition. Disney's dominance is attributable to various factors: the multimedia power of the brand, the technical quality of its production and its substantial investment in promotion. However, during the 1970s and 1980s there was growing industry belief that feature animation was no longer a profitable production avenue. Disney's animation had become closely associated with children's entertainment and lacked the 'crossover' appeal of Spielberg's and Lucas's live-action blockbusters. In 1984, a new corporate team headed by Michael Eisner, former President of Paramount Pictures, and backed by Walt's nephew, Roy E. Disney, assumed office. Eisner, alongside executives Frank Wells and Jeffrey Katzenberg, prioritized extending the company's traditional 'child' appeal to teenagers and adults. The live-action/animation fusion, *Who Framed Roger Rabbit* (Robert Zemeckis, 1988), was a breakthrough film in this regard. The following year, Disney released the fully animated film, *The Little Mermaid* (Ron Clements and John Musker, 1989), which grossed over $200 million. As Tino Balio notes, *The Little Mermaid* was 'Disney's first open attempt to court baby boomers and their children'.[20] The studio's later animated releases, *Beauty and the Beast* (Gary Trousdale and Kirk Wise, 1991) and *Aladdin* (Clements and Musker, 1992), were even more profitable.

Encouraged by animation's renewed box office appeal, Disney's rivals jumped on the bandwagon. Matt Mazer, whose company, Nest Family Entertainment, produced the $40 million animation, *The Swan Princess* (Richard Rich, 1994), argued that new entrants to Hollywood's animation market needed to adopt the same 'mythic storylines' as Disney.[21] However, whereas Disney's *The Lion King* (Roger Allers and Rob Minkoff, 1994) grossed over $200 million on its initial theatrical release, *The Swan Princess* (distributed by New Line, owned by Turner Broadcasting) and Fox's *The Pagemaster* (Joe Johnston and Maurice Hunt, 1994) each recouped only about $10 million.[22] Terry Thoren concluded that 'fairy tale is a dirty word in animation now', and 'a cutting-edge niche' was required for non-Disney animated features to succeed.[23]

Toy Story embodies a dialectic between consolidation and innovation. On the one hand, it signals a radical departure from the aesthetic conventions of hand-drawn cel animation, and fits squarely into Thoren's 'cutting-edge niche' bracket. Equally, its strategies of dual address – the techniques employed to engage with mixed audiences of children and adults – place it within recognizable generic and industrial contexts. It ascribes fairly closely to what I have elsewhere identified as the overarching generic conventions of the family film, including: (i) the reaffirmation of kinship and community; (ii) the foregrounding of literal or symbolic child figures and their experiences;[24] (iii) the exclusion and/or defeat of disruptive social elements; (iv) the minimization of 'adult' themes, such as representations of sexuality, violence, crime, profanity, drug abuse, poverty and gore; and (v) a story that, while acknowledging the possibility of an unpleasant or undesirable outcome, is finally upbeat, morally and emotionally straightforward and supportive of the social status quo.[25]

Stylistic and Narrative Innovations

By the time *Toy Story* was released, CG animation had already been used in Hollywood for over a decade. In early entries, such as Disney's *Tron* (Steven Lisberger, 1982), CG effects operate as loci of modernity, reaching towards an imminent, post-industrial technological future largely irreconcilable with daily realities. Conversely, CG animation since *Toy Story* is largely characterized by a patented hyperrealist aesthetic; what David A. Price calls 'a stylised realism that ha[s] a lifelike feel without actually being photorealistic'.[26] John Lasseter pioneered this approach in his celebrated Pixar shorts, *Luxo, Jr.* (1986) and *Tin Toy* (1988). It is predicated on rendering computer models in a believable, 'lifelike' way that disavows the overtly mechanical and the modernistic, and blurs the lines between live-action and animation – at least on a superficial level. To some degree, it follows *Who Framed Roger Rabbit*, which bridged the perceptual gap between the two media, subverting the common prejudice that cel animation is inherently juvenile ('cartoony') and suitable *only* for children. These late-1980s films restored a measure of credibility to animation among the teen and youth market, tapping the cross-demographic audience that *Star Wars*, *Close Encounters of the Third Kind*, *Raiders of the Lost Ark* (Spielberg, 1981), *E.T.* and *Back to the Future* (Zemeckis, 1985) had successfully mobilized.[27]

Who Framed Roger Rabbit is also marked by self-referential, occasionally risqué humour. In this sense, it eschews the largely non-comedic wholesomeness of classical Disney animation (a fact that led to the decision to release it under the company's more adult-orientated Touchstone banner) and anticipates the studio's pronounced reorientation towards comedy in the early 1990s. Robin Williams's ad libbing Genie in *Aladdin* is a watershed; as Paul Wells argues, 'the genie is located in the contemporary era and directly addresses a contemporary culture aware of the terms of reference Williams brings to the character.'[28] Moreover, 'the "laughs" . . . often occur outside the context of the narrative.'[29] The Genie's 'separateness' from the wider narrative is at least as significant as his contemporaneousness. But *Toy Story* goes further, embedding itself within the 'contemporary culture' that the earlier films merely gestured towards, and decisively breaking from the fairy-tale/musical aesthetic of 'classical' Disney. On its theatrical release, *Toy Story* was called 'Disney's [sic] neatest film ever' by the *New York Daily News*, which quipped that it 'makes other Disney flicks look as cutting edge as a bound volume of Reader's Digest.'[30] In turn, animation historian Leonard Maltin observed that: 'Disney's audience was always parents taking kids . . . Now they're going after young moviegoers, the same audience every other studio is going after. If you can expand your audience without excluding the one you already have, then you've hit paydirt.'[31] Finally, according to Lasseter, Jeffrey Katzenberg, then Chairman of Walt Disney Studios, 'very much wanted' *Toy Story* 'to be hip, adult.'[32]

Humour and Intertexuality

Toy Story is distinguished from its predecessors by the diversity and the multi-layeredness of its comic mechanisms. Like most child-orientated comedy films dating back to the beginnings of commercial cinema, it trades heavily in slapstick mechanisms; in one sequence, Mr. Potato Head is struck at high speed by the remote controlled car, RC and his detachable plastic facial features fly off his body in separate directions. But the film is also suffused with a wide array of 'postmodern' inflections. Its nominal antagonist is Sid, the neighbourhood child who 'tortures' toys by dismantling, dismembering and exploding them. But his villainy is subject to ironic treatment: like the monstrous baby of *Tin Toy*, he is just a child, a fact comically underlined when he is heard remarking, in his sleep, 'I wanna ride a pony!' For older, cine-literate audiences there are numerous self-conscious, parodic allusions to Hollywood films. Woody's anguished repetition of 'There's no place like home! There's no place like home!'

when trying to escape Sid's house back to his own recalls Dorothy Gale's famous refrain in the final scene of *The Wizard of Oz*. When the mutilated remains of the toys Sid has destroyed emerge from the soil and advance on him, we are reminded of similar sequences in various zombie movies. And Woody turning his head 360° when trying to frighten Sid out of his practice of destroying toys parodies Linda Blair's infamously grotesque revolving head in *The Exorcist* (William Friedkin, 1971).

This final example is particularly interesting, in that it invokes an 'R'-rated horror film that only audiences above a certain age would have seen. Several risqué sight gags are similarly present for the exclusive benefit of adults. In one instance, a pair of detached, stereotypically female legs can be seen walking about; the legs have a large hook attached to them, signifying 'hooker' (i.e. prostitute). In another, Mr. Potato Head makes an implied 'kiss my ass' gesture to Woody when he removes his plastic lips and bumps them repeatedly against his posterior. The latter gag is accessible to most children, but works by suggestion rather than explicit elaboration, lessening its profanity. In one notably 'adult' sequence, a disconsolate Buzz Lightyear, having become aware of his status as a children's toy, is seen taking afternoon tea opposite two headless dolls. His reference to them as 'Marie Antoinette and her little sister' demands knowledge of the fate of the eighteenth-century French queen, who was executed by beheading during the French Revolution. Furthermore, Buzz's evident depression and implied alcoholism in this scene invoke the seriousness of mental illness, which children cannot be expected to comprehend in its many intricacies but which will resonate with post-adolescent spectators.

It is important to emphasize that while the film's 'adult' modes of address require close analysis, they are never vital components of the scenes in which they are placed. As such, they do not exclude children (or any other faction) who are unable to understand them. Indeed, much of the film's comedy is doubly coded: either equally accessible to children and adults (e.g. slapstick and sight gags), or operating on more than one interpretive level. One example of the latter occurs when baby Molly misaligns Mr. Potato Head's face. He then turns to another character and quips, 'I'm Picasso!' In order to comprehend this reference, the spectator must know of Picasso's abstract paintings of human heads with their misaligned facial features. This level of cultural literacy is presumably beyond that possessed by most young children (and by many adults, too). But the joke also operates on a simpler level: the incongruity of the misaligned face still works as a sight gag. Similarly, the aforementioned scene in which a depressed Buzz is discovered by Woody drinking tea also functions as comic absurdity. Even young children understand that it is impossible to become intoxicated by drinking imaginary Darjeeling tea, so his slurred speech is a logical *non sequitur*. The related image of the exaggeratedly masculine Buzz wearing a flowery apron and drinking tea (with their feminine, maternal coding), meanwhile, is a comical visual incongruity that can be appreciated by audiences of all ages and backgrounds.

These various layers of narrative appeal nonetheless underpin the film's status as a paradigmatic postmodern cultural artefact. David Denby, in his *New York* magazine review, wryly observed that:

> The postmodernist jokes give the movie a spark . . . Have the filmmakers (too many of them to list) been reading Guy Debord, Jean Baudrillard, or some of the other French theorists of illusion and representation? It's possible. It's also possible they just picked up on an idea floating around everywhere: In our world, nature is dead, and everything is now a representation of one sort or another; we're all lost in the forest of simulacra.[33]

This invoking of seemingly unrelated texts (literature, film, television) and consumer products – as well as other ideas 'in the air' – is *de rigueur* in post-1980s North American youth culture. David Weinstein has identified *The Simpsons* (1989–), Pee-wee Herman, Max Headroom, Beavis and Butt-Head and *Seinfeld* (1989–98) as belonging to a 'wave of self-reflexive television programmes which . . . have offered viewers new ways of watching and understanding television'.[34] These TV shows draw freely on the 'postmodern' characteristics of irony, parody, pastiche, satire and self-reflexivity. They are further characterized by what Mike Featherstone calls 'stylistic promiscuity': an openhanded *bricolage* that works to assemble and order a disparate and multiply sourced set of images, iconography, story elements and tropes.[35] Intertextuality itself might be seen as an intertext. Fredric Jameson coined the term 'blank parody' to describe the postmodern pastiches that he sees as endemic to late-industrial society: a self-reflexive process of appropriation without creation.[36]

Since *Toy Story*, 'postmodern' narrative strategies have become closely associated with family-orientated animation, being viewed as integral to the medium's cachet with teenagers and adults. Far from being creatively bankrupt, such films are often celebrated for their ingenuity, providing multiple layers of narrative appeal that reward recognition of current trends, memes and representational elements in contemporary Western popular culture. Many of these textual allusions are throwaway, but not extraneous: in animation, everything on the screen carries performative functions. I would argue that one of the primary pleasures in such texts is the kind of cognitive play associated with puzzle-solving.[37] Such intertextual allusions need to be identified and interpreted, and this is not an autonomic process; it requires knowledge, and some degree of effort. Studies of children's humour development have suggested that children over the age of eight tend to find 'more cognitively challenging' humour – that is, that which requires 'work' to understand it – to be funnier than simpler forms, such as visual incongruity or nonsense wordplay.[38] By the pre-adolescent (age 9–12) stage there also tends to be greater pleasure derived from 'inside jokes' or 'metahumour'.[39]

Intertextuality, then, also functions to strengthen appeal to older children who (generally) are seeking to graduate from the fantasies of the child's world that continue to be linked with the 'children's film' in its simplest iterations. In his review of the Aardman/Sony Claymation film, *The Pirates! In an Adventure with Scientists* (Peter Lord, 2012), the British critic Peter Bradshaw approvingly noted: 'Some people think you can improve children's minds by playing them Mozart. I think you could treble the IQ of any child, or indeed adult, by putting them in front of an Aardman project like this.'[40] The fascination of such films lies partially in *making meaning*. That is to say, the active viewer has the task of decoding or interpreting multiply-sourced intertextual references. Foregrounding intertextuality has thus served an important role in Hollywood animation retaining its narrative distinctiveness from non-animated family films, where postmodern narrative strategies have never been as pronounced.

This clear line of demarcation is significant, because the boundaries between live-action and animated Hollywood family films have blurred in several other regards. Postmillennial live-action films are characterized by a generic reorientation towards fantasy, which can be attributed to several factors: the technological potentialities of computer-generated imagery (CGI), the particular popularity of fantasy among international audiences, and the manifold opportunities for licensing and merchandizing afforded by such subjects. Equally, *Toy Story* signalled a notable shift in Hollywood animation away from fairy-tale, and towards exploration of the associative world of everyday life. Post-2000 fairy-tale films, such as *Shrek* (Andrew Adamson and Vicky Jenson, 2001) and *Frozen* (Jennifer Lee and Chris Buck, 2013), are explicitly characterized by their parodic and/or revisionist treatment of their sources. Nevertheless, the self-reflexivity of Hollywood animation has clearly influenced live-action fairy-tale films such as *Maleficent* (Robert Stromberg, 2014), which rewrites the conventional endorsement of heterosexual romantic love in the *Sleeping Beauty* myth. All of these films recognize the outdated sexual politics of the fairy-tale genre (inherited from the likes of Charles Perrault, Hans Christian Andersen and the Brothers Grimm), acknowledging that its conventions enter into too great a conflict with lived experience to be presented without interrogative irony.[41] Furthermore, the various forms of interplay between animated and live-action family films – ranging from self-reflexive narrative and generic borrowings to parodic quotation – again demonstrate that we cannot view these forms as hermetically self-contained.

Indeed, *Toy Story* is a key text in contemporary Hollywood's tendency towards generic hybridization. Within its medium (animation) and structuring master-genre (family film), various subgeneric identities can be discerned. Conventions of the buddy movie (the friendship between Woody and Buzz), the domestic comedy (the comic interplay between the central characters) and the family drama (tensions within the domestic unit) are strongly apparent. There are also punctuating tropes of fantasy and horror in the anthropomorphism of inanimate, man-made technology, which is itself ironized when the toys deliberately menace Sid. Many of these generic elements are explicitly in reflexive dialogue with one another. Sid's grotesque torture and destruction of toys, and his cannibalizing spare parts to create bizarre hybrids (such as the fusion of a doll's head with spidery metallic legs) result in moments of genuine suspense. But horrific moments are always leavened or disavowed. Woody's and Buzz's terror as Sid's monstrous toy hybrids advance on them is quickly displaced by relief as they (and we) perceive the toys' benevolence. Other horror tropes are subject to comic treatment. Woody's using Buzz's dismembered arm from Sid's window in an attempt to convince Andy's toys that he and Buzz are now friends, but only convincing them that he has murdered Buzz when he inadvertently moves the arm completely into shot, is funny for two reasons: first, because we, the audience, understand the nature of the misunderstanding and its relation to the toys' growing mistrust of Woody and the latter's heightening neuroticism; and second, because of the incongruity of murder and dismemberment within the film's family-comedy generic framework.

But despite these programmed strategies of generic hybridization, the film is rooted within a recognizable, everyday setting. This reorientation from the fantastic settings of the fairy-tale film to the domestic environment is more significant than it may initially appear. Disney executive Thomas Schumacher claimed that the storyline 'was highly dependent on the computerized technique, which gave the characters a three-dimensional quality and thereby provided greater emotional weight'.[42] In contemporary Hollywood animation, emotional realism – the source of what is commonly (and vulgarly) known as 'relatability' – has attained particular centrality. Spielberg's live-action family films, *Close Encounters of the Third Kind* and *E.T.*, were key precursors in their focus on the emotional subjectivities of their protagonists. Both films explore the psychological impact on its characters of family breakdown. As with the children in those two films, *Toy Story*'s central child figure, Andy, is forced to grow up in a single-parent household with an absent father. All three films thus acknowledge the changing definitions of family, but *Toy Story* follows *Mrs. Doubtfire* (Chris Columbus, 1993) in normalizing single-parent families, rather than – as Spielberg's films do – characterizing it as a form of social malfunction. *E.T.*'s Elliott (Henry Thomas) is seen glumly lamenting his father's absence, and his mother (Dee Wallace) appears to be teetering on the brink of a nervous breakdown. *Mrs. Doubtfire*, released more than a decade later, is able to posit a possible future for 'family' *after* the divorce of the parents. *Toy Story* continues this work, presenting a functional domestic environment in which the absence of Andy's father – whether due to death, divorce, separation or surrogacy – is never remarked on.

Toy Story's contemporary, suburban setting also facilitates the juxtaposition between the everyday world and the fantastic, localized in the central conceit that inanimate toys can move, talk and think. But within the film's narrative logic, toys are motivated by universal human emotions, drives and neuroses. The dynamic between the toys humorously palimpsests a modern office environment on to the child's playspace, with Woody, the *de facto* leader, delivering vacuous motivational homilies, and the other toys responding with a mixture of deference, insecurity and resentment. These toys also live under constant fear of being usurped by newer, more technologically advanced iterations of themselves. They are relieved when Andy unwraps his birthday presents to discover a lunchbox, a bed sheet and a board game, but are horrified when Buzz Lightyear – who possesses 'more gadgets than a Swiss army knife' – is revealed as Andy's new toy. While Andy's other toys are impressed by Buzz, the newcomer elicits violent jealousy in Woody, who is terrified that his status as 'Andy's favourite' is being usurped. These anxieties are borne out when Andy is seen literally weighing his two favourite toys in each hand, and then when he chooses to take Buzz out on a playdate. Possessively, Woody warns Buzz to 'Stay away from Andy – he's mine, and no-one is taking him away from me', and then attempts to push his rival out of the window. Their mutual antagonism is the central problematic that the narrative must resolve. Ultimately, the 'buddy movie' structure functions as a mechanism through which platonic love can eventually flourish. Thus the film's much-lauded 'emotional realism' is firmly embedded within the larger conventions of the family film, where obstacles are ultimately overcome and kinship ties are reaffirmed.

Randy Newman's non-diegetic songs are also central to the film's strategies of projecting 'emotional realism'. Sung by Newman in his idiosyncratically homespun, sardonic drawl, the vocal performance is determinedly non-professional, bespeaking authenticity and negating the ingratiating professionalism of some of Disney's earlier musical numbers. As Jack Zipes has observed, most of Disney animated features from *Snow White* to *Aladdin* adhere to the conventions of the 1930s Hollywood musical.[43] Lasseter made a conscious decision to move away from diegetic songs, believing that characters spontaneously bursting into song would detract from the film's 'realist' credentials.[44] Diegetic musical numbers largely fell out of favour in live-action Hollywood family films during the 1970s. However, non-diegetic songs had been used to memorable effect in, say, *Back to the Future*, where 'The Power of Love' by Huey Lewis and the News underlines its youth and adult sensibilities. Newman's songs verbally express the inner thoughts and emotions of the characters in the usual fashion, but their more up-tempo and ironic style adds a further layer of adult appeal.

Modernity, Nostalgia and Childhood

The film's strategy of tapping adult desires is most visible in its deliberately cultivated modes of nostalgia. Newman's music, of course, is part of this: despite his success with Disney, he came to prominence as a singer-songwriter in the 1970s. Moreover, many of the toys are old enough to be familiar to adult audiences from their own childhoods; Mr. Potato Head and Slinky Dog first retailed in the United States during the early 1950s. Evoking adult nostalgia for childhood has been a constant of the family film, as Walt Disney himself recognized when he spoke of his films' appeal to 'the child of all ages', recuperating 'that fine, clean, unspoiled spot down deep in every one of us that maybe the world has made us forget and that maybe our pictures can help us recall'.[45] Relatedly, *Toy Story* is centrally preoccupied with the evanescence of childhood. The toys' omnipresent fear of Andy's growing up – the end of childhood – is rooted in the sure knowledge that his maturation signals their symbolic death; a future in which they are never played with, or shelved, or destroyed. The films look wistfully on childhood as an Arcadian realm of boundless imagination and uninhibited play that, once left, can never be returned to. While most children in the 'real world' actively look forward to adulthood for its supposed liberation from overbearing authority, the film's interpretation of childhood is rooted to adult subjectivities. Bert's (Dick Van Dyke) elaboration of childhood slipping 'like sand through a sieve' in *Mary Poppins* (Robert Stevenson, 1964) is typical of a broader trope in post-twentieth century adult-generated children's fiction, in which the spontaneity and unaffectedness of childhood are overshadowed by a regretful, nostalgic preoccupation with its transience.

In a sense, the film's obsession with growing up (and 'growing out' of childhood) reasserts the binary social distinction between 'childhood' and 'adulthood' that contemporary Western culture, and post-*Star Wars* live-action family films in particular, have worked to erode. Cultural critics such as Benjamin Barber have spoken against the 'infantilising' effects of neo-liberal economics and consumer capitalism, arguing that Western popular culture constructs and maintains a permanent childhood in adults in which reason and thought give way to the childish, instant desires of Freud's pleasure principle.[46] Doubtless Barber would see *Toy Story* as a cog in the machine of infantilism, but the film actually disavows such an ethos in two key regards. First, it clearly addresses child and adult audiences as *separate entities*, recognizing their partially discrete interests stemming from differing levels of cognitive development, knowledge and experience. Second, all of the *Toy Story* films actively repudiate the 'kidulthood' that Barber now sees as coterminous with Western society. There is no forecasting of lifelong play in their vision of Andy's adult life. Rather, the imminent threat of abandonment – or in the case of Jessie, Stinky Pete and Lotso in the second and third films, the traumatic memory of it – hangs heavy over every toy in the series. Andy's future is to be largely devoid of the artefacts of childish play, as is clearly signalled in *Toy Story 3* (Lee Unkrich, 2010) when he donates his toys to a younger child.

The only explicitly 'kidult' figure in the films, the stereotypically geeky toy collector in *Toy Story 2*, is unambiguously perverse. Indeed, he cannot be seen as anything but a satirical comment on the practice of adults – crudely reified in the figure of a small, fat, balding, middle-aged, socially inept single man – actively partaking of a children's culture that, by normative conventions of adult society, they should have left behind. If Andy's overall trajectory reaffirms the socially ratified progression from childish play to adult responsibility (or graduation to the more complex and profane pleasures of adolescence and young adulthood), the collector represents an all-pervasive, regressive obsession with the accoutrements of childhood. His rejection of adult behavioural norms (localized in his theft of Woody) confirms the extent of his dysfunction. This assault on kidulthood is one of several barely coded criticisms of late-modernity in the *Toy Story* series. The films pass comment on the wastefulness and greed of advanced capitalism and its strategies of inbuilt obsolescence. Andy's toys live in constant fear of being superseded by the next, putatively 'better', toy off the production line. In empathising with the fate of inanimate toys, and asserting the value of the old and apparently obsolete and the importance of recycling, the film takes aim at the festishization of the new, and the endless cycle of production, consumption and wastage that underpins advanced capitalism. In so doing, it also allegorizes contemporary green debates surrounding sustainability and emphasizes the need to raise ecological awareness.

Generally, Hollywood feature animation to this point had strenuously avoided explicit sociopolitical commentary of this kind.[47] The ideological potential of popular film as a vehicle for propagandist content had been recognized soon after the invention of the medium, and the mid-twentieth century children's cinemas of Soviet Russia, East Germany, Czechoslovakia and China were explicitly founded on this basis. However, this overtly political approach had never prevailed in the United States. The apparent apoliticsm of Disney's animated films is partly attributable to their temporal and/or geographic displacement, which encourages a mode through which political comment is allegorized. More importantly, overt politicking is incongruous with Hollywood's commercial mandate to appeal to as many consumers, and offend as few, as possible. The conservative racial and sexual politics of Disney's early features were not considered, at the time of their initial release, to have an ideological underpinning; rather, they were seen simply as reflecting contemporary social norms. By the 1980s, live-action Hollywood family films were engaging with sociopolitical concerns with greater directness. Particularly notable in this regard are the explicitly anti-war, pro-disarmament narratives *WarGames* (John Badham, 1983) and *Short Circuit* (Badham, 1986).[48] As with those films, *Toy Story*'s politics are hardly radical in themselves; few would argue that consumer culture is an unfair target for broad satire, and there is certainly no question of 'politicising the classroom', a charge levelled at Soviet children's films. However, *Toy Story*'s additional layer of sociopolitical awareness *is* important in building adult appeal, and engendering the belief that there is more to these films than meets the eye.

Disney's animated films had always proven phenomenally successful in addressing 'the child within the adult', presenting narrative pleasures designed to 'regress' adult spectators to symbolic childhood. While this form of 'undifferentiated address' is clearly present in *Toy Story*, the film presents a more diverse range of attractions – (the voices of) popular adult stars, verbal and visual puns, intertextual allusions, heightened emotional realism and social commentary – to appeal directly to more sophisticated sensibilities (including those of 'tweens' and teenagers). The success of these 'double address' strategies underpins the enormous popularity of Pixar, DreamWorks and, since the 1990s, Disney itself. In turn, this boundary-breaking appeal corresponds with an interesting phenomenon in which Hollywood's family-orientated animated features rank among the best films ever made according to user-generated IMDb ratings, as well as rating extremely highly on the aggregated review sites, Rotten Tomatoes and Metacritic.[49] With *Toy Story*, Pixar successfully differentiated itself from its competitors by branding itself as a purveyor of 'quality' family films that operate on multiple levels. This 'tradition of quality' is supported by Disney's machinery of promotion and distribution, as well as unparalleled resources in terms of funding, production personnel and equipment. Nevertheless, in its broad-appeal narrative strategies, *Toy Story* served as a template for the subsequent tradition of 'quality' animated family films in Hollywood since the turn of the century.

Conclusion

The technological barriers between live-action and animated Hollywood family films have broken down. 'Live-action' films routinely employ CG effects, while certain animated films strive for a photorealistic, almost live-action aesthetic; digital technologies such as performance capture proliferate in films of all types. However, the narrative and representational divisions between live-action and animation in Hollywood are perhaps greater than ever. While most feature animation continues to be rated 'U' or 'PG' by the Motion Picture Association of America (MPAA) – ratings that denote suitability for younger children – the majority of live-action family blockbusters are now rated 'PG-13', which cautions that 'Some material may be inappropriate for children under 13'. *Star Wars: The Force Awakens* (J. J. Abrams, 2015), *Jurassic World* (Colin Trevorrow, 2015) and the last five entries in the *Harry Potter* series are examples of 'PG-13'-rated Hollywood films that target child audiences, but broaden their appeal to teen and youth audiences with stronger representational elements that position them beyond the 'children's film' ghetto. A 2004 Harvard School of Public Health study argued that 'a movie rated PG or PG-13 today has more sexual or violent content than a similarly rated movie in the past' and accused the MPAA of tolerating more extreme content in family-friendly ratings.[50] The PG-13 rating had been introduced by the MPPA after accusations that Spielberg's *Indiana Jones and the Temple of Doom* (1984) was too violent for PG. In fact, in the words of former Disney executive Joe Roth, it was that film's precursor, *Raiders of the Lost Ark* (Spielberg, 1981), which spelled 'the beginning and the end of family films in America'.[51] In September 1996, Fox executive Bill Mechanic explained that: 'We made a strategic move to get out of the kid business, as we've known it, a year ago . . . [*The*] *Nutty Professor* [Tom

Shadyac, 1996] and *Independence Day* [Roland Emmerich, 1996] have become the kid movies, the new family films.'[52]

Since the late 1970s there has been a progressive shift towards a new aesthetic in live-action Hollywood family films. Indeed, they may not instantly be recognizable as family films at all; many do not feature child protagonists or even *contain* children, and reside on the borderline between 'child' and 'adult' suitability. Despite this, their vast international popularity rests on their ability to appeal to audiences of all ages. Since the turn of the millennium, Disney has expanded its family entertainment portfolio to include more adolescent- and youth-orientated brands, including *Star Wars* (via Lucasfilm) and various comic book icons (via Marvel). At the same time, its acquisition of Pixar in 2006 consolidated its traditional strength in animation. *Toy Story* appeared at precisely the point at which the definition of 'family film' was expanding and diverging. The family film continues to encompass more 'traditional' forms, such as cel animation, as well as familiar genres such as domestic comedy, fairy tale and literary adaptation. But it has also widened to include CG animation, live-action/animation hybrids, fantasy and blockbuster superhero films pitched at older children, teenagers and adults. This differentiation reflects industry recognition that the 'family audience' is inherently pluralistic, and that consumers (divided by gender, age, class, ethnicity and sexual orientation, as well as local, regional and national identity) may derive pleasure from different patterns of fantasy.

However, within these various forms, there are commonalities that continue to place them within the overarching category of the family film. *Toy Story* employs a diverse range of narrative and representational strategies to appeal to mixed audiences of children and adults. While some of its modes of address are relatively new, others have a much longer lineage. The use of spectacle, adult stars and the calculated arousal of nostalgia for childhood among adults are present in silent-era family films such as Mary Pickford's children's literary adaptation vehicles of the 1910s and 1920s. There is an even longer tradition of moral fables that evoke comfort and reassurance and reaffirm kinship ties. *Toy Story*, for all its ingenuity, is an explicitly didactic text that promotes family and friendship. It teaches good conduct such as determination and striving for self-improvement (in Woody's overcoming jealousy and possessiveness), and advocates moral virtues such as loyalty and kindness. It is also a symbolic maturation narrative, with Woody and Buzz having to come to terms with their status in the world. Buzz's realization that he is 'made in Taiwan' – and not an intergalactic superhero – allegorizes the child's growing awareness of the world-at-large, graduating from the self-perpetuating fantasies of early childhood. These didactic elements offer parents the gratification of seeing the kinds of moral lessons they attempt to impart to their children practically and attractively reinforced on the screen. Finally, the film's pleasurable repetition of formulaic structures, its provision of narrative closure (negating ambiguity and ambivalence) and its engendering emotional uplift in audiences of all ages are stable elements in the family film, transcending both the epoch and the medium.

Notes

1 Janet Maslin, 'There's a New Toy in the House. Uh Oh', *The New York Times*, 22 November 1995, p. C9.
2 David Ansen, 'Disney's Digital Delight', *Newsweek*, 27 November 1995, p. 89.
3 Jane Horwitz, 'Ode to "Toy": An Animation Sensation, *The Washington Post*, 23 November 1995, p. D7.
4 Judy Gerstal, 'Animated Toy Dazzler Lights Up the Season', *The Toronto Star*, 24 November 1995, p. D3.
5 Steve Persall, 'A True Treasure from the Toy Box', *The St. Petersburg Times*, 24 November 1995, p. 3.
6 Steven Rea, 'An Adventure in Animation That's Dazzling', *The Philadelphia Enquirer*, 22 November 1995, p. C1.
7 Leonard Klady, 'Toy Story', *Variety*, 20 November 1995, p. 2.
8 Adrian Martin, 'Bopping Toys Have Dual Appeal', *The Age*, 7 December 1995, p. 14.
9 Simon Rose, 'Talk of the Toon', *The Daily Mirror*, 21 March 1996, p. 3.
10 Adam Mars-Jones, 'A Film, Not a Plaything', *The Independent*, 21 March 1996, p. 8.
11 Kevin McManus, '"Toy": Animation Sensation', *The Washington Post*, 24 November 1995, p. N54.
12 Bruce Haring, 'Computer Animation No Longer Just a "Toy"', *USA Today*, 15 August 1995, p. 1D.
13 Marc Graser, 'Pixar Run by a Focused Group', *Variety*, 20 December 1999, p. 76.
14 On the 'family audience' in context of silent-era Hollywood, see Noel Brown, *The Hollywood Family Film: A History, from Shirley Temple to Harry Potter* (London and New York: I.B. Tauris, 2012), ch. 1.
15 On the beginnings of the 'family film', see Noel Brown, '"A New Movie-Going Public": 1930s Hollywood and the Emergence of the "Family" Film', *The Historical Journal of Film, Radio and Television*, vol. 33, no. 1 (2013): 1–23.
16 Peter Krämer, '"It's Aimed at Kids – The Kid in Everybody': George Lucas, *Star Wars* and Children's Entertainment', in Yvonne Tasker (ed.), *Action and Adventure Cinema* (London and New York: Routledge, 2004), pp. 358–70 (pp. 366–67).
17 See Noel Brown, '"Family" Entertainment and Contemporary Hollywood Cinema', *Scope: An Online Journal of Film and Television Studies*, no. 25 (2013): 1–22.
18 'New Plan to Put Warners in Family Way', *Variety*, 9 December 1991, pp. 1, 3.
19 Ryan Murphy, 'The Kids Are All Right', *Entertainment Weekly*, 16 April 1993, unpaginated.
20 Tino Balio, 'Hollywood Production Trends in the Era of Globalisation, 1990–1999', in Steve Neale (ed.), *Genre and Contemporary Hollywood* (London: BFI, 2002), pp. 165–84.
21 John Brodie and Jay Greene, 'Dwarfs Tell Disney: Draw! – Rival Studios Get Serious about Animation', *Variety*, 11 July 1994, p. 1.
22 John Brodie, 'Disney Wannabes Play Copycat-and-Mouse', *Variety*, 2 January 1995, p. 3.
23 Ibid.
24 *Toy Story* features both literal and symbolic children, with the human child figure of Andy and the childlike figures of the toys themselves.

25 Noel Brown, *The Children's Film* (New York: Columbia University Press, 2017), ch. 1; also Noel Brown, *British Children's Cinema: From The Thief of Bagdad to Wallace and Gromit* (London: I.B. Tauris, 2016).
26 David A. Price, *The Pixar Touch: The Making of a Company* (New York: Vintage, 2009), p. 213.
27 *Who Framed Roger Rabbit* was, in fact, audience-tested mainly with teenagers, a fact that underpins the perceived importance of securing the 'youth' market. See James B. Stewart, *Disneywar: The Battle for the Magic Kingdom* (New York: Simon & Schuster, 2005), p. 88.
28 Paul Wells, *Understanding Animation* (London and New York: Routledge, 1998), pp. 185–6.
29 Ibid.
30 Lewis Beale, 'At Long Last, Disney Is Shooting for the Hip', *New York Daily News*, 20 November 1995, p. 36.
31 Ibid.
32 Ibid.
33 David Denby, 'This Toy's Life', *New York*, November 1995, pp. 126–9.
34 David Weinstein, 'Of Mice and Bart: *The Simpsons* and the Postmodern', in Cristina Degli-Esposti (ed.), *Postmodernism in the Cinema* (New York and Oxford: Bergahn, 1998), pp. 61–72.
35 Mike Featherstone, *Consumer Culture and Postmodernism* (London: Sage Publications, 1991), pp. 7–8.
36 Fredric Jameson, 'Postmodernism and Consumer Society', in Hal Foster (ed.), *The Anti-Aesthetic: Essays on Postmodern Culture* (Port Townsend: Bay Press, 1983), pp. 111–25.
37 On the pleasures of cognitive play for film audiences, see Carl Plantinga, *Moving Viewers: American Film and the Spectator's Experience* (Berkeley: University of California Press, 2009), pp. 21–5.
38 Jennifer Cunningham, 'Children's Humour', in W. George Scarlett et al. (eds), *Children's Play* (London and New Delhi: Sage, 2005), pp. 93–109 (pp. 106–8).
39 Ibid.
40 Peter Bradshaw, 'The Pirates! In an Adventure with Scientists', *The Guardian*, 29 March 2012, p. 15.
41 It is too early to tell whether this parodic treatment of fairy-tale conventions will remain largely confined to animation; Disney's live-action remake of *Cinderella* (Kenneth Branagh, 2015) is notably strait-laced.
42 Jamie Portman, 'Toy Story Is Success Story for Disney', *The Gazette*, 21 December 1995, p. D5.
43 Jack Zipes, 'Once upon a Time beyond Disney: Contemporary Fairy-Tale Films for Children', in Cary Bazalgette and David Buckingham (eds), *In Front of the Children: Screen Entertainment and Young Audiences* (London: British Film Institute, 1995), pp. 109–26 (pp. 110–12).
44 Cited in Chelsie Lynn Akers, 'The Rise of Humour: Hollywood Increases Adult Centred Humour in Animated Children's Films' (unpublished Master's thesis submitted to Brigham Young University, July 2013), pp. 3–4.
45 'Interview with Fletcher Markle', 25 September 1963, in Kathy Merlock Jackson (ed.), *Walt Disney: Conversations* (Jackson: University Press of Mississippi, 2006), pp. 89–103.

46 Benjamin Barber, *Consumed: How Markets Corrupt Children, Infantilise Adults and Swallow Citizens Whole* (London and New York: W. W. Norton, 2007).
47 The same cannot, of course, be said of animated shorts.
48 See Brown, *The Hollywood Family Film*, pp. 166–75.
49 As of early 2017, the IMDb user-generated ranking of the top 250 films ever made includes *The Lion King* (#44), *WALL-E* (#76), *Toy Story* (#101), *Up* (#102), *Toy Story 3* (#108), *Inside Out* (#144), *Zootropolis* (#185), *How to Train Your Dragon* (#207), *Finding Nemo* (#210), *Monsters, Inc.* (#213) and *Beauty and the Beast* (#245); all these films have an average rating of at least 8/10. It is notable that all of these animated films are post-1990 releases, and that the vast majority are post-*Toy Story* CGI productions. See 'Highest Rated IMDb "Top 250" Titles', *IMDb.com*. http://www.imdb.com/search/title?groups=top_250&sort=user_rating&start=1 (accessed 18 June 2017).
50 Sharon Waxman, 'Study Finds Film Ratings Are Growing More Lenient', *The New York Times*, 14 July 2004, p. E1.
51 Bernard Weinraub, 'Fun for the Family Is No Longer "Pollyanna"', *The New York Times*, 22 July 1997, pp. C9.
52 Judy Brennan, 'Summer School Lessons', *The Los Angeles Times*, 12 September 1996, p. F1.

Chapter 3

THE COWBOY, THE SPACEMAN AND THE GURU: CHARACTER AND CONVENTION IN THE SCREENWRITING OF *TOY STORY*

Andrew Gay

> And thank goodness we were just too young, rebellious and contrarian at the time. That just gave us more determination to prove that you could build a better story. And a year after that, we did conquer it. And it just went to prove that storytelling has guidelines, not hard, fast rules.[1]
>
> — Andrew Stanton, co-screenwriter of *Toy Story*.

> A rule says, 'You must do it this way'. A principle says, 'This works . . . and has through all remembered time'. The difference is crucial.[2]
>
> — Robert McKee, screenwriting guru.

The Rules of the Game

Since launching into the feature filmmaking business with *Toy Story* (John Lasseter, 1995) – the first animated film in the history of the Oscars to be nominated for Best Original Screenplay[3] – the Pixar Animation Studios brand has earned an unrivalled reputation for powerful and effective storytelling. Of its eighteen features released to date, only *Cars 2* (John Lasseter and Brad Lewis, 2011) and *Cars 3* (Brian Fee, 2017) have disappointed critically,[4] and *The Good Dinosaur* (Peter Sohn, 2015) failed to meet box office expectations.[5] Otherwise, Pixar has enjoyed an unprecedented run with critics and audiences alike, and aspiring screenwriters have grown eager to learn the secret to Pixar's string of successful scripts.

Pixar's orientation to story and script emerged during the development process of *Toy Story* in the early 1990s, so if we want to understand the effectiveness of Pixar's screenwriting, it makes sense to return to the beginning – to *Toy Story*'s script and its writing process – to see what they can teach us. How did a group of animators with no experience of writing feature films learn to tell appealing screen stories? This chapter examines two contributing influences in the development of *Toy Story*'s screenplay: first, the character-shaping principles taught by screenwriting guru Robert McKee, whose popular weekend 'Story' seminar the Pixar team attended in 1992,[6] and second, the genre conventions of the buddy picture – or what McKee terms the 'Buddy Salvation' plot[7] – which the Pixar team sought to emulate.[8] I assess *Toy Story*'s adherence to McKee's principles as articulated in his book, *Story: Substance, Structure, Style, and the Principles of Screenwriting* (1997), published subsequent to *Toy Story*'s commercial release, and I also compare *Toy Story* with notable examples of buddy salvation that Pixar's John Lasseter and others have credited as having been genre influences, namely *48 Hrs.* (Walter Hill, 1982), *The Defiant Ones* (Stanley Kramer, 1958), *Midnight Run* (Martin Brest, 1988), *The Odd Couple* (Gene Saks, 1968) and *Thelma & Louise* (Ridley Scott, 1991). Before doing either, however, I offer an overview of *Toy Story*'s script development.

Requests by this author to access the many draft scripts of *Toy Story* that reside in Pixar's archives were denied. Without earlier script versions to study, this chapter draws from other published accounts of *Toy Story*'s early development in its analysis of the only publicly available draft of the screenplay, a release script dated November 1995 and marked 'FINAL DRAFT', with an original story credited to John Lasseter, Pete Docter, Andrew Stanton and Joe Ranft, and authorship of the screenplay itself credited to Joss Whedon, Andrew Stanton and the writing team of Joel Cohen and Alec Sokolow.[9] Working with a release script offers an imperfect solution. As Chris Pallant and Steven Price have observed, such authorized publications often 'impose a retrospective narrative upon the production of the film, generally privileging a linear version of production development, which in practice is frequently less straightforward than might at first appear . . . the published forms of screenplays and storyboards have tended to differ in crucial respects from the material that was actually created in the making of a film'.[10] Indeed, the release script for *Toy Story* includes none of the deleted or extended scenes available as bonus features on any of the film's various DVD or Blu-ray releases and appears to reflect all of the final changes made by the creative team prior to *Toy Story*'s theatrical opening. The only perceptible difference between the published screenplay and the distributed motion picture appears to occur on page six of the script, on which 'HAMM, the piggy bank, flips one last penny into his coin slot'.[11] In the film, Hamm flips a quarter into his slot instead, a minor but obvious change and the only clear detail I have found to otherwise distinguish the final draft from a word-for-word transcript of the completed film.

Story Toys: How to Write a Hit Pixar Screenplay

Toy Story's original treatment was co-written by director John Lasseter, supervising animator Pete Docter and character designer Andrew Stanton, with

Toy Story initially intended only as a working title.[12] In March 1991, Lasseter delivered the treatment to Jeffrey Katzenberg, then the head of Walt Disney Studios, just as Disney and Pixar were finalizing negotiations to partner on the co-production of their first fully computer animated feature motion picture.[13] According to David A. Price:

> It paired Tinny, the one-man band from [Pixar's short film] *Tin Toy* [1988], with a ventriloquist's dummy (known only as 'the dummy') and sent them on a sprawling odyssey, one that was to take them from the back of a truck to an auction, a garbage truck, a yard sale, a couple's house, and finally a kindergarten playground. Yet the core idea of *Toy Story* was present from the first treatment onward: that toys deeply want children to play with them, and that this desire drives their hopes, fears, and actions.[14]

Based on the strength of this first treatment, an agreement was finalized between Disney and Pixar by July 1991.[15] The most significant term of that agreement noted by Price, at least as it pertains to the screenwriting of *Toy Story*, is that it 'gave Katzenberg final control over all creative decisions. If dissatisfied with Pixar's script, Disney could bring in screenwriters of its choosing.'[16]

Katzenberg wielded a heavy hand over the development of *Toy Story* from the beginning. According to Price, 'Disney exercised its right to install outside screenwriters, hiring the comedy-writing team of Joel Cohen and *National Lampoon* alumnus Alex Sokolow to work with Pixar's story team on the script.'[17] Likewise, Katzenberg pushed hard for a more adult vision of *Toy Story*. According to Sokolow:

> [Katzenberg] really wanted it to have an edge. One of the things he kept saying to me and my writing partner, Joel Cohen . . . was that he wanted us to write an R-rated script . . . That was something lost in the narrative from Pixar about *Toy Story*. That first draft had characters breaking the fourth wall, cursing, and trying to kill themselves. It was a very dark script. We had Buzz, when he realised he was a toy, stick his hand in a light socket.[18]

Katzenberg may have also played a role in steering the Pixar team toward genre conventions to solve story problems apparent in the original treatment. 'At first there was no drama, no real story, and no conflict', says Katzenberg.[19] Price recounts how Katzenberg, concerned that the two leads 'wanted the same things for the same reasons', suggested that Pixar should pursue the structure of 'an odd-couple buddy picture in the mold of *48 Hrs.* and *The Defiant Ones*. Both films centred on two men thrown together by circumstance and forced to cooperate in spite of their hostility, eventually gaining one another's respect.'[20] Elsewhere, however, Lasseter claims more independence in Pixar's selection of genre and has framed the buddy picture direction as a kind of rebellion against the Disney house style:

> We actually made a list of what we wanted our movie *not* to be. We didn't want it to be a musical; we didn't want it to have like a good guy and a bad guy, and you know, sidekicks and all that stuff. Because that was all Disney's thing. So we started to look at different kinds of film genres and we landed upon the buddy picture. We loved *The Odd Couple* and *The Defiant Ones*, and *Midnight Run* . . . so we hit upon this buddy picture concept of an old toy that's a child's favourite, and a child's birthday gift – a new, real flashy, modern toy that becomes the new favourite, and how the old toy deals with that. So that became the essence of *Toy Story*.[21]

In their own public remarks on the subject, both Docter[22] and Stanton[23] have agreed with Lasseter that Pixar had to fight Disney to preserve their unique vision of *Toy Story* as a buddy picture unlike any animated feature that had come before it. Lasseter says: 'We realised that this was something no one had really done before. We felt it had a lot of potential, in terms of making a strong character film.'[24] As a result of their genre research, the plot of *Toy Story* began to more closely resemble its final iteration. According to author Charles Solomon:

> A draft [treatment] from September 2, 1991, shows the plot of *Toy Story* beginning to take shape. Tinny replaces an old ventriloquist's dummy as a child's favorite toy. The mismatched pair fall out of the car at a gas station when the family goes for pizza; on the way back, they're captured by a 'mean kid' who straps Tinny to a rocket. The dummy and Tinny help each other escape, and reach home safely. They become friends who play together 'as a team'.[25]

Both characters went through additional transformations after the treatment of 2 September, as reported by Price: '"As the story evolved it became clear that Tinny was too antiquated", Lasseter recalled. "So we started to analyze what a little boy would get these days that would make him so excited that he stopped playing with anything else"',[26] eventually landing on the Space Ranger concept. Likewise, given 'that a buddy picture is most compelling if its lead characters are opposites, Lasseter then heightened the contrast of old and new between the two toys by making the ventriloquist's dummy a cowboy figure'.[27] As Lasseter says, 'It would be like Roy Rogers meets Buck Rogers . . . something people hadn't seen before.'[28]

The in-house Pixar story team consisted of the original treatment writers with the eventual addition of story supervisor Joe Ranft, who joined Pixar in 1992. Fully aware of their liabilities as novice screenwriters, the story team sought expert guidance. 'Some attended McKee's seminar and got a lot out of it', says senior Pixar development executive Mary Coleman.[29] The script guru's three-day seminar in Los Angeles may have also helped the animators speak the language of the professional screenwriters installed by Disney. As Sokolow recounts, 'I had done [the McKee] lecture in '89 or '90. I don't know when they went. When I started working with them, they hadn't done it, but in the course of our tenure together, they did.'[30] Stanton confirms McKee's influence in an interview with *Premiere Magazine*:

> When we set out to make *Toy Story* we didn't know squat about anything . . . We didn't know how to make a movie let alone write one and I think it was John Lasseter and Pete Docter went down to [McKee's] course in L.A and they came back just raving. I mean we really really followed McKee almost to the letter of the law when we worked on *Toy Story*. *Toy Story*'s very much a product of McKee's system.[31]

Lasseter and Docter attended their McKee seminar sometime in 1992.[32] Throughout the rest of that year, the story team worked with Cohen and Sokolow to deliver a script. Katzenberg approved the first script for production on January 19, 1993, and Cohen and Sokolow departed the project after seven drafts.[33]

The *Toy Story* narrative faced its first significant test on 19th November 1993, when Pixar screened an initial story reel – storyboards set to vocal performances by the actors – for several Disney executives. Pallant and Price have noted how such reviews have been intrinsic to the development culture at Disney Animation since the company's inception, when 'the development was subject to almost Darwinian conditions of evolution, with only the strongest ideas being allowed to survive, and the reputation of the artist affording no protection to a weak idea'.[34] Pixar's story reel featured a cruel and remorseless Woody maliciously throwing Buzz out of a second floor window then threatening and verbally abusing Andy's other toys. 'Hey, it's a toy-eat-toy world', he replies, when accused by Bo Peep.[35] The rest of the toys then throw Woody out the window in an act of merciless revenge. Solomon notes the fallout: '"It was awful", Lasseter says bluntly. "Woody was just a jerk to everybody; the characters were repellent and hateful. I was so embarrassed by it"'.[36] Those in attendance were so disgusted with the dark tone of the reel that Disney immediately placed production on hold, giving Pixar a matter of weeks to get their house in order or face cancellation of the project. The screening proved so traumatic for the story team that it has become known in Pixar lore as Black Friday.

As a result of the Black Friday disaster, Disney reached out to screenwriter Joss Whedon for rewrites. According to biographer Amy Pascale, Whedon was immediately intrigued:

> It was 'a perfect structure with a ghastly script. If you have a pretty good script, but there's just something you can't put your finger on and figure out structurally, that's a nightmare', he says. 'When you read something where the structure was John Lasseter's story concept, which was rock solid, and you could just go in there and do a strong rewrite, that's good.'[37]

When Whedon arrived at Pixar, he found collaborators who 'were eager to jump back into the story and strip it down to the essentials', writes Pascale.[38] Accustomed to spitballing in a television writer's room in order to break a story, Whedon felt right at home with the Pixar team's approach to open collaboration. He and the team would brainstorm in a room together, then 'Joss would take all the ideas from the Pixar team and go into his office, crank up the music he needed to be inspired, and write. When he emerged, he delivered pages that evoked exactly what they had been trying to describe in the room as a group – but so much stronger, more economical, and so much more concise.'[39]

With the story back on track, Disney approved *Toy Story* to go back into production. While other titles were considered to replace its working title, including *Moving Buddies*, *The Cowboy & the Spaceman* and *To Infinity and Beyond*, it eventually became clear to the team that no title could top the simplicity of *Toy Story*.[40] Whedon finally left Pixar in April 1994 to pursue other projects, and substantial rewrites continued throughout the entire production process, now with Stanton primarily in the screenwriter's chair. According to Pascale:

> The Pixar Team didn't see Joss again until a test screening when the film was nearly finished. He seemed a little shocked at how much it had changed. A couple weeks [sic] after the movie came out and he had finally seen it two or three more times, he sent a letter to the team. '"I didn't get it at first, but now I GET it" – and I remembered he capitalized *GET*', Stanton says with a laugh. 'It just took a while for him to adjust from where he had left the film to what it became.'[41]

Katzenberg also left Disney in August 1994[42] and had no hand in guiding *Toy Story* toward the finish line in its final year of production, but his early insistence that the toys have adult personalities left a profound legacy that would resonate throughout the refinement of the characters and their desires.[43]

The Wisdom of the Guru

According to Mike Bonifer, who produced the original promotional website for *Toy Story* and also directed a television documentary about the movie's making, 'in its emergent and most entrepreneurial state, Pixar's mission was to *break rules* and test the limits of what was possible. The status quo was their enemy. They built the brand by defying a lot of conventional wisdom.'[44] While these claims fit the popular mythology surrounding Pixar, they do not easily square with reports that the *Toy Story* creative team drew heavily from the teachings of Robert McKee, a man who has been criticized both by screenwriters and by film critics for pushing a paint-by-numbers approach to storytelling.

'I'm starting to think Robert McKee has done more harm to writers and the state of the movie industry than Rob Schneider', writes television scribe Ken Levine, arguing that 'adhering to his method forces you into a formulaic model'.[45] After attending a McKee seminar for a profile on the guru, critic Jason Zinoman writes that McKee 'often has no idea what he's talking about . . . He's been criticised for turning the creative process into a series of rules, but this misses the real problem with his course, namely that the rules themselves are often banal and arbitrary.'[46] Nevertheless, Pixar's Stanton has defended McKee's utility: 'I think for people who have never had a story analyzed and broken down like it is in [McKee's] course, it's an epiphany . . . Regardless of whether you ultimately always adhere to it or agree with it.'[47]

McKee himself remembers meeting the Pixar team and has long counted it as a feather in his cap that he helped the fledgling storytellers find their wings: 'John Lasseter and his whole crew came to me years ago', McKee says. 'They said, "look, we're a bunch of computer nerds who can't tell a story worth shit and we're scared". And they showed me a short so talented, I said, "look, you guys are gonna be fine, just sit down and take notes"'.[48]

According to Price, the Pixar team returned from their experience at McKee's screenwriting seminar

> as true believers in McKee's principles . . . High among these was McKee's doctrine that a protagonist and his story become interesting only as much as the forces arrayed against him *make* him interesting; character emerges most realistically and compellingly from the choices that the protagonist makes in reaction to his problems . . . McKee's teachings became the law of the land at Pixar.[49]

McKee recalls of their meeting, 'I know that, when they took the class, their great concern was how to make toys into characters.'[50] Central to McKee's teaching of character-building is his distinction between 'characterization' and 'true character'. From his perspective, '*Characterization* is the sum of all observable qualities of a human being, everything knowable through careful scrutiny'.[51] On the other hand, 'TRUE CHARACTER is revealed in the choices a human being makes under pressure – the greater the pressure, the deeper the revelation, the truer the choice to the character's essential nature.'[52] Elsewhere he adds: 'The key to True Character is desire.'[53] McKee urges writers to design characters based on an inherent tension between characterization and true character. 'When characterization and true character match, when inner life and outer appearance are, like a block of cement, of one substance, the role becomes a list of repetitious, predictable behaviors . . . they are boring.'[54] Furthermore, 'The revelation of deep character in contrast or contradiction to characterization is fundamental in major characters.'[55]

Consider Woody's characterization in *Toy Story*: Woody is introduced in the script as 'a pull-string rag doll cowboy'[56] – a wholesome, classic toy of an heirloom quality. Lasseter explains he's 'definitely not a new toy. No kids get cowboy dolls these days. It really had a sense that the doll had been around for a long time.'[57] Not only is Woody a cowboy, he is also a sheriff, the default leader in Andy's room, and a visual representation of traditional values such as justice, bravery and responsibility. Woody claims to be driven by selfless principle when he says to the other toys, 'It doesn't matter how much we're played with. What matters is that we're here for Andy when he needs us. That's what we're made for.'[58] Nevertheless, the true desire of his heart is to be Andy's preferred toy which, according to Mr. Potato Head, he has been since Kindergarten,[59] so when Buzz Lightyear is introduced to block that desire, Woody resorts to underhanded tricks. As Stanton explains:

> We realized, you can make him kind, generous, funny, considerate, as long as one condition is met for him, [and that] is that he stays the top toy . . . we all live life conditionally. We're all willing to play by the rules and follow things along, as long as certain conditions are met. After that, all bets are off.[60]

Under pressure, Woody reveals a moral flaw. Jealous of the attention Buzz has received from Andy, Woody sets a trap for Buzz and tries to knock him behind Andy's desk to keep him from taking Woody's place on Andy's trip to Pizza Planet, a plan that runs against his iconic lawman characterization. Unfortunately, Woody miscalculates, creating what McKee calls 'the gap', accidentally knocking Buzz out the window and worsening his situation: 'Rather than evoking cooperation from his world, his action provokes forces of antagonism that open up the *gap* between his subjective expectation and the objective result, between what he thought would happen when he took his action and what in fact does happen.'[61]

Woody's actions illustrate McKee's requirement of conflict between characterization and true character. 'True Character waits behind this mask. Despite his characterization, at heart who is this person? Loyal or disloyal? Honest or a liar? Loving or cruel? Courageous or cowardly? Generous or selfish? Willful or weak?'[62] Woody's true character is revealed by his action to be that of a petty doll, driven by envy. Of course, there must be more to Woody's true character than these flaws, or *Toy Story* would not have succeeded. Indeed, the Black Friday *Toy Story* story reel failed so miserably in large part because Katzenberg had pushed the writers toward a Woody whose true character was flatly selfish and mean-spirited, intentionally throwing Buzz out the window. Woody, as written in that version of *Toy Story*, lacked dimension. '*Dimension means contradiction*', writes McKee.[63] Characters must have complex contradictions, or they will bore the audience. Woody is petty and partly driven by envy, sure, but he is also much more than that: he is clever, resourceful, burdened by a sense of duty to Andy's other toys, and deeply concerned with Andy's well-being. As

Stanton says, characters must have 'an inner motor, a dominant, unconscious goal that they're striving for, an itch that they can't scratch . . . And Woody's was to do what was best for his child'.[64]

Through characterization, Woody is introduced to the audience as a dutiful sheriff and beloved toy. Buzz's introduction uncovers another side to Woody, one driven by jealousy. Woody's response to this jealousy – his willingness to compromise his ethical principles to sabotage Buzz – reveals further depths of selfishness, but that is only the beginning of his journey, not his end. Woody spends the rest of the plot of *Toy Story* digging deeper into his true character, confronting his selfish jealousy to reach beyond it, into his inner loyalty, courage and resourcefulness. As McKee argues:

> The function of STRUCTURE is to provide progressively building pressures that force characters into more and more difficult dilemmas where they must make more and more difficult risk-taking choices and actions, gradually revealing their true natures, even down to the unconscious self.
>
> The function of CHARACTER is to bring to the story the qualities of characterization necessary to convincingly act out choices. Put simply, a character must be credible: young enough or old enough, strong or weak, worldly or naïve, educated or ignorant, generous or selfish, witty or dull, in the right proportions. Each must bring to the story the combination of qualities that allows an audience to believe that the character could and would do what he does.[65]

In its original design, *Toy Story* failed because a purely selfish Woody was not a credible protagonist to drive the structure the writers had developed, but the Whedon-led rewrites brought the script back to first principles to resolve this storytelling crisis. As McKee writes, 'The PROTAGONIST has the will and capacity to pursue the object of his conscious and/or unconscious desire to the end of the line, to the human limit established by setting and genre.'[66]

This phrase, 'the end of the line', appears seventeen times in McKee's *Story* and is fundamental to his teaching of character and structure. For McKee, both life and story are about exploring positive and negative values. 'Generally', he writes, 'the protagonist will represent the positive charge of this value; the forces of antagonism, the negative. Life, however, is subtle and complex, rarely a case of yes/no, good/evil, right/wrong. There are degrees of negativity'.[67] McKee identifies these degrees of negativity as the contrary, the contradictory, and at the end of the line, the negation of the negation, a phrase he repurposes from the German philosopher Hegel.[68] 'A story that progresses to the limit of human experience in depth and breadth of conflict must move through a pattern that includes the Contrary, the Contradictory, and the Negation of the Negation.'[69]

McKee defines the contradictory as 'the direct opposite of the positive'.[70] If the positive value at stake in *Toy Story* is friendship, we can define the contradictory value as enmity. 'Between the Positive value and its Contradictory, however, is the *Contrary:* a situation that's somewhat negative but not fully the opposite.'[71] In *Toy Story*, the contrary of friendship is rivalry. Rivalry is introduced in the script with the arrival of Buzz in Andy's room on page 21. '(Gasp!) Have you been replaced?' asks Rex.[72] Woody initially tries to brush this off by offering Buzz a relatively warm welcome while also reasserting his dominance: 'Howdy! My name is Woody and this is Andy's room. That's all I wanted to say, and also, there has been a bit of a mix-up. This is my spot, see, the bed here –' but Buzz cuts him off: 'Local law enforcement! It's about time you got here. I'm Buzz Lightyear, Space Ranger, Universe Protection Unit. My ship has crash landed here by mistake.'[73] Woody and Buzz talk past each other because Buzz does not accept his toy existence. Adding insult to injury, Woody's rival for Andy's attention does not even appreciate the sacred responsibility of his own toyness.

WOODY

All right, that's enough. Look, we're all very impressed with Andy's new toy –

BUZZ

Toy?

WOODY

T-O-Y. Toy.

BUZZ

Excuse me, I think the word you're searching for is Space Ranger.

WOODY

The word I'm searching for I can't say because there's pre-school toys present.[74]

Toys exist to offer their child play, but Buzz claims a different mission. It is easy to see why Woody would find this particularly galling.

Enmity arrives on page 49, where Buzz confronts Woody for throwing him out the window:

Buzz lunges for Woody. The two toys fly off the seat and out the open side door of the van.

EXT. GAS STATION – CONTINUOUS

Woody and Buzz hit the ground and roll under the van, locked in mortal combat.

WOODY

Ok! Come on! You want a piece of me?!

Buzz lands a punch that sends Woody's head spinning around.

Woody lunges with all his might. He smacks Buzz in the face, making it SQUEAK with every blow.

Buzz closes his helmet on Woody's hand.[75]

Here Woody and Buzz have progressed from rivals to enemies and the negative values in the script from the contrary to the contradictory, but that is not the end of the line. 'At the end of the line waits the *Negation of the Negation*, a force of antagonism that's doubly negative . . . Negation of the Negation means a compound negative in which a life situation turns not just quantitatively but *qualitatively* worse. The Negation of the Negation is at the limit of the dark powers of human nature.'[76] According to McKee, the negation of the negation is one of the principles that Pixar took most to heart after his seminar: 'I was told – I think this is true – that they won't OK a script for production until they can answer the question "What's the negation of the negation?" '[77]

In *Toy Story*, the negation of the negation is betrayal (or enmity masquerading as friendship). On page 92, for the very first time in the entire script, Woody refers to Buzz as his friend. When Sid's mutant toys surround Buzz to repair his broken arm, Woody attacks them, mistakenly believing them to be cannibals. When he realizes they have helped Buzz, he apologizes: 'Uh . . . sorry. I . . . I thought that you were gonna. . . (laughs nervously) . . . you know, eat my friend.'[78] This would appear to be an enormous breakthrough in their relationship, the first time Woody tries to help Buzz for selfless reasons and an apparent move from the contradictory value to the positive. Nevertheless, just one page later, when faced with the existential threat of Sid, it is every toy for himself as Woody abandons Buzz to his fate while scurrying for his own safety. 'Fine. Let Sid trash you. But don't blame me', he says.[79] Woody manages to hide in a crate but becomes trapped, and Sid straps Buzz to a rocket, threatening his annihilation.

This betrayal serves an important structural function in Woody's maturation by creating an opportunity for him to re-examine and purge his jealousies. 'Why would Andy ever want to play with me, when he's got you?' Woody asks.[80] 'I'm the one that should be strapped to that rocket.' A few pages later, when given another chance to leave Buzz behind and return to Andy free of his former rival, Woody commits instead to friendship. Rallying the mutant toys to his cause, he tells them, 'There's a good toy down there and he's – he's going to be blown to bits in a few minutes all because of me. I've gotta save him! . . . He's my friend. He's the only one I've got.'[81] Having navigated through rivalry, enmity, betrayal and finally arriving at true friendship, Woody is ready to risk it all to save Buzz. According to McKee, 'If a story stops at the Contradictory value, or worse, the Contrary, it echoes the hundreds of mediocrities we suffer every year . . . If a story does not reach the Negation of the Negation, it may strike the audience as satisfying – but never brilliant, never sublime.'[82] By taking Woody to the end of the line of his selfish jealousies and giving him an opportunity to redeem himself, the Pixar screenwriters succeed in designing a compelling and memorable character for the ages.

'They'll Probably Kill Each Other':[83] *The Conventions of Buddy Salvation*

McKee holds that all screenwriters are genre writers. Each one 'must not only fulfill audience anticipations, or risk their confusion and disappointment, but he must lead their expectations to fresh, unexpected moments, or risk boring them. This two-handed trick is impossible without a knowledge of genre that surpasses the audience's.'[84] Developing this knowledge requires study. According to McKee, 'Genre study is best done in this fashion: First, list all those works you feel are like yours, both successes and failures . . . breaking each film down into elements of setting, role, event, and value . . . What do the stories in my genre always do?'[85]

During the development of *Toy Story*, according to Price, the Pixar creative team 'screened a series of buddy pictures, including not only *48 Hrs.* and *The Defiant Ones*, but also *Midnight Run* and *Thelma & Louise*, among others, to study their structure'.[86] Lasseter has also listed *The Odd Couple* among the key films they studied.[87] I have viewed each of these films and have read their scripts to determine which of their conventions reverberate in *Toy Story*.

McKee has little to say in *Story* about the exact conventions of the buddy picture – or what he calls, 'Buddy Salvation' – though he categorizes it as a subgenre of the love story that 'substitutes friendship for romantic love'.[88] When asked in his online subscriber community *Storylogue* about the differences between love story and buddy salvation conventions, McKee offers a little more insight:

> I doubt very much that in Buddy Salvation stories you would have the rituals of romance, the rituals of beauty, the rituals of presentation, the rituals of fate, and so forth – those wouldn't seem appropriate, I don't think, in a buddy film – but they may have rituals of combat, rituals of struggle, rituals of defeating forces opposed to them, and that might substitute for a kind of romantic ritual.[89]

In *Story*, McKee argues that: 'The most important question we ask when writing a *Love Story* is: "What's to stop them?"'[90] What blocking force stands in the way of eternal love? However, my reading of *Toy Story* and the other five buddy pictures studied for this chapter suggests that the "What stops them?" question is reversed in buddy salvation narratives. The driving question is not 'what blocks them from getting together' but 'what keeps them from flying apart?'

The single most unifying convention of the buddy salvation subgenre, found in each of the studied films and screenplays, is that the buddies must be locked into their partnership by external forces. The pair may initially choose to team up and grow to eventually despise one another with no apparent route of escape, as in *The Odd Couple*,[91] or they may find an existing friendship tested to the limits when situations force them to commit fully to one another at the expense of everything else that matters to them, as in *Thelma & Louise*.[92] Two characters may even hate each other from the start but find themselves bound together by circumstances outside of their control, as in *48 Hrs.*,[93] *The Defiant Ones*[94] and *Midnight Run*.[95]

In these latter cases, the relationship begins as one of utility but grows into something more. In *48 Hrs.*, Detective Cates needs the convict Hammond to help him catch a cop-killer, while Hammond needs to cooperate with Cates in order to secure his fortune and freedom. In *The Defiant Ones*, prisoners Cullen and Jackson are chained together and must cooperate to escape pursuing lawmen. In *Midnight Run*, bounty hunter Walsh must return a bail jumper, 'The Duke', to California against his will in order to collect a reward. In all three films, the characters coordinate their efforts for purely selfish reasons or under duress. External forces of antagonism require their partnership, which cannot be dissolved until those forces of antagonism are resolved through McKee's rituals of combat and struggle.[96] In *Toy Story*, Woody and Buzz are bound together by Woody's need for Buzz to return with him to Andy's room as evidence of his innocence. As in *Midnight Run*, however, Woody's and Buzz's true desires are at cross-purposes because Buzz does not believe himself a toy. Woody must deceive Buzz and humour his Space Ranger delusions to persuade Buzz to cooperate with his efforts to get home.

Rituals of combat and struggle are often enacted not only between the buddy pair and the external forces of antagonism, but also within the partnership itself. Indeed, struggle between partners is typical of this subgenre, as succinctly observed in the Sheriff's remark in *The Defiant Ones* that his escaped prisoners will 'probably kill each before they go five miles',[97] a line that would aptly apply to most buddy salvation partnerships. In *The Defiant Ones* and in *48 Hrs.*, both of which feature interracial protagonists, prejudice drives much of the conflict, as the white character in each story repeatedly tries to assert his supposed racial superiority over his black counterpart. In *The Odd Couple*, Oscar's carefree sloppiness and Felix's fussy tidiness lead to endless arguments. 'If you look at the essence of a buddy picture', says Lasseter, 'you have two characters as opposite as you can get'.[98] In *Toy Story*, Woody and Buzz are opposites in their characterization – as cowboy and spaceman, old and new toy – as well as in their deepest self-identification: for Woody, his toyness is his purpose; for Buzz, it is a source of first denial then shame.

In most buddy pictures, this building tension between the opposite partners eventually leads to all-out war, and often physical blows are exchanged. In *48 Hrs.* and *The Defiant Ones*, the duos engage in prolonged fist fights. In *The Odd Couple*, no punches are thrown, but Oscar and Felix do confess brutal truths to one another by script's end. This having-it-out moment is usually a required step, making it possible for the two partners to shift their aggressive energies from one another toward the external forces of antagonism. In *Toy Story*, Woody and Buzz get their physical altercation out of the way at the start of their journey, in the gas station scene. While their fight does not resolve their enmity for one another, it releases enough tension for them to put their differences aside and work together to achieve their individual aims.

Often in the third act of a buddy picture, one or both partners are presented with an opportunity to prematurely dissolve the relationship at the expense of their counterpart, but they will choose instead to sacrifice personal gain for the good of their 'buddy'. The rituals of combat have humanized each partner in the eyes of the other, to the point that their partner becomes more than a means to an end. In *Midnight Run*, Walsh gives up his reward to set 'The Duke' free. In *The Defiant Ones*, Jackson gives up his fantasy life with a beautiful woman when he realizes she has misled Cullen into a dangerous swamp, and Cullen returns the favour when he leaps from the train that promises his freedom in order to stay behind with the injured Jackson. In *Toy Story*, Woody chooses to rescue Buzz from Sid at significant risk to his own well-being. Then again, in the final sequence when Buzz gets caught in a fence, Woody jumps down from Andy's van – perhaps in a direct echo of Cullen's leap from the train in *The Defiant Ones* – to help Buzz free himself. Buzz returns the favour moments later when he leaps on to Sid's dog's face to save Woody from certain death.

As with rituals of romance in the love story, these buddy rituals bring the partners closer together by the journey's end, even if they choose not to openly admit it. 'Buddy movies are about sublimating, punch an arm, "I hate you". It's not about open emotion', says Whedon.[99] *Thelma & Louise* stands out in this regard in that the title characters conclude their journey having formed a deeply intimate emotional bond. More typical are *48 Hrs.*, *The Defiant Ones*, *Midnight Run* and *The Odd Couple*, in which the concluding attitude is something closer to begrudging respect. Woody's last line in *Toy Story* falls in line with this tradition: 'Now Buzz, what could Andy possibly get that is worse than you?!'[100]

Avoiding Cliché: Characterization and Setting in Toy Story

'*Story* is about originality, not duplication', writes McKee,[101] but despite Pixar's reputation as an innovator, senior development executive Mary Coleman admits: 'We're not consciously trying to push the envelope . . . In some ways our movies are very conventional, in terms of story conventions like character arcs. If you look at all of our movies there's a protagonist who starts with a flaw, goes on a journey, and comes out the other end a better person . . . or rat . . . or fish.'[102] If *Toy Story* and other Pixar scripts adhere so closely to conventions of classical plot structure, character motivation and genre, why, then, have they earned their reputation for inventiveness? McKee offers a clarification: '[Conventions] do not inhibit creativity, they inspire it. The challenge is to keep convention but avoid cliché.'[103] How does Pixar avoid cliché?

While some screenplays make their mark through groundbreaking plot structures – Charlie Kaufman's send-up of McKee in *Adaptation* (Spike Jonze, 2002) comes to mind – Pixar has avoided cliché primarily through novel use of characterization and setting, exploiting the power of animation to realize whatever world the animator imagines. Woody's behaviour is not particularly surprising; nor are the basic stages of his journey with Buzz, all of which fulfill our genre expectations for buddy salvation. Instead, the sense of astonishment we experience reading or watching *Toy Story* comes from our recognition of familiar genre tropes and understandable human emotions emanating from a world of toys. We delight in being made to believe that a toy could feel the depth of envy, regret and ultimately selfless courage that Woody displays throughout his journey and find pleasure in the toyish twists on Buzz and Woody's buddy rituals.

Similar observations could be made about the genre maps and emotional landscapes explored in *Ratatouille* (Brad Bird and Jan Pinkava, 2007) with rodents, in *Finding Dory* (Andrew Stanton and Angus MacLane, 2016) with fish, or in any of Pixar's string of animated hits. Indeed, if there is one storytelling rule consistent across Pixar's most successful screenplays, it is this one: give recognizable characters unusual characterization and take them through familiar genre situations in an unexpected setting. As McKee writes, 'the source of all clichés can be traced to . . . one thing alone: *The writer does not know the world of his story.*'[104] *Toy Story* comes to life thanks both to its adherence to classical character arcs and genre conventions and to its vibrantly drawn characterizations set in an utterly believable world of sentient toys, an approach that plays to Pixar's strengths in visualization and world-creation. 'Because [Pixar has] a great foundation . . . what they do is the best stuff in Hollywood . . . They paid attention, they learned, and the results are – for me – gratifying, because I know that this works', says McKee.[105] In writing *Toy Story*, Lasseter and his team at Pixar authored characters and worlds capable of taking their audience to infinity and beyond. They succeeded by applying their own talents – and the considerable talents of their collaborators, from Katzenberg to Whedon – to the challenge of building new and extraordinary experiences upon the foundation of storytelling conventions.

Notes

1 Andrew Stanton, 'The Clues to a Great Story', *TED: Ideas worth Spreading*, 2012. https://www.ted.com/talks/andrew_stanton_the_clues_to_a_great_story?language=en (accessed 28 August 2016).

2 Robert McKee, *Story: Substance, Structure, Style, and the Principles of Screenwriting* (New York: Harper-Collins, 1997), p. 3.

3 Tim Dirks, 'Pixar-Disney Animations', *AMC: Filmsite*. http://www.filmsite.org/pixaranimations.html (accessed 28 August 2016).

4 'Cars 2', *Rotten Tomatoes* https://www.rottentomatoes.com/m/cars_2/ (accessed 28 August 2016); 'Cars 3', *Rotten Tomatoes* https://www.rottentomatoes.com/m/cars_3 (accessed 9 October 2017).
5 'Pixar Movies at the Box Office', *Box Office Mojo*. http://www.boxofficemojo.com/franchises/chart/?id=pixar.htm (accessed 28 August 2016).
6 Richard Neupert, *John Lasseter: Contemporary Film Directors* (Urbana: University of Illinois Press, 2016), p. 93.
7 McKee, *Story*, p. 80.
8 Lawrence French, '*Toy Story* Beginnings: An Animation Brain Trust Devised the Toys' Story', *Cinefantastique*, November 1995, p. 36.
9 Joss Whedon et al., *Toy Story* Final Draft Script (Pixar Animation Studios/Walt Disney Animation, 1995) http://www.pages.drexel.edu/~ina22/splaylib/Screenplay-Toy_Story.pdf.
10 Chris Pallant and Steven Price, *Storyboarding: A Critical History* (New York: Palgrave Macmillan, 2015), p. 22.
11 Whedon et al., *Toy Story* Script, p. 6.
12 David A. Price, *The Pixar Touch: The Making of a Company* (New York: Vintage Books, 2008), p. 121.
13 Ibid.
14 Ibid.
15 Ibid., p. 123.
16 Ibid.
17 Ibid., p. 127.
18 Alec Sokolow and Tony Camin, 'The God of Story: An Interview with Robert McKee', *VICE*, 1 July 2014. http://www.vice.com/read/the-god-of-story-0000339-v21n6 (accessed 29 August 2016).
19 Walter Isaacson, *Steve Jobs* (New York: Simon & Schuster, 2011), p. 286.
20 Price, *The Pixar Touch*, p. 124.
21 Aubrey Day, 'Interview: John Lasseter', *Gamesradar+*, 3 June 2009. http://www.gamesradar.com/interview-john-lasseter/ (accessed 30 August 2016).
22 Pete Docter and Richard Crouse, 'Pete Docter | In Conversation With . . . | TIFF 2015', *YouTube*, 19 June 2015. https://www.youtube.com/watch?v=iml_slMLBUs (accessed 30 August 2016).
23 Stanton, 'Clues to a Great Story'.
24 French, '*Toy Story* Beginnings', p. 36.
25 Charles Solomon, *The Toy Story Films: An Animated Journey* (New York: Disney Editions, 2012), p. 40.
26 Price, *The Pixar Touch*, p. 125.
27 Ibid.
28 French, '*Toy Story* Beginnings', p. 36.
29 Scott Myers, 'GITS Q&A Part 3: Mary Coleman (Pixar)', *Go into the Story: Official Screenwriting Blog of the Black List*, 29 February 2012. http://gointothestory.blcklst.com/2012/02/gits-qa-part-3-mary-coleman-pixar.html (accessed 29 August 2016).
30 Sokolow and Camin, "God of Story".
31 Daniel Goldin, 'Inside Screenwriting: Script Gurus in 21st Century Hollywood', originally in *Premiere Magazine Online*, n.d., republished with author's permission at *Screenplayology.com*, ed. Andrew Kenneth Gay. http://www.screenplayology.com/PremiereScriptGurus.pdf, 3 (accessed 30 August 2016).

32 Neupert, *Lasseter*, p. 93.
33 Price, *The Pixar Touch*, p. 128.
34 Pallant and Price, *Storyboarding*, p. 59.
35 'Black Friday: The *Toy Story* You Never Saw', disc 1, *Toy Story*, special edition (Pixar Animation Studios/Walt Disney Pictures, 2010), Blu-ray.
36 Solomon, *Toy Story Films*, p. 43.
37 Amy Pascale, *Joss Whedon: The Biography* (Chicago: Chicago Review Press, 2014), p. 72.
38 Ibid., p. 73.
39 Ibid., p. 74.
40 Germain Lussier, 'Pixar's Rejected "*Toy Story*" Titles Revealed', *Film*, 24 August 2011. http://www.slashfilm.com/pixars-rejected-toy-story-titles-revealed/ (accessed 30 August 2016).
41 Ibid., p. 76.
42 Kathryn Harris and Claudia Eller, 'Studio Chief Katzenberg to Leave Disney', *Los Angeles Times*, 25 August 1994. http://articles.latimes.com/1994-08-25/news/mn-31054_1_jeffrey-katzenberg (accessed 30 August 2016).
43 Lawrence French, '*Toy Story*: Walt Disney and Pixar Team Up to Launch the First Computer-Animated Movie', *Cinefantastique*, November 1995, pp. 20–22.
44 Mike Bonifer, 'Rule #23', *GameChangers*, 7 October 2013. http://www.gamechangers.com/rule-23/ (accessed 29 August 2016).
45 Ken Levine, 'Beware of This Man' . . . *By Ken Levine: The World As Seen by a TV Comedy Writer*, 1 March 2007. http://kenlevine.blogspot.com/2007/03/beware-of-this-man.html (accessed 30 August 2016).
46 Jason Zinoman, 'Robert Mckee's Unconvincing Story', *Vanity Fair: The Hive*, December 2009. http://www.vanityfair.com/news/2009/11/robert-mckee-200911 (accessed 30 August 2016).
47 Goldin, 'Inside Screenwriting', p. 1.
48 Ibid., p. 3.
49 Price, *The Pixar Touch*, p. 127.
50 Sokolow and Camin, 'God of Story'.
51 McKee, *Story*, p. 100.
52 Ibid., p. 101.
53 Ibid., p. 376.
54 Ibid., p. 103.
55 Ibid., p. 104.
56 Whedon et al., *Toy Story* Script, p. 2.
57 French, '*Toy Story* Beginnings', p. 36.
58 Whedon et al., *Toy Story* Script, p. 12.
59 Ibid., p. 11.
60 Stanton, 'Clues to a Great Story'.
61 McKee, *Story*, p. 148.
62 Ibid., p. 375.
63 Ibid., p. 378.
64 Stanton, 'Clues to a Great Story'.
65 McKee, *Story*, 105–6.
66 Ibid., p. 140.
67 Ibid., p. 319.

68 Sokolow and Camin, 'God of Story'.
69 McKee, *Story*, p. 319.
70 Ibid.
71 Ibid.
72 Whedon et al., *Toy Story* Script, p. 23.
73 Ibid., p. 25.
74 Ibid., p. 28.
75 Ibid., pp. 49–50.
76 McKee, *Story*, pp. 319–20.
77 Sokolow and Camin, 'God of Story'.
78 Whedon et al., *Toy Story* Script, p. 91.
79 Ibid., p. 92.
80 Ibid., p. 97.
81 Ibid., p. 101.
82 McKee, *Story*, p. 332.
83 Nathan E. Douglas and Harold Jacob Smith, '*The Defiant Ones* Script', in George P. Garrett, O. B. Hardison, Jr. and Jane R. Gelfman (eds), *Film Scripts Two*, The Film Scripts Series (Milwaukee: Applause Theatre & Cinema Books, 2013), p. 353.
84 McKee, *Story*, p. 80.
85 Ibid., p. 89.
86 Price, *The Pixar Touch*, p. 127.
87 French, '*Toy Story* Beginnings', p. 36.
88 McKee, *Story*, p. 80.
89 Robert McKee, 'Q&A: If "Buddy Salvation" Is a Sub Genre of the Love Story Genre, Which of the Love Story Conventions Apply to It?' *Robert McKee's Storylogue: The Education of a Writer*, 5 November 2013. http://www.storylogue.com/docs/question-answer.html?documentId=1544 (accessed 30 August 2016).
90 McKee, *Story*, p. 95.
91 Neil Simon, *The Odd Couple I and II: The Original Screenplays* (New York: Touchstone, 2000).
92 Callie Khouri, *Thelma & Louise* Final Shooting Script (USA: Metro Goldwyn Mayer, 1990), unpublished screenplay. http://www.dailyscript.com/scripts/thelmaandlouise.html (accessed 30 August 2016).
93 Roger Spottiswoode et al., *48 Hrs.* Undated Script (USA: Paramount, n.d.), unpublished screenplay. http://www.dailyscript.com/scripts/48hours.html (accessed 30 August 2016).
94 Douglas and Smith, '*Defiant Ones* Script'.
95 George Gallo, *Midnight Run* Shooting Script (USA: Universal n.d.), unpublished screenplay. http://www.weeklyscript.com/Midnight+Run.html (accessed 30 August 2016).
96 McKee, 'Q&A'.
97 Douglas and Smith, '*Defiant Ones* Script', p. 353.
98 French, '*Toy Story* Beginnings', p. 36.
99 Pascale, *Joss Whedon*, p. 73.
100 Whedon et al., *Toy Story* Script, p. 125.
101 McKee, *Story*, p. 8.
102 Myers, 'GITS Q&A'.

103 Ibid., p. 91.

104 McKee, *Story*, p. 67.

105 Tim Kashani and Robert McKee, 'ShowbizU: When Pixar Met Robert McKee', *YouTube*, 22 July 2014. https://www.youtube.com/watch?v=kpN7KeWfbmE (accessed 30 August 2016).

Chapter 4

NEW AND INHERITED AESTHETICS: DESIGNING FOR THE *TOY STORY* TRILOGY ONE FILM AT A TIME

Heather L. Holian

In January of 1993 Ralph Eggleston started his new job at Pixar Animation Studios as art director of the project that would become *Toy Story* (John Lasseter, 1995). Over the next two and a half years, Eggleston collaborated with his small team of artists to develop a visual style that enhanced and realized the vision of director, John Lasseter, while also exploiting the available technology of this first CG animated film. In the process, Eggleston and his crew unknowingly established a design aesthetic that would directly impact two more *Toy Story* films over the next fifteen years, and likely a fourth, scheduled (at the time of writing) for US release in June 2019.

The original *Toy Story* not only launched a new visual art in the form of the 3-D animated film, but it also established a rich cast of characters in a distinctive imagined world that audiences quickly came to recognize and associate with this film, and ultimately with Pixar. The following study demonstrates that Pixar artists who were cast[1] to design the first two *Toy Story* sequels necessarily worked within the iconic visual world of the initial film, while simultaneously seeking to make their own contributions in step with trilogy story developments, technological advances and changes of director. Not surprisingly, the origins of the *Toy Story* aesthetic originated with Lasseter and his collaborations with the film's crew, including its art and story teams. As such, this chapter will similarly begin with *Toy Story* and an exploration of those initial influences and design challenges of Eggleston and his artistic team, before considering how the art departments of *Toy Story 2* (Lasseter, 1999) and *Toy Story 3* (Lee Unkrich, 2010) inherited, reinterpreted and extended the trilogy's aesthetic.

From the start, it was clear to Eggleston that the style of *Toy Story*, would be shaped by two primary factors: story and available technology. 'The story and those creating it were the inspirational guideposts', he recalled. 'Building on that were the form, color, textural and lighting supports for the specific needs of the characters and story – mostly derived from the basic conceit that our story was to be told from the point of view of the toys.'[2] Over the course of the project's development, collaborative back and forth conversations between the story and art teams helped determine the look of the entire film, in direct response to the story's evolving emotional content. According to Eggleston, all successful film design starts with, and is grounded in, the deep investigation of 'the specifics of emotional content from a character point of view'.[3] Indeed, one of his most vivid memories from those initial months on *Toy Story*, involved Lasseter expressing a similar sentiment to two Disney executives who visited Pixar, and who were looking at some of the earliest art for the film with he and Eggleston. They wished to know how the film their company was partnering to produce and release was going to look in its finished state. Eggleston recalled that he was not sure how to respond, being not only new to the project, but also the computer animation medium and its processes. 'I wasn't yet sure [how it would look] – but before I could say that, John jumped in (thankfully) and said, "the film will tell us what it needs to be visually". Not only was I relieved, but it turns out that this is a true-ism.'[4] Therefore, as the story and its characters and emotional content evolved and eventually solidified, the art team under Eggleston's guidance – and with Lasseter's input – worked to develop what would become the visual language of *Toy Story*. As with future Pixar productions, this collaborative development process with Lasseter involved a level of creative freedom and artistic agency whereby the film's art team was empowered and encouraged to individually respond to the story, offering their own ideas whenever appropriate. According to Eggleston,

> John was always so great about corralling our ideas and using them like a chef making a great meal. He was very hands on, but *always* very open to new ideas from anyone if it helped bring his story to life. Once we had a clear direction, he left us alone to plow forward, reining us in when necessary if he felt the story might be changing in a way that affected what we were doing. And we'd all add little details along the way where appropriate – ALWAYS 'character' based.[5]

Of the second stylistic factor, that of technology, Eggleston observed in 2015, 'Plastic toys and wood were easier. Fabric, simulations of (cloth, hair, water), atmosphere, and depth of field [were] much harder. That we attempted humans at all is a wonder!'[6] These limitations meant that character clothing had to be tight fitting or modeled into the animation, which directly impacted and limited character designs, as did the fact that hair had to be modeled as well. As a result, hair was kept short or contained, like the ponytail of Andy's mom.[7] Skin also proved difficult for the computer. From a design perspective these technological realities meant that the human characters had to be stylized.[8] These creative limitations naturally affected the film's global aesthetic, but fortunately a stylized visual approach also harmonized with the exaggerated and abstracted forms of many real-world children's toys, which provided direct inspiration for those found on screen, and to a large extent guided the film's overall style.

Additionally, the work of visual development artists hired primarily by Lasseter offered another critical stylistic inspiration. In fact, *Toy Story* established the now routine Pixar practice of acquiring alternative creative viewpoints from freelance artists outside the studio, with the goal being that these works would further generate energy, excitement and new ideas. For *Toy Story* these artists, who included illustrators Steve Johnson, William Joyce, Dave Gordon and Bill Cone, offered Eggleston and his team various creative solutions for the stylization of form, texture and lighting. Their simpler approaches to hair, the rendering of fabric and the suggestion of detail through pattern and colour were especially inspirational as the *Toy Story* art group tackled the challenge of building a rich appealing world that was also computer-friendly.[9]

According to Eggleston, however, it was the work of Bill Cone that proved particularly significant for the film's aesthetic: 'He really found the right balance of cartoony and real for our uses, and his designs always have such an acute and specific character driven sense of humor.'[10] Cone started as a Pixar freelancer in 1992, and was later hired as a permanent member of the *Toy Story* art department, where he focused primarily on set design. One of his most significant designs was the exterior of Sid's house, which Cone envisioned as a visual counterpoint to the neat, Craftsman style home of Andy that he'd already designed. He did a series of exploratory drawings reflecting various approaches to how this contrast might be shown. Then after some lively creative conversations between Cone and Eggleston during which they imagined what Sid's parents might be like, Cone hit on the idea of Sid's dad being a kind of 'weekend warrior' who ambitiously starts home improvement projects, but never finishes them properly. As a result each door and window of Sid's house is a different architectural style, producing what Cone described as a 'sort of hybrid Tudor, stucco Frankenstein of a thing'.[11] This disturbing hybridity continues on the interior, where various, visually discordant wallpapers and flooring from different decades contribute to the sense of unease radiated by this not very home-y house.[12] Indeed, the unpleasant ambience of Sid's environment was pointedly perpetuated by Eggleston's conscious use of the distinctive carpet pattern from *The Shining* (Stanley Kubrick, 1980) for the upstairs carpet of Sid's house.[13]

Other visual inspiration was found in the work of American painter Grant Wood, and illustrator and painter Maxfield Parrish, artists who Lasseter admired and brought to the attention of his team.[14] Lasseter singled out Parrish for his saturated colour and use of luminous, bouncing light, which the director found appealing. Indeed, the influence of Parrish's palette and lighting can be found in the final film, most noticeably in the sunset shots of Andy's house exterior and bedroom. Here the saturated palette of the film is further lit by a rich, rosy hue while cast shadows appear as a vibrant violet in the style of Parrish.[15] As for Grant Wood, Eggleston noted that his stylized paintings sparked creative solutions to design problems posed by the current technology. For example,

Wood's use of strong light sources and his reductive approach to landscapes provided an inspiring model for how to use subtle shifts in texture, lighting or even the position of objects to imply a visual richness not possible digitally at the time.[16] Wood's influence is apparent in several *Toy Story* shots, including the views of Andy's living room from the opening sequence. Here bright cast sunlight combines with the careful use of shape, and changes in texture, pattern and colour to suggest the desired layers of visual detail.

Despite the emphasis Eggleston placed on Cone's important design contributions, or the key models provided by the paintings of Wood or Parrish, the final, synthetic style of *Toy Story* was most strongly shaped by its art director. 'I'd say Ralph Eggleston's style influenced what was to become the *Toy Story* we saw on film', observed Tia Kratter who served as Lead Digital Painter on *Toy Story*. 'He was unafraid to use bright colors or dark values as the needs of the story dictated.'[17] Robert Kondo, Sets Art Director for *Toy Story 3* shared Kratter's opinion, frankly observing to Charles Solomon in 2010, 'Ralph Eggleston is the aesthetic of *Toy Story*'.[18] Indeed, aside from creating dozens of concept works for the film, Eggleston also produced the studio's first colourscript, a critical and now-routine design document that indicates a feature's colour, mood and lighting through a series of drawings arranged in sequential order. Here the colourscript consists of 33–35 unframed panels of varying length executed in rich pastel on strips of black paper measuring three by thirty inches.[19] Eggleston's stylized yet atmospheric approach to rendering the film's key shots predictably eschewed detail in favour of clear visual communication, including the film's bright, saturated palette and distinct Parrish-inspired lighting. Ultimately, Eggleston's *Toy Story* colourscript became one of the touchstone design documents of the trilogy, and was referenced and studied by later Pixar artists attached to the sequels.[20]

Given the substance of the film's story, Kratter remembered that the art team also relied as much as they could on real-world reference to further develop *Toy Story*'s visual aesthetic. These influential materials included not just the dozens of toys owned by Pixarians or viewed on sale racks at local toy stores,[21] but also dozens of photos of children and ubiquitous suburban elements, such as minivans and intersections, which are preserved today in Pixar's archives. For her purposes as lead digital painter, Kratter recalled 'forcing' her seven-year-old son to get a flat top haircut like Sid's so she could take photos and investigate the hair's appearance and texture. She also photographed her niece's hairline as a reference for Andy's sister, Molly. In another case, a trip to a local garden nursery produced a useful houseplant that Kratter carefully studied in order to paint the digital model of the potted vegetation covertly used by the green Army Men in the film's opening moments.[22]

The small art team responsible for finding *Toy Story*'s design solutions and then putting them on screen numbered five, including Eggleston.[23] Their offices were together, in very close proximity, and among the story and technical teams. 'And people (including me) kept their doors open', Eggleston remembered. 'It was easier to hear folks beating their foreheads on their keyboards.'[24] Kratter, Cone and Eggleston fondly recalled a lively collaborative environment in which iteration happened very quickly,[25] problem solving was 'on the fly',[26] in person, and without the notes, email or meetings that often attend today's evolving designs at the studio.[27] The shout of a question frequently provided many humorous as well as useful suggestions from a group of people who not only clearly respected one another, but in terms of the artists, they also came from similar artistic backgrounds, and therefore spoke the same design language, struggled equally with the new medium and bonded as a result. (Interestingly, each of these artists still works at Pixar and several of them contributed to *Toy Story*'s later instalments.)

Toy Story 2

In 1996 the Walt Disney Company approached Pixar about the possibility of making a direct-to-video sequel to *Toy Story*.[28] Pixar agreed and work began by the fall of that year.[29] Within months, however, Pixar proposed to Disney that for internal cultural reasons, the film should become a theatrical release.[30] Due to the high quality and potential of the project Disney had simultaneously arrived at the same conclusion.[31] Disney approved Pixar's request, and soon the small studio was running two full-scale productions concurrently, *Toy Story 2* and *A Bug's Life* (Lasseter, 1998). The final, dramatic circumstances surrounding this project are well known, including the film's change of director and its story reboot ten months prior to the film's November 1999 release date.[32] Despite the many changes that did occur over *Toy Story 2*'s nearly three-year production period, no alteration was made to the global aesthetic of the film when it shifted from a video to a theatrical release, or when director changes were made in December 1998. Predictably, the budget enlarged significantly as the project evolved, but this allowed for greater visual richness, rather than prompting a shift in style.[33] Likewise, the late change in the film's production designers did not impact the movie's visual language

Jim Pearson was initially hired in December 1996 to serve as art director for the direct-to-video version of *Toy Story 2*. When the project was upgraded, so was Pearson's position. He became the production designer of *Toy Story 2* in 1997 and oversaw much of the film's visual development and design during its first two years.[34] Once Lasseter and Lee Unkrich assumed directing responsibilities for the final ten-month push, Lasseter brought in a trusted group of creative and administrative leads who had worked with him on previous projects. Bill Cone was part of this so-called 'swat team' and assumed the role of production designer. As such, Cone attended shading and model reviews, met weekly with Lasseter, supervised the final sequences of the film to go into production, and managed the same *Toy Story 2* art team, which included Pearson, who became Cone's co-production designer.[35] As Cone has stressed on several occasions, the re-envisioned film could not have been made in such a short period if Pearson and his crew had not successfully completed an 'enormous amount of work',[36] which included designing all of the characters and many of the sets prior to the reboot.[37] Considering that creative process, Pearson recalled: 'When we started it was part of our mandate to make sure that we visually related the world that *we* built to the first movie.'[38] Therefore, when Cone joined the team, the only revisionary work needed was the colourscript, which he did redo so that it corresponded to the revised story and better aligned with the first *Toy Story* in terms of palette.[39]

Cone's action and Pearson's design mandate both reflect one of the challenges of designing for sequels, namely maintaining the iconic look of the original film. This goal is particularly relevant to a medium where quantum leaps in technology can radically alter the appearance of the sequel, even one designed two years later. Indeed, Cone believes that 'determining what is necessary to retain from the original in terms of look or style, and also exploring how you can expand the film's palette, or solve its problems creatively without resorting to the same solutions that were used in the earlier film' are some of the most difficult production design challenges for sequels.[40] Moreover, as Eggleston noted, sequels depend upon characters and environments that audiences already know, but the design challenge – and excitement – both for the art team and the audience, comes from developing and expanding the world beyond what was previously seen.[41] For his part, Pearson acknowledged feeling some pressure designing for the theatrical sequel to the popular, profitable, groundbreaking *Toy Story*, but the positive collaborative dynamic of his art team mitigated those feelings as did the first film, 'They did *so* many things right in that movie . . . We had a really great, solid foundation of quality to build on.'[42]

This foundation, of course, included the design aesthetic established by Eggleston, and subsequently inherited by Pearson and his *Toy Story 3* successor, Bob Pauley, both of whom consulted Eggleston during their stints on each film.[43] The original set of Andy's room offers an excellent example of how the foundational stylistic and formal elements of *Toy Story* were both retained and revised by later Pixar artists. Despite appearing in a new house, the iconic, caricatured furniture designs of Andy's memorable room were carried over in both *Toy Story 2* and *3*, where they were appropriately aged. Moreover, Andy's new room also has a hardwood floor, and the same warm, reflected light of the first film. All of these features, recognizable to audiences, continued to contribute to the sense of Andy's room as 'home', and how home should feel – comfortable, safe, inviting and familiar. Even the wallpaper is essentially the same blue, although rather than a fluffy cloud, Pearson explained that he selected a gold star to reference both Woody and Buzz, through the sheriff badge and stars of outer space, respectively.[44] According to Cone, the visual continuity of this space as 'home', and especially for the toys, was an important touchstone to establish, as it allowed the art team 'leeway to imagine' and light the new sets of

Toy Story 2 differently, even in contrast to Andy's room.[45] Indeed, the exterior of Andy's new house and his room, seen very briefly at the end of the first film, were the only sets carried over, which gave Pearson, Cone and their team ample opportunity to extend the environments of the *Toy Story* world. This occurred most notably in Al's apartment and collection room, the airport set and especially Al's Toy Barn, referenced in film one.

In preparation for designing Al's Toy Barn, Pearson looked at the concept work Eggleston and Cone produced for the Pizza Planet set of the original *Toy Story*. Pearson explained that the two sets felt conceptually analogous, since they were both themed and caricatured. Moreover, the Toy Barn was 'this oddly anachronistic rural structure' originally set in suburbia, like Pizza Planet, although with changes to the story it was later moved downtown across from Al's apartment, further heightening the structure's absurd incongruity with its surroundings. From a design perspective, the interior of Al's Toy Barn offered a kind of space that Andy's toys had yet to encounter. It was filled with toys in bright, cheerful packaging and yet with a few exceptions, these beings were in a kind of eerie suspended animation. Pearson wanted to immediately convey that this was a disorienting, mysterious, even scary place for Andy's toys, and related design discussions focused on one of the central themes of *Toy Story*, namely that 'toys don't really come to life until they're played with'. As a result, Pearson explained that the crew decided to 'double down' on this idea, through the set's cool lighting, which evoked a 'kind of enormous cryogenic chamber for toys' that also served to provide the right level of foreboding. The only significant exception to this atmosphere was the late addition of the pink Barbie aisle, where dolls frolic outside their packaging in a patch of warmer lighting.[46]

Like Andy's room, the toy characters that inhabit this familiar space were also inherited designs Pearson and his team contended with when designing anew. For example, the appearance and production logic of Woody ultimately dictated the new character designs for each member of Woody's Roundup, challenging the artists in their designs.[47] Pearson and his team looked at Woody and imagined the kind of manufacturing processes needed to make a 1950s toy like him, and then applied those techniques to the design of the entire ensemble. Therefore, all three new characters – Jessie, Bullseye and the Prospector – are made from cloth, have the same stitched knees and hip joints, and the same hard plastic heads, hands, hooves and facial details. As a result, Woody's original design, which took some time to land upon, eventually gave rise to three more important characters, two of which were recurring.[48] Moreover, the Woody's Roundup conceit of *Toy Story 2* required the 'reverse engineering' of an entire backstory for Woody and an extensive set of related vintage memorabilia and packaging.[49] Pearson recalled: 'The opportunity to expand the *Toy Story* canon by giving Woody this colorful pop culture backstory was really one of the indelible things about this film, and I think for us as artists, as creative people, that was really kind of a cherry on top.'[50] Pearson and his team looked at Roy Rogers and Hopalong Cassidy paraphernalia, specifically studying the types of objects produced as well as how they were made and showed wear over time. Ultimately, the story and art teams closely collaborated to imagine the numerous physical items that finally populated Al's collection room.[51]

By the time *Toy Story 2* was in development, technology had greatly advanced allowing for a hyperrealistic environment akin to that glimpsed in *A Bug's Life*, and yet the computer still struggled with humans. Better skin shaders and improved hair and cloth simulation[52] enabled noticeable improvements over the characters of the first film, but encouraged a continued stylization in human design. As a result, Pearson acknowledged that one of the project's design challenges was consciously pulling back from a realism that was now digitally possible for items such as toys or tree bark, but not possible for humans.[53] This design approach, however, ensured a homogenous style that also perpetuated the established *Toy Story* look.

Toy Story 3

In early 2006, just over six years after the release of *Toy Story 2*, Lasseter asked his trusted co-director from that film, Lee Unkrich, to helm the franchise's third instalment. Unkrich, in turn, cast Bob Pauley, a character designer for film one as his production designer, while Pauley selected relative Pixar newcomer Daisuke 'Dice' Tsutsumi as his art director of lighting. These personnel choices would prove significant for the notable expansion of both the *Toy Story* world, and its aesthetic. For example, Unkrich is fascinated by horror stories and the macabre,[54] both of which find their way into this film through story elements as well as individual characters, such as the creepy, cymbal-playing Monkey, and the broken, shuffling Big Baby, whose head turns 180° in a particularly chilling scene, evoking *The Exorcist* (William Friedkin, 1973). Tsutsumi, who completed the colourscript for *Toy Story 3*, responded to Unkrich's personal inspirations by introducing both a moodier palette and overall lighting scheme that went beyond either earlier film. This expanded approach to lighting, which was encouraged by enormous technological advances since the previous film, is particularly notable throughout the daycare-as-prison sequences, where colour is desaturated and light is often stark.

As on *Toy Story 2*, Pauley and his crew inherited design assets like Pearson and his team, and they also shared a strong desire to connect their film with the style first introduced by Ralph Eggleston. They did this strategically, in a variety of ways. For example, they continued to use the recognizable set of Andy's room, and Tsutsumi employed the colour and lighting of film one within the early montage of video clips of Andy playing with his toys. Tsutsumi explained to Charles Solomon: 'We lit the montage like the *Toy Story* world where the shadows are bright purple and the sunlight comes through the window, bounces off the wooden floor and warms the entire room. That's one of the signature styles of *Toy Story* that John really pushed.'[55] Then, when the story picks up seven years later, Andy is preparing to leave for college, playtime is over and the future of the toys is uncertain. Tsutsumi lit the room indirectly with more desaturated light to signal this contrast of time and circumstance.[56]

Once the toys leave the safe confines of Andy's house, Pauley and his team were in new territory with the chance to again extend the trilogy's environments. One of these spaces was Bonnie's house. Although seen relatively briefly in the film, it was critical from a design and story perspective that this space not only felt like a safe, happy haven for toys, but was also stylistically consistent with the established *Toy Story* world. To do this, Pauley went back and looked at the shape language used in pivotal sets on *Toy Story* and *Toy Story 2*, such as the gas station, Pizza Planet, the airport and Andy's house. These repetitive shapes became guiding forms for designing Bonnie's space as well, which Tsutsumi then lit with dappled sunlight.[57] This distinctive lighting technique was purposely employed throughout the film as a visual signifier of Bonnie and her safe, imaginative world,[58] and thus established a new element of the trilogy's visual aesthetic.

The team's most ambitious new set designs, however, were those for Sunnyside Daycare, and the city dump. In the latter, the world takes on an especially photorealistic aesthetic, heightening the climactic drama. The toys stand among blowing debris and mounds of garbage, eerily lit by bulldozers and work lights that also illuminate the heavy air full of dust. Here, as elsewhere in the film, available technology permitted atmospheric effects not seen in either of the earlier films. Indeed, for the first time in the trilogy such realistic passages were stylistically feasible since the human characters could now more closely match environmental fidelity. Invaluable, inspirational field trips by Pixar artists to local daycares and the landfill helped the crew layer these sets with real-world details and light effects, which grounded the spaces in a tangible reality, intended to further enhance the audience's emotional engagement.[59]

Conclusion

When Ralph Eggleston and his team began work on *Toy Story* in 1993 they were forced to envision and design a cinematic world ultimately defined by the confining parameters of current technology. However, following a range of visual inspiration provided by director John Lasseter, children's toys, historical fine artists, freelancers and Eggleston's own crew, the *Toy Story* art team discovered design possibilities and innovative solutions to technical limitations. The final synthetic result under Eggleston's leadership was a bright, stylized world that became the *Toy Story* aesthetic. During design work for film two, Jim Pearson, and later Bill Cone, contended with an inherited and iconic visual style, as well as the challenges of current software to expand the world of *Toy Story* through elaborate new sets and important recurring characters. Stylization remained an aesthetic hallmark of *Toy Story 2* out of technological necessity, while also serving a strong studio desire for visual continuity. By the start of *Toy Story 3*, the computer offered no such limitations, and instead, Bob Pauley and his art team were challenged by how to employ new technology while remaining true to an inherited visual style intimately associated with Pixar's most recognizable franchise. Design strategies which borrowed heavily upon the colour, lighting and shape language of the earlier films allowed Pauley to do just that, while the cinematic tastes of Lee Unkrich and the design sensibilities of Dice Tsutsumi combined to dramatically extend and develop the trilogy's aesthetic.

Notes

1 This term is widely used in the industry today to reference the way in which individuals are chosen for or assigned to particular roles on specific films based upon their personal talents and creative strengths. At Pixar, directors cast their core creative team such as the production designer or head of story, who in turn casts some of the members of their own departmental crews. Walt Disney first employed the practice with his animators beginning in the early 1930s when he carefully selected animators for particular characters or sequences based upon their artistic skills. Michael Barrier, *Hollywood Cartoons: American Animation in Its Golden Age* (Oxford: Oxford University Press, 1999), p. 88.
2 Ralph Eggleston, interview by the author via email, 29 June 2015.
3 Ibid.
4 Ibid.
5 Ibid.
6 Ibid.
7 Ibid. The one exception was Scud, whose fur was created by *Toy Story*'s Lead Digital Painter Tia Kratter through the time-consuming process of digital painting displacement, whereby the digital model is manipulated in or out. With Scud, Kratter was displacing the model downward as she digitally painted tiny hairs to emulate fur. Tia Kratter, email message to author, 6 August 2015.
8 Eggleston also credited the particular production process of *Toy Story* for the appearance of the humans. 'Some people think the "look" of the humans or Scud in *Toy Story* were hampered by technical limitations – and some of that is true', he explained. 'But what affected that just as much was how we approached them from a production point of view. It wasn't as "whole-istic" as it should have been – but was understandable seeing as we were all wearing multiple hats and were juggling various phases of items in production'. Eggleston interview, June 2015.

9 Ibid.
10 Ralph Eggleston, email message to author, 16 July 2015.
11 Bill Cone, interview by author via email, 15 October 2015.
12 Eggleston interview, June 2015.
13 Tia Kratter, interview by author via email, 6 August 2015.
14 Maxfield Parrish is a personal favorite of Lasseter and returned as an inspirational reference point for the film *Cars*. His work had already been a touchstone for the earlier short, *The Adventures of André and Wally B.* (Alvy Ray Smith, 1984), when Lasseter used Parrish as an example of the color variation in tree leaves. See Michael Rubin, *Droidmaker: George Lucas and the Digital Revolution* (Gainesville, FL: Triad, 2006), p. 364. Moreover, Bill Cone, production designer for *A Bug's Life* believes that given Lasseter's fondness for Parrish's work he and his team also consulted the artist for Lasseter's second film. Bill Cone, email message to author, 11 November 2014.
15 In particular see Parrish's paintings, *Arizona* from 1950, and *The Millpond* of 1945.
16 Eggleston interview, June 2015.
17 Kratter interview, August 2015.
18 Quoted in Charles Solomon, *The Art of Toy Story 3* (San Francisco: Chronicle Books, 2010), p. 31.
19 Ibid.
20 Jim Pearson, email message to author, 28 May 2016; Amid Amidi, *The Art of Pixar: The Complete Colorscripts and Select Art from 25 Years of Animation* (San Francisco: Chronicle Books, 2011), p. 15.
21 Bob Pauley, interview by author, 23 April 2013.
22 Kratter interview, August 2015. The houseplant was also painted through the challenging displacement technique (see n. 7).
23 In addition to Bob Pauley, the final member of the team was Robin Cooper.
24 Ralph Eggleston, email message to author, 16 July 2015.
25 Cone interview, October 2015.
26 Kratter interview, August 2015.
27 Ralph and Tia both make mention of this change.
28 The practice of following a box office hit with a direct-to-video sequel starring the same characters had already worked well for Disney, as evidenced by *The Return of Jafar* (Tad Stones, 1994). Typically Disney's video sequels were made oversees, on a shorter schedule and for a fraction of the price. Charles Solomon, *The Toy Story Films: An Animated Journey* (New York: Disney Editions, 2012), p. 86.
29 By the time Jim Pearson joined the team in December as art director of the project, early visualization of the film had already started under the direction of Ash Brannon, who later became the film's co-director. Artists Laura Phillips and Randy Berrett were already working as full-time sketch artists and freelancers Dave Gordon and Sean Hargreaves had been hired to create visual development work for the project. Jim Pearson, interview by author, 15 October 2015; email correspondence with author, 1 June 2016.
30 Ed Catmull, *Creativity, Inc.: Overcoming the Unseen Forces that Stand in the Way of True Inspiration* (New York: Random House, 2014), p. 67.
31 Pearson interview.
32 For various accounts see Solomon, *The Toy Story Films*; Catmull, *Creativity, Inc.*; Karen Paik, *To Infinity and Beyond: The Story of Pixar Animation Studios*

(San Francisco: Chronicle Books, 2007), pp. 142–61; David A. Price, *The Pixar Touch: The Making of a Company* (New York: Alfred A. Knopf, 2008), p. 174ff.

33 Jim Pearson remembered that the project had a 'laundry list of things that we were then all the sudden allowed to do, or were capable of doing when we went theatrical, because they gave us basically another year and a whole bunch more money'. Among the items on their wish list was the ability to make the trees in Andy's yard blow in the breeze, like the vegetation did in *A Bug's Life*, which was nearing completion. The trees were built, but before the theatrical decision enlarged the project's funds, the production did not have the budget to allocate time to the technical team to make them move. Pearson interview.

34 Ibid.

35 Bill Cone, email message to author, 13 October 2015.

36 Bill Cone, email message to author, 15 October 2015.

37 Bill Cone, email message to author, 28 May 2015.

38 Pearson interview.

39 However, Cone's new *Toy Story 2* colorscript, which corresponded with the rewritten story is not complete because lighting had already begun on the film and there was no time to finish the colorscript. Instead, Cone and Sharon Calahan, director of photography, verbally discussed how some sequences should look. Cone, email, 13 October 2015.

40 Cone, email, 15 October 2015.

41 Eggleston interview.

42 Pearson interview.

43 Eggleston interview, Pearson interview.

44 Pearson interview.

45 Cone interview.

46 Pearson interview.

47 Originally a plastic squeeze toy named Señorita Cactus, whose appearance was inspired by Carmen Miranda and Lupe Vélez, was planned in place of Jessie. According to Pearson, her character was defined as 'being prickly', but ultimately 'cooler heads prevailed' as she was determined to be too limiting. Pearson interview.

48 Ibid.

49 Bill Cone specifically identified this as one of the biggest design challenges of *Toy Story 2*, along with Al's apartment and Toy Barn, while acknowledging he had 'next to nothing' to do with the solution since he was not then on the film. Cone interview.

50 Pearson interview.

51 Ibid.

52 Cloth simulation, while improved was not yet perfected, despite breakthroughs on *Geri's Game* (Jan Pinkava, 1997), and therefore Al's pants had to be sculpted into the model, as on the first film. 'We came up with a solution that worked and it was originally supposed to be a technical limitation, but we just found ways to get around stuff', Pearson proudly observed. Pearson interview.

53 Pearson interview.

54 Cone, email message to author, 28 May 2015.
55 Solomon, *Art of Toy Story 3*, p. 54.
56 Ibid., p. 55.
57 Ibid., p. 131.
58 Ibid.
59 Pauley interview.

Chapter 5

ROUGH AND SMOOTH: THE EVERYDAY TEXTURES OF *TOY STORY*

Lucy Fife Donaldson

As one of the first fully computer-generated imagery (CGI) films, it is not surprising that *Toy Story* (John Lasseter, 1995) figures prominently in debates about both the technical achievements of digital imaging and the anxieties concerning absence in digital filmmaking, particularly the perceived inherent lack of materiality in its processes and final product. As CGI exponentially enlarges the plasticity of a fictional world, the inevitable emphasis on plastic surfaces within a film that focuses on children's toys seems to magnify the concerns of the latter camp, causing writers to equate its constitution with insubstantiality, finding the film to be dominated by a processed smoothness that corresponds to the feel of CGI more generally. As Ian Garwood puts it, the concern is that 'the infinite manipulability of the image betrays its fatal lack of real-world robustness'.[1] The result is that connections between the plasticity of the technology and its plastic/in-organic look lead to the digital being conceptualized as too much surface and not enough depth, an absence or even a flimsiness in its efforts to form objects, characters and worlds. And yet, there are those that recognize its material possibilities, such as Giuliani Bruno who suggests there is a continuity to be found in the digital evolutions of media, 'in the digital age, materiality can be reactivated, because it was always a virtual condition'.[2] Thomas Elsaesser and Malte Hagener emphasize the malleability of the digital as a positive, suggesting that to focus on a movement from concrete to abstract 'is merely to paint the reverse side of its strengths'.[3] Following their leads, rather than focusing on the film's CGI animation as presenting a deficit of materiality, this chapter is based on the idea that looking at digitally composited space expands opportunities to discuss the sensory appeal of film. Michel Chion has recognized *Toy Story*'s attention to surface and the material qualities of certain objects as an effort to revitalize interest in texture: '*Toy Story* delights through conveying the toys' texture, which in real life we don't notice or consider interesting'.[4] I suggest that this interest in unnoticed everyday textures goes beyond the toys themselves, and is a crucial part of the film's development of a fully formed and dense fictional world and of the narrative's interest in rearranging our perspective to the scale and axes of movement inhabited by its characters.

Texture and Surface

Cinema of all kinds can be considered textured, the characteristics and appeal of its formal properties wrought through colour, shape, fabric, density and light. The resulting textures are intimately related to the nature of the film world, acting both as functional parameters of that world's consistency and as sensory contexts that inform our response to it. Surface characteristics are perhaps the most immediate to communicate the feel of a fictional world: a hard rough space might seem gritty or even threatening, while a smooth and soft environment can be luxurious or comforting. These particularities of décor and setting determine dynamics of mood and atmosphere; how a space materially feels informs how characters and audience respond to it. Coming from a spread of theoretical bases, work on the material qualities of cinema – its tactility and substance – has sought to emphasize its tangible properties, the different ways in which cinema conjures a range of sensory experiences beyond sight and sound, the way film moves us and works to immerse us in its worlds. Contemplation of texture in film offers a way to unpick the feelings evoked by the constituents of a film's form, by the qualities of its materials and how it uses them. *Toy Story* offers an ideal opportunity to think about the attention to texture enabled and necessitated by digital filmmaking, and to consider the expressive work of CGI.

Texture necessitates a focus on the fine detail, as well as precision about the specific qualities and consistency of the material that makes up the composition as a whole. As a critical concept it places attention on the hitherto overlooked, the minute choices that shape the fabrication and feel of film. Through a concern with texture, the surface of objects and environment become important to locating these detailed choices. As Victoria Kelley observes, although diminished in all sorts of ways, surfaces are worthy of our attention:

> Despite the fact that surface is frequently belittled or ignored in language and in discourse, in material practice surface layers are often given special attention, coated with substances or treated with processes that alter their appearance, including their colour and their feel (glaze on ceramics, varnish on wood, cosmetics on human skin) and that are two-dimensional applications upon three-dimensional objects. Thus the material complexity of the surface, as well as its assiduous formation, invites investigation.[5]

The material complexity Kelley describes here is important to my focus on the dramatic achievements of *Toy Story*. Surface prompts touch in the sense that this is the site of our tangible exchanges, whether through actual contact with an object or visually predicting its feel. Looking across the surface – a haptic contact whereby the eyes function like a hand brushing over an object – has become an important way of understanding the tactile appeal of cinema.[6] Although my account of *Toy Story*'s textures is not framed through an understanding of a purely haptic relationship with the image, this does have the benefit of drawing attention to surfaces and maintaining their importance to our understanding of the feeling of form. Moreover, the 'special attention' and 'assiduous formation' connected to the complexities of surface signal the importance of the effort that goes into the making of objects and surfaces.

Smoothness and Plasticity

It certainly seems appropriate that the primary focus of attention to *Toy Story*'s material qualities would concern its plastic surfaces. There is a clear correspondence between medium and material recognized by filmmakers and scholars alike,[7] the plastic qualities of CGI making it the ideal vehicle for a film that features plastic objects as its main characters. Through this embedded responsiveness to surface, the film explores the complexities of plastic as a material: the plastic of Mr. Potato Head is hard and rigid, causing his component parts to clatter to the floor whenever he is knocked, while the moulded surface of the squeaky claw-worshipping aliens is soft and yielding. This rendering of a smooth and shiny tactile world prompts responses like that of William Schaffer who observes '*Toy Story* as a whole resonates with the *feel* of plastic'.[8] As noted by Vivian Sobchack through her observation that the 'tactile, kinetic, redolent, resonant, and sometimes even taste-full descriptions of the film experience'[9] are more frequently found in popular accounts of cinema and not academic ones, *Toy Story* is a film noted in reviews for its careful production of touchable surfaces: 'A Tyrannosaurus rex doll is so glossy and tactile you feel as if you could reach and stroke its hard, shiny head.'[10] The touchability highlighted by Glieberman's review here was important to the film's makers too. Thomas Schumacher, former President of Walt Disney Feature Animation, connects this tactility to the believability and integrity of its fictional world: 'the sense that you can reach out and hold what you see on the screen – is very significant to the appeal of the film. If you tried to make it look like real life, you would fail, because it will never look like real life, but it can be touchable life.'[11] Echoing these ideas, Jennifer M. Barker sees the film as an example of a Hollywood blockbuster 'whose critical success owes much to the human need for touch and texture', going on to suggest a significant connection between the appearance of its surfaces and the qualities of the fiction, whereby 'nostalgic charm and its kid-appeal are inseparable from its tactile allure'.[12]

While the tactile correspondences between medium and material are seen to buoy up engagement with *Toy Story*'s fictional world through consistencies of nostalgic appeal, they are also registered as somewhat less than, insufficient in complexity or depth. Barker's discussion of the film continues as a critique of the absence of texture, both in the smooth surfaces of its world and in its digital form, describing its touchability as contingent on a surface that is as 'cool and smooth as a Fisher-Price toy', devoid of imperfections.[13] She goes on to elaborate further on these qualities of plastic perfection:

> Its texture is completely manufactured and processed, and even if we didn't know that this film was the first feature in history to consist entirely of computer-generated imagery, we would *feel* it. This film's skin has no grain to it, no roughness, no messiness: it is as smooth as a plastic Magic Eight ball. Its giddy Play-Doh colors are manufactured, so rich and bright that they could hardly exist outside toy stores and candy counters: every red is a smooth candy-apple red, and every pink is a squishy bubble-gum pink.[14]

Garwood has already observed that this criticism of *Toy Story* as smooth and cold, or 'too *pristine*',[15] is overstated. For him, writers such as Barker, Darley and Schaffer 'reinforce the view that a plastic consistency characterizes the texture of CGI'.[16] Garwood goes on to suggest that in *Toy Story* and its sequels 'There are many moments where the plastic sheen of the CGI image is deliberately roughened up'.[17] Garwood addresses variations in image texture through moments in which video games and video recordings are brought into the fictional world, highlighting how changes in image resolution offer playful explorations of different visual schemes that are used to distinguish between characters (good versus bad), and in the layering of narrative spaces this achieves, which ultimately suggest 'continuities between media formats'.[18] Picking up from Garwood's nuanced discussion of the film's exploration of media textures and how these relate to the sensory aspects of storytelling – that is the texture *of* the film as imagined through its narrative structures and attitudes to character development and the fictional world – this chapter addresses the moments when the smooth surfaces of the film are 'roughened up' by focusing on textures *in* the film. The precision of CGI strategically reproduces imperfection and roughness, so that the world of the film is not merely smooth but *textured.*

Imperfection and the Everyday

In coherence with the care afforded the plastic construction of its characters, *Toy Story* pays consistent attention to developing the intricacies of their environment. What this reveals is an everyday mundanity rather than a falsely rendered and flimsy fantasy, where the inclusion of scuffs, scratches, chips and knocks to the edges of doors and windowsills work to flesh out the dimensions of the space. In the first moment when narrative action switches from the make-believe scenario of Andy's (John Morris) playtime to the toys as a community, the detailed rendering of surface imperfections is made apparent. On Woody's (Tom Hanks) prompting that 'the coast is clear', RC, the toy car, emerges from its hiding place in a cupboard and peers around the door, the edge of which is visibly scratched, scuffed and indented. Similar marks of everyday wear and tear are repeated throughout Andy's home, typically in the background of the action, such as the bottom of the door in front of which the green soldiers freeze in a tableau before Andy's mom bursts through to step on one of them, or on the window frame behind Buzz Lightyear (Tim Allen) as he first encounters his new home. Elsewhere, details of irregularity, roughness and corrosion are woven into the broader fabrication of the film's spaces and the objects in them, from the rusty edging of the Pizza Planet delivery truck to the heavily scored and pitted surface of the desk in the room of neighbouring toy-torturer Sid (Erik von Detten). While there are elements of its design that evoke an American past, especially the kinds of colour and shapes we might associate with a mid-century modernist sheen,[19] this is a fictional world that shows signs of ageing and wear, of use and life.

The presence of marks and scuffs on skirting boards and doors map the dramatic action and setting of *Toy Story* directly on to the surface qualities of our own lives. Through these additions the filmmakers' emphasis is on a lived-in world, an environment that has been used and worn over time: 'We wanted to do more dirt and dust bunnies – the stuff you really see in your house instead of some perfect place that exists inside a computer program.'[20] Eggleston's comment here makes a clear connection between design and a desire to immerse the audience, to connect the world of the film to their daily routines. The inclusion of roughness and imperfection is thus a strategy to counteract the potential false feeling of CGI, the perfect virtual space. Control of the surface texture shapes the world as lived-in, a shaping Eggleston connects to believability over strict reality, and perhaps it is these kind of minute details that can make a virtual space feel like one that you might really inhabit (as opposed to trying to appear 'real', a distinction I take to be the avoidance of a photo-realist style).[21]

In their explorations of surface, Glenn Adamson and Victoria Kelley (alongside their contributors) note the temporality of texture, picking out surfaces that mark the passage of time – the softened and defaced funerary monument of Ralph of Shrewsbury, Bishop of Bath and Wells in Wells Cathedral – and those that have been deliberately altered to simulate age – the distressed patina of faked antiques. Their emphasis on surface texture's connection to temporality in a multitude of design contexts bears noting: 'Because they are impacted upon by the world around them, surfaces are usually subject to change over time (soiling, fading, creasing, cracking)'.[22] Building on their discussion of texture and temporality, we might come back to that skirting board with scratches and dents to consider how such marks inform us that the skirting board has existed long enough to be scratched, and furthermore that there is a history of contact between it and the inhabitants of the house, which could be mapped with no small amount of specificity. The particular marks and chips point out the routines and habits, the spots where contact is regularly made – doors and windows that are opened frequently, cupboards that are used all the time. As Bruno notes, 'an affect is actually "worn" on the surface as it is threaded through time in the form of residual stains, traces, and textures'.[23] Texture and its relation to temporality are thus involved in telling us a story about everyday life, filling in a history of activity and motion prior to this part of the narrative.

Coming back to the tactility of the film, while the sheen of a plastic surface might provoke a desire to touch, there is a way in which marks and dirt add to a surface's touchability, in that there is something to feel. Too shiny a surface might deflect touch – the coldness that Barker notes – whereas a scored or roughened surface invites exploration and tells a story about prior interactions. Texture thereby adds depth, in aesthetic and narrative terms. For CGI, the process of creating these textures involves a layering and fabrication that reveals deep concerns with the material:

> In order to provide the withered, old look that has been painted multiple times, it is divided into more than five layers: a layer for the wood grain, a hand painted layer to indicate where the base coat of paint lies, another painted layer to describe where this paint is chipped and scratched, more layers of paint for color, and finally, a layer of dirt and scratches to provide the aged affect.[24]

I will come back to discuss the intensity of this work, but for now it is worth contemplating the relative 'thickness' of the design, and the extent to which this kind of layering is expressly focused on creating a narrative of patina and textures.

If roughened edges describe frequent contacts and use, these details present not just the abstract notion of a world that is inhabited, but moreover, how the world is used and moved through. As in live-action film, the design of a particular space supplies clues and ideas about its inhabitants, from basic socio-economic information to indications of culture and taste, even to details about how people (or toys) move through the space, their habits and the nature of their activities. These might include: being rough or gentle with door openings; heavy footed or clumsy with possessions; in the habit of sitting in one particular chair, or in one spot at a desk; and so on. In an article that focuses on the phenomenological aesthetics of fictional worlds in film, Christopher Yates describes the importance of the 'subtlety of specific things', those material details of the film's world not strictly necessary to plot but constitutive of the nature of the world and the people that live in it.[25] He attends to the kind of world-building details that fill in information about the place and time, but also how it feels to be in that world (e.g. tasks which cause heat and dirt, natural elements of landscape and wildlife). The fairly limited environment of *Toy Story* features two key spaces: Andy's bedroom and Sid's bedroom. The textural differences of these are chosen to dramatize the differences between their inhabitants, and by extension, the experiences of the toys who move through them.

The contrast of the bedrooms connects to the differences in the boys' temperaments, and the responses of the toys to them. While Andy's room is scuffed here and there, the colour scheme – dominated by sky blue and white – shiny wood floors and abundant windows make for a bright and light space, a room of clean lines and ample proportions where the toys feel safe. This is the site of many happy playtimes with areas specifically designated for the toys – a chest, as well as open shelving and cupboard space – which offer them a certain mastery over their environment. If we are to understand this as a place of work, in which toys have staff meetings, these are considerations that provide a degree of comfort and security, perhaps akin to modern open-plan offices. In contrast, Sid's room is a dark and cluttered landscape, where toys are left to hide wherever they can, clustering in dark corners under the bed, lest they be pulled apart and repurposed. The freedom of movement enabled by Andy's room is replaced by a restrictive and threatening space, conveyed through more abrasive and coarse textures that communicate discomfort and perhaps even destructive impulses towards objects that cannot be contained. It is also a space of many textures: 'Before [Tom Porter, shader and visual effects lead] worked on it, Sid's room looked like a collection of smooth, abstracted shapes; when he was done, the place overwhelmingly conjured the wretched, stuck-in-the-'70s mood that Eggleston was looking for – right down to the bits of glitter in the stucco ceiling.'[26] In the context of an emphasis on inorganic smoothness from prior scholarship, the movement from smooth to textured described here expressly addresses the desire to roughen the space, making an explicit connection between textures chosen and the mood that the room should express. The textures of the space concentrate the feeling that Sid's room is a place to escape from, where toys are not safe but rather subject to Sid's subversive and destructive attentions that mark the space within. The feel of the space, especially in its direct contrast to Andy's room, is evoked through a correlation between mood, as described above, and the textures of the room. The old-fashioned (textured rather than smooth and clean) and worn out (rough and coarse) surfaces of décor and furniture conjure a space that is neglected and dreary, where things (such as toys) are not cared for and perhaps overused. Scale is an important consideration here, as, given the diminutive size of the toys in relation to the space, human-scale textures become exaggerated and potentially impinge further on the possibilities of movement. When Buzz and Woody are left stranded on Sid's desk, the setting provides an example of how the child's destructive impulses have been mapped on the textures of his space, the scored desk and pitted window frame evoking the physical precariousness of the toys' situation – including his ability to mark and score *them* – as they remain trapped there. These marks describe the ways in which Sid moves through his world, his interactions with surfaces and how they are presented dramatizing his character's roughness, and thus inviting us to feel for the toys and share their anxieties.

Design Coherence

The contrast of feel in the design of the bedrooms connects to the central thematic and dramatic tension of the film's narrative, the pull between old (rough and dirty) and new (smooth and clean). This conflict is of course embodied most dynamically in the clash between Woody as the much-loved faithful toy and Buzz as the new favourite (underlined by their respective iconography as cowboy and spaceman), but these anxieties around temporality and change seep throughout the world of the film, playing out through the narrative structures (e.g. in the upheaval of the impending house move) and the textures present in the film's design.[27] While the roughness of the material world that I have noted is primarily in the background, the counterbalance it represents to the more prominently smooth surfaces of the toys themselves, can be considered central to the overall aesthetic of the film.

In support of their dramatic conflict, design distinctions between Woody and Buzz are also mapped on to a contrast of rough/textured and smooth/hard. The bright whiteness of Buzz marks him out as emphatically new, devoid of dirt or scratches, so that he stands out from the other toys and even the background environment (for instance, the white window frames of Andy's room).[28] While Woody is not noticeably worn,[29] his plastic surfaces are less shiny and reflective than Buzz (and those of other toys, such as Rex [Wallace Shawn]) and the majority of his figure is made of fabric, which, while colourful, is of a more subdued tone. The relative contrasts of rough/smooth and soft/shiny are foregrounded in a key moment that uses texture to cement the profound change Woody experiences with Buzz's arrival. Buzz's incorporation into Andy's affections and into the team of toys at the cost of Woody's increasing isolation is dramatized in a montage sequence during which the room's décor changes to reflect Buzz's new status, and Buzz is shown to be involved in leading the other toys (encouraging them to work out, grooming and coaching them to improvement). The passage of time that is evoked through the edits is intensified by changes to the surfaces of the toys themselves as Buzz announces to the toys accompanying him – Rex and Slinky (Jim Varney) – that he has been marked by Andy, lifting his foot to reveal 'Andy' scrawled on the bottom. Alone and at some distance from this little group, Woody lifts his foot to compare his own mark of ownership. Whereas Buzz's foot is bright and smooth, the hardened plastic revealing no wear and the black ink of the name freshly applied and clearly defined, Woody's own foot is scuffed, Andy's signature worn and faded. Texture is thus incorporated into the climax of this significant character and narrative moment, acting as a tangible sign of Woody's feelings, a mark of age and irrelevance.

The textural connections of the design of the world to its feel within the fiction further establishes coherence in the way it connects our experience to that of the toys. The kind of textural details that I've foregrounded here, the marks on skirting and window frames, places us in their world, the everydayness of which connects to our own. We would not normally notice these marks, but as we are at toy height and scale we do. Through the examples of the bedrooms and the design of the central toy protagonists, we can see how the concerns of the narrative are embedded into the material constitution of the fictional world. In this sense, the textures *in* the film support the texture *of* the film. The compositional details of specific surfaces contribute to the feel of the whole, and support the central threads of dramatic tension and conflict.

Achievements in Detail

As we've seen, attention to the instances of texture and roughness uncovers a remarkable degree of detail in the design of the film. Of course, animation of all kinds places emphasis on the fictional world as fabricated (a revelation that in reality applies just as much to live-action film). In every film there will be details included that remain in the background or that will never be seen, though in animation – and perhaps even more so in digital animation – the decision to put so much time and energy into creating something that will go so unnoticed seems to represent a remarkable level of effort and creativity. For investigating the materiality of a fictional world, the meticulous labour of the makers is an important consideration. Making a connection between the work done and its affect could even constitute an intervention into the criticism of the digital as lacking substance.

During the discussion of Sid's bedroom on the DVD commentary, Eggleston refers to the balance of bringing detail into the design while being careful not to overstep its importance: 'A lot of times . . . you'd think that, "look at all this work we did, let's show it off, let's put lights back there", when no, it's not important.'[30] This attitude speaks to a clear coherence of the relation between form and content, whereby the elements of style or design are not pursued simply for their own ends, but only in service of supporting the narrative, or the development of character. The intertwining of design and narrative is one consistently referred to by film designers, as production designer Paul Sylbert puts it: 'Style in film results from every part of it, and those parts must cohere, and they must be directed at some effective result. Design is not self-expression. It is an expressive use of objects, forms, and colors in the service of the script.'[31] In the context of this design process dealing with a new medium, Eggleston's comment also draws attention to the consistency of his (and the others') work with previous approaches and methods. It is not only that particular aspects of the work done are not shown off, but also that the ground-breaking achievements of the digital are not made more important than anything else. Coming back to the idea of the look and feel of *Toy Story* (and CGI more generally) being too plastic or pristine, it is worth noting that many of the artists working on the film were expressly working against the perfection of CGI. Modeler Damir Frkovic explains his work: 'I add lots of little detailing that nobody tells me to do . . .

It's always the goal to add that little layer to make the set look less perfect, less of the computer world and more like a messy believable place.'[32] If animation can be described as acting, as proposed by Tom Porter,[33] it is worth considering the material qualities of this work; acting is of course a highly embodied practice, invested in conveying emotion and mood through gesture and expression. Although the body is hidden, the precise work of the animator is likewise concerned with expression and feel, their detailed efforts bringing tangible impact to the ways in which stories are told.

Surface Contribution

Key to the texture of surfaces in digital animation is the visual effects team, and especially those who work with shader programmes: 'Shaders are the surface textural descriptions of an object, including its color, reflectivity, transparency, patterning, dirt, and scratches.'[34] As with textures in other forms of visual art (and in real life for that matter), CGI incorporates the way light is used to register the qualities of different surfaces: 'The shader program then instructs . . . layers to "talk" to each other in ways that mimic the play of light over real objects.'[35] Those who work with shaders are specifically focused on surface and materiality, their efforts towards 'touchableness' through surface descriptions being concerned with precise questions about the consistency of objects which determine their appeal to feel and touch. Consider the exacting variances of surface in the design of the toys. Both Hamm (John Ratzenberger) and Bo Peep (Annie Potts) could be characterized by a smoothness in their textures, but while Hamm has a matt appearance, Bo Peep is reflective and shiny. Their shared smoothness suggests a certain degree of similarity in their make-up, especially in their molded fabrication, but the subtle differences present clear distinctions between the toys in visual and tangible terms – it is clear they are made out of distinct materials which determine movement through their world and how they are handled.

Visual effects artists can be added to those other members of a filmmaking team, such as foley artists, whose work attends in great detail to the character of surfaces in the fictional world, balancing the reality of a surface with the communication of the specifics of its feel in order for the audience to remain immersed in the film. And like foley artists, whose work thickens a film's aural texture and adds to the ways in which sound enlarges space beyond the screen, visual effects artists are concerned with adding dimensionality: 'Like some ultimate contact paper manufacturer, [Porter] takes flat, surface-pattern visual information, then writes a customized mathematical "shader" program to "wrap" it around the three-dimensional geometry of a modeled object.'[36] The layered qualities of the work involved in creating these digital textures further reminds me of the layering involved in sound work, and the extent to which this too involves an imaginative, or even performative, process for the filmmaker: 'Sid's desk, for instance, boasts four separate layers of hand-depicted detail: a "splatter" layer of paint marks, a "bump map" where the artists imagine Sid hit it with hammers or scraped it with blades, a "specularity" layer to specify where light is more or less reflective around those pocks and irregularities, and a "dirt" layer for general grunge.'[37]

Attention to the complexities of texture and surface – in their making and affect – therefore involves an appreciation of the substantive, significant contributions of those less celebrated participants in the digital animation process. In consideration of the changes to filmmaking structures necessitated by CGI work, we might further point to Pixar's structures of labour, which champion the efforts of the team, as a sign that digital filmmaking is more visible as a collaborative art form.[38]

Conclusion

In an article that considers the more organic aesthetic of Pixar's short films *Day & Night* (Teddy Newton, 2010) and *La Luna* (Enrico Casarosa, 2011), Helen Haswell returns us to the conflict of CGI precision and roughness:

> differently from the 'perfection' of computer-generated images . . . Pixar's experimentation with textures suggests a more expressive aesthetic than has previously been accomplished in digital animation. Although this could be interpreted as a way of increasing realism through the mimicking of real textures, thus moving away from a traditional aesthetic, it is the expressiveness that these textures evoke that, I argue, has facilitated a more organic aesthetic.[39]

Despite the fact that Haswell is addressing expressive and technological developments made since *Toy Story*, I would argue that we can see the seeds of the expressive textures she describes here in that earlier film. It is true that there are limits in the film's textural intricacy when it comes to organic matter, this being one type of surface where the animation reveals its age most prominently: the rendering of human skin misses crucial details of skin's softness and elasticity, of its complex surface of muscles, hairs and folds. However, as this is the result of technical limitations rather than expressive intentions, I do not consider this to undermine my arguments concerning the film's achievements in building a textured world.[40] In joining Ian Garwood's rejection of the limiting associations of the film with smoothness and perfection, the 'feel' of plastic, this chapter has sought to re-evaluate the ways in which the film's achievements in textural detail can be considered to be both expressive and dramatic. Attention to texture demands a more precise approach, calling on us to notice the fine details and 'subtlety of specific things' that flesh out the fictional world on screen. This necessitates attention to the complex work of the designers involved in the making of the film, presenting their meticulous efforts as central to grounding the experience of the audience. The layered complexity of their work further pulls against the potential insubstantiality of CGI, refusing to characterize it as thin or insubstantial, but rather as richly crafted and materially full as any other film's design.

Notes

1 Ian Garwood, *The Sense of Film Narration* (Edinburgh: Edinburgh University Press, 2013), p. 72.
2 Giuliani Bruno, *Surface: Matters of Aesthetics, Materiality, and Media* (Chicago: University of Chicago Press, 2014), p. 8.
3 Thomas Elsaesser and Malte Hagener, *Film Theory: An Introduction through the Senses* (London: Routledge, 2010), p. 173.
4 Michel Chion, 'The Sensory Aspects of Contemporary Cinema', in John Richardson, Claudia Gorbman and Carol Vernallis (eds), *The Oxford Handbook of New Audiovisual Aesthetics* (Oxford: Oxford University Press, 2013), pp. 325–30 (p. 327).
5 Glen Adamson and Victoria Kelley (eds), *Surface Tensions: Writings on Popular Design and Material Culture* (Manchester: Manchester University Press, 2013), p. 13.
6 Laura U. Marks is a key reference point here, as her work is central to developing understanding of what she frames as 'haptic visuality'; see *The Skin of the Film* (Durham: Duke University Press, 2000), p. 2.
7 Ralph Eggleston, 'Filmmakers commentary', *Toy Story* [DVD] (Los Angeles: Walt Disney Studios Home Entertainment, 2010).
8 William Schaffer, 'The Importance of Being Plastic: The Feel of Pixar', *Animation Journal*, no. 12 (2004): 72–95 (p. 86).
9 Vivian Sobchack, *Carnal Thoughts: Embodiment and Moving Image Culture* (Berkeley: University of California Press, 2004), p. 54.
10 Owen Glieberman, 'Plastic Fantastic', *Entertainment Weekly*, 14 November 1995, p. 74.(Glieberman, 1995: 74)
11 John Lasseter and Steve Daly, *Toy Story: The Art and Making of the Animated Film* (New York: Disney Editions, 1995), p. 18.
12 Jennifer M. Barker, *The Tactile Eye: Touch and the Cinematic Experience* (Berkeley, CA; London: University of California Press, 2009), pp. 44, 45.
13 Ibid., p. 45.
14 Ibid., pp. 45–46.
15 Andrew Darley, *Digital Visual Culture* (London: Routledge, 2000), p. 86.
16 Garwood, *The Sense of Film Narration*, p. 73.
17 Ibid., p. 74.
18 Ibid., p. 85.
19 As described by Marcus Maloney in *The Search for Meaning in Film and Television: Disenchantment at the Turn of the Millennium* (Basingstoke: Palgrave Macmillan, 2015), pp. 25–30.
20 Art Director Ralph Eggleston, quoted in Lasseter and Daly, *Toy Story: The Art and Making of the Animated Film*, p. 22.

21 See Helen Haswell, 'To Infinity and Back Again: Hand-drawn Aesthetic and Affection for the Past in Pixar's Pioneering Animation', *Alphaville: Journal of Film and Screen Media*, no. 8 (2014): 1–17.
22 Adamson and Kelley (eds), *Surface Tensions: Writings on Popular Design and Material Culture*, p. 13.
23 Bruno, *Surface: Matters of Aesthetics, Materiality, and Media*, p. 5.
24 Mark Henne, Hal Hickel, Ewan Johnson and Sonoko Konishi, 'The Making of *Toy Story*', *COMPCON '96: Proceedings of the 41st IEEE International Computer Conference* (Santa Clara, CA: IEEE, 1996), pp. 463–68 (p. 466).
25 Christopher S. Yates, 'A Phenomenological Aesthetic of Cinematic "Worlds"', *Contemporary Aesthetics*, no. 4 (2006). http://www.contempaesthetics.org/newvolume/pages/article.php?articleID=394 (accessed 8 January 2013).
26 Lasseter and Daly, *Toy Story: The Art and Making of the Animated Film*, p. 78.
27 And indeed beyond the fictional world, as Elsaesser and Hagener point out, this movement between old and new is part of *Toy Story*'s material construction, as it is, for them, 'the emblematic film that allegorizes the shift from analog to digital in a number of ways' (*Film Theory: An Introduction through the Senses*, p. 171).
28 The newness of Buzz through his pronounced whiteness is noted as a deliberate design choice by the contributors to the DVD commentary (2010).
29 Woody's scruffiness becomes a narrative point in *Toy Story 2* (John Lasseter, Ash Brannon & Lee Unkrich, 1999) when he is accidentally sold to a toy collector and refurbished for sale in Japan.
30 Eggleston, 'Filmmakers commentary'.
31 Qtd. in Vincent LoBrutto, *By Design: Interviews with Production Designers* (Westport, Connecticut: Praeger, 1992), p. 85.
32 Qtd. in Lasseter and Daly, *Toy Story: The Art and Making of the Animated Film*, p. 69.
33 Tom Porter, 'Creating Lifelike Characters in *Toy Story*', *ACM SIGART Bulletin*, vol. 8, nos. 1–4 (1997): 10–14 (p. 14).
34 Henne et al., 'The Making of *Toy Story*', p. 465.
35 Lasseter and Daly, *Toy Story: The Art and Making of the Animated Film*, p. 78.
36 Ibid.
37 Ibid.
38 A point also made by Berys Gaut. 'digital cinema has made possible a broadening out of the realm of filmmaking activities in which collaboration is possible, with new artistic possibilities either being made available or being rendered more artistically powerful'; see *A Philosophy of Cinematic Art* (Cambridge: Cambridge University Press, 2010), p. 140.
39 Haswell, 'To Infinity and Back Again: Hand-drawn Aesthetic and Affection for the Past in Pixar's Pioneering Animation', p. 5.
40 The extent of the technical challenge and difficulties presented by human appearance and clothing is recounted by various members of the visual effects team in Lasseter and Daly, *Toy Story: The Art and Making of the Animated Film*, pp. 88–91.

Chapter 6

TOYING WITH PERFORMANCE: *TOY STORY*, VIRTUAL PUPPETRY AND COMPUTER-ANIMATED FILM ACTING

Christopher Holliday

In the early 1990s, during the emergence of the global fast food industry boom, the Walt Disney studio abruptly ended its successful alliance with restaurant chain McDonald's – which, since 1982, had held the monopoly on Disney's tie-in promotional merchandise – and instead announced a lucrative ten-film licensing contract with rival outlet, Burger King. Under the terms of this agreement, the Florida-based restaurant would now hold exclusivity over Disney's array of animated characters, and working alongside US toy manufacturers could license collectible toys as part of its meal packages based on characters from the studio's animated features *Beauty and the Beast* (Gary Trousdale and Kirk Wise, 1991), *Aladdin* (Ron Clements and John Musker, 1992), *The Lion King* (Roger Allers and Rob Minkoff, 1994), *Pocahontas* (Mike Gabriel and Eric Goldberg, 1995) and *The Hunchback of Notre Dame* (Gary Trousdale and Kirk Wise, 1996).[1] Produced by Pixar Animation Studio as its first computer-animated feature film but distributed by Disney, *Toy Story* (John Lasseter, 1995) was likewise subject to this new commercial deal and made commensurate with Hollywood's increasingly synergistic relationship with the fast food market. To coincide with the North American theatrical release of *Toy Story* in November 1995, for example, Burger King manufactured a range of collectible plastic toys representing the film's main characters: Woody the Cowboy, Buzz Lightyear, Rex the dinosaur, Hamm the piggy bank, RC the remote control car and the Green Army Men soldiers. However, also available as part of the restaurant's 'Kid's Club' meal (a children's meal programme inaugurated by Burger King in 1989) was a set of four collectible hand puppets marketed under the 'Toy Story Pals' label and again featuring Woody, Buzz, Rex and Hamm. Produced by the New York-based advertising agency Ammirati Puris Lintas, the five television commercials celebrating Disney's tie-in with Burger King depicted children excitedly manipulating their puppets' heads and arms from the 'inside out', throwing voices into their models and orchestrating their bodies into the most dynamic poses within the spectacle of repertory theatre. Indeed, as the exchange between two (presumably fictional) Burger King employees in one of these US television adverts proclaimed, some of the children at the restaurant 'have been here for hours' because 'they can't put their puppets down'.[2]

The strengthening of cross-promotional activity between the entertainment and fast food industries throughout the 1990s (including the considered targeting of the child audience beyond the cinema auditorium) suggested, of course, a far from ideologically innocuous version of puppetry operating both in excess of and as a direct consequence to the 'animated' activity of the chain's pre-teen clientele. Fuelling the younger consumer's collective (and *collecting*) mentality, the volume of tie-in merchandise readily available as a result of the Disney/Burger King union, including the range of *Toy Story*-themed puppets, not only offered potent promotion for Pixar's debut computer-animated feature, but in their new role as controlling puppeteer actually inverted their ideological position as the puppets of consumer culture.

Manoeuvring beyond Disney's highly visible 'culture of commercialization' and profitable merchandising of childhood, this chapter takes its cue from the loaded image of puppetry promulgated as part of *Toy Story*'s promotional discourse, and in particular the vision of its popular toy characters as discrete puppet forms.[3] Most notably, this chapter argues that it is the analogous image of puppet/puppeteer interaction that recurs throughout *Toy Story* that readily confronts the vexed relationship between animation and discourses of digitally animated performance, and spotlights how puppetry as a conceptual framework functions as a lever for understanding issues surrounding computer-animated film acting. Whether human (Andy) or non-human figurations (Woody, Buzz), all computer-animated film characters are ostensibly virtual marionettes that belong to a new breed of cyber puppetry. The jointed segmentation and individual limbs of computer-animated bodies provide specific articulation points for the animator, who remotely operates each character's armature and steer their complex endoskeletons utilizing a series of *avars* (animation variables). The specificity of such processes – compared with how animated movement is achieved in cel animation or stop-motion techniques – implicates computer-animated film 'acting' into the centuries-long tradition of 'performing objects'. Understood through Western discourses of puppet theatre and typically held distinct from cinema, performing objects have been defined by Frank Proschan as 'material images of humans, animals, or spirits that are created, displayed, or manipulated in narrative or dramatic performance'.[4] The frequent scenes in *Toy Story* of toys under Andy's puppet-like manipulation thus creatively 'doubles' how computer-animated film performance is engineered through a similar encounter between occluded performer and visible performing object. By acknowledging how the toys are initially *acted upon* by Andy (before they are puppeteered into another animated life beyond his perception and control by the film's animators), this chapter argues that *Toy Story* discloses how performance in the computer-animated film might be conceptualized as an innovative form of modern puppet entertainment. Throughout its narrative, Pixar's debut film ultimately establishes an acceptance of the (digital) puppet as a replacement for the live, lively and living human body, and this chapter suggests how *Toy Story* celebrates – rather than disguises – the on-stage/off-stage partition fundamental to the stagecraft of computer-animated film acting.

Digital Puppetry and Performing Animation

The advent of digitally assisted or computer-mediated acting within contemporary Hollywood cinema has prompted widespread critical debate and popular consternation as to digital technology's intercession into, and corruption of, profilmic human presence.[5] The received narrative telling the history of digital actors, avatars, synthespians and vactors (a neologism of virtual and actors) across moving image culture often defines the digital as a frustrating prosthesis that obstructs, disguises and reorients the foundational reality of human performance. Several scholars, such as Lisa Bode, Lisa Purse, Chris Pallant and Sharon Carnicke have extended the parameters of digital acting by unpacking the aesthetic and even ethical uncertainty surrounding a type of performance that is 'digitally enabled'.[6] Pallant makes clear that animated performances or graphically/digitally mediated forms of acting tend overwhelmingly to move away from the psychology of the 'method', which held such sway as an acting style throughout the 1950s following the demise of classical studio-era Hollywood.[7] Yet as a technique that conventionally transcribes and encodes human activity and movement (bodily, facial) through motion sensors (physical *avars*) that are relayed via computer software, the technique known as motion-capture is a form of digital puppetry that typically maintains the human body as the primary control mechanism. In this way, motion-capture has dually revised preexisting paradigms surrounding 'actorly' performance in cinema, yet equally satisfied something of a spectatorial desire for the nuances of human connection and (preservation of) the 'minutiae of human emotion' demanded in, and of, cinema's characters.[8] Popularized in blockbuster (often franchise) films such as *The Lord of the Rings* (Peter Jackson, 2001–03) and *The Hobbit* (Peter Jackson, 2012–14) trilogies, but also *King Kong* (Peter Jackson, 2005), *The Curious Case of Benjamin Button* (David Fincher, 2008), *Avatar* (James Cameron, 2009), *Tron: Legacy* (Joseph Kosinksi, 2010), *Rise of the Planet of the Apes* (Rupert Wyatt, 2011), *Real Steel* (Shawn Levy, 2011), *Dawn of the Planet of the Apes* (Matt Reeves, 2014) and *The BFG* (Steven Spielberg, 2016), 'mo-cap' technology has placed computer graphics on a collision course with the alleged sanctity and immediacy of human performance in the digital age. Although contentious among animation purists and still subject to ongoing industry scepticism, motion-capture technology has been credited with nonetheless manifesting an immediacy of performance through the real time articulation of labour, with imperceptible pauses or lags within the computer's processing of the human 'data' and resultant digitized action. Kenny Chow notes that 'the correspondence between motion capture and full body puppetry has drawn the attention of performance studies'.[9] Multiple scholars with a background in puppet theory have certainly identified the degrees of overlap between the traditional manipulation of the physical puppet and the 'capturing' of human information, which has distinguished motion-capture as a controlled form of digital puppetry.[10]

The upward trajectory of motion-capture as a digital tool in service of animated performance across contemporary filmmaking practice has cued a more focused interest in the epistemology of the technique as a mode of digital puppetry. Addressing the problematic body politics engendered by mo-cap's transcription of human movement, John Bell asks suggestively: 'who performs the digital image?'.[11] Bell's point is a salient one, anchored to the production of the computer-animated film *Happy Feet* (George Miller, 2006) which, as he notes, raises significant questions about the visibility of renowned American tap-dancer Savion Glover, 'whose body was recorded via motion-capture to manipulate the digital puppet of [penguin protagonist] Mumble'.[12] Inspired by the popular nature documentaries *Life in the Freezer* (David Attenborough, 1993) and *March of the Penguins* (Luc Jacquet, 2005), *Happy Feet* marries Glover's convoluted footwork with an ensemble cast of recognizable star names (Hugh Jackman, Nicole Kidman, Elijah Wood, Brittany Murphy, Robin Williams) within the construction of its penguin characters. For Bell, the absence of Glover-as-author in the film's publicity material strongly evidenced certain longstanding assumptions underpinning film performance (which, uniformly, gravitate towards star personnel), while likewise bearing out the central problem inherent to digitally mediated acting. Ultimately the tap dancer's contribution to *Happy Feet* is occluded at the expense of its more marketable star voice cast, a dynamic that has been openly critiqued by Tanine Allison. Allison argues that the 'division between voice and action, mind and body' in protagonist Mumble reflects a more problematic racialized project of white appropriation, which coerces the film towards neo-minstrelsy as enacted by its dancing hordes of penguin 'blackface' bodies.[13] At the same time, however, the hierarchical (even 'puppetlike') arrangement between the star vocal performer, Glover (as 'invisible' motion-capture performer), and the skilled animators at Animal Logic raises questions about the very attribution of animated performance and the anxieties that surround the division of labour. Mihaela Mihailova has recently argued for greater emphasis to be placed on animator craft in motion-capture performances, while identifying how the universality of 'collaboration' as a totalizing label in motion-capture production rhetoric actually downplays the 'impact and significance' of the animators' labour.[14] Even with mo-cap's recourse to (and promise of) degrees of indexicality and human embodiment, the primacy afforded to the motion-capture performer as the central site for performance is, as Mihailova argues, a common feat of misdirection popular among the visual effects industry. Bell's validation of the input of Glover in *Happy Feet* thus becomes part of a persistent, and for Mihailova troubling, discourse that systematically works to partition off ownership of digitally mediated acting from the labour of animators and artists.

The omission of the animator within critical and popular discussions of motion-capture appears notably at odds with the received narrative being told elsewhere in animation studies, which organizes and celebrates the human animator as the locus for animated performance. This conflict is due, in part, to its sparing use across postmillennial computer-animated filmmaking, and the manner in which critical scholarship has consistently isolated the technique from any animated heritage despite its contiguities with earlier rotoscope processes.[15] As Yacov Freedman puts it, the resistance by filmmakers to motion-capture remains 'indicative of a larger dispute over the use of modern technology within the pantheon of animation techniques'.[16] At the heart of such opposition among animation purists lies the place of mo-cap technology within established relationships between animation and discourses of performance, which have conventionally been conceptualized as resting on the skills, abilities and expertise of the animator. Critical labels such as 'animator/actor' and 'animator-as-actor' bear out the durability of this perspective, one that has been maintained across a wealth of practitioner manuals and guidebooks that coach animators in the successful creation of persuasive characters replete with alert personalities.[17] Heather Holian makes clear that this kind of animator/actor synonymy has a venerable tradition in animated filmmaking, and ultimately finds a lineage in studio animation of the 1930s. By affixing animated acting to a discourse of 'masquerade' as a way of outlining the practitioners' own self-effacement and masked presence behind their characters, Holian suggests that 'animators are then arguably the most sophisticated, versatile and total – that is entirely masked and anonymous – professional masqueraders working in the entertainment business today'.[18]

Despite a relatively coherent critical narrative that commonly anchors animated acting to the creative capacities of the animator, computer-animated feature films such as *Toy Story* and its digital brethren are not immune to the same kinds of theoretical problems that have enveloped other modes of digital acting. Performance in the computer-animated film must be appreciated as a highly discursive enterprise: an expansive and fluid construction born out of a unique combination of dubbed vocal tracks, animated gestures, mimes, acute choreography, staging, postures and poses. To disentangle vocal and behavioural cues of the computer-animated film character is therefore to separate out a range of constitutive performance details or elements that are linked to the believability and coherence of a viewable performance in cyberspace. *Toy Story*'s duo of Woody and Buzz, for example, undeniably bear the imprint of Tom Hanks and Tim Allen (and the familiarity of their star voices), but the characters' acting credentials are equally rooted in the work of other creative personnel, including directors, artists, animators, designers, shaders, painters, story and layout artists and sculptors. The 'performance *of* animation' (Donald

Crafton's term for the invisible industry of the animators) is rarely singular, but a result of interconnecting and interdependent spheres of labour.[19] Within the context of the Pixar studio, for example, the assignment of individual shots or sets of shots (rather than specific characters) to animators means that they 'ultimately complete between 90 seconds to less than ten minutes of final footage, which is usually scattered throughout the film'.[20] The industry-level division of performance among multiple 'actors' working together more obviously codes computer-animated film acting as fundamentally collaborative. In a typical Pixar feature film, 'twenty to thirty animators frequently contribute incrementally to the same character throughout the course of a production', thereby disclosing the schizophrenic identity of computer-animated characters and the hybridized nature of the resultant performance.[21] Within this highly fractured and fissured process of animated acting, it is ultimately the voice that provides a unifying consistency to the performance, a common denominator that smooths over such divisions of production and blinds spectators to the identity of fictional characters as a complex accumulation of labour.

The appreciation of 'acting' within a feature-length computer-animated film context (and in particular the entwined issues of authorship and attribution) becomes increasingly complicated by the set of conditions that govern and guide the creation of its many screen performances. Computer-animated films, as Stephen Prince argues, offer 'some of the most affecting performances in modern cinema'.[22] Yet these are films that demand new ways of elucidating how their range of performers do not 'act' in the same way as in live-action cinema. Incremental 'tweaks' replace 'takes' within the work of computer-animated film acting as each gesture, posture and movement of the digital body is the result of careful composition and management. Computer-animated films are not replete with the same kinds of 'mindful' bodies inhabiting live-action cinema who are conscious of the recording apparatus, or who rehearse and perform 'on set'.[23] But this shortage of human actors on screen spotlights the unique spectrum of bodies that computer-animated films are sated with, and those conditions under which their bodies are able to perform. To offer a more expansive concept of animated performance, this chapter uses *Toy Story* as an exemplary case study to argue that puppetry can be understood as an altogether more inclusive category that pulls multiple computer-animated films into its orbit, and reveals the sliding scale of puppet processes involved in their creation of performance. Within the many creative practices and contributions involved in the crafting of computer-animated film performance, the puppetry of *Toy Story* gives greater shape and definition to the kinds of labour and actorly activity conventionally prescribed to the animator. Computer-animated films ultimately expand a discussion of puppetry beyond those (exceptional) films that use motion-capture technology, and it is *Toy Story* that most explicitly identifies the particular methods by which their performances – not fully explainable in terms of 'acting' – can be both achieved and appreciated.

Toy Story, *Puppetry and Play*

Visions of the puppet enacted in performance are, perhaps expectedly, notably pronounced across Pixar's *Toy Story* films. Scenes of puppet–puppeteer interaction open the very first *Toy Story*, with a protracted sequence that stresses the spectacle of the puppet as 'a theatrical figure moved under human control'.[24] During the first few seconds of Pixar's debut feature, the camera descends from an opening shot of painted cloud wallpaper (a self-reflexive manipulation of expectations surrounding the verisimilitude of digital imagery) into a cardboard-constructed interior space immediately recognizable as a child's playful interpretation of a western. Replete with the stable units of the genre, such as the wanted poster, saloon door and array of gunfighters – what Rick Altman might call the western's 'semantic' building blocks upon which generic meaning is founded – a Mr. Potato Head Doll is suddenly thrust into the film frame as the spectator becomes instantly folded into the fantasy space of childhood play.[25] Remaining off-screen and partial, an unseen animator (toy owner Andy) not only handles his readymades, but also narrates a story about them, adopting the role of voice artist as he constructs Mr. Potato Head's standout opening performance.

The toys' avatarial relationship with Andy is predicated on his degrees of attachment with them *and* their identity as objects to be worked on: from the modulation of Andy's voice in accordance with culturally informed notions of 'gender', to his projecting of personalities onto each figurine. This sequence as it unfolds is particularly significant insofar as it illuminates the film's overwhelming emphasis on the figure of the toy *as puppet*, but equally the very process of 'narration' that is intrinsic to the toy's story first told without their autonomous agency. Most significantly, the heroic stature of Woody the cowboy is the key structuring principle within Andy's fictional saviour narrative. Compared with Molly's (Andy's infant sister) destructive behaviour of the toys (notably Mr Potato Head, who utters 'Ages three and up! It's on my box! Ages three and up!'), or Sid's brutalizing of branded commodities, it is here that *Toy Story* awards space to Andy's affectionate handling and enthusiastic puppeteering of his beloved doll.

In his examination of children's play and the 'imagination-encouraging' process of toy manipulation, Kevin J. Wetmore Jr. explains, 'Like action figures, the toy theatre variant of performing object theatre can stimulate famous, professional narratives in the home.'[26] Safe within the sanctity of his bedroom, Andy's solitary performance *with* (and *through*) Mr. Potato Head, who here assumes the fictionalized role of villainous 'One Eyed Bart', begins and ends with the possibilities engendered by the toy. Not only does the process of ventriloquy only commence when the doll appears via Andy on screen, but the toy owner even shakes the plastic doll on certain vocal beats to physicalize the rhythms of the improvised speech ('All right, everyone! This… is a stick-up. Don't anybody move!') in ways that gesture to the contribution of the voice to animated acting.

As a dramatic moment of interference and collision between humans and objects, Andy's 'objectified' engagement with his toys-as-puppets invokes the education of young children in subject–object relations as far back as Victorian England, and in particular the educative 'object lessons [that] were designed to teach children to make careful observations of discrete objects and their own surroundings through a language educed from the objects'.[27]

The extension of a child's general knowledge through objects as stimulus material across nineteenth-century English classrooms is an 'object-centric methodology' that anticipates Andy's own curious behaviour with his cherished toys. His object investment leads him to a wider personalized master narrative drawn from the western genre, a (toy) story that self-reflexively extends across the franchise as Andy repeatedly observes his toys while casting them in new roles. For example, the story of One Eyed Bart is followed up in *Toy Story 2* (John Lasseter, 1999) with Hamm assuming the role of Evil Dr. Porkchop in Andy's fictionalized narrative, albeit one containing many of the same characters and gendered voices. Both villains are then revisited in the false opening of *Toy Story 3* (Lee Unkrich, 2010), which transplants the action of the first two films into a seemingly authentic, 'live-action' Old West. Here unfolding within an ordinary domestic setting, these puppeteered performances that open *Toy Story* allow the film subsequently to unravel tensions between Andy's projected characterizations and their truthful personalities as sentient toys. This even includes Woody, whose heroism within Andy's authored story is (re)made increasingly ambivalent by his later vengeful actions towards Buzz. Indeed, it is not until the 'reflexive nostalgia' of *Toy Story 3*'s bombastic opening sequence that Andy's toys are permitted a return to such well-defined heroic (and, in the case of Hamm, villainous) characterizations.[28]

Whether inviting questions of generic allegiance and 'genre play'; suggesting complex gender relations by the positioning of Buzz Lightyear as a 'hypermasculine action hero' as a counterpoint to Woody; or even nostalgically portraying the toy as mass-produced industrial commodity, many scholars have become increasingly acquainted with *Toy Story*'s opening sequence, recognizing its place within the development of the American cartoon tradition and emergence of the computer-animated film.[29] Many have also been quick to identify how *Toy Story* self-reflexively folds its identity *as computer-animation* back into the mechanisms of its puppeteerly sensibility. Thomas Elsaesser and Malte Hagener have argued how the intensity of owner Andy's connections with his toys is fully entwined with discourses of agency and mastery, particularly as the opening sequence of *Toy Story* narrates the dichotomy between the 'hapless and the manipulated toys' and the veiled presence of Andy 'beyond the frame'.[30] The manipulation of toys therefore functions both as an emblem and as allegory: Andy's throwing of his voice through ventriloquy into his plastic playthings and their later sentience in excess of any that their puppet master accords them, works to repeat the film's own status as a bridge between the earlier 'traditional opto-chemical photographic process' and its new digital exclusivity.[31]

Andy's decision between pull-string Woody and the laser-adorned Buzz certainly erects a duel between the characters upon which the jeopardy of *Toy Story* is founded. Yet Andy's identity as a child is one seduced, unlike Woody, by the red laser (or, 'a little light bulb that blinks') of his Space Ranger from Sector 4 of the Gamma Quadrant. This recalls Massimo Riva's notion (from a chapter on Pinocchio narratives and the ambivalence of puppet machinery) that adolescence and technology are inextricably entwined, fundamentally embroiled since 'young people are nowadays both the main producers and consumers of technological change'.[32] The features of Buzz as a state-of-the-art toy, including flashing lights, 'impressive wingspan' and internal vocal mechanism (that Hamm heralds as 'quality sound system. . . probably all copper wiring'), are thus more than just analogous to the old/new frontier ushered in by computer-animated 'cinema'. Rather, Buzz's technological attributes make him seductive as a modern puppet, an attractive proposition for Andy as he develops and matures a stronger technological consciousness.

The alignment of old and new is, however, made entirely visible as Andy's hand (and the grasped puppet) intervenes into his authored play-space, an act that marks the full realization of computer graphics and its possibilities for dimensionality. Tom Kemper argues that as Mr. Potato Head 'pops down into the frame . . . the action effectively pops out the three-dimensional qualities of computer animation'.[33] Yet the abrupt intervention by Andy actually substitutes a hand-drawn image of Mr. Potato Head (on a wanted poster pinned to the cardboard set) with a three-dimensional puppet equivalent. The newly hidden 'drawn' image cast aside by the pristine digitally rendered toy narrativizes the forward momentum of technological progress, as the crude graphic of One-Eyed Bart drawn by Andy is replaced with the computer-animated replica.[34] At the same time, the image of Andy's hand suspended in the centre of the frame as he manipulates the doll draws explicit attention to the spectacle of the puppet/puppeteer relationship. The occlusion of Andy's own physiognomy, the metonymic presence of his dextrous hands, and his marginal status as both voice artist and animator more broadly within *Toy Story*'s opening scenes, all work in service of mounting an increasingly apparent vision of puppetry. Puppets, of course, lack interiority and motivation, and thus the on screen/off-screen separation fundamental to the stagecraft of puppet theatre is reprised in *Toy Story* through Andy's play patterns, his formation of toy identities and the literal staging of questions around engagement and proximity. Positioned here front-on to this theatrical stage, spectators only become fully immersed into the film's action with the introduction of toy subjectivity a few minutes later, a formal device that is able to dislocate and disrupt this performed marionette theatre through the toys' ascension to independent agency.

In its opening moments, *Toy Story* breaks down the dynamic chemistry between human and non-human performers, paying full attention to the activity of agents performing alongside – and as a consequence of – human performers. The film's foregrounding of non-human objects and artefacts 'acting' within Andy's authored theatrical production thus more readily acknowledges the structures that support computer-animated films as an equivalent to traditions of puppet manipulation. In his self-edited 1983 issue of the journal *Semiotica*, North American puppet theorist Frank Proschan discusses the strengths of the 'performing object' in ways that usefully anticipate both the display and manipulation of toys by Andy in *Toy Story*. Proschan conceives such 'performing objects' in relation to the *materiality* of the objects themselves, underscored by a wide-ranging tradition of *material* imagery: puppetry and marionettes, but also other objects such as 'scroll paintings, peepshows, masks, and narrative sculptures' which are orchestrated to achieve dramaturgical performance.[35] Proschan's work has been taken up in earnest by puppet theorist Bell, who has expanded this original definition of performing objects to include any kind of 'stuff, junk, puppets, masks, detritus, machines, bones, and molded plastic things that people use to tell stories or represent ideas'.[36] Although puppetry and puppet theatre have been described as the most developed form of performing objects, a multitude of material artefacts can function as such sites of significance and signification, inserted between the human performer and spectator who are simultaneously trained upon the object engaged in performance. Indeed, Bell's diagrammed triad (adapted from experimental Soviet and Russian theatrical director Vsevolod Meyerhold) conceptualizes the humbling of humanity by the object, but also the terms of object/performer contact, and he outlines the following set of relationships:

Performer →→→ object ←←← spectators

Bell argues that the very *dynamics of concentration* supporting object performance recall the 'dynamics of painting or sculpture', insofar as the activity both of performer and spectator are trained not on themselves but on the object (painting, sculpture) itself.[37] Whereas dance performances involve a conscious human body performing before an enthralled audience, the object (as newly performing 'stuff') is made to intervene into – and ultimately take hold of – this spectatorial relationship. The object becomes the subject of the performer *and* the spectators' gaze simultaneously, marking most explicitly a 'focal but also an ontological shift from humans . . . to the world of inanimate materials'.[38] The performer manipulates, puppeteers, orchestrates and activates the object into a performance (even providing its voice when needed), yet the spectator is no less trained on, and guided by, the movement, agency and sudden volatility of the object as it undertakes such a performance. In the 'performing object' model, then, the object in performance (material or virtual, tangible or intangible) is always maintained at the centre. In this way, animation more broadly, and the computer-animated film in particular, fits safely into Bells's diagramming of these relationships:

Animator →→→ virtual object [computer-animated film] ←←← spectators

Of course, for the Pixar animators Andy is no less a virtual or cyber puppet than the toys he manipulates, and thus he is equally implicated within the film's puppeteered performances:

Animator →→→ Andy/toys [*Toy Story*] ←←← spectators

It is now the animator (as performer) who takes as their focus the object engaged *in* performance with the spectator sharing in this focal arrangement.[39] Whereas live-action cinema might be considered closer to dance – given how the human performer and spectator are to some extent 'focused' on each other – in the computer-animated film there is a shared investment in an intermediary object 'designed or designated by another human' as it is engineered into a presentable performance.[40]

Within the workflow of computer-animated film production, it is the organization of computer-animated film bodies – their skeletal structures, articulation points and segmented bodies – that further manages the movements of these characters and supports their identities as 'performing objects'. Aylish Wood has stressed a greater need to comprehend the 'complexities of software' within the construction of computer graphics, suggesting that animators and the computer must be understood to 'fold together in the action of making moving images'.[41] Not only does the language of 'software studies' here recall the rhetoric of puppet manipulation through the emphasis on puppeteer/puppet proximity, but also the versatility of certain software tools (Wood's example is the Autodesk Maya programme) both facilitates and guides the animator's 'actorly' choices as they work within three-dimensional virtual space. With regard to the 'integrity' of the computer-animated body and its potential degrees of pliability, 'thinking through a movement requires taking into account the hierarchy of the model'.[42] Whereas the modellers give volume to two-dimensional artwork by sculpting three-dimensional virtual characters viewable from every angle, the process known as 'rigging' involves the addition of controls or *avars* (animation variables) to this wireframe digital mesh that permits animators to remotely operate a character's armature. Rigging Technical Directors design how the character moves, introducing joints, fat and muscle under the digital skin so that the animators can effectively *become* animator/actors and manipulate the digital puppet so as to act *with it*. Deformers are also added during this preparatory 'rigging' stage to the surface of the characters, which allow certain behavioural relationships to be defined between multiple points effected by a singular motion. Alvy Ray Smith, the co-founder of the Pixar studio alongside Edwin Catmull and Steve Jobs, argued back in 2000 for a distinction in computer-animated film production between the 'art of acting and the representation of actors'.[43] The deformation of skin, wrinkles and plotting of facial expression as part of a character's physical nuance therefore suggest that rigging is more implicitly involved in the 'representation of actors', as it involves making actors *out of models*.

Alongside the creative contributions of three-dimensional character riggers, animators are no less embroiled in the 'art of acting', since their puppeteered manipulation must generate a performance *from these actors*. As Smith puts it, the animator 'is just that special kind of talented actor who can make us believe that a collection of colored polygons has heart, gets angry, and outfoxes the coyote'.[44] Most notable in this respect is *Toy Story*'s Woody, who both 'has heart' and 'gets angry' (mostly at and due to Buzz), but was also a character initially conceived as a ventriloquist dummy rather than a cowboy doll during the original treatment for *Toy Story*. However, Kemper argues that even in his new guise of a cowboy, Woody remains essentially 'still a ventriloquist dummy'.[45] The complexity of Woody as a digital puppet within the production of *Toy Story* facilitated the character's range of emotional expressivity, which relied upon a synchronicity in his operation between control and resultant movement. Steve Tillis argues that 'The number of avars that might be involved in a complex model is astonishing: the model for *Toy Story*'s Woody had 212 avars in his face alone, 58 of which were dedicated to his mouth, allowing him an exceptional range of expression and a capacity for shaping his mouth for each particular phoneme he would speak.'[46] Individual points on the cowboy's face enabled him to furrow and arch his painted eyebrow, contributing to a complexity and specificity of motion within his fluid, malleable physiognomy. Despite his painted, plastic visage, Woody's range of controllable features achieved using facial and bodily rigs both qualify and articulate the nuances of his performance. Indeed, *Toy Story* regularly exploits his broad spectrum of motions and emotions, particularly noticeable when Woody suddenly learns of the imminent arrival of riotous children at Andy's birthday party, or when the Sheriff laughs hysterically at Buzz's erratic and impulsive behaviour.

By reducing Woody to his most basic workable geometry, comprised a series of surface faces (known as polygons), Pixar's animators are more akin in their labour to puppeteers insofar as they 'control', 'direct' and 'orchestrate' his body, rather than engage in the drawing/redrawing of individual frames. It comes as little surprise, then, that not only has puppetry entered the lexicon of computer-animated film production as industry shorthand to describe the interrelationship between the *performer* (animator) and *performed* (character), but animators often reflect upon their work as a specific form of live virtual puppetry. *Toy Story 3* animator Bobby Podesta remarks: 'Imagine having Pinocchio in the computer that you move around frame by frame, but instead of having a dozen strings, you've got hundreds and hundreds and hundreds. It gets very nuanced.'[47] Supplemented by the development of Marionette, Pixar's proprietary software program and animation toolset, the inscription of the animator as puppet master in collaboration with other spheres of production codes a computer-animated film world as an alternate kind of live performance setting in which figures are 'worked' within a three-dimensional (rather than scenic) screen space.[48] Computer-animated films can therefore usefully be conceptualized as a puppet progeny of marionette theatre, a variation of digital puppetry that is predicated upon a particular quality of collaborative contact (what Henryk Jurkowski calls the 'constant pulsation' of puppetry as a performing art) that exists between the object in performance and the human performer.[49] The proximity of subject/object distance, the adjustment of particular bodily and facial controls, and the manipulation of a geometric wireframe model throws into relief how computer-animated bodies both act, and are acted upon, more like puppets. In this way, Andy's activity during *Toy Story*'s opening moments doubles the creative interaction or 'pulsation' that exists between animators and their digital objects, folding the production of computer-animated films back into the diegetic spectacle of puppet performance.

Conclusion: Computer-Animated Films as Modern Puppet Entertainment

To conceptualize the characters in *Toy Story* as puppets operating within the tradition of performing objects is to speak more generally to the ways in which computer-animated films can be viewed as a unique form of puppet entertainment. Coexistent with the labour of Pixar's creative team of artists, character riggers and sculptors (as well as voice artists and sound designers), puppetry certainly illuminates the creative bargain that is struck in computer-animated films between animators and those 'actor-objects' that are cast in primary roles and ultimately individuated as people.[50] Performance within the context of animation, as Wells makes clear, remains an 'intriguing concept', not least because it 'properly represents the relationship between the animator and the figure, object or environment that he/she is animating'.[51] Within the complex labour relations that support computer-animated film production, puppetry, puppetry sharpens our awareness of this encounter, exposing how the moving force and apparent agency of virtual bodies are determined extrinsically through puppet-like or puppeteerly manipulation. This is particularly resonant given the many computer-animated film characters that have been extra-textually reconjured as spectacular digital puppets. In her discussion of where animation and puppetry hold the potential to overlap, Colette Searls argues that *Shrek The Musical*, a theatrical adaptation of the 2001 DreamWorks computer-animated film, 'used digital puppetry to make an animated character perform live onstage', thereby extending the practices central to computer-animated film production into the theatre.[52] Since November 2004, an interactive Disney theme park attraction, 'Turtle Talk with Crush', has utilized digital puppet processes to allow a fictional computer-animated character from Pixar's *Finding Nemo* (Andrew Stanton, 2003) to interact and improvise with a live audience in real time. Opened in 2007 at Walt Disney World's Magic Kingdom in Florida, the 'Monsters Inc. Laugh Floor' attraction operates using similar principles of virtual puppetry, and is again marketed on the theatrical spectacle of monsters from Pixar's fourth computer-animated feature appearing to perform 'live'.

Beyond the multimedia afterlives of computer animation and the co-option of its characters away from the cinema auditorium, the scenes of puppetry made explicit throughout *Toy Story* supports a critical investigation into computer-animated film performance because the discourse of puppetry ultimately preserves, rather than obscures, their specificity as a particular type of contemporary digital animation. Within the emergent, but significant, body of work on digital performance, notions of digital puppetry have been collapsed predominantly into a framing discourse of motion-capture.[53] However, despite Pixar animator Gordon evoking 'mo-cap' technology when describing animated acting as 'more like a *suit*, you're *really feeling* the physicality of *that* thing', the adoption of a performing objects model permits puppetry to account for the specificities of computer-animated film acting.[54] The internal 'hands-in' quality of motion-capture (as the dominant form of cyber or digital puppetry) is replaced in computer-animated filmmaking with the externalized 'hands-on' encounter between 'performing object' (puppet) and performer (puppeteer) that is rooted in new kinds of object orchestration.

Back in 2000, Andrew Darley asked of *Toy Story* 'is it cartoon animation, three-dimensional (puppet) animation, live-action or, perhaps a combination of all three?'.[55] Such a question of identity was directed at the critical uncertainty that troubled Pixar's first feature, and essentially sought to ask who was 'pulling the strings' in a computer-animated film that appeared to amalgamate and recombine prior animated forms and traditions. However, the visions of puppet manipulation inscribed into *Toy Story*'s opening sequence – as Andy balances, poses and choreographs his plenitude of popular toys in a dramatic routine – are revelatory insofar as they self-reflexively acknowledge the very techniques of puppetry fundamental to its illusion. Andy's operation, control and generation of Woody and Buzz's movement was not only rehearsed by the childlike delirium of America's youth demographic that marked Burger King's tie-in advertisements, but also more readily alluded to the new practices of puppet–puppeteer collaboration upon which the toys' story was able to be told.

Notes

1 In 1996, the same year that the former head of marketing for Burger King, John Cywinski, joined Disney, the Disney Corporation signed a new ten-year global marketing agreement with McDonald's. As Robert J. Sodaro and Alex G. Malloy note, 'burned' by the Burger King/Disney relationship that presented Burger King 'access to killer promotions', the 1996 deal showed how 'McDonald's worked aggressively to lock up the rest of the Disney pantheon'. Robert J. Sodaro and Alex G. Malloy, *Kiddie Meal Collectibles* (Iola, Wisconsin: Krause Publications, 2001), p. 8.

2 Burger King Toy Story Puppets, Christmas Commercial (1995).

3 Henry A. Giroux and Grace Pollock, *The Mouse That Roared: Disney and the End of Innocence* (New York: Rowman & Littlefield, 2010), p. 100.

4 Frank Proschan, 'The Semiotic Study of Puppets, Masks, and Performing Objects,' *Semiotica*, no. 47 (1981): 1–4 (p. 4).

5 The recent of digital likenesses of actors Peter Cushing and Carrie Fisher used in the production of *Rogue One: A Star Wars Story* (Gareth Edwards, 2016) showcases the (often uneasy) proclivity of digital processing for artificial resurrection that operates in excess of actor mortality. With reference to the digital recreation of Brandon Lee in *The Crow* (Alex Proyas, 1994) and Oliver Reed in *Gladiator* (Ridley Scott, 2000), Lisa Bode has discussed how such simulation of actors via computer graphics 'when they have died during film production' and the digital repurposing of past performances has a rich history. See Lisa Bode, 'No Longer Themselves? Framing Digitally Enabled Posthumous "Performance"', *Cinema Journal*, vol. 49, no. 4 (2010): 46–70.

6 For critical discussions of digital acting in their increasing variance see Lisa Bode, 'From Shadow Citizens to Teflon Stars: Reception of the Transfiguring Effects of New Moving Image Technologies', *animation: an interdisciplinary journal*, vol. 1, no. 2 (2006): 173–89; Lisa Bode, '"Grave Robbing" or "Career Comeback"? On the Digital Resurrection of Dead Screen Stars', in Kari Kallioniemi, Kimi Kärki, Janne Mäkelä and Hannu Slami (eds), *History of Stardom Reconsidered* (Turku: International Institute for Popular Culture, 2007), pp. 36–40; Lisa Bode, 'Fleshing It Out: Prosthetic Makeup Effects, Motion Capture and the Reception of Performance', in Dan North, Bob Rehak and Michael S. Duffy (eds), *Special Effects: New Histories/Theories/Contexts* (London: BFI/Palgrave, 2010), pp. 32–44; Lisa Purse, 'Digital Heroes in Contemporary Hollywood: Exertion, Identification, and the Virtual Action Body', *Film Criticism*, vol. 31, no. 1 (2007): 5–25; Chris Pallant, 'Digital Dimensions in Actorly Performance: The Aesthetic Potential of Performance Capture', *Film International*, no. 57 (2012): 37–49; and Sharon Carnicke, 'Emotional Expressivity in Motion Capture Technology', in Joerg Sternagel, Deborah Levitt and Dieter Mersch (eds), *Acting and Performance in Moving Image Culture: Bodies, Screens, Renderings* (Piscataway, NJ: Transaction, 2012), pp. 321–38.

7 Pallant, 'Digital Dimensions in Actorly Performance', p. 37.

8 Ibid, p. 40.

9 Kenny Chow, *Animation, Embodiment, and Digital Media: Human Experience of Technological Liveliness* (Basingstoke: Palgrave Macmillan 2013), p. 104.

10 See also Steve Tillis, 'The Art of Puppetry in the Age of Media Production', in John Bell (ed.), *Puppets, Masks and Performing Objects* (New York: New York University and Massachusetts Institute of Technology, 2001), pp. 172–85; Stephen Kaplin, 'A Puppet Tree: A Model for the Field of Puppet Theatre,' *TDR: The Drama Review*, vol. 43, no. 3 (1999): 28–35; Colette Searls, 'Unholy Alliances and Harmonious Hybrids: New Fusions in Puppetry and Animation', in Dassia N. Posner, Claudia Orenstein and John Bell (eds), *The Routledge Companion to Puppetry and Material Performance* (New York and London: Routledge, 2014), pp. 294–307.

11 John Bell, *American Puppet Modernism: Essays on the Material World in Performance* (New York: Palgrave Macmillan, 2008), p. 163.

12 Ibid.
13 Tanine Allison, 'Blackface, *Happy Feet*: The Politics of Race in Motion Picture Animation', in Dan North et al. (eds), *Special Effects: New Histories, Theories, Contexts* (London: BFI/Palgrave Macmillan, 2015), pp. 114–26 (p. 114).
14 Mihaela Mihailova, 'Collaboration without Representation: Labor Issues in Motion and Performance Capture', *animation: an interdisciplinary journal*, vol. 11, no. 1 (February 2016): 40–58. (pp. 41–42).
15 For a discussion of animation's rotoscoped bodies (that anticipates Allison's racialized analysis of *Happy Feet*), see Joanna Bouldin, 'Cadaver of the Real: Animation, Rotoscoping, and the Politics of the Body', *Animation Journal*, no. 12 (2004): 7–31.
16 Yacov Freedman, 'Is It Real. . . or Is It Motion Capture?: The Battle to Redefine Animation in the Age of Digital Performance', *The Velvet Light Trap*, no. 69 (2012): 38–49 (p. 38).
17 Paul Wells, *Animation: Genre and Authorship* (London: Wallflower Press, 2002), p. 23; Stephen Prince, *Digital Visual Effects in Cinema: The Seduction of Reality* (New Jersey: Rutgers University Press, 2012), p. 110.
18 Heather Holian, 'Animators as Professional Masqueraders: Thoughts on Pixar', in Deborah Bell (ed.), *Masquerade: Essays on Tradition and Innovation Worldwide* (Jefferson, North Carolina: McFarland, 2015), pp. 231–40 (p. 231).
19 Donald Crafton, *Shadow of a Mouse: Performance, Belief, and World-Making in Animation* (Berkeley: University of California Press, 2013), p. 15.
20 Holian, 'Animators as Professional Masqueraders', p. 232.
21 Holian elaborates that 'Two to three minutes of final footage per animator per feature-length film is the Pixar average. During production, a typical Pixar animator completes approximately 100 frames every one to two weeks, depending on the number of characters involved'. Ibid., pp. 232–37.
22 Prince, *Digital Visual Effects in Cinema*, p. 102.
23 Alex Clayton, 'Performance, With Strings Attached: *Team America*'s Snub to the Actor', in Tom Brown and James Bennett (eds), *Film Moments: Criticism, History, Theory* (London: BFI, 2010), pp. 127–30.
24 Paul McPartlin, qtd. in Steve Tillis, *Toward an Aesthetics of the Puppet: Puppetry as a Theatrical Art* (New York: Greenwood Press, 1992), p. 21.
25 Rick Altman, *Film/Genre* (London: BFI, 1999), 24.
26 Kevin J. Wetmore Jr., '"Great Reckonings in Little Rooms", or Children's Playtime: Shakespeare and Performing Object Theatre of Toys', in Jennifer Hulbert, Kevin J. Wetmore Jr. and Robert L. York (eds), *Shakespeare and Youth Culture* (New York: Palgrave Macmillan, 2006), pp. 43–56 (p. 48).
27 Marlis Schweitzer and Joanne Zerdy, *Performing Objects and Theatrical Things* (London: Palgrave Macmillan, 2014), p. 1.
28 Jason Sperb, *Flickers of Film: Nostalgia in the Time of Digital Cinema* (New Jersey: Rutgers University Press, 2016), p. 101.
29 Tom Kemper, *Toy Story: A Critical Reading* (London: BFI, 2015), p. 39; Shannon R. Wooden and Ken Gillam, *Pixar's Boy Stories: Masculinity in a Postmodern Age* (Lanham: Rowman and Littlefield, 2014), p. 35. Jason Sperb further identifies a discourse of nostalgia inscribed within *Toy Story* channelled through the figure of director John Lasseter and his predilection for collecting vintage toys, a commodity consciousness that Sperb argues 're-enacted the aging baby boomer's

fond memories of growing up within the material properties of postwar America'; Sperb, *Flickers of Film*, p. 101.

30 Thomas Elsaesser and Malte Hagener, *Film Theory: An Introduction Through the Senses*, 2nd edn (New York: Routledge, 2015), pp. 194–95.

31 Ibid., p. 194.

32 Massimo Riva, 'Beyond the Mechanical Body: Digital Pinochio', in Katia Pizzi (ed.), *Pinocchio, Puppets, and Modernity: The Mechanical Body* (New York and London: Routledge, 2012), pp. 201–14 (p. 202).

33 Kemper, *Toy Story: A Critical Reading*, p. 38.

34 A similar gesture to technological representation occurs during the final shot of a clouded blue sky in *Toy Story 3*, which in their spacing and identical formation recall the design of Andy's wallpaper, but are here rendered with pristine illusionism.

35 Frank Proschan, 'Puppet Voices and Interlocutors: Language in Folk Puppetry', *The Journal of American Folklore*, vol. 94, no. 374 (October–December 1981): 527–55 (p. 542).

36 Bell, *American Puppet Modernism*, p. 2.

37 Ibid., p. 5.

38 Ibid.

39 The transformation of the human performer into a unique performing digital object in 'mo-cap' digital acting and its popular(ized) discourse of physical embodiment potentially place the mo-cap performer in two places within Bell's triad, as both 'animator' *and* performing object:
Animator/mo-cap performer →→→ virtual object (mo-cap performer) ←←← spectators

40 Bell, *American Puppet Modernism*, p. 5.

41 Aylish Wood, *Software, Animation and the Moving Image: What's in the Box* (Basingstoke: Palgrave Macmillan, 2015), p. 3.

42 Ibid., p. 43.

43 Alvy Ray Smith, 'Digital Humans Wait in the Wings', *Scientific American*, vol. 1, no. 13 (2000): 72–76. (p. 72).

44 Ibid., p. 75.

45 Kemper, *Toy Story*, p. 36. Woody's original puppet form can be glimpsed as a drawing suspended on the wall behind the cowboy doll when he makes his heroic entrance (assisted by Andy) in *Toy Story*'s opening western narrative.

46 Tillis, 'The Art of Puppetry in the Age of Media Production', p. 176.

47 Bobby Podesta quoted in Melena Ryzlk, 'Animation Advocacy, Pixar Style', *The New York Times*, 9 February 2011). http://www.nytimes.com/2011/02/10/movies/awardsseason/10bagger.html?_r=0 (accessed 18 March 2017).

48 Starting life as a programme written by computer programmer Tom Duff titled *md* (motion doctor), MENV (an abbreviation of modelling environment) is a tool-based package rewritten by original Pixar employees and computer graphics pioneers Eben Ostby and Bill Reeves and used during the production of *Toy Story*. Affectionately labelled 'Marionette', it has since been renamed 'Presto' as a tribute to Doug Sweetland's 2008 Pixar short film of the same name, which premiered with the theatrical exhibition of *WALL-E* (Andrew Stanton, 2008).

49 Henryk Jurkowski, 'Transcodification of the Signs Systems of Puppets', *Semiotica: Journal of the International Association for Semiotic Studies*, no. 47 (1983): 123–46.

50 Suzanne Buchan, *The Quay Brothers: Into a Metaphysical Playroom* (Minneapolis and London: University of Minnesota Press, 2011), p. 155.
51 Wells, *Understanding Animation*, p. 104.
52 Searls, 'Unholy Alliances and Harmonious Hybrids', p. 297.
53 See Scott Balcerzak, 'Andy Serkis as Actor, Body and Gorilla: Motion capture and the Presence of Performance', in Jason Sperb and Scott Balcerzak (eds), *Cinephilia in the Age of Digital Reproduction, Vol. 1: Film, Pleasure and Digital Culture* (London: Wallflower Press, 2009), pp. 195–213; and Nicholas Bestor, 'The Technologically Determined Decade: Robert Zemeckis, Andy Serkis, and the Promotion of Performance Capture', *animation: an interdisciplinary journal*, vol. 11, no. 2 (July 2016): 169–88.
54 Andrew Gordon, qtd. in Holian, 'Animators as Professional Masqueraders', p. 237.
55 Andrew Darley, *Visual Digital Culture: Surface Play and Spectacle in New Media Genres* (London and New York: Routledge 2000), p. 84.

Chapter 7

Toy Stories through Song: Pixar, Randy Newman and the Sublimated Film Musical

Susan Smith

From the initial sunny bars of Randy Newman's solo rendition of 'You've Got a Friend in Me' near the start of *Toy Story* (John Lasseter, 1995) to the Gipsy Kings' flamenco version ('Para El Buzz Espanol') during the closing credits of *Toy Story 3* (Lee Unkrich, 2010), this popular and much covered song reverberates throughout Pixar's famous trilogy, articulating its evolving treatment of friendship (and even romance) and knitting the films together thematically. In addition to the Oscar nominated 'You've Got a Friend in Me', two other original songs composed and performed by Randy Newman[1] appear in *Toy Story*: 'Strange Things' and 'I Will Go Sailing No More'. *Toy Story 2* (John Lasseter and Lee Unkrich, 1999) features two more songs written by Newman: 'Woody's Roundup', sung by the Western quartet Riders in the Sky, along with Sarah McLachlan's moving rendition of 'When She Loved Me' (also Oscar nominated). *Toy Story 3* includes 'We Belong Together', for which Newman – performer as well as composer – earned his first 'Best Original Song' Oscar for the *Toy Story* series in 2011, his second overall in this category, having already won in 2002 for the thematically similar 'If I Didn't Have You' (sung by Billy Crystal and John Goodman) from *Monsters, Inc.* (Pete Docter, 2001). Yet despite *Toy Story*'s importance in establishing a style of song that would be revisited and reworked throughout the series, this aspect of the film has received scant academic attention, often overshadowed by its technical advances in computer-generated imagery (CGI).

Even biographical studies of Randy Newman – the singer, song-writer and film composer who created all of the above songs as well as the scores for *Toy Story*, its sequels and several other Pixar movies[2] – find little of substantive interest in his film work, while the two main scholarly articles devoted to Newman's music were published in 1987 and 1992,[3] pre-*Toy Story*. Regarded as a maverick singer/song-writer whose sardonic outlook subverts the romantic conventions of North American popular song, ironically singing not for himself but from the vantage-point of fictional characters who espouse often unpleasant views antithetical to his own, Newman's film work tends to be regarded as a more commercial (if popular), artistically diluted departure from his usual style. His music for the *Toy Story* films does receive praise on account of its knowledgeably allusive scores[4] and the 'predominantly quirky as well as romantic' tenor of Pixar animated features is felt to provide Newman with 'a more spacious canvas to work with' than elsewhere in his movie composing.[5] Generally, though, his authorial world view is deemed to centre on a satirical vision of North American society that's at odds with Pixar's more wholesome, upbeat fare. As Kevin Courrier observes:

> Where Randy Newman sheds his sardonic pose and plays it straight is in his movie music, which might explain why his scores, well-crafted and unaffecting, are also ultimately forgettable . . . Randy Newman's voice tends to be invisible in his film scores, or in the case of movie songs like 'You've Got a Friend in Me' (*Toy Story*), little more than placidly charming.[6]

This tendency to treat Randy Newman's film music as an aberration in the composer's *oeuvre* is not altogether surprising given the *auteur* focus of such biographical studies, the priorities of which lead Courrier to deduce that: 'it's not a question of the quality of Newman's music for the movies, it's a question of what is absent in the work.'[7] Elsewhere, in the fields of sound studies and musicology, Pixar has received *some* scholarly attention but, in the case of Daniel Goldmark's chapter on 'The Pixar Animated Soundtrack',[8] the emphasis is on this studio's innovative investment in scoring and sonic design more broadly, while its two main case studies are *WALL-E* (Andrew Stanton, 2008) and *Up* (Pete Docter, 2009), neither of which feature Randy Newman as composer.[9] Central to Goldmark's argument, moreover, is Pixar's rejection of the Disney animated musical format, a key element of which is deemed to involve the privileging of diegetic numbers or songs over underscoring.[10] As Goldmark observes, the irony of Disney's purchase of Pixar in 2006 'is that the one thing that the powers that be at Pixar always agreed upon – and apparently still do – is that they did *not* want to make a musical film in the tradition of the Disney feature'.[11] Contending that: 'all but a few features by Disney animation have had at least one musical number in the course of the story', meaning that 'the rhetorical bond between Disney and musicals has become all but unbreakable',[12] Goldmark maintains that:

> Of the many ways in which Pixar differentiates itself from the classic animated shorts and films produced by Disney, the complete shunning of the Disney musical archetype may be the most pronounced. As Disney re-established its hold in the animated and live action film musical throughout the 1990s and 2000s, Pixar seemed far more intent on revisiting old narrative tropes of the animation world (and the childhoods of many an adult): robots, insects, toys come to life, and superheroes. And though Pixar could not escape the

historical legacy of Disney as the source of so many modern cartoon film protocols, the people most involved in steering the studio, including John Lasseter, Brad Bird, Pete Docter, and Andrew Stanton, made a deliberate decision to avoid the formulaic Disney musical.[13]

Arguing that 'the first four Disney features – *Snow White* (David Hand et al., 1937), *Pinocchio* (Ben Sharpsteen et al., 1940), *Dumbo* (Sharpsteen et al., 1941) and *Bambi* (Hand et al., 1942) – established the guidelines for music in feature-length cartoons (following similar trailblazing for general cartoon scoring in the first Disney sound cartoons in 1928)',[14] Goldmark concludes that: 'all four films basically adhered to the dominant structure of the late 1930s film musical, with songs dominating the soundtrack and significantly outweighing original underscoring.'[15] Pixar's refreshing innovations with music and soundtrack[16] are contrasted, therefore, with the 'formulaic' nature of the Disney animated musical (no longer, he claims, the dominant model of production in feature film animation)[17] and the latter's tendency to trade in the kind of 'conventional claptrap' that a film such as *Enchanted* (Kevin Lima, 2007) pokes fun at.[18] Goldmark's argument would appear to find some support in Pixar's widely reported decision not to make *Toy Story* in the manner of a Disney animated musical. Apparently, 'Lasseter made a conscious decision to move away from diegetic songs, believing that characters spontaneously bursting into song would detract from the film's "realist" credentials.'[19] Yet, precisely how Newman's songs are utilized in *Toy Story*, the ways in which its theme tune is redeployed as the series progresses and what all of this reveals, in turn, about Pixar's relationship with the Disney musical remain largely unexplored.

While recognizing that there are understandable reasons why Randy Newman's songs for Pixar have suffered academic neglect, then, my aim with this chapter is to begin to rectify this lack of attention by focusing on their place and use in *Toy Story*. In doing so, I consider Newman's three songs for this movie not as negative departures from the songwriter's other work nor as outright, unambiguous rejections of the Disney musical formula but in terms of how they interact and connect (as part of the collaborative filmmaking process) with *Toy Story*'s thematic and aesthetic concerns, and how this invests the use of song, in turn, with a deeper rationale that helps account for its evolving role within the series. Above all, the chapter argues that the significance of Randy Newman's songs in *Toy Story* and beyond is inextricably bound up with the toys' dual status as supposedly inanimate beings who are endowed with a secret life of their own beyond the ken of the human characters. Addressing questions of who owns the songs, from which space such music emerges and the extent to which their use differs (or not) from that found in Disney animated film musicals, it argues that this duality in the toys' condition lends a persuasive internal logic, complexity and interpretative force to the varying deployment of Newman's melodies at certain points on the soundtrack.

'You've Got a Friend in Me'

Compared with the diegetic song and dance numbers with which Disney has become associated, the opening track, 'You've Got a Friend in Me' (like the other two Newman songs that crop up later), is not performed by a character from within the story space (not in the way, say, that the songs are in *Pocahontas* [Mike Gabriel and Eric Goldberg], also released in 1995). This approach may well have been dictated by the previously stated desire on the part of Pixar's senior creative team not to emulate the Disney animated musical yet, considering the film's subject matter, could *Toy Story*'s opening song have been fashioned as a conventional diegetic number anyhow? The film's central premise that the toys can not come alive when humans are present means that the only character capable of performing this ode to the friendship between child and favourite toy is Andy, who still could have appeared running around the house but now singing this song to Woody as he does so. Such a decision would not have required much, if any, compromise to the film's realism, moreover, since Andy could easily have been shown humming and singing like an ordinary boy in naturalistic style as he plays with his toy, with the child actor who voices him (John Morris) replacing Newman as singer of the song. Bar that last point, this is the approach taken in *Toy Story – The Musical*, a one-hour stage show conceived by Walt Disney Creative Entertainment for Disney Cruse Line and performed in the Walt Disney Theater on board the Disney Wonder Cruise Ship, from 2008–16.[20] As that show demonstrates, however, to have reconstrued the film's opening sequence in this way would be to distort *Toy Story*'s perspective by suggesting that the narrative is orientated around the child's point of view,[21] when in fact it's the toys' outlook that forms its main focus of interest.

This is indicated by the film's title, of course, the appearance of which – just as Newman's rendition of 'You've Got a Friend in Me' strikes up (and directly after Andy has grabbed Woody away and out of frame) – seems timed to imply that it's the *toys' stories* the songs are designed to tell. That this song is, more specifically, an expression of *Woody's* devotion to Andy is gently but firmly intimated by the particular manner of its presentation (the impact and significance of which are lost in the translation of the film into a cruise liner stage show). Following on immediately from the cowboy doll's set phrase: 'You're my favourite deputy!' (triggered by Andy pulling the cord in the toy's back), the song seems to arise like a musical extension or outgrowth of this avowal of comradeship by sheriff Woody, encouraging us to read the lyrics' second-person mode of address as directed by him towards Andy ('*You're* my favourite deputy!'/'*You've* got a friend in me'). The song is also performed by Randy Newman who, aged 52-years-old around the time of the film's release, seems far more suited to voicing the thoughts and feelings of a cowboy doll iconic of America's mythic roots in the West than the young boy (whose child-like exclamations are heard throughout this opening sequence anyway). The lyrics support this notion, registering as they do the greater maturity of the song's owner: 'Just remember what *your old pal* said/*Boy*, you've got a friend in me' (the italics are mine).[22]

The creators of *Toy Story* did not have to rely on these subtle suggestions of the song's relevance to Woody, of course – they could have chosen to attach it more explicitly to him, presenting Newman's song directly from the cowboy doll's point of view. But to have made Woody the obvious source of the song – and the thoughts and feelings expressed therein – would have dissolved that very sense of distance between him and Newman's non-diegetic singing that's so suggestive of his lack of voice (and reliance on another's) during these passages of human-centred play. It's fundamental to the deeper irony of this sequence that Newman's voice should remain to a degree untethered and at one remove from Woody. Enriching the visual contrasts throughout between Andy's gleeful physicality and Woody's stillness, the song's non-diegetic status articulates the poignant paradox that Woody cannot openly express his loyalty and affection for Andy during the very moments of play that are so emblematic of their friendship. Whatever his dedication to the child, as a supposedly inanimate toy, he can never truly be close enough to Andy to admit this openly in the manner of a conventional production number (unlike Woody, Andy has no such problem in vocalizing his feelings, as his uninhibited outbursts during this and the preceding playtime prologue make clear).

Woody's silence throughout this introductory episode showing Andy playing with him thus invests Pixar's cheerfully upbeat song with its own special pathos: unable to project his feelings on to the external world while in Andy's presence, Woody, the impassive toy, is denied the musical's quintessential freedom – namely, that ability to burst into song and dance when ordinary words and actions become inadequate. The joyous rapture to which the musical number gives expression otherwise seems perfect for conveying the heightened experience that the toy feels on being played with by a child. As Jessie bitterly remarks to Woody in *Toy Story 2*, before Sarah McLachlan's melancholy rendition of 'When She Loved Me' reveals the cowgirl doll's abandonment by her owner Emily, it's the sense that 'when Andy plays with you it's like, even though you're not moving, you feel like you're alive, 'cos that's how he sees you'. The overriding optimism of 'You've Got a Friend in Me' (so different in tone and outlook from 'When She Loved Me', its tragic inverse) is also very much in tune with the musical's utopian sensibility. As David and Caroline Stafford observe: 'It's a perky song, cheerful, open-hearted and folksy. As soon as the intro kicks in you get the impression that the clarinet player's embouchure is being compromised by his inability to stop smiling. The tuba's smiling. Randy Newman's smiling.[23]

Contrary to what Pixar's creative team might explicitly state, therefore, there's a sense in which 'You've Got a Friend in Me' (in expressing the unswerving loyalty that Woody feels for Andy but can not declare openly to the boy) *wants* to be a musical number but *can not*, necessitating the emotions conveyed by the song to find release instead via the non-diegetic layer of the soundtrack. The dramatic law that requires Andy's playroom toys to regress to a silent, impassive state when this child or other humans are around nevertheless means that the opening song is still fulfilling a role equivalent to that of the musical's production number. Indeed, if the main purpose of a number is to enable a character (or group of characters) to give vent to what can not be revealed in the ordinary 'reality' of the narrative then this is precisely what 'You've Got a Friend in Me' is enabling Woody to do. The song's ability to articulate what the cowboy doll feels inside for Andy therefore complicates any sense that it is unambiguously non-diegetic,[24] giving rise to the possibility (furthered by the next two songs and Jessie's 'When She Loved Me' in *Toy Story 2*) that musical moments like this are about externalizing a subjectivity otherwise trapped inside the toy.

That 'You've Got a Friend in Me' is an outward, musical expression of Woody's thoughts and feelings is consistent with the idea put forward earlier that the song builds on and enlarges the sentiment inherent in this toy's spoken phrase: 'You're my favourite deputy!' The notion that the song is an extension of Woody's speech here is not hindered either by the shift that takes place from Tom Hanks's speaking voice to Randy Newman's singing voice, the tone and timbre of which if anything appear fairly similar. In seeming to trigger Newman's song, then, Woody's spoken line fulfils a role comparable to the musical's traditional cue for a song and, in showing how it is Andy's act of pulling the cord in his back that prompts the cowboy doll to make this declaration, the film draws attention to the ventriloquism on which animation and the animated musical depend. Based on this line of reasoning, therefore, what the film's opening song offers, ultimately, is a much more expansive and personal assertion of Woody's unwavering friendship for Andy than this toy can articulate to the child through the restrictions of his voice box's pre-recorded, generic catchphrase.

The desire on the part of Pixar's creative team to break free from Disney's musical formula may well have influenced the film's overall aims and design but *Toy Story*'s opening use of what, for argument's sake, I continue to refer to as non-diegetic song works so well because it harmonises with the story's internal rationale. Rather than appearing merely the forced outcome of some externally imposed motivation, this song emerges organically out of the particular needs of the story in ways that make sense in terms of the kind of characters involved and the narrative rules by which they operate. The song's effectiveness in this regard is reinforced by Randy Newman's contribution as singer, not just composer. In his chapter within this collection, Noel Brown relates 'Randy Newman's non-diegetic songs . . . to the film's strategies of projecting "emotional realism"', finding in the singer's vocal delivery a more naturalistic, anti-Disney quality that chimes with 'the film's "realist" credentials': 'Sung by Newman in his idiosyncratically homespun, sardonic drawl, the vocal performance is determinedly non-professional, bespeaking authenticity and negating the ingratiating professionalism of some of Disney's earlier musical numbers.'[25] Newman's unpolished, characteristically nasal voice and occasionally strained delivery certainly seem far removed from the more stylized, 'performed' Broadway-like singing one associates with contemporary Disney numbers, in particular. Based on this, one can only speculate on the appeal that his vocals (and mordant outlook) might have held for Pixar's senior creative team, given their rejection of the Disney animated musical format.

The non-sugar-coated imperfection in Newman's voice is also extremely well-suited, however, to the needs of character and story, perfectly befitting a figure drawn from the rustic primitivism of the American west and, coupled with the song's mainly upbeat rhythm and lyrics, suggesting a hardy resilience to the rough and tumble of Andy's boyish play. While the rigours of the latter are nowhere near as extreme as Sid's dismantling and blowing up of toys, this opening sequence nonetheless shows what has to be borne by Woody if he's to remain the child's favourite plaything. The contrast between the song's cheerful ode to friendship and the film's visual portrayal of the stresses suffered by Woody as he's hurtled forward in a battery-operated car, hurled down a staircase banister or launched from a chair seems designed to demonstrate precisely this, implying the strength of Woody's commitment in spite of everything inflicted on him. This disparity between the song's optimism and the physical hardship that Woody endures might have been difficult to reconcile but it's held in artful counterbalance by Newman's endearing but unsentimental performance. A more saccharine or polished delivery would have jarred with the uncomfortable realities that come from being Andy's favourite toy – instead, Newman's unrefined vocals, complementing the song's simple bouncy rhythm, at once register and suggest an ability to withstand the bumps and knocks to which Woody is subjected along the way.

Perhaps what Newman's voice manages to do so effectively, above all, then, is reconcile this broad tension in the opening sequence between joyful celebration of the close bond between child and toy on the one hand and sensitivity to the more exacting demands that such a relationship involves for the latter on the other. It's a tension that's inherent in the composer's lyrics, too, the cheerful tone of which is occasionally undercut by characteristically (for Newman) unromanticized lines which gesture (prophetically, as it turns out) towards tougher times: 'When the road looks rough ahead/And you're miles and miles/From your nice warm bed'. Held non-diegetically apart from Woody yet delivered with evident feeling, Newman's singing is perfectly suited to a film that does not want to appear like a Disney animated musical but remains committed to the emotional and psychological depth that song can bring – especially, as here, to a type of animated character (toys) whose enforced muteness (masking a secret inner life) renders them most in need of its expressive power. Often associated with ironic distance, Newman's earnest, almost conversational style of delivery on this occasion evokes a warmth and sincerity that chime with the song's theme of unstinting friendship and the sequence's brightly coloured *mise-en-scène*. A sense of distance persists, though, in the non-diegetic origins of his singing which, never fully embedded in character in the way that Tom

Hanks's voicing of Woody's speech is, keeps it at one remove from the toy from whose vantage-point he sings.

Considered this way, Newman's vocal presence allows *Toy Story* to appear far removed from a Disney musical and yet, if we consider to whom the songs belong within the story, covertly a musical at heart. In allowing 'You've Got a Friend in Me' to give outlet to the otherwise imprisoned feelings of a mute (socially servile) character, *Toy Story* therefore employs its opening song in ways comparable with what Disney practiced decades before in *Dumbo*.[26] While such a connection again highlights the importance of song in Disney feature animation, it complicates the idea that this early classical phase in that studio's output unilaterally established its live action-influenced musical format. Instead, it points to elements of innovation in Disney's use of song then that seem to anticipate Pixar's in the contemporary era.

'Strange Things'

In giving vent to periods of crisis in first Woody's and then Buzz's life, the next two songs[27] are closer, tonally, to Newman's authorial outlook. Displaying his skill in writing for character, they remain creatively attuned to the toys' existential condition, however. In the process, 'Strange Things' extends the film's rationale for using songs non-diegetically, whereas 'I Will Go Sailing No More' expands their function beyond Woody's character. In the case of 'Strange Things', this second song now clearly relates to Woody, with Andy only appearing intermittently and the cue for the song provided by a line of dialogue that the sheriff toy this time speaks freely for himself (rather than as a result of Andy pulling the cord in his back). 'You know, in a couple of days everything'll be just the way it was. They'll see. They'll see. I'm still Andy's favourite toy', he insists defiantly (on witnessing the other toys gather around Buzz excitedly after the space ranger figure has fortuitously managed to pull off the illusion of flying around the room) only for such bravado to be undermined by what follows. In contrast to the selfless and outwardly directed 'You've Got a Friend in Me', 'Strange Things' is decidedly introspective in articulating Woody's trauma ('Strange Things Are Happening *to Me*!'). The impact of this is reinforced by the visual focus throughout on his startled reactions while the shaky point-of-view 'camerawork' to evoke the effect of being held by Andy as the boy jumps up and down at the start of the song renders literal this toy's sense of disorientation. The editing is also paced to match the urgency of the song's rhythms: condensing a series of events into just two minutes, this musical montage evokes a sense of how the passage of time must feel to the devastated Woody during this period of (to him) seismic upheaval. The repetition of the song's title refrain after the first and final verses also intensifies the emotional impact on him of Buzz's arrival. The obsessive reiteration of lines like: 'Strange things are happening to me/

Strange things/Strange things are happening to me' is particularly effective in conveying Woody's panic and turmoil on seeing the décor, furnishings and established order of Andy's bedroom turned upside down.

Although Woody is technically free to sing 'Strange Things' to the other toys (during those sections of the montage when Andy is absent), in practice this song arises precisely to give vent to feelings that he is unable to admit to them. An earlier exchange with Bo-Peep revealed Woody to be too proud to divulge his pain at no longer being Andy's undisputed favourite. His increasing alienation from the other toys as they are shown growing closer to Buzz in the middle part of the song only heightens this all the more, with the lyrics expressing his fear of losing their friendship altogether:

I had friends
I had lots of friends
Now all my friends are gone
And I'm doing the best I can to carry on.

I had power (power)
I was respected (respect)
But not any more
And I've lost the love of the one whom I adore.

Woody's marginalization from the group is suggested even before the song begins when he is shown hanging back as the other toys crowd around Buzz to congratulate him on his 'flying' demonstration. Woody is left alone instead with Slinky who then also recedes from frame as the 'camera tracks in' on the cowboy doll, as he defiantly insists he's 'still Andy's favourite toy'. Woody's dispossession is thus two-fold since not only does he lose his privileged place in Andy's affections (literally, by the end of the song, since he's relegated to the toys' chest while Buzz occupies the child's bed at night), but his position as loyal friend and leader of the other toys is also thrown into jeopardy. And it's this double disempowerment (linked to feelings of alienation and abandonment) that justifies the song's displacement once more onto the non-diegetic layer of the soundtrack. Woody's weakened position within the narrative is reflected, narrationally, in the fact that, even in Andy's absence, he still can not take ownership of Newman's singing voice and (as we find out soon) is on the verge of losing that too.

'Strange Things' is transitional, therefore, and in more than one sense. Serving as a musical bridge between Woody's life before and after Buzz's arrival, it draws on the emotional impact and innocence of 'You've Got a Friend in Me', helping us to understand how Woody must be feeling now everything that first song celebrated is under threat. As a result, it prepares us for his spiteful action later when, in an attempt to sideline Buzz (to prevent him from being the sole toy chosen by Andy to go with him to Pizza Planet), he causes the space ranger figure to fall accidentally out of the bedroom window. Newman, the maverick singer/song-writer with a penchant for composing for unlikeable characters, is perfectly suited to bringing out this more shadowy undertone to Woody who was originally conceived far more unsympathetically[28] and who, in the finished film, still finds himself struggling with unpalatable feelings of jealousy and resentment towards Buzz. But 'Strange Things' is also pivotal in being the last song to use Newman's voice as a conveyor of Woody's thoughts and feelings and so marks the point at which this toy is required to hand over the musical reins to Buzz.

'I Will Go Sailing No More'

The film's final track – 'I Will Go Sailing No More' – arises when Buzz, convinced that he is a real space ranger, finds out from a television advert he overhears in a room in Sid's house that he is in fact (as Woody has previously tried to tell him) a mass-produced toy. By far the most wry and melancholic of the three songs, it articulates the devastation felt by Buzz at this news as he walks away downcast only to leap from the stair-railings with his wings out in defiance of the TV advert's customer warning that he is 'NOT A FLYING TOY'. The crushing effect of this stipulation is reinforced by a voiceover reminder of Woody's similar insistence a while ago that: 'You are a toy! You can't fly!', the emergence of which – in the midst of Newman's song – once again blurs the distinction between diegetic and non-diegetic sound. Aiming for an open window, he falls to the floor instead (hitting a step on the way down), the impact causing his left arm to break from his body as he lies there, utterly dejected. Once again, the song is not 'performed' by the character, as in a conventional diegetic number and, realistically, how could it be? Buzz is hardly likely to burst out singing in the middle of being chased by Sid's fearsome dog and with what appears to be the boy's father dozing in a nearby room. But there's no doubt the song belongs to Buzz, the only figure present during this sequence and whose emotional state the lyrics evoke so unequivocally.

The decision to transfer Newman's voice from Woody to Buzz could have been unsettling from an audience perspective, potentially interrupting the earlier attachment of the first two songs to Woody and challenging humanist assumptions about the integrity of the individual self in the process. That this assigning of Newman's singing voice to more than one character is not as destabilizing as one might expect (at least not to this author's knowledge) may have something to do with *Toy Story*'s status as a work of animation, a form that by necessity has to construct its fictional beings in a composite way that involves animated bodies being married with voices (both speaking and singing) sourced from elsewhere. Even in the context of animation, however, where identities are expected to be more hybrid and animated characters often rely (as in Woody's case) on more than one voice, the allocation of Newman's singing to two different characters has the potential to jar with our sense of them as individuals. That Newman's singing voice is never totally embedded in Woody's character prior to this musical switch and hence seems less integral to his identity than Hanks's speaking voice may help to explain why this does not in fact happen. The film's use of non-diegetic song is therefore instrumental in endowing Newman's voice with a degree of flexibility. As such, it enables his singing to be reassigned to another character in a way that would be much harder to accept in an animated musical where the success of a production number (unless totally dance-based) typically depends on the vocals appearing to issue from a character's mouth. Considering the number's importance in articulating a person's sense of selfhood, *Toy Story*'s eschewal of all this in favour of dividing Newman's songs across more than one character perhaps marks the point where the film moves furthest away from the Disney musical (a form especially reliant on the idea of individualism). Indeed, it's difficult to imagine a situation where the singing voice of a Disney protagonist would be reassigned to another character since the conventions and demands of the diegetic number would militate against this.

Another factor to consider here is that Woody and Buzz are *toys*, not just animated characters, and so however anthropomorphized they might be they remain apart from humanity, making the allocation of Newman's voice to both of them arguably more acceptable, dramatically. It therefore seems apt that the moment where Buzz appropriates Woody's singing voice is precisely when the space ranger discovers that he's a toy. Arising at this exact point, the conferment of this non-diegetic style of singing on Buzz confirms the reality of his newfound condition. Faced with the realization that he's a manufactured, mass commodity product rather than a real space ranger with his own individual identity, there's a logic to the way he articulates his despair through a means of expression that's so symptomatic of a toy's constrained existence. In this respect, Buzz's reliance on Newman's voice underlines his fractured sense of self, since he now has to resort to another human voice borrowed from his former rival to give expression to his feelings. His lack of freedom in being unable to fly (contrary to what he previously thought) is thus reflected in his inability to own the song diegetically. There is a paradox here, however, since if Buzz's acquisition of Newman's voice denotes his discovery that he is 'merely' a toy, then it also bestows on him a capacity for subjective expression at the very point where he feels most disempowered within the narrative. No longer the outsider – for the first time in the film – he becomes endowed with an inner life to which we are granted access. What that inner life expresses here may be utter disillusionment, but the song affirms Buzz's subjective state at the very point when he feels his individuality has been destroyed, bearing out Woody's and the film's underlying conviction in the emotional enrichment and strength of identity and purpose that come from being a toy.

There is another justification to this decision to reassign Newman's voice to Buzz given how it mirrors the space ranger's ousting of the cowboy doll as

Andy's favourite toy within the narrative. Indeed, if the previous song, 'Strange Things', expressed Woody's disorientation and growing jealousy at this, then 'Sailing No More' confirms the reality of such displacement since the singing voice that had formerly given expression to his innermost feelings is now no longer (solely) his. Hence, just as he lost his spot as favourite toy in Andy's bed, so now Woody has to relinquish his privileged position as centre of the film's subjective space. This transfer of Newman's singing voice from Woody to Buzz therefore amounts to a *sharing* of the musical narration between them, and so is indicative of their growing equality as protagonists, *both* of whom now warrant the emotional depth that songs can bring. In a sense, 'I Will Go Sailing No More' does for Buzz what 'Strange Things' did for Woody, revealing a vulnerability that punctures the space ranger toy's former self-confidence and sense of invincibility. Not only that, but this apportioning of Newman's voice to each of these characters also points to Buzz's developing friendship with Woody: as emerging buddies rather than rivals, what could be more fitting than that they should share Newman's songs between them?

Toy Story's *Reprise of 'You've Got a Friend in Me'*

Given Woody and Buzz's growing friendship during the second half of *Toy Story*, there's a sense in which the film's first song increasingly relates as much to them as to Woody and Andy. That 'You've Got a Friend in Me' is never explicitly reassigned to them during the narrative perhaps reflects Pixar's ultimate privileging of the child–toy relationship over the friendship between toys, not to mention this studio's resistance to having Woody and Buzz perform the song in the form of a diegetic number (tempting as that might have been). Instead, this song is reprised as a duet between Randy Newman and Lyle Lovett during the closing credits sequence. Following on directly from the privileging of Woody and Buzz as best buddies in the film's final scene (and shot) at Andy's new family home, this version of the song appears like a thinly veiled tribute to their friendship. The duet structure is certainly more expressive of these toys' relationship than Woody and Andy's, the easy reciprocation of the title line suggesting a freedom of interaction between the two that is not a feature of the cowboy doll's bond with the young boy (hence the logic of presenting this song initially as a Randy Newman solo, sung on Woody's behalf outside the objective diegetic world in a way that the child can not hear).

This reworking of 'You've Got a Friend in Me' as a duet represents the culmination of the film's changing use of Newman's songs and singing voice to articulate Woody and Buzz's growing friendship. Whereas these two toys had previously shared Newman's voice across different songs (with Woody 'handing over' Newman's voice to Buzz for 'I Will Go Sailing No More'), now they implicitly inhabit the same tune, jauntily exchanging the song's title line and other lyrics, with Newman again representing Woody (as in the opening rendition of the song) while Lovett sings (by inference) on Buzz's behalf. That Woody and Buzz do not perform this song together in the final scene may be ultimate proof of Pixar's decision not to make *Toy Story* in the manner of a Disney animated musical but to find other expressive opportunities through the use of non-diegetic song instead. In this particular instance, there's a delightful aptness to the way that Newman and Lovett's duet harmonizes with the conventions of the buddy movie. Indeed if, as Andrew Gay observes in his chapter, Woody's final line ('Now Buzz, what could Andy possibly get that is worse than you?!' as they await news of the boy's first Christmas present) typifies the 'begrudging respect' that usually characterizes the partners' 'concluding attitude' at the end of the buddy movie,[29] then how these two toys really feel about each other arguably finds freer outlet beyond the narrative in this duet reprise of 'You've Got a Friend in Me'.

It is a central tenet of this chapter, then, that Randy Newman's songs are central to the narrational fabric of *Toy Story* due to the access they grant us to the toys' inner life. As playthings who cannot speak or reveal themselves as sentient beings in the presence of the human characters (except for the one flouting of this rule involving Woody and Sid near the end of the film) Andy's toys project an obligatory impassivity and silence which make sense of the sheriff doll's dependency on the singing voice of Randy Newman to articulate his innermost thoughts and feelings. Even where humans are not present and the toys are technically free to speak and sing, the song's non-diegetic status remains warranted, articulating the otherwise ineffable insecurity and isolation that comes from being a toy and, in Buzz's case, acknowledging a subjectivity that seems contingent on his discovery that he is indeed just that.

In the process, the songs acquire a poignancy and substance that help explain their enduring appeal. As an affirmation of the staunch loyalty of a special pal through thick and thin, 'You've Got a Friend in Me' has the capacity to enhance the child's animistic belief and emotional investment in the companionship of toys while affording comfort to those undergoing the pains of separation from parents and the fear of isolation at school. Woody's 'Strange Things' articulates the anxieties and uncertainties arising from the discovery that things do not stay the same, normalizing more troubled feelings such as jealousy and resentment of the popular other and the need to feel loved. And, finally, 'I Will Go Sailing No More' (notwithstanding Woody and Buzz's later success in 'falling with style' during the narrative climax) challenges the wish-fulfilling nature of the (Disney) musical's "I Want" song, confronting the possibility that in reality ambitions and desires may not always be satisfied nor obstacles and limitations overcome.

Yet, as I also argue, while these three songs are not presented diegetically in the manner of a Disney animated musical, there is nonetheless a sense in which they still manage to fulfil the function of the production number by allowing the toys to give vent to feelings they otherwise can not express. In this respect, *Toy Story* reminds me of Michel Chion's notion of 'the sound cinema [as] an art of palimpsest',[30] underneath which (according to him) a silent film exists, its 'silent image vibrating with a sound we never hear'.[31] In the case of *Toy Story*, though, it's almost like (from the toys' perspective) there's a musical buried beneath this text's surface, suppressed but waiting to announce itself. It's deeply fitting, therefore, that, as the films become increasingly focused on the friendship (even romance) between the toys, the toys in turn discover a greater capacity to perform and become audiences to the songs within the diegesis (in the absence of humans, of course). With this in mind, it seems telling that during the rescue mission towards the end of *Toy Story* that forges Woody and Buzz's friendship, Andy's younger sister, Molly, is at one point shown catching a brief glimpse of (and giggling at) these two figures in the wing mirror, swinging across the road in their battery operated toy vehicle, while 'Hakuna Matata' from *The Lion King* (Roger Allers and Rob Minkoff, 1994) plays in her mother's car. Humorously counterpointing Timon and Pumbaa's 'problem-free philosophy' with Woody and Buzz's fraught attempts to reach Andy, such intertextuality heralds an occasion where the Disney animated musical breaks through into the world of *Toy Story* – and via a song that, in celebrating the coming together of meerkat, warthog and hungry lion cub in an unlikely friendship, mirrors the key thematic drive being played out here.

As the toys' friendships become ever more central as the series develops, there's an increasing trend towards rendering their songs diegetic and therefore capable of being performed and heard. Jessie's song in *Toy Story 2* is transitional in this regard. Although 'When She Loved Me' is performed non-diegetically by Sarah McLachlan as an accompaniment to a flashback charting Jessie's relationship with and ultimate abandonment by the child Emily, as the song draws to a close and the movie dissolves back to the present, Woody's astonished, transfixed stare at Jessie suggests that, along with us, he has heard it too (or, if not literally the song itself, something approaching its affective power). Jessie is never actually shown singing (she turns away to look out of the window just as the melody and flashback begin) but, somewhere in the space of this song, McLachlan's heartrending vocals and Newman's stirring music seem to punctuate the diegetic layer of the soundtrack, raising the possibility that 'When She Loved Me' becomes audible to another character.[32]

Musical Reverberations of 'You've Got a Friend in Me' in Toy Story 2 *and 3*

Elsewhere, the series' developing use of song can be illustrated by the films' constant reworking of the anthemic 'You've Got a Friend in Me'. This song's original significance as a declaration of the toy's unfaltering allegiance to his child owner is clearly still relevant by the end of *Toy Story 3* when Woody (sitting on the porch, having been handed over to Bonnie along with the other toys in an act of kindness by Andy) softly says: 'So long partner' as he watches the young man drive away to college. Woody's fond farewell is echoed in Newman's score which gently plays its instrumental theme 'So Long' throughout this closing sequence, strains of which even seem to nostalgically rework elements from 'You've Got a Friend in Me'. This moment movingly reaffirms, therefore, the strength of Woody's bond with Andy while at the same time confronting its inevitable finality. As such, this closing sequence bears out what is subtly intimated during two earlier sung reprises of 'You've Got a Friend in Me' in *Toy Story 2* and 3. In both cases, the song's invocation of this child–toy relationship is relayed through nostalgic framing devices that still contemplate it with great affection but now register – knowingly from a more distant viewpoint – its transitory nature.[33] In *Toy Story 2* the reprise in question occurs two thirds of the way through when Woody watches his marionette self singing (in the voice of Tom Hanks) 'You've Got a Friend in Me' on 'Woody's Roundup' show via a videotape played on an analogue television set. In *Toy Story 3*, Newman's original rendition of the song accompanies a succession of shots showing Andy playing with Woody (along with his other toys) in an unmistakable evocation of *Toy Story*'s melodious opener, but this time the sequence is ironically mediated through the viewfinder of the boy's mother's video camera as she records her son growing up.[34]

In contrast to such nostalgic, retrospective reworkings, the series contains two other dynamic reprises of 'You've Got a Friend in Me', each of which attests to the toys' increasing ability to appropriate this song and perform it proactively in the manner of a diegetic musical number that signals some form of emotional rebirth or breakthrough. The sequence just mentioned from *Toy Story 2* where Woody watches his marionette counterpart singing the song while strumming on a guitar could be regarded as another possible example of this, especially given the use of Tom Hanks (the speaking voice of the main Woody from *Toy Story* onwards) to sing the song. Yet despite the fact that 'You've Got a Friend in Me' is now located diegetically within the film's fictional world and Woody can hear the song, he still does not perform it. Instead, he experiences it second-hand via an old television monitor and in the rudimentary form of a puppet show, both of which distance the tune from him, spatially and temporally. Moreover, in prompting Woody to change his mind and return to Andy rather than go to the museum in Japan with the rest of the 'Roundup Gang', this reprise is also very much subservient to the needs of both human child and narrative, reminding Woody of his loyalty to the boy and precluding the kind of uninhibited self-expression associated with the musical number.

The same cannot be said of the next reworking of this song. Arising at the end of *Toy Story 2*, it's Wheezy (with backing from a group of Barbie dolls) who – in celebration of his vocal rejuvenation, Woody's rescue of him, and the wider camaraderie among the toys – belts out the song in the style of a big production number that knowingly acknowledges the conventions of the musical genre: 'I feel swell. In fact, I think I feel a song coming on!' he declares before, toy microphone in hand, launching into 'You've Got a Friend in Me' in the rich baritone voice of Robert Goulet, doyen of stage and screen musicals.

And, after the high drama of the toys' narrow escape in the incinerator and the poignancy of Andy handing them over to Bonnie, *Toy Story 3* follows up with an unabashedly utopian closing credits sequence that culminates in Jessie and Buzz's Paso Doble-inspired dance to the Gipsy Kings' flamenco version of 'You've Got A Friend in Me' ('Hay Un Amigo En Mi'). This is aptly preceded by a sequence featuring 'We Belong Together', a non-diegetic song performed by Newman that rejoices in the toy community's newfound collective strength and comradeship (typified by the changed outlook of post-Lotso Sunnyside where all of the toys now look out for one another). In one sense, Jessie and Buzz's Spanish dance seems to entail a shift to a more conventional romantic perspective of the kind traditionally associated with the Disney musical (at least pre-*Moana* [Ron Clements and John Musker, 2016]) and the musical genre generally. Yet, together with Wheezy's high-spirited performance, Jessie and Buzz's exuberant Paso Doble (danced to the diegetic sound of the Gipsy Kings' track on a record player and surrounded by friends) at the same time represents a kind of celebration – through the vehicle of the production number – of the toys' identities and lived experience outside their relationship with humans. As a result, the original meaning of the song (and the human/toy hierarchy inherent therein) is loosened and unfixed during such moments of musical performance. In contrast to the song's first rendition near the start of *Toy Story*, when Woody was unable to sing in Andy's presence and Newman could only perform it on his behalf as a paean to this toy's devotion to the human child, these two musical reprises of 'You've Got a Friend in Me' now enable the toys to sing and dance for themselves.

Of course, when Wheezy belts out 'You've Got a Friend in Me', it still is not 'his' voice that we hear any more than it's Woody's when Randy Newman sings or Tom Hanks speaks on the cowboy doll's behalf. But, within the world of an animated film, this is as close as a character can get to performing a big production number (albeit perhaps more in the style of stage than screen musical). During sequences like this and the one where Jessie and Buzz perform the Paso Doble together, it's as if, now freed from the constraints formerly placed on them, the toys – and the *Toy Story* trilogy as a whole – can finally admit to their innermost musical desires by succumbing to the joys of song and dance.

All of the above reworkings of 'You've Got a Friend in Me' attest to Pixar's creative, flexible approach to song as well as the lasting contribution made to the series by Randy Newman, the combined achievements of which bear out Victor Perkins's contention that, contrary to the long-standing claims of *auteur* theory, 'authorship of movies may be achieved not despite but in and through collaboration.'[35] That this song continues to evolve in rich and meaningful ways is central to understanding the series' ability to remain fresh and inventive.

The evolution of the song is partly due to the sequels' readiness to revisit its original meaning from a more ironic standpoint. But the imaginative progression of 'You've Got a Friend in Me' also stems from the films' deepening grasp of their own musicality and the benefits to be gained from allowing the toys to take ownership of the song. Those moments where Wheezy, Jessie and Buzz embrace the song as an expression of their friendship or (in the case of the last two characters) their romantic feelings for each other are significant, therefore, constituting points at which the *Toy Story* films blatantly become musicals[36] and occasions when the series recognizes that its toys and this genre really do belong together.

Notes

1 Born in a family of major film composers, Randy Newman is nephew of Alfred, Lionel and Emil Newman and cousin of Thomas and David Newman. Thomas Newman has also composed several scores for Pixar films, including *Finding Nemo* (Andrew Stanton and Lee Unkrich, 2003), *WALL-E* (Andrew Stanton, 2008) and *Finding Dory* (Andrew Stanton, 2016). See Kevin Courrier, *Randy Newman's American Dreams* (Toronto, Ontario: ECW Press, 2005), p. 26.

2 To date, Randy Newman has composed scores and songs for seven Disney-Pixar films: *Toy Story*, *A Bug's Life* (John Lasseter and Andrew Stanton, 1998), *Toy Story 2*, *Monsters, Inc.*, *Cars* (John Lasseter, 2006), *Toy Story 3* and *Monsters University* (Dan Scanlon, 2013). *Cars* is the only one of these films to include songs composed by others. Newman is also the composer of score and songs for Disney's *The Princess and the Frog* (Ron Clements and John Musker, 2009) and *James and the Giant Peach* (Henry Selick, 1996).

3 Peter Winkler, 'Randy Newman's Americana', *Popular Music* vol. 7, no. 1 (1987): 1–26, reprinted in Richard Middleton (ed.), *Reading Pop: Approaches to Textual Analysis in Popular Music* (Oxford and New York: Oxford University Press, 2000), pp. 27–57; also Sara Dunne, 'Randy Newman and the Extraordinary Moral Position', *Popular Music and Society*, vol. 16, no. 3 (1992): 53–61.

4 Biographers David and Caroline Stafford praise the musical literacy inherent in Randy Newman's scoring of *Toy Story*'s opening sequence:

> Perhaps more in evidence here than in any previous score is the breadth of Randy's musical vocabulary and his surefooted confidence in leaping from one style to another. The cue identified on the soundtrack album as 'Andy's Birthday', for instance, starts with a couple of flourishes that live somewhere between Sousa and Tchaikovsky, segues into a grand symphonic theme from maybe 1850s Germany or 1950s Hollywood, and then slides effortlessly into an Elmer Bernstein western theme – we're still less than a minute into the cue – then into a few bars of Prokofiev, a few bars of Leonard Bernstein and a jazz walking bass takes us into a show-tune-overture variation of 'You've Got a Friend In Me' . . . and so on. And still it's good to listen to (David Stafford and Caroline Stafford, *Maybe I'm Doing It Wrong: The Life & Music of Randy Newman* (London: Omnibus Press, 2016), pp. 201–02).

Kevin Courrier makes a similar point about Newman's scoring of *Toy Story 2*, observing:

> As in *A Bug's Life*, Newman gives *Toy Story 2* as varied a score as any animated film has ever had. In the opening credits, as Buzz works the video game, Newman does playful variations on John Williams' *Star Wars* themes and Strauss' *Also Sprach Zarathustra* (from Kubrick's *2001*). When Andy's toys meet up with a Barbie collection in Al's Toy Barn, Newman cleverly incorporates a few bars from the Safaris' surfing hit, "Wipeout"'. (Courrier, *Randy Newman's American Dreams*, p. 236)

5 Ibid., p. 235. According to Courrier, 'the Pixar films don't provide Newman the opportunity to use fully the sardonic humor of his pop albums', despite the fact 'they've still allowed for some clever and witty musical ideas' (ibid.). He also quotes Newman himself as preferring the songs he's composed outside of the movies despite their weaker commercial appeal:

> By 1999, Newman was mostly familiar to people because of *Toy Story*. 'You know, people like "You've Got a Friend in Me", which I wrote for a movie so it's not saying "fart" or "piss" in it', Newman explains. 'They're not inferior songs . . . but "Davy the Fat Boy" or "Shame" or "Better Off Dead" [are] the things that interest me'. But they didn't interest the record company enough to promote Newman's new album. *Bad Love* may have been a boldly funny collection of songs about how love is an absurdist farce, but that didn't keep it from going largely unnoticed. And given the strict, conventional radio playlists in the late nineties, what station would find room for offbeat songs like 'The Great Nations of Europe' or 'The World Isn't Fair'? (ibid., p. 299).

Describing Newman's 'movie tunes' as 'terribly lifeless' (ibid., p. 28), Courrier nevertheless finds greater merit in the composer's scoring for Pixar compared with his other movie work. He even goes so far as to claim that such work poses a challenge to Carl Stalling's bleak view of animation's disregard for music in favour of too much dialogue, observing that:

> Newman, a composer famous for writing songs around dramatic ideas, understands the value of dialogue and how music can enhance it. His sense of drama and satire in his music for Pixar not only puts the lie to Stalling's pessimistic outlook, but ultimately does his best hopes proud (ibid., p. 237).

6 Ibid., pp. 25–26.

7 Ibid., p. 27.

8 Daniel Goldmark, 'Pixar and the Animated Soundtrack', in John Richardson, Claudia Gorbman and Carol Vernallis (eds), *The Oxford Handbook of New Audiovisual Aesthetics* (New York: Oxford University Press, 2013), pp. 213–26; See also Paul Wells, 'To Sonicity and Beyond! Gary Rydstrom and Quilting the Pixar Sound', *Animation Journal* (2009): 23–35.

9 The composers of *Up* and *WALL-E* are Michael Giacchino and Thomas Newman, respectively (for the latter, see also Note 1).

10 Underscoring is a term that refers to the practice of creating instrumental music that lies underneath the dialogue and action on screen. See Jason M. Gaines, *Composing for Moving Pictures: The Essential Guide* (New York: Oxford University

Press, 2015), pp. 8, 13. Kathryn Kalinak, *Film Music: A Very Short Introduction* (Oxford and New York: Oxford University Press, 2010), p. 62.

11 Goldmark, 'Pixar and the Animated Soundtrack', p. 215.

12 Ibid.

13 Ibid.

14 Ibid., p. 214.

15 Ibid.

16 Goldmark's rationale for choosing *Up* and *WALL-E* as his main case studies is that they:

> address different senses of loss or longing, whether for a person, a location, or an ideal. In each case, the music and sound design are instrumental in creating the sense of space and in turn amplifying the feeling of longing created not only in the characters, but also in the audience, which is naturally meant to empathize with the protagonists (ibid., p. 220).

In the case of *Up*'s 'Married Life' montage, he observes that: 'The scoring here is originally composed and is thus unburdened by the structure (or lyrics) of a preexisting song or tune (assuming that no one recognizes the theme's progenitor in "Alice Blue")' (ibid., p. 221).

17 Goldmark maintains that in the contemporary era of feature animation where Disney's dominant position has been challenged by a number of studios, 'the standard Disney production template is now only one of a variety of successful options' (ibid., p. 214) and 'Musically we find that musicals are no longer the de facto format of choice' (ibid., p.225).

18 Ibid., p. 215. In the footnote in which this phrase appears, Goldmark admits:

> I would be curious to see what Pixar might do if it faced the challenge of creating an animated antimusical – that is, an animated musical film that does not fall into the conventional claptrap that was parodied quite well in the live-action Disney film, *Enchanted* (Lima, 2007) (ibid.).

He also concludes his chapter by ruminating: 'Perhaps maybe even Pixar will do a fully formed musical . . . someday' (ibid., p.225).

19 See Noel Brown's chapter in this collection.

20 For more information about this production, see '*Toy Story – The Musical*', *DIS* website. https://www.wdwinfo.com/wdwinfo/cruise-new/ToyStoryMusical.htm (accessed 20 April 2017]
I have been unable to find confirmation that *Toy Story – The Musical* closed in 2016 but an audition notice by Disney Cruise Ships reposted online suggests that the show was expected to finish then. See, for example, Scott Sanders, 'Disney Cruise Line's Toy Story – The Musical Aboard the Disney Wonder Closing in 2016 [Updated]' (posted November 24, 2015), *Disney Cruise Line Blog*. http://disneycruiselineblog.com/2015/11/disney-cruise-lines-toy-story-musical-aboard-disney-wonder-closing-2016/ (accessed 20 April 2017).
One wonders what Goldmark would make of the Disney Cruise Liner production of *Toy Story – The Musical*.

21 In *Toy Story – The Musical*, this distorting effect is compounded by the fact that Andy is played by an adult actress (Laurel Hatfield in the original cast), presumably due partly to employment regulations preventing anyone under

21-years-old from working on the liner. See 'Overview: Preparing to apply', *Disney Cruise Line/Disney Careers.* http://dcl.disneycareers.com/en/prepare-to-apply/overview/ (accessed 20 April 2017).

22 Lyrics like: 'Some other folks might be a little smarter than I am/*Bigger and stronger too*' [my italics] also point to Woody given his diminutive stature.

23 Stafford and Stafford, *Maybe I'm Doing It Wrong: The Life & Music of Randy Newman*, p. 202.

24 In film music studies, the distinction between diegetic and non-diegetic (or extradiegetic) has been contested. For a discussion of this and the pitfalls of invoking such a distinction unquestioningly, see Daniel Goldmark, Lawrence Kramer and Richard Leppert, 'Introduction. Phonoplay: Recasting Film Music', in Goldmark et al. (eds), *Beyond the Soundtrack: Representing Music in Cinema* (Berkeley and Los Angeles, CA: University of California Press, 2007), pp. 1–12. There, the editors observe:

> This distinction is often useful and probably unavoidable. Sophisticated treatments of it have increasingly enhanced its usefulness by recognizing that it is not absolute; there are many cases in which the music's status is at least temporarily uncertain, and others in which the relationship between the types is transitional rather than oppositional: one flows into the other (ibid., p. 4).

Elsewhere, Daniel Goldmark argues more boldly for the limited value of these terms in relation to animation, pointing out that:

> Occasionally [they] can be helpful for analyzing particular situations in cartoons, but they fail to take into account that music is far more integral to the construction of cartoons than of live-action films because the two forms are created in completely different ways (Goldmark, *Tunes for 'Toons: Music and the Hollywood Cartoon* (Berkeley and Los Angeles: University of California Press, 2005), p. 4).

25 See Noel Brown's chapter in this collection.

26 See my analysis of this film – especially musical sequences like 'Baby Mine' and 'Pink Elephants on Parade' – in Susan Smith, 'The Animated Film Musical', in Raymond Knapp, Mitchell Morris and Stacy Wolf (eds), *The Oxford Handbook of the American Musical* (Oxford and New York: Oxford University Press, 2011), pp. 167–78.

27 Neither of these songs appears in *Toy Story – The Musical*, the stage show performed on the Disney Wonder Cruise Ship, while six new songs composed by Valerie Vigoda and Brendan Milburn feature instead. See Andrew Gans, '*Toy Story – The Musical*, by GrooveLily and Dickstein, Will Debut on Disney Cruise Line', *Playbill* (7 March 2008). http://www.playbill.com/article/toy-storythe-musical-by-groovelily-and-dickstein-will-debut-n-disney-cruise-line-com-148213 (accessed 21 April 2017).

28 See David A. Price, *The Pixar Touch: The Making of a Company* (New York: Vintage Books, 2009), pp. 131–32.

29 See Andrew Gay's chapter in this collection.

30 Michel Chion, 'On a Sequence from *The Birds*: Sound Film as Palimpsestic Art', in *Film, A Sound Art*, translated by Claudia Gorbman (New York and Chichester, West Sussex: Columbia University Press, 2009 [2003]), ch. 10, pp. 162–85 (p. 171).

31 Ibid., p. 170.

32 Robynn J. Stilwell theorizes on the significance of what happens when the boundary between diegetic and non-diegetic music is crossed in 'The Fantastical Gap between Diegetic and Nondiegetic', in Goldmark et al. (eds), *Beyond the Soundtrack*, pp. 184–204.

33 For different discussions of these sequences in relation to nostalgia, technology, texture, touch and the sensory nature of film, see Ian Garwood, *The Sense of Film Narration*, 'Storytelling through the Imperfect Image', ch. 3 (Edinburgh: Edinburgh University Press, 2015), pp. 63–98; and Colleen Montgomery, 'Woody's Roundup and WALL-E's Wunderkammer: Technophilia and Nostalgia in Pixar Animation', *Animation Studies Online Journal*, no. 6, 2011. https://journal.animationstudies.org/colleen-montgomery-woodys-roundup-and-walles-wunderkammer/ (accessed 20 April 2017).

34 According to David and Caroline Stafford,

> In concert, where violent rebellion would result from any disinclination to include ['You've Got a Friend in Me'] in the set list, [Randy Newman] warns the audience not to be fooled by the sentiment' inherent in it. 'It's a fucking lie, of course. What do you expect? It's a cartoon' (Stafford and Stafford, *Maybe I'm Doing It Wrong: The Life & Music of Randy Newman*, p. 202).

Contrary to this anarchic assertion by Newman, though, the ironic reprise of the song near the start of *Toy Story 3* is one instance where the reliability of this tune's sentiment is questioned. In particular, the fading out on Newman's lines: 'And as the years go by/Our friendship will never die' only to fade in to the film's present (where a now grown-up Andy is shown preparing to go to college while his toys face an uncertain future without him), invites scepticism about the viability of such a claim.

35 Victor Perkins, 'Film Authorship: The Premature Burial', *CineAction* no. 21/22 (November, 1990): 57–64 (p. 61).

36 In a surprising shift in his argument, Daniel Goldmark suggests (in a section towards the end of his chapter) that WALL-E 'may be as close as Pixar has yet come to creating a film that typifies some of the characteristics – or expectations – of the mainstream Disney musical' (ibid., p. 222). Such a claim implies a potential connection with my approach after all, despite some of this scholar's assertions elsewhere in his chapter (cited earlier).

Chapter 8

From Shelf to Screen: Toys as a Site of Intertextuality

Sam Summers

Intertextuality, as defined by Julia Kristeva, is 'the passage from one sign system to another',[1] or rather, the inherent interconnectedness of all signs and, by extension, all texts. 'Any text', she claims, 'is constructed as a mosaic of quotations; any text is the absorption and transformation of another'.[2] It is true that no text is created or received in a vacuum, and all authors and readers bring with them their past experiences, whether textual or otherwise. A text such as *Toy Story* (John Lasseter, 1995), though, explicitly activates and draws upon these links more than most. Noel Brown's chapter in this book highlights some of the cultural references found in the film's script, and the ways in which these intertextual gags contribute towards its dual address by reaching out to multiple demographics. Here, though, I focus on the connections established by the toys themselves, and in particular the meanings they can create for a child audience. With its combination of world-famous products licensed from companies such as Hasbro and Mattel, and original characters who can not help but bring to mind other real-world toy box fixtures, *Toy Story* goes out of its way to make sure that it includes recognizable toys that any kid watching can own or play with. In this chapter, I look at the various effects and uses of this particular form of intertextuality in the film, which range from world-building and establishing tone to informing thematic concerns. Crucial to all of these functions is the fact that, while toys can be understood as texts themselves, their inclusion in the film amounts to more than a quotation of one work of fiction appearing in another. Rather than alluding to another film, book or song, the hypertext to which *Toy Story* refers is reality itself, with the toys functioning as quotations from the 'real world'. It is this desire to anchor itself to the everyday life of its audience which runs through the various uses of intertextuality here, setting the film apart from other animated works which use anachronistic or otherwise contextually inappropriate intertexts to place themselves at a remove from reality.

There are three main ways in which the toys of *Toy Story* are tethered to those that exist in the real world. Foremost, there are the *specific* characters who literally represent existing commodities, their appearance sanctioned by the relevant manufacturers, allowing them to be imported directly and more-or-less unchanged into the films. Officially licensed toys in the first *Toy Story* include Mr. Potato Head from Hasbro, Slinky Dog from James Industries, Etch A Sketch from the Ohio Art Company, Troll Doll from the Troll Company and Toddle Tots from the Little Tykes Company, while Mattell's Barbie and Ken, Fisher-Price's Chatter Telephone and a Totoro plush from Studio Ghibli join in the sequels. These toys were licensed to appear in the franchise following negotiations with their respective rights-holders, requiring the manufacturer's approval of the character's on-screen actions, characterization and role in the story.[3] The arrangement is a mutually beneficial one, with the toys' profiles receiving a significant boost from the films' success: Mr. Potato Head saw a reported 800 per cent increase in sales following *Toy Story*, while Etch A Sketch sold a remarkable 4,000 per cent more units.[4] Second, there are the *generic* toys which are well-known and widely recognizable staples of many children's bedrooms, but whose rights are not tied up with any particular company. Traditional playthings, such as the little green army men or Hamm the piggy bank, fall into this category, as does Rex, who stands in for the many hundreds of plastic dinosaurs around the world. The use of these longstanding, public-domain figures helped to boost the ranks of Andy's toys without the need to consult copyright holders, while still remaining faithful to the kinds of items one could conceivably find in a real toy box. Deviating further from specific depictions is the third category, *archetypal* toys, wholly fictional characters created by Pixar to serve as analogues for well-known products for which they could not secure the rights. Perhaps most explicitly, Sid's ill-fated 'Combat Carl' is a clear ersatz G. I. Joe, whom Hasbro would not allow to appear in *Toy Story*.[5] Other examples include 'Mr. Spell', a version of Texas Instruments' Speak & Spell, and Lots-O'-Huggin' Bear, a villainous take-off of Kenner's Care Bears from the third film. In fact, as I explore later on, Buzz and Woody themselves play heavily on the conventions of character-based action figure fads.

Given the list above, it should not need pointing out that *Toy Story* employs its intertextual connections in an entirely different manner to the rapid-fire pop culture comedy found in *Shrek* (Andrew Adamson and Vicky Jenson, 2001) and its sequels and imitators. While DreamWorks' ogre frequently encounters modern music, products and brands wholly at odds with the series' medieval fairy-tale setting, all of the toys in *Toy Story* are perfectly at home in the fictional world of Andy's room. In *Shrek*, these inclusions are intentionally illogical. They act to create dissonance in the service of comedy, spoofing fairy stories by loudly disrupting the genre's lexical code. In the Pixar film, however, they have an oppositional effect, and one which functions with much more subtlety. The use of real-life toys to populate the diegesis anchors it to our own world, making it clear that the story takes place in a familiar setting. This is important because it is one of many factors which sets *Toy Story* apart from the prevailing trends of the animated features which came before it. In addition to its groundbreaking and unique technology and visual aesthetics, its story of toys inhabiting a recognizably contemporary suburban environment stands in contrast to the fantastical stories which dominated the market at the time. By 1995, the output of market leaders Disney and their closest competitor, Don Bluth, consisted mostly of fairy tales, historical epics and talking animal pictures. The makers of *Toy Story* were not only able to more closely mimic reality with their computer animation, but were also apparently determined to make it clear that the world inhabited by Andy is meant to be a version of our own. This is something that can be taken for granted in the average live-action film, in which the world is photographed and transposed directly on to the screen, but this is not the case in animation, where the diegesis is constructed from scratch, and can only ever constitute at best a representation of reality.

Toy Story, then, makes use of its intertextual reference points to immediately present the animated world as a familiar one; the first toy seen on screen is not Woody, the fictitious protagonist, but Mr. Potato Head, possibly the most well-known of the real-world toys in Andy's room. The next shot features the Toddle Tots and the Troll Doll, mixed in with generic toys such as Hamm and archetypes such as Rocky the plastic pro-wrestler. The familiar is depicted alongside the ersatz, neatly establishing the recognizable setting while slowly acclimatizing the audience to the fact that not all of the movie's characters will be taken from reality. Only then are we introduced to Woody, his unfamiliarity mitigated by the fact that he is brought into a recognizable context; the audience are encouraged to discern for themselves his place in the plastic ecosystem based on information they bring with them to the cinema. This kind of world-building – surrounding original protagonists with a supporting cast drawn from recognizable figures – can be seen in other animated films which take texts and commodities as their subject matter. In *Who Framed Roger Rabbit* (Robert Zemeckis, 1988), for instance, Roger Rabbit, his sidekick Baby Herman and his wife Jessica are 'toons' who live in a version of Hollywood populated by such icons of 'Golden Age' animation as Bugs Bunny, Mickey Mouse and Donald Duck. *Wreck-It Ralph* (Rich Moore, 2012), meanwhile, follows the villain of a fictional arcade game called *Fix-It Felix, Jr.*, who interacts with actual videogame heroes such as Sonic and Q*Bert, as well as attending a support group full of famous gaming antagonists. In addition to providing a draw for the characters' existing fan-base, the use of preexisting icons to populate these worlds helps to establish the films' conceits. It is easy to understand that we are watching a world in which cartoons or video game characters can interact with one another if we see this illustrated using diverse examples that we recognize from our own experience. It also works to convey the essence of the original characters by showing how they relate to the established ones, implying that Roger is a star of the stature of Mickey and Bugs, or that Ralph is Felix's enemy in the vein of *Mario*'s Bowser or *Sonic*'s Dr. Robotnik. In addition to locating the setting and anchoring the diegesis to the real world, then, *Toy Story*'s intertextual network plays an important role in situating the original story and characters firmly among the familiar.

Andy's Room and Playing with the Familiar

This carefully exploited sense of familiarity is crucial to the diametrically opposed aesthetic and tone of the films' two key locations, Andy's home and Sid's. The sole setting for almost the entirety of the first act, Andy's room is depicted as beholden to tradition and routine, the better to accentuate the disruption caused by the arrival of the high-tech interloper, Buzz Lightyear. The *in media res* opening and subsequent day-in-the-life montage detailing a typical play session between Andy and Woody establishes the status quo of the bedroom as simple and repetitive from the child's perspective, while the regimented 'staff meeting' does the same from the perspective of the toys. The cumulative effect is a sense of Andy's room as a lived-in environment, a permeating air of familiarity which preempts the characters' reactions, whether excited or fearful, to the introduction of the new and unknown Buzz. The cast of existing toys, then, extends this familiarity to the extra-textual level, populating the setting with common items that both adults and children are liable to own, or at least be aware of. The commitment to including recognizable objects goes beyond just the characters and reaches into the set dressing, with boxes of board games such as *Twister*, *Operation*, *Candy Land* and *Mousetrap* visible in the background, and a barrel of Playskool's Tinker Toys used as a lectern. Every inch of the space is layered with potential touchstones from the lives of the audience. This aids with the construction of Andy as a relatable 'every-child'; despite the idiosyncrasies of his cowboy posters and old west-style bed sheets, necessary to convey his particular attachment to Woody, the variety of playthings on display and the fact that any number of them could conceivably be found in the bedrooms of the child audience helps those children to see themselves in the character. What could otherwise be an overly specific environment is again imbued with that all-important familiarity.

The toys' real-life roots also provide a useful point of reference with which to contrast Buzz, both as a brand new toy foreign to their self-contained community, and as a character with delusions of being an actual space ranger. As he meets them for the first time, we hear this exchange:

Hamm: So, where you from? Singapore? Hong Kong?

Buzz: Well no, actually, I'm stationed up in the Gamma Quadrant of Sector 4. As a member of the elite Space Ranger Corps, I protect the galaxy from the threat of invasion from the Evil Emperor Zurg, sworn enemy of the Galactic Alliance!

Potato Head:	Oh really? I'm from Playskool
Rex:	And I'm from Mattel! Well, I'm not really from Mattel, I'm actually from a small company that was purchased in a leveraged buyout . . .

Buzz's ignorance of these major manufacturers is one of the early clues that he is unaware that he is a toy rather than a space ranger, and the script's name-dropping of these ordinary household brands lends a measure of bathos to the humorous back and forth. The fact that these companies are likely well known not only to the characters, but also to much of the audience aligns our subjectivity with that of Andy's toys, not with Buzz, highlighting his alien qualities and positioning him as a disruptive force. There is little doubt that his arrival will upend the bedroom's cosy familiarity, so concretely established through both formal and intertextual means in the film's first fifteen minutes.

Despite the simplicity of the techniques outlined above, questions may arise as to the efficacy of using intertextual connections to create meaning, especially when its primary purpose is to convey a sense of familiarity in a film ostensibly aimed at children. Needless to say, in order for a child to identify with Andy, or feel at home in his room, as a result of his collection of recognizable toys, they must first be able to recognize the toys. Writing on intertextual references in children's literature, Christine Wilkie-Stibbs points out that 'the writer/reader relationship is asymmetric because children's intersubjective knowledge cannot be assured.'[6] While any kind of extra-textual allusion always runs the risk of being missed by uninformed readers, this is much more likely when writing for children, whose exposure to popular culture is drastically limited. Although toys, like nursery rhymes and fairy stories, would seem likely to form part of the common cultural experience of most children, specific brands can fluctuate in popularity from generation to generation. As such, the toys that registered as iconic for the makers of *Toy Story* might not necessarily have had the same cultural cachet for the children of 1995, or indeed for the generations to come. Wilkie-Stibbs observes a similar phenomenon, which she describes as 'a curious kind of hegemony in children's books, in which adults who write for children . . . consciously or unconsciously operate in and are influenced by the intertextual space which is the literature they read as children.'[7] This can be seen in the selection of toys used in the film: Etch A Sketch, Troll Dolls and the plastic version of Mr. Potato Head were all introduced in the 1960s, coinciding with the childhood of director John Lasseter (b. 1957) and story artists Joe Ranft (b. 1960) and Andrew Stanton (b. 1965). Each has since seen its popularity ebb and flow, with the Troll in particular enjoying a resurgence in the early 1990s. Not as lucky was the slinky dog, which debuted in 1952, and was discontinued before the release of the film,[8] implying a much lower profile among the children of 1995. These vintage products may certainly hold a nostalgic appeal for older viewers, and thereby contribute to the film's dual address. How likely is it, though, that *Toy Story*'s original target audience of children would have recognized the toys of this earlier generation, or having done so interpreted and understood their presence in such a way as to produce the effects I have suggested earlier? Does it matter?

The influential structuralist scholar Michael Riffaterre claims that 'when it activates or mobilises the intertext, the text leaves little leeway to readers and controls closely their response.'[9] Taking this view, then, a film such as *Toy Story* should be able to engineer the intended effect of an intertext in its audience through its formal qualities alone, regardless of their degree of familiarity with the reference point. Riffaterre's apparently absolutist approach has since been countered by critics including Jonathan Gray, who writes that his 'faith in intertextuality as conditioning and guaranteeing the "proper interpretation" is unrealistic, holding out for a world of perfectly informed readers.'[10] It is crucial, then, to add the caveat that the text can control a reader's response *only if they are already familiar with the intertext*, influencing only their interpretation of the reference rather than conjuring associations in the mind of the uninformed. As long as the reader has some idea of the text to which the reference is directing them, their response can be shaped to correspond with what was intended. To that end, Riffaterre suggests that, when presented with outmoded intertexts, 'when the culture which the text reflects is still within reach, the readers' task is facilitated by the frequency of references to well-known intertexts, or just by chance encounters with them.'[11] This is certainly possible in our case. Most of the older toys seen on screen were still in production in 1995, as well as having had their brand bolstered and disseminated through multimedia paratexts, animated series and the like. It is, then, highly possible that even children who have never played with these toys will be aware of their existence, but the fact remains that many will not be, especially when international audiences are taken into account. Wilkie-Stibbs concludes that it is important, in these instances, to ask 'what sense children make of a given text when the intertextual experience cannot be assumed'?[12] This inevitably raises a second question: to what extent do the text's formal elements work to compensate for this by creating similar effect without relying on any specific external referents?

In the case of *Toy* Story, the film generally provides enough textual information to compensate for any lack of extra-textual knowledge. In the above exchange about the toys' places of origin, one does not need to be aware of Mattel and Playskool as companies to understand the comic difference between Rex and Potato Head's straightforward and mundane responses and Buzz's fantastical space-faring bluster. There is nothing inherent in the joke which presupposes specific awareness of the manufacturers; it only asks that we understand them *to be* manufacturers, which is implied by the context and Rex's follow-up dialogue. Meanwhile, the many jokes in *Shrek* and its sequels about, say, Pinocchio's nose growing when he lies, rely upon knowledge of the character that extends beyond the information offered up in the films themselves. In *Toy* Story, only the toys' immediately obvious properties are invoked, such as Potato Head's interchangeable parts, or Slinky's stretchy spring.[13] Going beyond humour and returning to the case at hand, familiarity with the specific toys is not necessary to appreciate the coding of Andy's room and its inhabitants as traditional and familiar, or by extension the contrast with Buzz's alien modernity. This juxtaposition is explicit in the film's introduction of this character, who is revealed via a close shot of his legs standing on the bed, Woody's head positioned between them, seemingly miniscule by comparison. Woody's frightened expression and the swelling, ominous music as the camera tilts up to show Buzz's face establish the character as a potential threat to the dominant order. This is closely followed by a point-of-view shot as Buzz surveys Andy's room, his concerned look reflected in his clear plastic visor. Forced to view the mundane scenery from the perspective of a character who is not only new to this world, but also as a 'space ranger', assumes that he has landed on an alien planet, the audience is shown the suspicion with which he views a setting we are accustomed to, revealing the extent of his detachment from the familiar.[14] Hence, it is clear that recognizing the specific toys is in no way *necessary* to understanding this juxtaposition of the familiar and the new: the contrast is clearly illustrated elsewhere, and is simply – although potentially very effectively – reinforced by creating links to the real world.

Sid's Room and the Familiar Made Strange

The scenes set in Sid's room rely less on specific toys, and instead foreground archetypal and generic characters, exploiting the familiarity with which these figures are imbued to create an altogether different effect. The lack of licensed characters is partly out of necessity; while many companies were happy to let Andy play with their products, they were clearly less forthcoming when it came to having them maimed by Sid. Hasbro, in particular, was unwilling to consent to their iconic soldier doll, G. I. Joe, being blown up by a firework. They were keen to downplay Joe's violent image, and so 'Combat Carl' was created as a stand-in.[15] Similarly, the 'mutant toys' which populate Sid's bedroom and eventually befriend Woody and Buzz are cobbled together from parts that *could* belong to specific, real-world products, but are never identified as such. One is a combination of what looks like a Fisher Price Melody Push Chime, a Mickey Mouse arm and a G. I. Joe (or Combat Carl) head, while one has a head and neck that could pass for a PEZ dispenser and another is a fishing rod with legs that resemble Barbie's. Even the pterodactyl that Sid combines with Janie Doll is a dead ringer for a figure from Kenner's *Jurassic Park* line. Much as in Andy's room, the purpose of the recognizable, or semi-recognizable, toys is to invoke their familiarity, but in this case rather than making the audience feel at home, they instead suggest the desecration of the home.

Sid's handiwork is made all the more visceral by the fact that the characters he has tortured resemble items the child viewer could own, and could have formed an attachment to. Indeed, a 'mutant' toy formed from completely unrecognizable constituent parts could just as well not be a 'mutant' at all, simply an original toy with a monstrous design. However, if we are familiar with the toy in its complete, undefiled form we are fully aware of the extent to which it has been mutilated. This taps into the feeling of the uncanny as outlined by Freud, distilled by Nicholas Royle as 'a peculiar commingling of the familiar and unfamiliar'.[16] He cites as specific examples 'the fear of losing one's eyes . . . or in realising that someone has a missing or prosthetic body part',[17] afflictions from which many of the mutants suffer. He also cites 'the return of the dead', perhaps an apt description of their state, and one which is compounded by the fact that the audience is likely already familiar with how they looked when they were 'alive'.[18] In this case, though, 'unhomely' – the literal translation of the German *unheimlich* – seems more appropriate than 'uncanny', referring more directly to the violation of the domestic space. Here that space is represented by toys, a specific feature of the child's bedroom quoted by the film to incite fear of, and later empathy for, the mutants.

The toys that can have the greatest potential impact in this area, though, are the generic items, those which have no ties to any specific product or company and are therefore likely to be familiar, in their myriad permutations, to children of many generations and backgrounds. This is palpable in the way they are deployed in the film. The first mutant toy we see is their leader, 'Baby Face'. A frightened Woody shines a torch beneath Sid's bed, revealing the shaved but otherwise normal head of a generic baby doll, in profile, its body shrouded in darkness. The audience is briefly led to believe that this is an ordinary doll, along with Woody, who instantly calms down and starts speaking to it as if it were a child. It then scuttles out from beneath the bed, exposing its spider-like body, made from Erector Set-style metal parts. It suddenly spins its head to face Woody and the camera, showing its hollow right eye-socket. This bait-and-switch – a minor one, considering the doll is already visibly unsettling to begin with – nonetheless presents the audience with the familiar first, allowing them to collect any associations they have with baby dolls, in general or from personal experience, before introducing the body-horror element to the equation. This is followed by a similar shot as the rest of the mutants begin to emerge, which features an apparently ordinary jack-in-the-box being wound up, playing the tune 'Pop Goes the Weasel' as per tradition. When it pops open, instead of Jack, a monstrous green hand bursts out.

In addition to being generic representations of extremely common toys – essentially blank slates on to which any child can project their own dolls or jack-in-the-boxes – these particular examples are especially potent because their extra-textual connotations are of early childhood innocence. They are both playthings one would associate with very young children, with Scott G. Eberle noting that baby dolls out of all toys 'seem to best exemplify the innocence of child's play, [and as such] we find it particularly unsettling when they betray those expectations'.[19] In addition to embodying this innocence, of course, the baby doll is a representation of the child itself. Sid's mutilation of the doll, then, is doubly coded as an attack on childhood, the actions of a kid attempting to pose as a grown-up by lashing out at the past. The figure of Baby Face is also doubly uncanny, as it is both eerily reminiscent of a baby and a twisted reflection of the familiar doll. The character's familiarity, its potential to evoke beloved dolls from the lives of the child audience, is later used as the central point around which the film's presentation of the mutants pivots. Initially presented, from the point of view of Buzz and Woody, as villainous 'cannibals', it transpires that they are in fact kindly creatures, helping out to fix Buzz's arm and rallying together to free the space ranger from Sid's rocket. The Baby's fixed smile, initially appearing sinister, now appears sincere. In light of its heroic actions, the audience is asked to empathize with, not fear, the toy. While it remains doubtlessly uncanny, this process is helped along by Baby Face's ability to serve as a stand-in for the audience's childhood dolls, tapping into a collective knowledge of the innocence and love embodied by such dolls and thereby underscoring the character's status as a victim.

Woody, Buzz and Toys with Character

It would seem, then, that while *Toy Story*'s success relies to some degree on the intertextual connections activated by its characters, allowing children to recognize their own collection in the toys seen on screen, it is also important that intertextual baggage be kept to a minimum. This allows the filmmakers the freedom to create personalities for the toys, and to decide what befalls them, accounting for the distinct lack of specific real world products in Sid's room. It is also why the more prominent characters are generic, traditional toys, such as the piggy bank or the dinosaur; they can be and do whatever the writers and animators see fit. This reflects how children actually play with these toys: Susan Willis says of dinosaur toys in particular that 'extinction has turned [them] into vessels for all sorts of encoded meanings. Because they are produced by the imagination . . . dinosaurs can be molded and shaped to . . . serve a range of personal needs.'[20] This also applies to many of the specific toys in the film; the whole point of products such as Mr. Potato Head or Etch A Sketch is that their personalities and functions are subject to the whims of the child. In some cases it was this very inherent flexibility which caused a character to be deemed unfit for use. This was the case with Barbie when Mattel, according to John Lasseter, 'believed that little girls, when they play with [her], make up the personality of the toy. They didn't want us to say, "When Barbie comes alive, she's like this" '.[21] This underscored the importance of including toys which, while recognizable either as specific products or as types, lacked the intertextual baggage which would tie the hands of the storytellers.

There is a problem with this approach, however. The reliance on generic toys, or those with 'blank slate' personalities, means that Andy's room is not an accurate depiction of a boy's bedroom in 1995. Since the late twentieth century, the average American toy box has contained more and more 'character' toys, action figures drawn from popular multimedia entertainment franchises. Jeffrey Goldstein, David Buckingham and Gilles Brougère identify this trend, asserting that 'toys, games, and media today are increasingly enmeshed in webs of "integrated marketing", which depend on what marketers call the "synergy" between different types of products.'[22] Whether a spin-off of a popular film franchise such as *Star Wars*, or the subject of its own promotional cartoon series such as *The Transformers* (1984–87), a toy is no longer just a toy, but rather a single link in a chain of products designed to increase one another's visibility and desirability. Dan Fleming traces the development back to the 1960s, during which time 'the toy industry became increasingly dependent on cinema and, especially, on television for play-worthy objects that could borrow the popularity of a screen character or story.'[23] Given the state of the toy industry in 1995 – Saban's *Power Rangers* were the biggest sellers of 1994, spurred on by a hit TV show and joined in the top 10 by *The Lion King*, *Batman* and *G. I. Joe* merchandise[24] – it would be unrealistic for Andy not to own at least a few action figures based on a multimedia franchise. Of course, toys like this present serious issues in terms of characterization: 'Instead of being a Native American or "Red Indian" in some general sense', Fleming writes, 'a small plastic toy might represent Tonto from *The Lone Ranger*, and consequently a familiar set of story ideas and character relationships.'[25] This intertextual baggage, while theoretically restricting children's play, would have resulted in much more stringent restrictions for the film's storytellers if they chose to populate their world with not only pre-established toys, but also pre-established characters.

In order to present a recognizable bedroom landscape while also retaining the freedom to build its toys' personalities from the ground up, *Toy Story* imbues its original protagonists, Woody and Buzz, with the distinctive characteristics of franchise action figures. The film works to suggest the existence of a 'familiar set of story ideas and character relationships' for its two leads without actually showing any of their accompanying franchise media.[26] This creates the impression for the audience of a lived-in world in which these characters have an extra-textual life outside of their plastic forms, thereby drawing connections between Woody, Buzz and the real world transmedia figures encountered by children on a daily basis. For example, Woody's voice-box features, in addition to simple phrases such as 'You're my favourite deputy', more specific quotes such as 'There's a snake in my boot!' and 'Somebody's poisoned the waterhole!', which seemingly allude to his fictional adventures. Meanwhile, Buzz, perhaps befitting his more modern aesthetic, is surrounded by references to a much more complex fictional mythology, with mentions of 'Star Command', the 'Gamma Quadrant' and the 'Evil Emperor Zurg' found in his packaging, his prerecorded phrases and his deluded 'space ranger' dialogue. He also has extensive ancillary merchandise, with bed sheets, a 'Deep Space Code' wall chart and character posters visible in Andy's room.

The clearest links between Buzz and contemporary character toys such as the Power Rangers, though, can be found in the commercial he witnesses on Sid's TV. First and foremost, it tells us that 'The world's greatest superhero is now the world's greatest toy!', solid confirmation that Buzz as a fictional character has already seen success in other media before his translation into plastic. Whether from a comic book, TV show, video game or movie, the children of Andy's world are familiar with Buzz's backstory and ostensible personality to the extent that he has some claim to the title of 'world's greatest superhero'. Further, the commercial adheres perfectly to the conventions of action figure advertising in the 1990s as outlined by Ellen Seiter:

> Close-ups of the toys in action are the rule, rather than shots of children playing with them. On the soundtrack we hear boys' voices making sound effects (engine noises, weapons) and providing speaking parts for the characters ... Boys' play with cars and action figures involves the boy impersonating the doll rather than interacting with it or establishing a relationship to it. Boys *become* their toys in play.[27]

Sure enough, we see a series of close-ups of Buzz demonstrating his various features as a pair of children wave him about, providing voices for Star Command ('Calling Buzz Lightyear') and Buzz himself ('On the way!'). The filmmakers recreate these tropes to the letter, strongly evoking real-life character toys and their paratexts in a way which, when combined with the rest of the above evidence, is enough to position Buzz as a fictional stand-in for those products. As such, the audience is encouraged to identify the real with the fictional, allowing their knowledge of, and experience with, these action figures, and their attendant multimedia franchises, to inform their response to the character.

The key debate surrounding character toys, and one which duly plays out in the depiction of Buzz and Woody in *Toy Story* and its sequels, revolves around the extent to which the pre-established narratives and characters attached to the figures restrict the parameters of play and limit the child's imagination. As Fleming puts it, 'pessimists view the opportunities to explore problems and to experience emotions as too tightly scripted in advance to allow any genuine imaginative activity; all that the child can do is copy the formulae.' Meanwhile, 'extreme optimists say that play has the inherent capacity to transcend such pre-imposed limitations, to use given identifications and opportunities merely as starting points, as resources to be imaginatively reworked.'[28] Although they may not necessarily express or understand it in these terms, this is a conflict which all parents and children must experience when playing with character toys, provided, of course, that they are aware of the fictional narrative and the characters' roles in it. When they pick up, say, a Power Ranger figure, the child must on some level make the decision either to follow the plot of the TV show or to place the character in an original scenario of their own design. To use *Power Rangers* as a contemporaneous example, almost every episode of the show follows the same structure: first the Rangers must fight a small army of generic enemies, before fighting the episode's unique monster. When defeated, the monster grows to a gigantic size, forcing the Rangers to combine their robot 'Zords' into a huge 'Megazord' to beat the monster again. As a child playing with these toys, you may feel compelled to follow this formula exclusively or, more likely, you would come up with your own stories for the rangers, perhaps even combining them with toys from other franchises.

This form of play, put forward by Fleming's 'extreme optimists', is clearly championed in *Toy Story*. When we are introduced to Andy, he is shown mixing all of his toys together, resulting in a western-style showdown featuring a dinosaur and a 'force-field dog'. This kind of fluid, hyperactive bricolage is revisited whenever we see Andy play in the series, and is taken up by Bonnie in *Toy Story 3* (Lee Unkrich, 2010). Moving beyond the literal depictions of play, we see this debate literalized in the form of Buzz Lightyear. For much of the film, he embodies the pre-established narrative with which he is packaged, fully believing in the existence of Star Command, Zurg and other aspects of his franchise's story-world. This Buzz, it is implied, is effectively the character as he is portrayed in other media, complete with exaggerated machismo and an unwavering dedication to his 'mission'. Everything he encounters in Andy's world, from the other toys to Pizza Planet to Sid, he adapts to make it conform to this narrative; the pizza truck becomes a 'space freighter', for instance, while Sid is trying to torture Woody for information. However, this is known to Woody and to the audience to be a delusion, and Buzz's arc ends with him realizing that this narrative is a fiction, and that he is free to decide his own path. As Woody tells him, 'being a toy is a lot better than being a Space Ranger', because as a toy he is able to be played with by Andy and make the boy happy. Free from the constrictions of his pre-established back-story and personality, he is able to live his own life, making new friends, and carving out his own place in Andy's room. By *Toy Story 2*, his personality has even subtly shifted, as he sheds much of his bluster. His arc, then, addresses the issues raised by Fleming and others head-on, taking a clear stance on the matter of whether action figures with built-in multimedia stories must restrict play, and potentially resonating with the many children who have made the decision to deviate from the path set out for them and their toys.

Returning to Fleming's summation of the optimist's position – that children have 'inherent capacity to transcend such pre-imposed limitations, to use given identifications and opportunities merely as starting points, as resources to be imaginatively reworked'[29] – it can just as easily be applied to the work of Pixar's animators and storytellers when it comes to the way they incorporate so many familiar toys, products and archetypes into the film. They refrain from using toys with enough extra-textual baggage to restrict their roles in the plot, or their depiction on screen, allowing them to rework these recognizable figures into a completely original story not beholden to any earlier material, or reliant on the specific foreknowledge of the audience. It is integral, though, that these existing toys are used as starting points, as they contribute significantly to the anchoring of the story in a world analogous to our own. As we have seen, no matter how far the on-screen action, or, in the case of Woody and Buzz, the toys themselves, deviate from these 'starting points', they are always palpably connected to real-world artefacts. Whether these connections are used as shorthand through which to elicit particular emotions, or as the bedrock of the film's theme of self-actualization, their contribution to the finished product is, if not essential to its enjoyment, an added layer of meaning through which we can relate to *Toy Story* and its characters on yet another, more personal, level.

Notes

1 Julia Kristeva, 'Revolution in Poetic Language', in Toril Moi (ed.), *The Kristeva Reader* (Oxford: Blackwell, 1986), pp. 89–136 (p. 111).

2 Julia Kristeva, *Desire in Language: A Semiotic Approach to Literature and Art* (Oxford: Blackwell, 1980), p. 66.

3 Damon Wise, 'Buzz, Woody . . . and Barbie Plays Too', *The Observer*, 5 December 1999. https://www.theguardian.com/film/1999/dec/05/2 (accessed 4 September 2016).

4 'The *Toy Story* Effect: How the Film Franchise Has Increased Toy Sales', *Hollywood Branded*, 17 November 2014.https://www.hollywoodbranded.com/toy-story-effect-how-film-franchise-increased-toy-sales/ (accessed 4 September 2016).

5 Wise, 'Buzz, Woody . . . and Barbie Plays Too'.

6 Christine Wilkie-Stibbs, 'Intertextuality and the Child Reader', in Peter Hunt (ed.), *Understanding Children's Literature* (London: Taylor & Francis, 2005), pp. 168–79 (pp. 169–70).

7 Ibid., p. 169.

8 Alex Witchel, 'Talking Toys With: Betty James; Persevering for Family and Slinky', *The New York Times*, 21 February 1996. http://www.nytimes.com/1996/02/21/garden/talking-toys-with-betty-james-persevering-for-family-and-slinky.html (accessed 4 September 2016).

9 Michael Riffaterre, 'Compulsory Reader Response: The Intertextual Drive', in Michael Worton and Judith Still (eds), *Intertextuality: Theories and Practices* (Manchester: Manchester University Press, 1990), pp. 56–78 (p. 57).

10 Jonathan Gray, *Show Sold Separately: Promos, Spoilers, and Other Media Paratexts* (Chesham: Combined Academic, 2010), p. 32.

11 Riffaterre, 'Compulsory Reader Response', p. 58.

12 Wilkie-Stibbs, 'Intertextuality and the Child Reader', p. 171.

13 Gags which lean more heavily on extra-textual knowledge can be found in *Toy Story* but, as when Mr. Potato Head jokes that his rearranged face looks like a Picasso painting, they tend to be throw-away moments aimed squarely at an adult audience.

14 It should be noted that both of these shots are accompanied by intertextual references on the soundtrack, which imitates the *Also sprach Zarathustra* fanfare from *2001: A Space Odyssey* (Stanley Kubrick, 1968) and the heavy breathing associated with *Star Wars*' (George Lucas, 1977) Darth Vader.

15 Wise, 'Buzz, Woody . . . and Barbie Plays Too'.
16 Nicholas Royle, *The Uncanny* (Manchester: Manchester University Press, 2003), p. 1.
17 Ibid.
18 Ibid., p. 2.
19 Scott G. Eberle, 'Exploring the Uncanny Valley to Find the Edge of Play', *American Journal of Play*, vol. 2, no. 2 (2009): 167–94 (p. 179).
20 Susan Willis, 'Imagining Dinosaurs', in Beverly Clark (ed.), *Girls, Boys, Books, Toys: Gender in Children's Literature and Culture* (Baltimore: John Hopkins University Press, 2000), pp. 183–95 (p. 187).
21 John Lasseter, quoted in Wise, 'Buzz, Woody . . . and Barbie Plays Too'.
22 Jeffrey Goldstein, David Buckingham and Gilles Brougère, 'Introduction', in Jeffrey Goldstein, David Buckingham and Gilles Brougère (eds), *Toys, Games, and Media* (London: Routledge, 2004), pp. 1–10 (p. 2).
23 Dan Fleming, *Powerplay: Toys as Popular Culture* (Manchester: Manchester University Press, 1996), p. 102.
24 Stacy Botwinick, 'Power Rangers Deliver Knockout Punch', *Playthings*, 1 December 1994.https://www.highbeam.com/doc/1G1-16540112.html (accessed 4 September 2016).
25 Fleming, *Powerplay*, p. 102.
26 While *Toy Story 2* introduces the audience to *Woody's Roundup* and the *Buzz Lightyear of Star Command* video game, the first film only gestures toward their existence.
27 Ellen Seiter, *Sold Separately: Children and Parents in Consumer Culture* (New Brunswick: Rutgers University Press, 1995), pp. 130–31.
28 Fleming, *Powerplay*, p. 30.
29 Ibid.

Chapter 9

FEAR, GUILT AND THE FUTURE OF PLAY IN *TOY STORY*

Karen Cross

Although rarely considered of critical importance within the field of media and cultural study, representations of childhood play form part of an important part of cinema heritage. This is particularly apparent in the case of *Toy Story* (John Lasseter, 1995), which, through its own particular depiction of play provides a critical insight into contemporary social and cultural concerns, which relate to the changing nature of family life, the role of new technologies and shifting patterns of production and consumption, especially in response to ecological crisis. More specifically, and as this chapter seeks to show, the setting of play depicted within *Toy Story* forms a primary site for the creative expression and working through of fears and anxieties relating to loss – especially the loss of analogue materialities, something inherent in the computer-generated animation process. This allows the animation to be read as a means of re-establishing and normalizing masculine forms of cultural production, and as that which sustains patriarchal interests (especially through the use of heroic figures and storylines). However, my contention here is that the particular setting of play depicted within *Toy Story* intends to draw attention to a deeper emotional landscape of transitional experience, which involves, but precedes masculine identification. With this in mind, I employ a psychoanalytic object-relations approach inspired by the work of Melanie Klein and Donald Woods Winnicott to help elaborate upon the precise emotional dynamics of mourning that the narrative of the film represents. By doing so, I show how *Toy Story* represents a particular kind of transitional experience, which allows the gap between the past and present, analogue and digital, to be bridged, and thus the future of play and creative life to ultimately be ensured.

Beyond Nostalgia

Broadly speaking, *Toy Story* sits within the postmodern tradition of film, which is evident from the various allusions it makes to other artistic sources, ranging from the paintings of Picasso to the horror movie genre, including such films as *Freaks* (Tod Browning, 1932) and *The Exorcist* (William Friedkin, 1973).[1] Combined with the fact that the toys that appear within the film will be familiar to adult audiences, this suggests a playful air of nostalgia and a clever use of important symbolic forms that relate to twentieth-century culture. It is important, then, that we think carefully about the particular memorial function that these references to the past perform. *Toy Story* reproduces the very same toys that were played with by the parents – on the verge of becoming the grandparents – of the children that once formed the (putative) primary audience for the film. Thus, the reappearance of toys from this era may suggest a circumspect reattachment to the ideological attitudes and patterns of production of late-modernity.

As the cultural theorist Roland Barthes argues, there is a sense in which modern toys offer the child nothing more than 'a microcosm of the adult world',[2] in relation to which they have little option other than to become consumers and users, rather than taking on the role of producer. They are that which rationalize patterns of global consumption, certain forms of nationalism and involve limiting social attitudes relating to the performance of class and gender. Here, we can think of the early example of the pull-along telephone as prefiguring social mobility and the network of contemporary global communications; the soldier as rationalizing modern warfare and commitment to the nation; and the baby doll and toy kitchen as providing a space for the young girl to accept her future role as a mother.[3] Thus, the reappearance of toys that connect with this history within *Toy Story* implies an investment within the ideals that once framed this setting of play.

As Paul Wells has written, however, *Toy Story* seeks to 'reconcile the personal and experimental with the popular and generic'.[4] The use of toys provides a chance to bridge the apparently opposed forces of new digital techniques of production with something highly familiar and known. There are also the practicalities of technique to consider. As John Lasseter has described, the initial lack of success with animating the human form is what led to the idea to build a narrative around toys. The forms chosen were supposedly those that worked best with the processes available at the time.[5] The limitations of the medium resulted in the anthropomorphic performance wherein toys speak as if they are human. Some suggest that this represents a problematic power dynamic in which ownership, notably signified through the inscription of the child's name on the feet of his toys, refers us to a history of slavery and commodity fetishism. It would thus seem appropriate to argue that *Toy Story* offers a lesson in 'how a subject is to appreciate the value of objects',[6] and this extends right through the 'toyetic'[7] culture of the film, which supports the sale of goods. Another way of looking, however, is to see the film as playing with the idea of ownership and control.

Toy Story arguably opens up other possibilities, which reshape, if not disturb, market terms. Indeed, the argument previously put forward by Barthes that modern toys only allow the child to 'identify himself [sic] as owner, as user, never as creator'[8] becomes complicated within the memorial frame of *Toy Story*, and the investment it makes within the retro toy. Andy's toys (especially Woody, who is a family heirloom) have had a long life. Within the film and its sequels there are also numerous references to garage sales, donations to day care and online sales sites, such as eBay, which point toward the reuse of objects made redundant by the endless flow of commodity production, and to the new market economies of recycling and reuse. On the surface, *Toy Story* appears to involve a longing for a return to a halcyon time of childhood play. Throughout all three films, Andy clings to his toys, which effectively form archetypes of a past era of play. The attachment intensifies as the boy advances towards adolescence, and, with this, we become aware of the adult market for nostalgia, which the film feeds but also seeks to problematize. We can understand *Toy Story* as that which provides an insight into the particular filters of memorialization, which constitute a contemporary fascination with analogue materialities within the digital age. As I argue, we can view the renewed attachment to the modern playthings represented within *Toy Story* as that which points more toward a delicate negotiation of past modalities of consumption and its normative investments within the toy.

The very fact that the narrative of *Toy Story* centres upon a story of the toy cowboy facing redundancy suggests a complicated return to the modern setting of play. It suggests that much more is at stake within the film than simply sustaining the toy industry, and that the story of the cowboy provides an important access point for understanding contemporary preoccupations and concerns relating to recent history. In his book *Fractured Times*,[9] Eric Hobsbawm observes the essentially 'macho' mythology that is persistently invested within the figure of the cowboy throughout the course of the twentieth century. This mythology translates through the rise of monopoly capitalism, which allows for more feminine evolutions, including the arrival of a yodelling cowgirl in the form of Jesse in *Toy Story 2* (Lasseter, 1999) and the reconfiguration of the heroic adventurer in the form of the space-ranger. As is widely acknowledged, even within contexts of popular film production, however, the figure of the cowboy now represents a controversial history of hero representation.

From the outset of the first film, it is apparent that the cowboy – especially the toy cowboy – represents a spectre of venture capitalism that has come under strain. The limp and lifeless figure of Woody, whose speech, rather tellingly, can only be activated by the child, stands to undermine any sense of masculine authority that is usually associated with the cowboy. Here, we are witness to the elaborate cardboard construction of the Wild West within which the child uses his toys to construct a scene of battle between the 'baddy' One-Eyed Bart (performed by Mr. Potato Head) and the 'goody' Sheriff (embodied by Woody) as he saves the day. As the crayon-daubed cardboard walls of the town come into view, the flimsiness of the fantasy construction becomes apparent as does the way that play functions as a zone where archetypes can be contested. In *Toy Story*, there is an intense awareness of industrial relations, evident, for instance, when the toys discuss global brands and factory specifications. As greater attention is focused upon the nature of the attachment to the toy within the setting of play, we also see how *Toy Story* constructs a space for reaching beyond any remaining traces of nostalgia carried within the form of the cowboy or continuing market interests invested in newer plastic forms.

Toy Story thus represents a fundamentally challenged world, which involves an intermingling of 'the old' and 'new'/analogue and computerized. This becomes evident through the make-believe characters of the 'attack-dog with a built-in force field' and by Rex the dinosaur, who later expresses anxiety about his ability to perform. The arrival of Buzz Lightyear again suggests the importance of a hyperreal configuration of masculinity, which is reflective of a continuing fantasy of the father. As Judith Halberstam argues, the arrival of the new toy becomes a way of the boy child negotiating his relation to 'the prosthetic and phallic capabilities of his male toys'.[10] And yet *Toy Story* effectively holds a mirror up to the past and asks us to consider the role of the modern toy and the meaning it holds today. The film not only invites us into the world of child's play, but it also asks us to see through the child's eyes. As we see at the outset of the first film, Woody, the favourite toy, is infused with the comfort of the familial past, but it is also made evident that he is a containing object for the expression of the child's fears and anxieties. As I argue here, this represents an important psychodynamic process, wherein the toy is invested with the unconscious wishes and desires of the child.

Using Winnicottian terminology, Holly Blackford also describes *Toy Story* as a 'transitional space' which allows absent fathers to be reconfigured as 'overgrown playmates and capitalist-infused toys'.[11] However, *Toy Story* is not simply about the evolution of masculine identification and the bonds between men that occur within the contested space of postmodernity, and the more recent turn to digital technologies. It is also about the particular psychological processes involved within the development of the child, and this can be described as that which precedes any identification with the father. Indeed, the capacity to play and make use of toys finds its roots in an earlier primordial moment, which is defined by the relation to the breast and can be reactivated in subsequent moments of transitional experience, including the loss of the father, the home and even childhood itself.

Within *Toy Story* we witness change on many levels, ranging from the passage from boyhood toward adolescence and the transfer of mythical status from the cowboy to the space-ranger. The intense focus on performativity within *Toy Story* actually serves to undermine the hero narrative, and, as I suggest here, pushes at the boundaries of masculine identification. With the fading lines of the theme song 'You've Got a Friend in Me', Woody is tossed lifeless on to the couch as Andy's attention is diverted to the festivities of his birthday party. This represents a critical moment in the film, where the real use of toys coincides with the child's 'unconscious phantasy',[12] to use a Kleinian term, and from here a whole fantasy of loss plays out through the world of the magically animated toys. Within this, we also witness certain defensive mechanisms of survival.

Defensive Mechanisms and the Tyranny of Play

For Sigmund Freud, dreams form the 'the royal road to the unconscious',[13] but for Melanie Klein it is play that enables access to the symbolizing processes of the infantile mind. As Klein found in her work with young children, 'the game of acting the part serves to separate those different identifications at work in the child which are tending to form the single whole'.[14] By this she means not only the differentiated internalized figures of the mother and father, but also the emotional experiences that produce their recognition within the mind of the infant. According to Klein, it is the relation to the mother established in infancy that forms the basis of all subsequent relations, including between the child and the father, siblings and other social attachments that follow in later adult life.

Klein observes that the mother and baby are initially held in the union of the nursing couple. This provides an important space of growth where the inherently aggressive actions of 'introjection and projection',[15] which are key to the process of feeding and survival, establish the entire experience of relating to the world. The first few months of life are defined by what Klein describes as the 'paranoid-schizoid position'[16] wherein the infant splits apart the breast into supposed 'good' and 'bad' parts, and thus casts out the frustrating and punishing elements of feeding that hinder omnipotent union. As Klein describes, 'the frustrating breast – attacked in oral-sadistic phantasy – is felt to be in fragments; the gratifying breast, taken in under the dominance of the sucking libido is felt to be complete.'[17] Hatred and aggressive feelings are projected onto the 'bad' mother, who forms the basis of what Klein calls a form of 'projective identification'[18] – the object into which the unbearable aggression of the ego is poured.

The destructive force of splitting enables the infant to proceed to internalize the gratifying breast, and then subsequently go on to form a sense of that which Donald Woods Winnicott later describes as the 'good enough'[19] object: an internalized sense of the mother and the self as whole and complete. Splitting allows the infant to defend the loved object and protect it from destructive forces, and this becomes a way of managing guilt and shame. Over time, and as the different aspects of the mother are no longer so widely separated, the infant begins to experience a sense of fear and loss – 'states akin to mourning and a strong feeling of guilt'.[20] This period, which occurs from about six months onwards, marks the transition to that which Klein refers to as the 'depressive position',[21] and it forms one of the most basic and important aspects of being able to relate to others. Within this, the infant experiences a flood of emotion and desire to repair and protect the injured object, and offers 'restitution for all the sadistic attacks'.[22] No longer driven by purely selfish concerns, the infant releases paranoid defences and develops the capacity to show concern for others. This allows for a more integrated sense of the self, and greater sense of autonomy, but also a sense of responsibility toward others.

Earlier defences can, and will, be reactivated any time the object is felt to be under attack. This is why Klein's work is important to the analysis of *Toy Story*, which provides access to the challenged world of the child and offers an analogy of the wider ways in which transitional experiences are negotiated and managed. Especially important here is Klein's understanding of schizoid object relating and the depressive states that follow in the awakening of self-realization. As I have already suggested, *Toy Story* represents the inner world of the child who is faced with negotiating the loss of the home. The world of the film thus forms a space for the activation and working through of 'unconscious phantasies', which take on the qualities of the first experiences of the breast.

In spite of its surface friendliness, Andy's playroom forms an embattled zone of play where toys marshal to monitor the boundaries of the home and maintain the distance of the outside world. Like the feeding infant, they seek to protect the loved object, which is both represented by the child and his world of play. The arrival of Buzz challenges this, along with the cowboy's reign over the terrain of the playroom. The presence of the spaceman also suggests a broader difficulty in negotiating the presence of new technologies. Against the backdrop of the changing bedroom, which becomes stripped of all Woody-related paraphernalia, the cowboy is forced to negotiate his position as Andy's 'special toy'. With his sense of omnipotence undermined, the cowboy increasingly becomes a volatile presence within the playroom, which is suggestive of a form of sibling rivalry. Woody's annoyance initially manifests itself as mild comic attacks on Buzz, who is yet to realize he is a toy. As he increasingly takes on the characteristics of a protesting child who is caught in the throes of envy – or 'laser envy', as Mr. Potato Head aptly calls it – this eventually hatches into a more dangerous plot to rid the playroom of the new arrival. With the surfacing of fears, a tipping point is reached where Woody's emotions spill out of the playroom and on to the surrounding streets. Buzz is pushed out of the window, whereupon he flees the safety of the home to seek out his spaceship. At this point, the audience becomes more deeply aware of the defensive operations needed to secure play.

Buzz unwittingly takes himself, and a now sorry Woody, ever further into the hands of danger. The terrain of the film dissolves into a more dark and dangerous landscape. Working against the clock and the bravado of the spaceman who refuses to awaken to the reality of his toy status, Woody is confronted with a stark reality that is signified by the 'Dinoco' oil company sign that is raised over the forecourt of the gas station. This emphasizes the dying and outmoded world of fossil fuel consumption along with the ephemeral nature of the toy, as it becomes the lost object. This moment also echoes an earlier scene in the film where the offerings on Andy's bookshelf, including such titles as *Red's Dream*,

Tin Toy and *Knick Knack*,[23] point toward the theme of obsolescence and the struggle of the toy to appeal to the child. Other titles, such as *Grimm's Fairy Tales* and *Help the Planet*, which stands next to *Pale Cowboy from Texas*, provide a degree of reassurance about the morality of the child. With the signs of more radical change afoot, however, *Toy Story* reveals a more threatening world of play, which challenges any previous faith.

Buzz and Woody eventually end up within the torture chambers of Sid's locked bedroom wherein they encounter the fragmented forms of Frankenstein-esque operations, including 'Legs' (a fishing rod mounted on a Barbie base) and 'Baby Face' (a one-eyed doll head mounted on spider's legs). These toys scurry about in the shadows like frightened automata and provide a stark contrast to Andy's bubbling world of colourful, inviting and friendly play. Their form is suggestive of the psychic disintegration of the alienated world of peeling paintwork marked by a lack of parental care. A further indication of the psychotic underpinnings is apparent when the toys are heard, first by Hannah, who responds to Woody's voice emulating her mother's call, and then by Sid in the gruesome scene in the backyard.

At first indirectly through a mechanical voice box, and then directly as he raises himself from the barbeque, Woody speaks to Sid and warns him to 'play nice'. This marks a crossing over of the threshold between reality and fantasy. Upon seeing the toy come alive, the child flees the scene and experiences a total breakdown in his ability to be in the presence of toys, never mind to be able to play with them. This is until later in *Toy Story 3*, where we see Sid working as waste collector sifting through the garbage to retrieve toys. This scene implies a holocaustic final solution, and forms a recognition that toys may ultimately be little more than the debris of history. The sea of waste displayed at the dump configures a landscape of melancholic suffering; a scar born of overconsumption.

Just like the Angelus Novus (angel of history) described by Walter Benjamin in his thesis on history, we are bearing witness to the 'the storm that we call progress'.[24] There is little choice other than to move with the flow, but looking back also awakens the temptation to try to preserve the past. *Toy Story 2* develops the theme by punishing the adult who unnaturally fetishises toys as a form of commodity. Within the context of the *Woody's Roundup* archive, the cowboy forms the missing piece of the toy collector's haul. Woody must decide between the different futures of his post-commodity status: either the kinship of his 'real' television family, which here also means the stasis of a museum object, or the child's bedroom. The temporary indulgence in the gaze of the 'cleaner', who is employed to erase the traces of previous signs of play, signals a momentary narcissism and a failure to recognize the needs of others. This parallels Buzz's experience in the first film when he refuses to recognize that he is a toy. The moment when he tries, but fails, to fly through the open window of Sid's house results in a symbolic castration, or that which Lilian Munk Rösing describes as the Lacanian 'subjective destitution'[25] – or the becoming pure waste after the ecstasies of consumption. As he is lying shattered on the ground, Buzz gives up hope, and from here is transferred to a hysterical world of feminine play, which is populated by headless dolls seeking solace in the confines of Sid's sister's bedroom. This scene underscores a fear of feminization that is often understood to be a key feature of *Toy Story* and its fantasy world,[26] and the dangers of going 'beyond' are further refracted through the challenged world of the destructive child for whom the veils between reality and fantasy have become severely eroded.

Adult tools, in the form of matches, become the incongruous objects of 'bad' play, and relate to an adolescent rejection of childhood. In relation to this, Bill Brown has written of the way that *Toy Story* 'instructs its viewers against misuse – against irregular exchange –as though the toy industry should have the final say on the shape of the world and the world to come'.[27] Sid's play, Brown argues, suggests an alternative in which 'curious composites are the things that materialize an otherwise unexpressed wish to transfigure things as they are.'[28] Within this realm, toys initially seem melancholic and then 'poignant as [they] quietly and heroically rally to aid the film's main heroes'.[29] They are in a way representative of the playful *bricolage* of postmodernity, which stitches together everyday and banal forms to create new objects of meaning. This makes them not-too-distant relatives of Andy's playroom, but the very fact that Sid's fantastical creations are never permitted to leave the confines of the wasteland that forms their home suggests a desire to see the boundaries of 'good' and 'bad' play maintained.

Toy Story thus seems to leave the toy and the child fragmented as either wholly 'good' or wholly 'bad'. In this way, it frames what Patricia Holland describes as popular culture's 'active struggle to maintain childhood – if not actual children – as pure and uncontaminated'.[30] The child is either with the toys or against them, persecuting and persecuted or valiant and triumphant. That said, it is imperative that we also recognize that we are witnessing the world from the perspective of the toy as it takes on the psychic fantasies of the child experiencing loss. The overidentification with the 'good' toy thus forms a necessary form of ego defence, which helps secure a sense of safety.

The 'Good-Enough' Toy and the Reconfiguration of Play

Woody's initial attempt to escape Sid's world fails quite simply because he remains motivated by purely selfish concerns. Running down the stairs to escape, we hear him chanting like Dorothy from *The Wizard of Oz* (Victor Fleming, 1939) – 'there's no place like home, there's no place like home' – and we are reminded not only of the toy's wish to be cradled within the comfort of the child's loving arms, but also the fact that home is on the verge of disappearance. The deadline of the removals van serves as further reminder of the constantly shifting ground upon which the whole notion of 'home' is built, but it is the continuing attachment to it that provides a motivation for escape.

As we learn, it is not the challenge to his masculinity that Woody must defend against, but, rather, the greater threat of the devastation that will occur if he fails to make amends. Woody admits to needing Buzz's help, but the bid to escape has been thwarted by the awakening produced by the commercial shown on Sid's father's television. This informs Buzz once and for all that he is a toy. He is not *the* Buzz Lightyear but just *a* Buzz Lightyear – one of many reproductions. In the wake of this realization, a depression sets in, along with the release of the illusion upon which his ego has thus far been built. 'Andy's house, Sid's house; what's the difference? It's all the same', he says. Woody tells Buzz that he must not be thinking straight, but, just as he argues, he is thinking more clearly than ever before. Buzz concedes that Woody was right all along and that he is just a toy – 'a stupid little insignificant toy' – but Woody will not allow Buzz to accept the impoverished sense of self that this realization brings. Instead, Woody insists that 'being a toy is a lot better than being a space ranger'. Sinking low into a dejected state, Buzz arrives at two realizations. The first is that he is no longer guided by the technological fantasy which constructs his toy's character. The second is that it is precisely this disillusionment that enables him to relate to the feelings of the child, and thus experience a renewed sense of self, which Winnicott describes as the process of sensing the 'good-enough mother'.[31]

This becomes the moment in which the infant recognizes the mother as having a state of externality beyond pure projection, a state of being 'found instead of placed by the subject in the world'.[32] As Winnicott also explains, the value of the object is the fact that it '*survives*'[33] destruction following on from the aggressive acts of introjection and projection. This is what enables the infant to make use of (and continue to feed off) the object as if it were the 'good' and gratifying breast, and it is the very process by which the infant begins to 'live a life in the world of objects'[34] and enter fully into the process of play, regardless of the underlying feelings of shame and guilt that remain active within the unconscious.

It is the awareness and the growing acceptance of their toy status that enables both Woody and Buzz to deconstruct the ideological imaginary (e.g., the idea of existing for the sole reason of defeating the Evil Emperor Zurg or being marvelled at by visitors in a museum). Buzz is valuable to the child precisely *because he is a toy*. This is what makes him so special. As Woody states, Buzz is a 'cool' toy, against which no other toy stands a chance. Here we see Woody experiencing his own depression, as he says that it is him and not Buzz that deserves to be strapped to the rocket. Woody tells Buzz to leave him and escape while he has the chance, but it is Buzz who, upon seeing the name that Andy has inscribed upon his foot, recognizes the need to defend against the loss of the 'good' child and the family home.

The idea of replaceability is challenged, and it is the markings of ownership that enable the toy to understand the needs of the child and how deeply invested they are within the life-world of the toys. The resolve in *Toy Story* to return to the setting of the family home does not necessarily provide a neat resolution to the experience of loss. In spite of appearances, the warm glow of the Christmas tree in the setting of the new family home contains other sources of disturbance, including the bark of a puppy, which reminds the toys of the endless threats that are posed by external forces. New arrivals increasingly take on the more dangerous characteristics of the outside world, but playtime is permitted (at least temporarily) to continue. In *Toy Story 3* the challenge is different. Andy has to decide who will follow him on his travels to college. Here, we find the toys clinging to the narrative of loss and return, but this itself increasingly represents an illusion. Andy is set to go to college and only one favoured toy will be permitted to accompany him. The obvious choice is Woody, but as we see Andy struggles with the decision. All the toys hold a certain value, otherwise they would not have been preserved within the space of the adolescent's bedroom.

When Andy rejects his sister's taunting he plays into the stereotype of the moody teen bravely distancing himself from home,[35] and this reminds us of the myth of masculine independence framing the experience of the cowboy. Just as both Klein and Winnicott observe, each stage of life provides another opportunity for working through unconscious content, including the fears and defences relating to loss. The suspended animation of the adolescent bedroom must finally come to an end and Andy must once and for all release his toys. In a moment of confusion they are nearly dispensed with among the trash, and Woody has to work hard to convince the toys that they were intended for the attic. The alternative is to go to Sunnyside, the day care centre where toys are at least played with. This repeats an earlier theme of separation and border control between the oral-sadistic drives of the drooling infant and the psychologically developed space of careful play.

Here, the punishment of Sunnyside's tyrannical ruler Lotso (a bitter bear who has been unable to cope with loss) parallels the earlier construction of the 'bad' child. To be a 'good' toy, as we know, means being there for the child, whenever he needs you, at whatever stage of life. The resolution to return home suggests a perhaps deluded investment in the future, but the payoff ultimately arrives in the form of the new child, Bonnie, to whom Andy finally entrusts his beloved toys. With one final attempt to control the setting of play, Andy relays a full character profile of each of the toys, and restages the heroic scenes of action that are seen within earlier films. As the young child laughs and looks on at the toys in awe, she reaches toward the cowboy. Andy regresses and, in a moment of protest, reluctantly hands Woody over. With this comes the realization that toys are meant to be played with and that the child becoming an adult must release their toys into a new setting of play which, as we later see in the television short *Toy Story That Time Forgot* (Steve Purcell, 2014),[36] is defined by a more chaotic and unfixed set of fantasies.

For now though, the world of *Toy Story* leaves us with the process of mourning and the recovery of what is attained in early childhood – an experience which, as the makers of the animation know, will permit the continuation of play. Through this narrative, the film makes clear that it is not just the experience of recovering the past that is important, or allowing its (analogue) forms to persist within the present moment. The point is, rather, to allow past objects of play to take on a new meaning: to become the future objects of investment for a new child, or, as it may be, the new audience who will draw ever greater value from the processes of meaning-making that the world of children's animation represents.

Notes

1 On this point see Alan Kirby, *Digimodernism: How New Technologies Dismantle Postmodernism and Reconfigure Our Culture* (London: Continuum, 2009), p. 8.
2 Roland Barthes, *Mythologies*, trans. Annette Lavers (London: Vintage, 2000), p. 53.
3 Ibid.
4 Paul Wells, 'From "Sunnyside" to "Soccer": Reading upon Animation . . .', *Animation in Practice, Process and Production*, vol. 1, no. 1 (2011): 3–9 (p. 7).
5 John Lasseter, 'The New Audience: Moviegoing in a Connected World,' talk held at The Samuel Goldwyn Theater on 14 September 2015. Hosted by Oscars Academy. https://www.youtube.com/watch?v=3eQZie6DUNg (accessed 24 March 2017).
6 Stefan Herbrechter, 'Toying with the Postmodern "To Infinity and Beyond"', in Ivan Callus and Stefan Herbrechter (eds), *Post-Theory, Culture and Criticism* (Amsterdam: Rodopi, 2004), p. 158.
7 Dan Fleming, *Powerplay: Toys as Popular Culture* (Manchester: Manchester University Press, 1996), p. 94.
8 Roland Barthes, *Mythologies*, p. 54.
9 Eric Hobsbawm, *Fractured Times: Culture and Society in the Twentieth Century* (London: Little, Brown, 2013), pp. 272–89.
10 Judith Halberstam, *The Queer Art of Failure* (Durham: Duke University Press, 2011), p. 30.
11 Holly Blackford, '"Luke, I Am Your Father": Toys, Play Space and Detached Fathers in Post-1970s Hollywood Family Films', in Noel Brown and Bruce Babington (eds), *Family Films in Global Cinema: The World Beyond Disney* (London and New York: I.B. Tauris, 2015), pp. 137–51 (p. 137).
12 See, for instance, Melanie Klein, 'The Development of a Child' first written in 1921 and included in *Love, Guilt and Reparation* (London: Vintage, 1998), pp. 1–53.
13 Julia Kristeva, *Melanie Klein* (New York: Columbia University Press, 2001), p. 48. In 'The Psycho-analytic Play Technique: Its History and Significance'. 1955. Melanie Klein also refers to her approach as corresponding to 'free association', in *Envy and Gratitude* (London: Vintage, 1997), p. 123.

14 Klein, *Love, Guilt and Reparation*, p. 133.
15 Ibid., p. 262.
16 Klein, 'Notes on Some Schizoid Mechanisms' (1946) in *Envy and Gratitude*, pp. 1–24.
17 Klein, *Envy and Gratitude*, p. 7.
18 Ibid.
19 D. W. Winnicott, *Playing and Reality* (London: Routledge, 2005), p. 119.
20 Klein, *Envy and Gratitude*, p.14.
21 Ibid.
22 Klein, *Love, Guilt and Reparation*, p. 265.
23 All are names of short films made by Lasseter made in 1987–89.
24 Walter Benjamin, 'On the Concept of History' 1940. Translated by Dennis Redmond. 2005. https://www.marxists.org/reference/archive/benjamin/1940/history.htm (accessed 24 March 2017).
25 Lilian Munk Rösing, *Pixar with Lacan: The Hysteric's Guide to Animation* (London and New York: Bloomsbury Academic, 2016), p. 19.
26 Ellen Scott, 'Agony and Avoidance: Pixar, Deniability and the Adult Spectator', *Journal of Popular Film and Television* vol. 42, no. 3 (2014): 150–62 (p. 154).
27 Bill Brown, 'How to Do Things with Things (A Toy Story)', *Critical Inquiry*, vol. 24, no. 4 (1998): 935–64 (p. 964).
28 Ibid., p. 964.
29 Tom Kemper, *Toy Story: A Critical Reading* (London: BFI, 2015), pp. 137–8.
30 Patricia Holland, *What Is a Child? Popular Images of Childhood*. (London: Virago, 1992), p. 98.
31 Winnicott, *Playing and Reality*, p. 14.
32 Ibid., p. 126.
33 Ibid., p. 120.
34 Ibid., p. 121.
35 Laurie Markham and Jane Chiu, 'Toy Story 3', *Journal of Feminist Family Therapy*, vol. 24, no. 2 (2012):. 182–9 (p. 187).
36 *Toy Story That Time Forgot*. Directed by Steve Purcell. ABC, 2 December 2014.

Chapter 10

MIRRORS AND SHADOWS: DUALITY, ILLUSION AND THE DIVIDED SELF IN *TOY STORY*

Jane Batkin

> Somewhere we have a sinister and frightful brother, our own flesh-and-blood-counterpart, who holds and maliciously hoards everything that we would so willingly hide under the table[1]
>
> — Ann Casement

Pixar's cinema is one of friendship, family and the bonds that are created within its seemingly child-centric universe. Beneath the surface, however, lie shadows, otherness and a curious fracturing of self. Ellen Scott writes about Pixar's ability to broach 'dark existential themes' with its audience;[2] it becomes a cinema of maturity and one that is unafraid of confrontation. Such themes resonate with us, from the absence of the parent in *Monsters, Inc.* (Pete Docter, 2001) to the lost child in *Finding Nemo* (Andrew Stanton, 2003), identity crisis in *Inside Out* (Pete Docter, 2015) and bereavement in *Up* (Pete Docter, 2009). Pixar invites its audience to view the image as offered, but also to consider what lies beyond it. Peripheral images are inferred through the slow, considered pacing of their films. In *Toy Story* (John Lasseter, 1995) shadows emerge, and the mirror reflects what is present on the screen and what may also be hinted at beyond it; the shine and luminosity of this film point to the darker recesses within it. The looking glass becomes a portal between the character and their murky twin, the shadow hovering somewhere in that unfamiliar world at the edge of what we know, awaiting what Casement calls 'an eruption . . . into consciousness'.[3]

Cinema is often viewed as a mirror in motion, offering visions of truth and non-truth. Henry Giroux sees it as a site of 'critique, understanding, and struggle',[4] a mirror that needs examining and exploring. Cinema, like art, offers up the image for us to consider, but we may view it in a way that questions its validity, choosing to see what is hidden, both within the frame and beyond it. As

John Berger explains, images conjure up an appearance of something 'that was absent'.[5] The camera distorts truth and clarity, so that illusion and absence create a cinema of hidden meanings. We view what we see and also what we imagine we see, but only if the screen draws us into that world. This can be applied to *Toy Story* particularly well; the film hints at shadows while dazzling us with its lustre. Its dark themes of fractured lives and selves reflect society today to create a cinema that becomes relevant to a more mature audience. These issues are scattered throughout the film to offer meanings that may appear concealed, in that they lead to the audience needing to extrapolate and infer truths and non-truths about the characters and story. Family, often a stable (or at least present) existence in children's film, more worryingly represents absence in *Toy Story*, which is revealed through the mirroring that occurs between its worlds and characters. Examples of this, to be discussed further in this chapter, include the breakdown of Andy's family unit (suggested through the absence of the father), and of Sid's largely solitary existence in the house next door. There are shadows looming in the looking glass and the double or *doppelgänger* lurks at the edge of the frame. Ignaz Cassar writes about the projected image in cinema and finds a secret, ghostly doppelgänger that forever haunts us, an image that we can either steer towards or away from.[6] It is the *Other* that occupies our peripheral vision while we consider the image before us. Marie Louise von Frantz ponders the meaning of the shadow, suggesting 'whatever form it takes, the function of the shadow is to represent the opposite side of the ego'.[7] Without the shadow or Other, we remain half-formed.

The focus of this chapter is on the physical and symbolic mirrors in *Toy Story* and the duality and fracturing that occurs within objects and characters (and objects *with* character) to create duality and shadows. I discuss the notion of what the shadow infers and apply it to the characters of Andy and Sid and to Buzz and Woody. I also explore the idea of the image hovering on the edge of a character's, and our, vision; that dark spot at the corner of one's view, which is almost there, almost not. Presence becomes absence and absence becomes presence as we engage with these ideas. Are these half-formed characters real or imagined? Significantly, what do the reflective surfaces reveal about *Toy Story*'s world, and what does the shadow really represent?

Mirrors, Reflections and Objects

James Clarke writes that in Pixar's films 'the images have space to linger'.[8] This is particularly interesting when we apply it to *Toy Story*. Andy's world is established pensively, representing both home and bedroom as central to the story, and the computer-generated (CG) world as a pioneering space, where surfaces reflect and bounce off each other. When we are introduced to this world, it is through the shiny objects that are at its core; the playthings that form the narrative, against a backdrop of summer sky walls and polished floors. The radiance of Pixar's visual style and the sheen of its cinema were inspired by the American painter Maxfield Parrish, renowned for his use of an extreme cobalt blue, and Clarke comments that the studio was 'grappling with visual realism in a way that Renaissance painters had done'.[9] Pixar's *Toy Story* celebrates a medium that is pioneering through its sharpness and shine, a 'newness' that demonstrates its innovative stamp on animation. Future Pixar features would seek to embrace a more organic, natural feel to their textures, striving for grit and grain rather than glaze, but *Toy Story* is unashamedly luminous, producing reflections and refractions that invite and hold our gaze.

Clarke's comment about lingering images plays on the mind. It dwells on the screen presence of physical things that are imbued with a sense of the 'real'. There is a feeling, in *Toy Story*, of a place that represents solidity and truth and yet there is a dreamlike pace to the film that is accentuated through the careful reveal of events, such as Andy's birthday party, or the pausing for breath of Woody and Buzz as they ponder their own fates. Lingering images grow darker as we watch Scud the dog's quiet but palpable fear of the sleeping man in Sid's house. If there is something haunting about this scene that stays with us, it is the hint of unseen violence inferred from Scud's encounter, the question of what is seen and what might exist beyond the lens. This slow, deliberate pace invites a sense of belief and investment from the audience, and also exemplifies the deep maturity of Pixar's work.

The actual mirror (be it helmet visor, window or wing mirror) is significant in *Toy Story*. It offers interpretations of truths and secrets and at times questions both the toyness and the reality of objects. When Molly spies Buzz and Woody flying in the wing mirror of her mother's car, she squeals with delight: the toys are alive. However, the image is fleeting and broken; toys *cannot* live. Clinton Lanier et al., however, suggest that the key to the film is how it maintains the human/toy relationship through Woody and Buzz who, rather than being toys, are fictional characters; thus what is being anthropomorphized is not the object itself, but what it represents. These toys therefore exist 'as independent ontological beings' with their own identities.[10] Buzz and Woody become real to Molly because they are fictional characters, rather than 'dead' objects. The mirror reveals a secret truth and acts as a portal for Molly to mentally enter the 'real' world of toys.

The stability of this world is repeatedly and crucially challenged through the use of these mirrors. They reveal cracks within identities and these ultimately allow shadows to enter, introducing darker themes and characters. Sigmund Freud often reflected on the uncanny (*unheimlich*) and the homely (*heimlich*), believing that the domestic, in particular, leads towards 'the notion of something removed from the eyes of strangers, hidden, secret'.[11] What is familiar, that is, the home, becomes less so the longer we fix our gaze upon it. Much as when we stare unblinkingly into a mirror, we encounter a darkening of our vision and an awareness of something hinted at, just beyond our sight. *Toy Story* reveals multifaceted layers and establishes itself as an important film that bridges the gap between the child and adult audience. Within Andy's seemingly harmless, happy world, we can find glimpses of duality, absence and voids. Mirrors serve as gateways, offering versions of images (particularly the 'self') that may be contested and otherness that needs closer inspection. Jacques Lacan's mirror stage theory is relevant to this discussion as it focuses on the unreality of the image seen;[12] the looking glass must be perceived as a fiction, a lie, in order for viewers to achieve wholeness, otherwise we remain fragmented, broken selves. In other words, we should be able to decipher what the mirror means, and recognize that its image is only an image. If we take this theory and apply it to *Toy Story*, we can see it in action with Buzz in particular, through his lack of understanding of, rather than knowledge of, his mirrored image.

We are initially introduced to Buzz as he surveys his 'crash site' through his helmet visor. Significantly, he first sees his own reflection in his visor, and then, second, views the bedroom beyond it. He is captivated by the charm of the reflection he sees here. The mirrored image is important; it is replete and splendid, offering him the representation of a genuine hero, and Buzz sees this as absolute truth. He is narcissistic in nature at this point, his character utterly self-absorbed, and he exudes confidence in his knowledge of himself and his prowess as space hero. Recently unboxed, Buzz is 'new' to his environment. We are aware that he does not possess the sophisticated consciousness of Woody, but he is only aware of his supposed purpose: to return home and defeat Zurg.

Joseph Henderson argues that 'every individual can reconcile the conflicting elements of his personality; he can strike a balance that makes him truly human.'[13] Identity and wholeness, or lack thereof, is key to *Toy Story* and our belief in its characters. Buzz's understanding of 'self' is limited to the false mirror image; he views and believes in his reflection as whole and his ego as heroic. The other toys' acceptance of their own status and selves has already been established and cemented before Buzz's arrival; a toy is, as Woody retorts, 'a child's plaything'. Buzz, however, retains an insistent belief in the mirror and what it reveals to him, as he remains caught up in his own image. Woody, by contrast, is viewed as a much more complex character (and therefore more 'human'). He is fallible, with flaws that conflict with the group as they serve his own purpose, and he is particularly prone to the trait of jealousy. His 'toyness' is both reinforced and challenged (e.g. in the scene where he conceives of Buzz's downfall so that Andy will choose to take him to Pizza Planet, aware that he is no longer the favourite *toy*). The sophistication of Woody's personality often alludes to a 'human' status, but he acknowledges his place in the world as Andy's possession while Buzz, infatuated by his own glorious image, retains a false and only half-formed identity.

The mirror offers Buzz an enticing lie; his purpose centres on fixing his spaceship so that he may return to his planet and thwart the evil Emperor Zurg, unaware that this directive is printed on the rocket ship packaging, hidden on the reverse side of his window to the outside world. Woody discovers and acknowledges this fact with a smirk, alluding to his awareness of what is real and what is not, while Buzz's vision is polarized; his ego is unfettered by the shadow that normally occupies its dark side. This shadow is what defines Jungian philosophy, in which, according to Henderson, 'ego and shadow, indeed, although separate, are inextricably linked together'.[14] This breaks down, in our discussion, to the idea that self requires its shadow to create wholeness. We see the shadowy half of Woody's personality through his envy and frustration but, because Buzz does not recognize the falsity of his own identity, he is unable to acknowledge the shadow.

It may seem ambitious to apply Lacan's mirror theory or Jungian philosophy to *Toy Story* because we are, of course, discussing toys (although they themselves are not real toys but CG objects). It would be prudent, therefore, to pause for a moment to consider animation itself, the validity of CG and particularly how empathy is achieved within it. Characters in animation are obstacles to the 'real'; they are artificial constructs. Lanier et al., as we have seen earlier, argue about the ontological properties of such objects and their embracing of the fictional. As fictional characters rather than objects, toys are able to achieve a different sort of real that drives their narrative. Wassily Kandinsky argues that all inanimate objects themselves are dead but that everything dead quivers into being, everything possesses a secret soul.[15] We have seen how Molly spies the toys in the wing mirror as animated, lively characters, far removed from dead objects. Alan Ackerman, meanwhile, longs to believe that the toys of Pixar break and repair, that the 'thingness' (i.e., the three-dimensional solidity) of the medium lends it a realism that other animation does not achieve.[16] CG, using this argument, lends characters solidity, a sureness, that *feels* closer to the real. We have already discussed Woody's human traits that remove him from toyness; if we engage with Woody and believe in his emotions, we remove him from his position as an artificial construct. This is the same spell that animation seeks to cast over its audience.

Alan Cholodenko argues that animation has the ability to subsume live-action; it is an important medium because in fact 'every encounter with film is an encounter with animation'.[17] Belief in animation as a viable and valuable medium is crucial within Pixar's work. When *Luxo Jr.* (Lasseter, 1986) was screened at Siggraph, Lasseter was thrilled that the audience engaged more with the characters of the two lamps than with the ground-breaking technical innovation being showcased.[18] Story and character are paramount, while the suspending of disbelief in what is artificial is crucial for connection. For all Pixar's luminous wonder, belief is what leads us into its world and allows us to empathize and engage with its characters. Fundamentally, Lasseter's intention is to entertain and connect with his audience through his stories and characters, and this mirrors the concerns, conflicts and themes of live-action cinema.

This connection between film and its audience is vital; according to Pieter-Jan Decoster & Nancy Vansieleghem, cinema can be seen to represent an important vessel 'of a collective consciousness',[19] in that Hollywood films belong to a discourse about American society, culture and politics. Pixar, too, belongs to this discourse, drawing its audience in and creating an engagement that is shared by others. This is due in part to the complexity yet familiarity of its characters. Woody exhibits traits of loyalty but also of jealousy; he is emotional and paranoid, seeing his displacement at the hands of Buzz as a betrayal. Woody, like Buzz, must accept the divisions and discords that naturally exist within every individual (because they, and we, believe that they are individuals). Buzz's displacement occurs later than Woody's; he is the calm to Woody's rage, the logic to his emotion until he discovers the truth and meaning of his own existence. Each character represents something of a fragmented self, but the two together form a whole. Woody needs to embrace a more heroic, less paranoid self (the traits he is missing), while Buzz's lesson is acceptance of his own reality. At first, Buzz can be seen as the shadow to Woody's safe existence; he is the threat as yet unrealized, the metaphorical 'thing' in Woody's peripheral vision. Buzz's emergence as the new favourite cements him as a core character in the narrative but, because of Woody's more realistic, troubled self-consciousness, Buzz inevitably remains the shadow.

Light and Dark, Presence and Absence

It is the nature of film to offer truths and fictions for audience dissemination and, within the established world that is created, the idea of what is not immediately obvious to the eye (an 'absence') is able to move into the space that presence occupies, seeping and creeping through the little cracks of this on-screen world. We have established that Pixar's world is complex and multilayered; there are mysterious characters that hover in our peripheral vision, such as the sleeping man and a parent's disembodied voice. These in turn lead us to consider their meanings; for example, neglect, alienation and the dysfunctionality of the family. As previously noted, Scott suggests that Pixar revives the notion of cinema needing to reach all audiences, and does so through its tackling of dark themes. It is this darkness that both complicates *Toy Story* and vitalizes it. The divide between Andy's and Sid's rooms is particularly significant here as a signpost of light and dark spaces, and the mirroring that exists between these 'worlds'.

Fernando Pessoa, the Portuguese poet, wrote under multiple pseudonyms and was intrigued by life, death and identity: 'We are phantoms made of lies,' he writes, 'shadows of illusions'.[20] Pessoa was concerned with the fracturing of self, with the difference that could be captured through creating multiple identities and alter egos. He questioned the life we physically live, finding more merit in the idea of otherness. This can be applied particularly well to Sid and Andy; Andy's life is the life *lived* while Sid's life is its shadow; the life *thought*, or imagined through the eyes of others. He remains an enigma, an unknown entity, until Woody and Buzz enter his world and their fear – through preconceived ideas about him – becomes palpable. Yet Sid potentially appears as a more colourful, 'whole' character for many viewers than his counterpart, once we enter his bedroom. Andrew Stanton himself suggests that the kid who blows up toys is more normal than Andy, 'the gentle soul'.[21] Thus Sid, Andy's mirror image, steps into the audience's consciousness and challenges its notion of right or wrong, real or illusionary. Which boy is the mirror image and which one is 'real'?

Andy's world is familiar; it is one filled with bright, glazed objects and a sense of family. His bedroom is a mirror to Pixar's universe, where nostalgia for childhood is a prevalent theme. Andy represents the good child who loves his mother, his sister and his toys. His activities centre wholly on these objects of love (reinforcing the view of the complex relationships between objects and humans) but we see little independence in Andy, no outside play, no venturing beyond the tightly drawn boundaries of his world. In embracing the ideal of 'good child', his identity is incomplete and divided; he may therefore represent less the life lived and more a shadow of illusion, as Pessoa suggests. Andy essentially remains a half-formed child and his lack of wholeness is the key to the otherness that slips into the narrative from the shadows, in the form of Sid.

The Shadow

Sid is the entity that Andy spies through the looking glass, darkly. Beyond the childlike wholeness that Andy imagines lies the world of the unconscious and, it is this world that Sid inhabits. According to Malcolm Bowie, for Lacan the unconscious is 'where the Other performs his darkest deeds'.[22] Andy's world of parental love and cherished toys is threatened unconsciously by Sid's shadowy presence next door. We imagine that Andy may be dimly aware of Sid as the boy who plays loudly in his back yard and abuses his toys; one boy is light and the other, darkness. If Andy passes the mirror and glances in quickly, he might become aware of this otherness, this idea of the fragmented self, this shadowy nemesis; it lies on the periphery of his vision, waiting to grasp his arm and pull him inside. This mirroring of boyhood occurs in a very similar way in Ray Bradbury's novel *Something Wicked This Way Comes* (1962). Will and Jim, like Andy and Sid, are deliberate reflections of each other: one light, one dark, but each is a fragmented half of a self. Bradbury alludes more explicitly to the mirror image than Lasseter does; the 'shadows flickered in the Mirror's Maze, as if parts of someone's life, yet unborn, were trapped there, waiting to be lived'.[23] Boyhood is emphasized as a life force in *Toy Story* as it is in Bradbury's novel, but with the added sense of a dark, unformed Other lurking in the mirror; a peripheral presence.

This notion of the peripheral has been referred to widely in the visual arts. Michael Bird finds, in the seventeenth-century painting, *The Cholmondeley Ladies* (c. 1600–10), that when we focus on one lady, the other becomes restless in the background; not quite present and not absent either.[24] Similarly, Frank Stella, the US painter, discusses seeing and not seeing and the importance of inferring 'what is not there, what we cannot find'. Stella suggests that the artist is aware of a presence, 'something in the dark spot that makes up his view'.[25] He claims that the painter looks to the mirror for reassurance about what is present and what is absent. This can equally be applied to cinema in its alluding to a dark presence that extends beyond the truth of the image that the audience beholds, and certainly to our discussion of Andy and his dark reflection, Sid, in *Toy Story*.

Sid lives in the dark spot of Andy's vision. Andy may be aware of Sid through the window (a further mirror) as their bedrooms align across the alleyway, one light, one dark, divided by a narrow strip of space that is, significantly, a divider of worlds. Andy's window is a portal through which the toys attempt to traverse between these two biospheres, empowered by the safety that one bedroom offers and fearful of the other. Woody is aware of the *idea* of Sid. He is the unknown, the dangerous Other. Woody and Buzz only attain a true awareness of Sid once they become trapped in his bedroom. He is the torturer of the object, the embodiment of every toy's ultimate fear that they will be broken. Indeed, Sid's dismembering of the inanimate is brutal (although creative) and the scenes within his darkened bedroom are reminiscent of the work of Jan Švankmajer and the Brothers Quay, in which the abject is emphasized to create shock value, and dead objects are conjured into being. They still, crucially, retain a jerky liveliness that emphasizes horror, reiterating Kandinsky's earlier idea of the inanimate quivering into being. Is the act of torturing toys as disturbing as the reanimating of those disfigured, dismembered objects?

Robert Bly, intrigued by the idea of the shadow, believes that everything we repress in life is kept in a bag we drag behind us. He notes, however, that 'the substance in the bag takes on a life of its own, it can't be ignored.'[26] The idea of Other, situated under the bed or on the periphery of one's vision, takes on a half-formed shape and becomes a shadow that, we imagine, has dark, malicious intentions as well as an awareness of us, characterized by Marie Louise von Frantz as feeling 'as if something is looking at me, something that I do not see but that sees me'.[27] Buzz and Woody, trapped in Sid's bedroom, allow their paranoia about his cruelty to extend to the things beneath his bed. These disfigured toys scuttling about in the darkness of their various hiding places are objects imagined about and then glimpsed by Woody's torchlight on the perimeter of his, and Buzz's, vision. They form a collective, horrific presence, hovering at the edge of what is known and what is not. Mirrors and their meanings apply once more here: Sid's toys are a darker reflection of Andy's; they are broken, mutilated, afraid: victims of a sadistic master. It is only when the shadows fall away and daylight fills the room that we more fully grasp the extent of Sid's cruelty and begin to see its cause as childhood boredom. In the absence of positive reinforcement (we are invited to believe that the invisible parent is the cause of the child's mischief), he amuses himself in various ways, such as stealing his sister's doll and preparing to blow up Buzz. Absence is at the core of Sid's world; meanings are made in Pixar's cinema and the audience is asked to consider the shadow and what it really represents.

Initially, Sid is depicted as Andy's sinister twin. He tortures, rather than plays with his toys and responds reluctantly to the distant, disembodied voice of the parent. We imagine that Sid might view Andy's window and wonder about the solidity of that bright, luminous world, where the presence of family seems constant and reassuring and where there are no shadows (however this view is not as accurate as it appears, and the fractured family and absent parent in Andy's world as well as Sid's, is discussed in due course). Andy, conversely, might glance furtively and fearfully into the gloom of Sid's bedroom. Each half of a boy hints at a fragmented self that needs stitching to the other, however reluctantly, in order to create a more rounded whole, formed essentially of both light and dark elements. Apart, these boys are shadows of each other; neither one is complete, but we imagine each must be disquietingly aware of the other.

Within *Toy Story*'s world of dualities, Lacan's mirror theory strikes a chord and Jung's idea of the shadow resonates. Cassar recognizes the haunting properties of the doppelgänger that exists on the projected screen, discussed earlier, and the question 'haven't I seen you before?' becomes all the more unsettling when we consider that our double may be watching us. Is Andy aware of Sid's shadowy presence? The alignment of their bedrooms would hint at some level of consciousness between them. The double, or doppelgänger, occupies the darker recesses of our minds and Derrida notes that a sense of displacement occurs when 'one feels oneself looked at by what one cannot see'.[28] The double in *Toy Story* occupies a space close to Andy. Sid can be seen and heard; he is the shadow of Pixar's luminous child, more unsettling yet growing ever closer the more the film unfolds, until he steps forward and occupies the void left by Andy. Because of Andy's fragmented identity (arguably he is too gentle to achieve wholeness and depth, as Stanton claims, the space for the shadow opens up. It seems that the more we encounter *Toy Story*, the more we discover Sid shifting in our periphery as he emerges from the shadows to embody the 'real' child. This is, in part, because of the familiarity that becomes established between Sid and the audience, but it is also certainly worth considering him as a product of our time.

Family

Presence and absence are driving motivators within Pixar's cinema, evident in *Finding Nemo*, *WALL-E* (Stanton, 2008), *Monsters, Inc.* and others. Presence seems to reinforce the safety and stability of Andy's world, just as absence establishes Sid's. The parent in each, however, suggests further fragmentations of family life. Andy's mother is caring, busy and active, but she is alone and in transition (the house is being sold and there appears to be no mention or sight of a partner). We imagine the division that has already occurred, fracturing the parental unit and reverberating through Andy's world. This luminous and stable environment hints of isolation, disruption and loneliness. Sid's mother, meanwhile, remains a ghostly echo, rather than a physical presence. She is the voice calling out 'pop tarts'. Woody mimics her, suggesting her absence is all too familiar, and Sid's sister, Hannah, responds to the fake voice in the same manner as she responds to the real one. The only physical adult presence is one alluded to inside the television room where a sleeping man slumps in a chair. In the absence of parent, the dog assumes the role of gatekeeper, defending the home at all costs, but, as we discussed earlier, Scud creeps tentatively into this room and retreats quickly, unwilling to disturb the adult there, suggesting a history of maltreatment and forcing us to wonder if this applies only to dogs or perhaps to children too. The truth of twenty-first century family life, through the Pixar lens, feels disturbingly real.

The nuclear family unit, consisting of husband, wife and children, experiences its demise here. Reflecting US society is important for and reaffirms Pixar's culture of addressing dark themes. *Toy Story*'s apparent fracturing mirrors the US Census of 2007, which looks back to reveal a rise of 75 per cent of the national divorce rate for women and 78 per cent for men between 1960 and 2006.[29] The family was in decline, having changed in structure due to the increase of many women entering the workforce, as well as other societal shifts, and US children began living with a single parent, typically their mother.[30] Twenty-first century childhood is viewed as a 'protected space'[31] and one that is extended to an older age to enable more nurturing of the child to take place, yet the idea that childhood is cosseted exists uneasily alongside the statistics given previously. The child of today is raised in a setting where shadows may be formed from absence and wholeness has become increasingly cracked.

Pixar is a mirror to modern US society. Andy's mother and Sid's sleeping 'father' remain the only real physical adult presences in *Toy Story*. The two adults create an illusion of wholeness that remains just that, nothing more, while Sid's mother is a disembodied, distant voice that only hints at presence but does not materialize. Sid's ability to disfigure Hannah's doll without parental intervention is a potent reminder of this. As Audrey Niffenegger reflects, 'I know, how absence can be present, like a damaged nerve, like a dark bird.'[32] The shadow lurks in the mirror, frees itself and floats like a ghostly presence through Andy's and Sid's worlds, defining the modern North American family as cracked, broken, absent.

Conclusion

Jung argues that there is no energy without a tension of opposites.[33] The conscious seeks out the unconscious; self seeks Other in identity formation, as we have seen. The mirror image offers a duality of truths for the individual; it establishes the ego and the shadow and opens portals to other worlds. The mirror reveals the double, as well as its connections with the image and with fear. We might only glimpse the shadow on the periphery of our vision but we are aware of its potential, both as a damaging force and, conversely, as an essential part of self.

Pixar creates a world of fascinating dualities in *Toy Story*. Characters exist in light and in darkness, striving for wholeness, yet achieving a more compelling (and arguably more 'real') fracturing of self. The issues of both humans and toys are equally important; from Andy's wholesome play to Sid's soulless torturing, from Buzz's yearning for illusion, to his acceptance that he is 'just a toy', and from Woody's elevated status to his acceptance of his own fallibility. The film presents a tension of opposites through its divisions; the mirror reflects self and other and the spark of opposites is dynamic and appealing. It is necessary to the characters' development, to their rise, fall and ultimate understanding of self and Other within the Pixar world. There is no 'dumbing down' in Pixar's cinema; the audience engages in a film essentially about the secret life of toys, but as we have seen Lanier et al. argue, the toys become characters rather than objects. The distance between us and them is reduced and the looking glass is multilayered; it reveals glimpses of doubles and otherness in its translucence, of family breakdowns and multilayered shadows, a rejecting of wholeness in favour of the incomplete and ever-shifting 'self', and these become images of a more complex truth the longer we gaze upon them.

Notes

1 Ann Casement, 'Encountering the shadow in rites of passage: a study in activations', *Journal of Analytical Psychology*, vol. 48, no. 1 (2003). 29–46 (p. 30).
2 Ellen Scott, 'Agony and Avoidance: Pixar, Deniability, and the Adult Spectator', *Journal of Popular Film and Television*, vol. 42, no. 3 (2014): 150–62 (p. 151).
3 Casement, 'Encountering the shadow in rites of passage', p. 32.
4 Henry Giroux, quoted in Pieter-Jan Decoster and Nancy Vansieleghem, 'Cinema Education as an Exercise in "Thinking Through Not-Thinking"', *Educational Philosophy & Theory*, vol. 46, no. 7 (2014): 789–804 (p. 793).
5 John Berger, *Ways of Seeing* (London: Penguin Modern Classics, 2008), p. 10.
6 Ignaz Cassar, 'Viewed from Behind: The Projected Image and Its Doppelgänger', *Parallax*, vol. 14, no. 2 (2008): 115–25 (p. 124).
7 Marie Louise von Frantz, 'The Process of Individuation', in Carl Jung (ed.), *Man and His Symbols* (London: Penguin, 1978), pp. 157–254 (p. 182).

8 James Clarke, *The Films of Pixar Animation Studio* (Harpenden: Kamera Books, 2013), p. 49.
9 Ibid., pp. 50–52.
10 Clinton Lanier, Scott Rader and Aubrey Fowler, 'Anthropomorphism, Marketing Relationships, and Consumption Worth in the *Toy Story* Trilogy', *Journal of Marketing Management*, vol. 29, nos. 1–2 (2013): 26–47 (pp. 29–31).
11 Sigmund Freud, *The Uncanny* (London: Penguin Classics, 2003), p. 133.
12 R. A. Lynch, 'The Alienating Mirror: Toward a Hegelian Critique of Lacan on Ego-Formation', *Human Studies*, vol. 31, no. 2, (2008): 209–21 (p. 214).
13 Joseph Henderson, 'Ancient Myths and Modern Man', in Carl Jung (ed.), *Man and His Symbols* (London: Penguin, 1978), pp. 95–156 (p. 156).
14 Ibid., p. 110.
15 Aniela Jaffé, 'Symbolism in the Visual Arts', in Carl Jung (ed.), *Man and His Symbols* (London: Penguin, 1978), pp. 255–332 (p. 292).
16 Alan Ackerman, *Seeing Things: From Shakespeare to Pixar* (Toronto: University of Toronto Press, 2011), p. 3.
17 Alan Cholodenko, quoted in Tom Gunning, 'Animating the Instant: The Secret Symmetry between Animation and Photography', in Karen Beckman (ed.), *Animating Film Theory* (North Carolina: Duke University Press, 2014), pp. 37–53 (p. 37).
18 Karen Paik, *To Infinity and Beyond: The Story of Pixar Animation Studios* (San Francisco: Chronicle Books, 2007), p. 80.
19 Decoster and Vansielegham, 'Cinema Education as an Exercise in "Thinking Through Not-Thinking"', p. 793.
20 Fernando Pessoa, *The Book of Disquiet* (London: Penguin Modern Classics, 2015), p. 302.
21 Tad Friend, 'Second Act Twist: Andrew Stanton, The Director of "Finding Nemo" and "WALL-E", Faces the Complications of Live Action', *The New Yorker*, 17 October 2011. http://www.newyorker.com/magazine/2011/10/17/second-act-twist (accessed 20 October 2016).
22 Malcolm Bowie, *Lacan* (Cambridge: Harvard University Press, 1993), p. 83.
23 Ray Bradbury, *Something Wicked This Way Comes* (New York: Simon and Schuster, 1962), p. 13.
24 Michael Bird, 'The Perception of Symmetry', *Tate Etc.*, 1 May 2004. http://www.tate.org.uk/context-comment/articles/perception-symmetry (accessed 20 October 2016).
25 Bowie, *Lacan*, p. 169.
26 Robert Bly, quoted in A. J. Mahari, *The Shadows and Echoes of Self – The False Self Born Out of the Core Wound of Abandonment in Borderline Personality Disorder* (Ontario: Phoenix Rising Publications, 2007), p. 84.
27 von Frantz, 'The Process of Individuation', p. 164.
28 Jacques Derrida quoted in Cassar, 'Viewed from Behind', p. 124.
29 Holley Tankersley, '"What Is Family?" Defining the Terms of the U.S Welfare State', in Dennis Wiseman (ed.), *The American Family – Understanding Its Changing Dynamics and Place in Society* (Illinois: Charles C Thomas, 2008), pp. 21–38 (p. 25).

30 Natasha Zaretsky, *No Direction Home: The American Family and the Fear of National Decline, 1968–1980* (North Carolina: The University of North Carolina Press, 2007), p. 11.
31 Suzanne Bianchi, John Robinson and Melissa Milke, *The Changing Rhythms of American Family Life* (New York: Russell Sage Foundation, 2006), p. 7.
32 Audrey Niffenegger, *The Time Traveller's Wife* (New York: Scribner, 2003), p. 516.
33 Les Oglesby, *C. G. Jung and Hans Urs Von Balthasar: God and Evil – A Critical Comparison* (East Sussex: Routledge, 2014), p. 85.

Chapter 11

WOODY, BUZZ AND THE KOONS COROLLARY . . . OR WHY *TOY STORY* IS ART

Paul Wells

You Can't Rush Art

— Geri, the Restorer (*Toy Story 2*)

It has long troubled me that popular entertainment rarely finds itself talked about as 'Art'. There are numerous reasons for this, of course. Art culture, unsurprisingly, insists upon defining the terms about what the contexts, techniques and conditions of art are, for example, and there remains a certain intellectual snobbery about finding Art in more mainstream commercially orientated practice. By way of illustration of this point, I once recall sitting with the director of an arts centre, who was considering screening animation programmes, but who vociferously refused to mix Pixar shorts with the films of the Quays or Švankmajer. On another occasion, too, a vice chancellor of a leading university sat with me after a presentation by Pixar personnel and a showing of *Toy Story* (John Lasseter, 1995), and cheerfully summed up the evening by saying 'There wasn't much to that, I don't know what you see in this stuff.' At the very least, this was bemusing, as the Pixar speakers had revealed the complexity and challenge of their craft, and the film itself renders few viewers unaffected. I was left to conclude that sometimes, genuine appreciation and recognition only comes with time. Now, more than twenty years after the initial release of *Toy Story*, and taking into account its subsequent sequels, and the plethora of critical and public response it has accrued, it is surely time to see the *Toy Story* trilogy as the 'Art' it undeniably is. This, then, is the preoccupation of the following discussion.

I am immediately reminded of Italo Calvino's remark that 'a classic is a book that is never finished saying what it wants to say', and it is clear that *Toy Story* takes on this 'classical' definition by the fact that it has remained constantly in dialogue with the culture that produced it. This might readily be seen in three clear contexts: the *personal*, the *social* and the *artistic*. The first aspect – the *personal* – is essentially biographical, and situates *Toy Story* in my own experience. *Toy Story* was the first film my son, Freddie, relentlessly played the video of; back-to-back showings in which as a young child he was inspired to talk to me about the complexity of emotions experienced by Woody, such as jealousy, guilt and loneliness. Woody and Buzz remain the only childhood toys he has kept. My daughter, Lola, was to have the same affinity with Jessie from *Toy Story 2* (John Lasseter and Lee Unkrich, 1999), a film that I only got to enjoy much later, as on the initial occasion I saw it, I had to leave the cinema early as my wife thought that her waters were breaking and our baby was on the way! I include these remarks merely to illustrate that 'family' films often facilitate important family memories, and as such, may inform wider *social* discourses. By the time *Toy Story 3* (Lee Unkrich, 2010) emerged, such social narratives were concerned with everything from the phenomenon of grown *men* crying at the films; whether the *Toy Story* films constituted the greatest trilogy ever (vying with *The Godfather* [1972–90], *Back to the Future* [1985–90] and *Lord of the Rings* [2001–03]); the fact that the films were prompting children to hoard their toys and preventing parents throwing them out; and inevitably, more adult fare, in which Woody and Buzz become sex toys in memes and private behaviour. Without question, the *Toy Story* trilogy transcended its status as a series of films, and prompted a range of cultural considerations about childhood and growing up, the relationship between children and their toys, the role of parents and family, the function of memory and nostalgia, and crucially, the values that accrue around toys as symbolic objects.

The films essentially suggest that at one level toys have no intrinsic value and are disposable playthings subject to destruction and loss. At another, toys possess the value prompted by a child's emotional investment. At yet another, in the way that the monetary value of toys may shift from their initial cost as a manufactured commodity to their economic potential as a collectible. It is in this latter context as a 'collectible' that there is the implied suggestion that the toy has historical presence and longevity, and has transcended its function, to become something with abstract connotations. In becoming a conserved and preserved 'object' it may be defined within the parameters of both archival and artistic contexts. To that end, I wish primarily to concentrate on the *artistic* aspects embedded in the *Toy Story* films. I address how Woody, Buzz and the other toys speak to what I am terming 'the Koons Corollary', a method by which the work of the artist Jeff Koons can be used to prove the artistic credentials of *Toy Story*. This will also chime with a further address of one of my own conceptual ideas, 'the scripted artefact', and a broader engagement with the ways in which *Toy Story* may help us deal with laser envy, falling with style and other difficult issues in which aesthetic gesture can be accorded with philosophical meaning and affect – surely the fundamental social premise of Art per se.

Toy Story and the studio's oeuvre in general have inevitably prompted a range of critical as well as public discourses, of course. Meinel, for example, situates Pixar's texts as a re-engagement with the United States' core myths and symbols, reactivating debates about manifest destiny, American Exceptionalism, Puritanism and the maintenance of a consensual notion of an 'American Dream' even in the midst of a post-facts, postmodern relativist order.[1] It is not hard to view Woody and Buzz as exemplary representational figures in these respects, playing out tensions between nostalgic yearnings for a middle-class, conservative American past and a more future-directed late capitalist fear of progress, underpinned by in-built obsolescence. Indeed, as Harari has claimed, there has been a major shift from the emergence and necessity of the *working* class in the nineteenth century to the possibility of the emergence of a *useless* class in the near future, with little economic or military function, which will struggle to find meaning in existence.[2] The *Toy Story* films, then, offer an underpinning prescience in posing one of the most challenging political questions about the nature of work, play, space, time and value in a neotechnologically determinist projection of the future.

Herhuth, taking another tack, embraces the sublime, the uncanny, the fantastic and sensation as core elements that resonate in Pixar texts when the films are read through the particular aesthetic filter of computer animation as a specific vocabulary of expression.[3] Though these analyses still place the Pixar texts within significant political and technological debates, the stress here becomes upon how the films prompt affect in the audience, and potentially revise received notions of human exchange and cultural logic. These are important observations because in privileging aesthetics and contemporary acts of mediation, in *animation*, this offers a platform for the ways in which such texts may aspire to the condition of art outside the parameters of contemporary market or business practices. This challenges, or at least intervenes in, Gurevitch's thesis that Pixar texts offer a continuum between emotion-based idioms of design and the political and market economy that they speak to.[4] Essentially, he argues that the design codes and conventions in the films effectively familiarize and encourage modes of engagement with late capitalist conditions of cross-platform manufacture, merchandizing and market-orientated behavioural orthodoxy in the service of brand identity. In this context, Woody and Buzz effectively go way beyond infinity in representing a particular place in markets and mindsets, simultaneously informed by brand essentialism and a codification that extends the perceived Disney tradition of creating multiple contexts for consumer opportunities.

This tension has long standing in Disney, and now Pixar criticism, in that it pits left-wing concerns about the primacy of the films as vehicles merely to sell toys and other products (and, further, largely as works which misrepresent or exclude virtually all social and cultural groups outside the white, middle-class male), against more liberal readings that suggest that the films have wider humanitarian and aesthetic discourses than this allows.[5] I should own up that

I may be an ideological defeatist in this debate, as I essentially concede that Western cultures have become so commodified that all cultural products exist with, through and for, late capitalist inscription. As such, to reduce those products to a place only in a political economy, and not address the wider implications for the millions of people who *unconsciously* consume, beyond conscious concerns with the market forces that form them, seems a limited address. In this respect, I am reminded of Schaffer's work in response to Darley's reading of *Toy Story*, in which Schaffer challenges Darley's assumptions about the complicity of Pixar in using a *new* technology in the service of the *same old* ideological practice of servicing commercial ends.[6] Resisting notions of such technological determinism, and, indeed, any limited reading of 'cartoon' representation, Schaffer claims that the 'feel' of Pixar renders it beyond the constraints of the market economy, servicing much greater possibilities of affect than the mere encouragement of ancillary sales, arguing: '*Toy Story* addresses parents and children through these characters in terms that at once acknowledge, make ironic, and promise to ameliorate the intervention of marketing in the most intimate relations of family life.'[7] In this view, it is clear that the sheer familiarity of the object relations, and the 'plasticity' embedded in them – however 'virtual' – makes the practical knowledge about, and memory of, the objects render notions of the technology or the consumer culture they exist within *subordinate* to emotional and imaginative engagement and empathy.

I wish to argue here, then, that it is in this that Pixar's films – and, in this case, the *Toy Story* trilogy – have the greatest affordance and resemblance to the cultures of Art. The fundamental response to the art object, first and foremost, is reception and contemplation of the artefact in and of itself. The gallery – the white cube – essentially verifies the purity of this ambition, localizing the art object in a non-distracting space purely directing the viewer to 'look', and arguably, in the first instance, 'feel', and thereafter to 'think' and, nearly always, *not* to 'touch'. It is the optical that suggests the kinetic and the haptic, and prompts the nature of what is experienced and thought about. It is pertinent here too, to recognize that the fundamental affect of Art is usually thought of as emotional, contemplative and serious, and that this often negates the role of humour and amusement. As Klein has noted, art historians have only limitedly taken into account how comic inflections drive and inform contemporary art, and this serves both to misrepresent some of its purpose, but importantly, to absent the role of humour in works of art per se.[8] This inevitably has the consequence of making self-evidently 'serious' art supposedly more valued than 'comic' art – the latter also inherently bound up with the cultural category of '*light* entertainment'. Such hierarchical 'demotion' marginalizes works that use humour consciously to critique established positions and offer alternative perspectives. This is especially significant when considering the artistic value of the *Toy Story* films, and is a key point I return to later in my discussion. First, though, it is important to address the context in which *Toy Story* emerged in relation to North American arts culture, since this is fundamental to the recognition of the component elements of *Toy Story* (its characters and environments) and its narrative themes (all associated with the construction of a certain 'Americana') as a model of (pop) art.

It should be remembered that in the early 1990s, largely right-wing fundamentalist groups – among them the American Family Association – were convulsed by the impact of two key pieces of art: Andres Serrano's *Piss Christ* (1987) and Robert Mapplethorpe's *X Portfolio* (1989). The former was an image of a crucifix immersed in urine; the latter included photographs of extreme sadomasochistic homosexual practice.[9] By labyrinthine rather than direct means, both pieces of work were supported with minimal sums of money donated by the National Endowment for the Arts [NEA], and this prompted the political outcry that taxpayers' money should not be funding such 'immoral' work. This had called into question not merely issues of taste, decorum and the profane, however, but the assumed value of art as a force for quasi-therapeutic 'good'. The United States' long tradition of landscape painting associated nature with God, and such imagery operated as a model of spiritual inspiration and uplift, antipathetic to the rise of American materialism. Even when art became more secular in the late nineteenth century, subliminally suggesting anxiety in landscapes that were strangely divorced from representations of the Civil War, it still became the focus of the public-facing project of the museum sector. Museums were dedicated to education and making art accessible in the service of an institutional view of national identity free from social bias and historical resentments. Crucially, at the point at which Modernist art came to define American art per se, the Museum of Modern Art actually maintained the idea of therapy in the avant-garde by insisting that modern art needed to be judged in two ways. First, on its own aesthetic terms and conditions – essentially 'art for art's sake' – or second, as an aspirational intervention in which entirely provisional (virtual?) alternatives for culture and society were privileged in a spirit of 'progress'. Serrano and Mapplethorpe, in the first instance, seemingly did not fit into this agenda, though both were referring explicitly to previous models of art historical formalism and theme, and made work pertinent to the ideological climate.

So, what of this in relation to *Toy Story*? Simply, the defence of Serrano and Mapplethorpe and their work slid uneasily between unpersuasive claims for aesthetics *or* forced readings that overstated political significance. Hughes notes both 'the kind of exhausted and literally de-moralised aestheticism that would find no basic difference between a Nuremberg rally and a Busby Berkeley spectacular, since both, after all, are examples of Art-Deco choreography' or a view of the works (particularly Mapplethorpe's) as 'moral spectacle, stripping away the veils of prudery and ignorance and thus promoting gay rights by confronting us with the outer limits of human sexual behaviour, beyond which only death is possible'.[10] Hughes's chief fear here, though, is not the banality of aesthetic reading or ideological overstatement, but, influenced by what was viewed as the new 'multi-culturalist' discourses advancing political correctness, art would *inherently* be judged as a vehicle for politics and *not* as art. Evaluations of *equality* would effectively override issues of *quality*. Even though, in this context, the impact of academic deconstruction properly reclaimed lost narratives of race, gender and class, and foregrounded the history of white male oppression, there was a reactionary backlash that championed the status quo. Even in the Museum of American Art's 'The West as America' exhibition in 1991, which employed a more obviously deconstructed approach to past art works, there was critical resistance to the seemingly inappropriate or wilful 'misreading' of American history and the mythology embedded in it. What kind of art, then, could reconcile a culture that craved to be backward looking and conservative, and comforted by the emotional therapy of aesthetics, while also acknowledging the formal practices of art in the service, at the very least, of a newly coined, politically infused revision of 'melting pot' America? These were the conditions in which the art-making of Jeff Koons and the Pixar animators were to thrive.

Koons was part of a loosely defined movement known as neo-geometric conceptualism, in which figurative elements were used in experimental forms as a rejection of nonobjective abstract works. More important, though, was the shift of perspective that informed this; no longer was there an imperative to be in dialogue with art history or modernism, but with consumer culture and the popular media. As Collings has noted, Koons

> saw art as equilibrium, as everything leveled. It was something people should love like they loved anything – like babies and sunshine and smiling. And it turned out to be quite a strange and unpredictable idea, after all, to think about what people actually want and then try to give it to them. Not from a Hollywood position, but from a position of extreme avant-gardism.[11]

Here, then, was a nostalgic art, a progressive form, and a therapeutic discourse, all fundamentally tuned to how people actually respond to their lives – a mix aped in *Toy Story*'s mobilization of new computer technologies in the service of popular art, rooted in the fresh propositions about personal and social identity, embodied in the abstract community of 'toys' – toys defined by their past in the present and subject to change in the future.

Kemper has noted that: '*Toy Story* looks like a veritable work of Pop Art dominated by glossy, brightly colored commodities, the film's artists relishing in their glimmering reflective surfaces: vibrant toy packages with shiny transparent windows; glowing primary colors; rounded, precisely moulded, industrial plastic forms.'[12] This situates the film in relation to the pop art of Lichtenstein, Warhol and Oldenberg, a point confirmed and extended by former Pixar Supervising Animator, Andy Schmidt: '*Toy Story* is like a compendium of Rockwell Americana but put through the mixer with Dali, Magritte, and Andy Warhol. It is a mixture between the naïve and the symbolic.'[13] He adds: 'Caricature is a form of abstraction; it exaggerates and focuses. The shapes, forms, and colors in *Toy Story* push this kind of abstraction even further, imagining, for example, how the soldiers move, or the slinky dog, or even Woody as a puppet-style toy.'[14] It might be recalled here that 'caricature' is normally situated within a more satirical or rhetorical tradition of expression, and becomes a vehicle for the parodies, paradoxes and puns that were played out in pop art forms. It is in this that *Toy Story* should more properly be recognized as in the tradition of the later pop exponents, and as the corollary to the pop art of Ed Pascheke, Frank Stella, Jim Nutt and, most specifically, Koons. If the first wave of pop was essentially about imitation and mimicry, then second wave pop is about the inscription of caricature and moving image, and the purposing of incongruity to both amuse and rethink established cultural logic. Koons, like the animators at Pixar, are reinscribing the virtual object with its past meanings but at one remove, repositioning artefacts and their associative cultures into a *transubstantiated* condition. Jean Piaget suggests:

> To know is to assimilate reality into systems of transformations. To know is to transform reality in order to understand how a certain state is brought out . . . To my way of thinking, knowing an object does not mean copying it – it means acting upon it. It means constructing systems of transformations that can be carried out on or with this object.[15]

Koons and the animators at Pixar speak to this view of 'knowledge'; a knowledge shared with the spectators in *reception* of it. This is a 'bottom up' *personal* knowledge, then, rather than a 'top down' *social* knowledge. This is to privilege the *personal as political* model rather than the ideologically charged curatorial imperatives emergent in the galleries that operated as a *social as political* model. Though some may argue that this is reactionary, and resistant to historical reconstruction in the name of more accurate and truthful forms of representation, this is a deliberate strategy to speak to common notions of humanity; more universal terms and conditions; and, crucially, privileging the context of the arts for the alternative languages of aesthetic intervention. Interestingly, it is also in the cases both of Koons and the Pixar animators a method of speaking to 'adult' cultural logic in which people would recognize the very infrastructure of art as a context in which they, too, participate. As *Toy Story* director, and Pixar CEO, John Lasseter reminded his audience at the twentieth-anniversary celebration of the release of the film: 'The fundamental thing that we did was we always viewed the toys as adults. We viewed them in a way that when Andy leaves the room it becomes a work place. What we wanted was for Woody to be the leader, he was Andy's favorite toy but he made sure everybody got played with and they had staff meetings.'[16] This sense of directly speaking to the adults and the children almost through 'blue collar' normality again leavens the sense of 'middle-class-ness' of art, 'leveling' it against other social expression, in the Koonsian sense noted above.

I was privileged to briefly meet Koons around the time of the retrospectives held at the Chateau de Versailles, Paris, in September 2008, and the Serpentine

Gallery, London, in June 2009. Having always believed that Koons's work is in some way related to Pixar's aesthetic and conceptual outlook, most specifically, in relation to the *Toy Story* films, I asked apropos of his sculpture of Popeye – a key 'blue collar' American icon – whether he liked animation, and more specifically, whether he liked *Toy Story*. He answered: 'Sure, I love cartoons. Popeye just says 'I Yam What I Am' to me, and I love the self-acceptance in that. I loved *Toy Story*. I loved the way it looked. I loved the way it felt. I don't feel comfortable with film, but Pixar do it great. Those movies are about self-acceptance too, aren't they, don't you think?'[17]

At one level, it is clear that the *Toy Story* films are concerned with the discourses that inform 'self-acceptance', in its way one of the most clichéd 'messages' of much contemporary Hollywood cinema, but this is partly the point – instead of the notion of 'be yourself', this kind of work refreshes stereotypical or archetypal views. It becomes essentially about the notion of how you have *become* yourself through the relationships you participated in with the material world. Being yourself is ultimately about recognizing and accepting who you were and are in material culture, in the service of how you might function within its terms and conditions. The caricatural transubstantiation achieved in the film both uses aesthetics to *re-emote* objects in new contexts, and to *satirize* the conditions that have made this necessary. This is not, then, 'top down' conservative nostalgia, but 'bottom up' provocations of empathy. Woody and Buzz can be loved like babies, smiling and sunshine because they are signifying aspects of a natural order based on 'feeling', perhaps (and ironically) genuinely therapeutic. This is because it is implicitly acknowledging that late capitalist material culture – however commercialized, superficial or seemingly inauthentic – actually constitutes an everyday 'natural' order of lived experience for most people in modern nations. As film critic A. O. Scott confirms, when writing about *Toy Story 3*: 'Therein lies its genius, and its uncanny authenticity. A tale that captured the romance and pathos of the consumer economy, the sorrows and pleasures that dwell at the heart of our materialist way of life, could only be told from the standpoint of the commodities themselves, those accretions of synthetic substance and alienated labor we somehow endow with souls.'[18] It is this idea that informs the 'scripted artefact', a concept I have discussed elsewhere, that I wish to reintroduce here as a core aspect of the way in which Koons and Pixar create their Art, and importantly, how animation serves to take 'things' and endow them with souls.

Following on from Norman Klein's notion of 'scripted spaces'[19], which conceives of the environment as a prescripted narrativized journey in which the viewer is rapidly stimulated into an elevated mode of perception ('a slender epiphany'), the concept of the 'scripted artefact' works as 'an embodied object whose meaning and affect is revealed through its use and reuse, demonstrating an oscillation between its status as a design idiom, its functional purpose, and its associative and symbolic implications and interaction'.[20] So, '[w]hen animation employs an Artefact, it changes the "mode of perception" by which an object is understood, placing it within a "system of transformation", creating the "slender epiphany", which reveals its "script"".[21] I argue here that Koons and the Pixar animators have the same modus operandi in constantly working with objects to reveal their inherent 'script' and, as such, implicitly to request of the viewer an empathetic realization both of personal memory *and* of socially constructed artifice. This *self-conscious* illusionism speaks to Art as a conduit for reappropriation and disguise; a transposition of what might be seen as 'lowbrow' into new forms that use irony to challenge normative assumptions. There is further irony in the fact that this may better service new discourses of equality and political correctness beyond more emphatic ideological rhetoric and dogma. Fundamental to the effectiveness of such Art is its capacity to communicate on terms that might readily be understood. (There is no desire to 'make strange' here, but rather to *re-familiarize.*) At the heart of this is not only the role of humour, but also, crucially, the role of animation.

After many years in which I have sought to disassociate animation from the assumption that it is fundamentally children's entertainment, I now wish to reassociate it with children and childhood, on the basis that animation, in the eyes of the public, retains its innocence. This notion of 'innocence' is largely predicated on two assumptions. First, that animation is predominantly encountered in, and throughout, childhood, and is reassuringly *familiar*, and second, that animation, as such, is a vehicle by which a certain kind of playful 'unreality' is tethered to moral and ethical codes that are humane and unaffected by overtly politicized adult interventions. The 'script' of the animated objects in the *Toy Story* films, then, is informed first by the expectation of something unthreatening and open to 'child-like' participation. It is a condition that is also aspired to in Koons's work:

> Children come to the studio or to exhibitions [and] they usually enjoy the experience and respond well to things. There's just an acceptance of everything. There isn't a segregation; there's nobody in any way circling around, informing or creating segregation, creating a hierarchy, creating some form of rules of what can be in play, what cannot be in play and, really, disempowering.[22]

This idea of an unconditional space that allows everything 'in play', and seeks to empower, also facilitates the investment in objects as archetypes. Both Koons and the Pixar animators seek to use objects as reflections of material culture, personal investment and primal memory. This enables the objects simultaneously to represent contemporary life, the ways in which individuals interact and participate in it, and the more deep-rooted emotional feelings common to human experience. As René de Guzman, senior curator of art at the Oakland Museum of California, noted on the occasion of the 'Pixar: 25 Years of Animation' exhibition:

> I think one of the most powerful things about the exhibition is that it gives people the sense that great creativity and artistic accomplishment is a tangible thing. It is not something that is beyond their reach. It's there in front of them; it just takes an eye and a lump of clay, an eye and some watercolors, to create magical experiences. It's empowering.[23]

In echoing Koons's remark about the empowerment in making both the 'objects' and the process in creating artistic outcomes accessible, de Guzman insists that Pixar's work speaks directly to the creative and aesthetic sense, and its potential value in everyone.

Koons's 'Celebration' series is focused on this concept, using children's playthings to insist upon an open unconditional response more geared towards prompting the interrogation of 'selfhood' rather than the 'social', though the series is not without significant cultural worth. 'Play-Doh' (1994), 'Building Blocks' (1996–2009) and 'Shelter' (1996–99) all use toys to embody a particular set of feelings. 'Shelter' is the most reminiscent of *Toy Story* in that it stages a number of toys in the frontier West, including Lego characters, a rocker, an M&M figure, Frosty the Snowman, popcorn and a windmill. Koons recalls: 'I was making these archetypal childhood images in "Celebration", which were the driving force in trying to communicate with [my son] from a distance [during the custody case].'[24] The choices seem highly particular to Koons's memories, perhaps, but like the toys in *Toy Story* they become both Proustian madeleines for *personal* discourses, and inevitably speak to the *social* and the *artistic* because they have been transubstantiated from their function as toys to their embodiments as scripted artefacts. Arguably, all toys are made as *projections* of ideas and feelings in the first instance; objects representing already lost worlds (prehistory, the frontier, etc.) or worlds lived by some but only imagined by others (living on a farm, being in a circus, etc.). These are the staging posts of the 'scripts', then acted upon in the narratives of Koons and the Pixar animators. This is the nature of the art endemic to material culture as it is perpetually processed from the idea to the physical to the experiential back to the virtual. As Koons notes: 'When a very controlled vocabulary, a very precisely articulated vocabulary in two dimensions or in three dimensions, is brought together it emulates our kind of human experience in the way we see the world both in the form of body and idea. That's what I feel is very special about having these objects.'[25] The *Toy Story* films play out this idea in a very specific way: Andy, the owner of Woody and Buzz, essentially sees his toys as 'ideas', while the toys themselves become aware of their own 'bodies'. More specifically, Andy projects narrative on to his toys, while the toys become increasingly knowledgeable about their own material existence, and the narratives (the 'script') they are created with, and how far they have some notion of 'freewill'. A more incisive commentary on this idea might be seen in the actions of Sid, Andy's neighbour, who projects far more inventively and creatively on his toys, reconstructing them to his own specifications and intent. Sid is often seen as the abandoned son of blue-collar indifference, creating a gothic playground for his toys, informed by inherent violence and cruelty. Simply, I do not view Sid in this light, and advance him as a far more interesting child driven by his own perspective, rather than the banality of Andy's more predictable activity. Sid uses the toys as mere materials in the service of his play, while Andy uses his toys in the service of received narratives about them. When Koons makes 'Split Rocker (Orange/Red)' (1999), a rocking horse with a split mismatching head, made up of two different kinds of horse/material, he is effectively making the same point. This is the representation of idea and body inscribed through the toys that are effectively scripted mediations between the personal and the social. Sid interprets and adds to the script; Andy understands and reinforces the script; Woody and Buzz challenge but ultimately cannot move beyond their script. Koons and the Pixar animators place these discourses into abstracted relief, and as such, aestheticize both gesture and concept. This, surely, is fine art.

Ultimately, these are fundamentally gestalt narratives, rooted both in the function and the potential of 'things', partly tethered to known and controlled aspects of existence, but open to the freedoms of invested experience. As Koons notes, 'abstraction is a connection to the different potential of things and that's the metaphysical spice, I guess.'[26] In this sense, both Koons and the Pixar animators are repurposing the idea of the 'ready made', but infusing it with contemporary processes of aesthetic and technological intervention. Elyse Klaidman, director of Pixar University and Archives, insists: 'we define art as either a process or a product of organizing and assembling objects to create something that initiates an emotion or response. It's obvious that all of these objects are doing that. They are art.'[27]

Both Koons and the Pixar animators are dedicated to this principle of provoking emotion, not merely in the sense of creating feeling, but in heightening the awareness of how the object has prompted emotion. To merely feel is not to know why and how the emotion has been aesthetically catalyzed, and the art here insists upon this realization. In some senses, this has co-opted the imperative of *transaction* from the commercial sector, but rather than placing it in a market economy, or indeed, an explicitly political frame, it works in the larger context of emotional affect and contemplation – an aesthetic sublime that refuses to be absolutely located, speaking to spaces outside orthodox ideas of the personal relationships, media forms or consumer contexts the work is ostensibly about. Koons's work, 'Caterpillar Ladder' (2003), for example, where a large caterpillar inflatable toy is moving through a step ladder, is 'about being able to retain one's course in life – these objects can go through things, but do not lose their course.'[28] This is the fundamental principle of the *Toy Story* films – Woody, for instance, moves through his roles as pull-string cowboy, as quasi-adult alpha male, his frontier identity in the TV show, 'Woody's Round-Up', his place as Andy's favourite toy, his function as friend and mentor, and his potential as a collectible object, but even more significantly, as the virtual embodiment of an animated character (with all the procedural elements of its creation: design, maquette, computer-generated imagery etc.), endowed with soul; a soul endangered until in the face of death in *Toy Story 3* he is plucked to safety by his alien toy friends. Woody has transcended artifice to prompt the deepest emotion in others of *fearing for* him, while also prompting intimations of God and the afterlife – this is indeed the vastness of infinity and beyond. It is surely the proper place of art in signifying and catalysing considerations of the potential meanings or purpose of life itself.

As Koons again has remarked:

> I think art can perform as a medium to get you to a state where everything can be revealed. It is just down to the self to open oneself up to the experience, just letting life and knowledge reveal themselves. It's all there, you just have to open yourself up to it. I think art can be a medium that does that.[29]

This mutuality of acceptance and transcendence resides in the aesthetic sublime of both Koons's work and the Pixar texts, and most redolently, the *Toy Story* trilogy. Using the same elements, the same component object 'scripts', the same 'animated' inscription, Koons and the Pixar animators embody the idea and transubtantiate the notion of 'transaction' from function to feeling. This has been the central concept in the work of Koons and Pixar since the late 1980s to the present day, perhaps ultimately finding its zenith in the parallel use of the 'gazing ball'. A quintessentially North American concept, the gazing ball is a coloured reflective ball sometimes placed outside houses or exchanged by family and friends – 'Their reflection deals with identity, but also excitement, affirmation and the possibility of going into a higher state.'[30] While Koons places such gazing balls in the midst of other ready-made objects, so that they are seen afresh, Pixar's Pete Docter uses the gazing balls as the shape of explicit memories in *Inside Out* (Pete Docter and Ronnie Del Carmen, 2015). Ultimately, Koons and Pixar situate their art then in the proper recognition of what it is to recall and know again the feeling of the most fulfilling human connections; to fall with style, but not lose course.

Notes

1 See Dietmar Meinel, *Pixar's America: The Re-Animation of American Myths and Symbols* (Basingstoke and New York: Palgrave Macmillan, 2016).
2 See Yuval Noah Harari, *Homo Deus: A Brief History of Tomorrow* (London: Harvill Secker, 2016).
3 See Eric Herhuth, *Pixar and the Aesthetic Imagination: Animation, Storytelling, and Digital Culture* (California: University of California Press, 2017).

4 See Leon Gurevitch, 'Computer Generated Animation as Product Design Engineered Culture, or Buzz Lightyear to the Sales Floor, to the Checkout and Beyond!', *animation: an interdisciplinary journal*, vol. 7, no. 2 (2012): 131–49.
5 See Henry Giroux and Grace Pollock, *The Mouse That Roared: Disney and the End of Innocence* (New York and Oxford: Rowman & Littlefield, 2001).
6 See William Schaffer, 'The Importance of Being Plastic: The Feel of Pixar', *Animation Journal*, vol. 12 (2004): 72–95.
7 Ibid, p. 77.
8 See Sheri Klein, *Art & Laughter* (London and New York: I.B. Tauris, 2007).
9 See Robert Hughes, *Culture of Complaint* (Oxford & New York: Oxford University Press, 1998).
10 Ibid, p. 188.
11 Matthew Collings, *This Is Modern Art* (London: Weidenfeld & Nicolson, 1999), p. 248.
12 Tom Kemper, *Toy Story: A Critical Reading* (London: BFI, 2015), p. 8.
13 Personal Interview with the author, November 2011.
14 Ibid.
15 Jean Piaget, quoted in Sherry Turkle (ed.), *Evocative Objects: Things We Think With* (Cambridge, Massachusetts and London: MIT Press, 2007), p. 38.
16 See Jacob Bryant, 'John Lasseter, Ed Catmull and "Toy Story" Team Celebrate 20th Anniversary', *Variety*, 2 October 2015. http://variety.com/2015/scene/vpage/toy-story-20th-anniversary-john-lasseter-ed-catmull-1201608613/ (accessed 18 April 2017).
17 Personal exchange with the author, September 2009.
18 See A. O. Scott, 'Voyage to the Bottom of the Day Care Centre', *The New York Times*, 17 June 2010. http://www.nytimes.com/2010/06/18/movies/18toy.html (accessed 18 April 2017).
19 Norman Klein, *The Vatican to Vegas: A History of Special Effects* (New York and London: The New Press, 2004), pp. 7–12.
20 Paul Wells, 'Chairy Tales: Object and Materiality in Animation', *Alphaville: Journal of Film and Screen Media*, vol. 8 (2014). http://www.alphavillejournal.com/Issue8/HTML/ArticleWells.html (accessed 18 April 2017).
21 Ibid. http://www.alphavillejournal.com/Issue8/HTML/ArticleWells.html (accessed 18 April 2017).
22 Jeff Koons and Norman Rosenthal, *Jeff Koons: Conversations with Norman Rosenthal* (London and New York: Thames & Hudson, 2014), p. 159.
23 René De Guzman, *Pixar: 25 Years of Animation* (San Francisco: Chronicle Books, 2010), p. 13.
24 Koons and Rosenthal, *Conversations*, p. 155.
25 Ibid., p. 136.
26 Ibid., p. 34.
27 De Guzman, *Pixar: 25 Years of Animation*, p 13.
28 Koons and Rosenthal, *Conversations*, p. 169.
29 Ibid., p. 272.
30 Ibid., p. 73.

Chapter 12

STORY IS KING: UNDERSTANDING THE *TOY STORY* FRANCHISE AS AN ALLEGORY FOR THE STUDIO NARRATIVE OF PIXAR ANIMATION

Helen Haswell

When *Toy Story* (John Lasseter) was released in 1995, analyses of the film suggested it was an allegory for the popularization of computer-generated (CG) animation and the subsequent displacement of hand-drawn methods.[1] According to this view, *Toy Story*'s narrative implies that Disney's traditional 2-D animation, represented by Woody, the outdated pull-string cowboy doll, has been rendered irrelevant by Pixar's pioneering digital animation, represented by Buzz Lightyear, the new and more advanced space ranger toy. While this is apparent, I would argue that the *Toy Story* franchise as a whole is representative of the history and development of Pixar Animation Studios and its relationship with the Walt Disney Company. This twenty-five-year relationship, which was formalized in 1991 when Disney agreed to finance the development, production and distribution of Pixar's first feature film, has been both turbulent and mutually beneficial. While the success of *Toy Story* enabled Pixar to renegotiate its contract terms with Disney, agreeing to produce a further five original films together, the first two *Toy Story* narratives reflect the friction between these two animation studios. By the time *Toy Story 3* (Lee Unkrich, 2010) was released, Pixar had been a subsidiary of the Walt Disney Company's Studio Entertainment division for four years, following a deal that cost Disney $7.4 billion and saw the appointment of Pixar co-founders Ed Catmull and John Lasseter to president and chief creative officer, respectively, of both Pixar and Walt Disney Animation Studios. In this regard, the apparently harmonious ending to the narrative of *Toy Story 3* is reflective of the post-acquisition period between Pixar and Disney.

Each film in the trilogy exemplifies the growth and progression of Pixar at that time, and consequently highlights the significance of the franchise to the fundamental ideals of the studio, which include the concurrent development of digital technology and CG aesthetics, and the value and precedence given to narrative. Twenty years after the release of *Toy Story*, Pixar's filmmakers continue to reiterate the importance of storytelling and the studio's commitment to narrative. This is also apparent when we take into consideration the industrial studio narrative of Pixar, which has been partly constructed by the studio and subsequently perpetuated by the media. While allegorical readings of the films are not made explicit, the release of each film in the *Toy Story* series punctuates key moments in Pixar's history, and the films' narratives appear to address the relationship between Disney and Pixar during this fifteen-year period. I use these readings of the films to highlight a familiar industrial narrative of Pixar to explore the studio's prominent role in the development of CG animation and the legacy and significance of the *Toy Story* franchise. Through an analysis of the narrative of the *Toy Story* trilogy, I argue that Pixar's focus on narrative development suggests that *Toy Story* is representative of the story of Pixar Animation Studios, and that the series exemplifies the foundational principles established by the company. Against the backdrop of the industrial analysis of the Disney–Pixar relationship and the narrative development of the *Toy Story* trilogy, the chapter argues that the films comment on the growth of Pixar and the studio's new position in mainstream American animation as a subsidiary of the Walt Disney Company.

Story Is King

Since 1986, when the company was founded, Pixar's mission statement has been to create 'memorable characters and heart-warming stories that appeal to audiences of all ages'.[2] The influence of Pixar's 'Braintrust' on the development of the studio's stories, and the introduction of Disney's 'Story Trust' – implemented by Lasseter following the 2006 Disney–Pixar merger – underlines the importance given to narrative. Pixar's emphasis on the value it places on storytelling was established early on through interviews with the studio's filmmakers and reiterated in documentaries about the company and in behind the scenes and making-of featurettes. Catmull notes that during the production of *Toy Story* the studio's now well-documented mantra and principle, 'story is king', quickly became pertinent to the foundations of the fledgling studio. For Catmull, it meant that Pixar would 'let nothing – not the technology, not the merchandising possibilities – get in the way of [the] story'.[3] This is emphasized in two extensive, company-endorsed accounts of Pixar's history: *To Infinity and Beyond: The Story of Pixar Animation Studios* by Karen Paik and *The Pixar Touch: The Making of a Company* by David Price. Both Paik and Price note that while Catmull and Pixar co-founder Alvy Ray Smith were technically capable, they required equally talented story artists in order to achieve their goal of creating a computer-animated film.[4]

This common understanding that Pixar's filmmakers place a great deal of importance on well-developed stories transcends the film world and extends to the industrial studio narrative of the animation company, and is often linked to the studio's success and the development of its creative culture. In attempting to uncover Pixar's 'winning formula' for the phenomenal and sustained commercial and critical success of the studio's films, analysts have turned to the production practices employed at the studio. Business self-help and industry-focused texts such as *Innovate the Pixar Way* (Bill Capodagli and Lynn Jackson, 2010) and *The International Film Business: A Market Guide Beyond Hollywood* (Angus Finney and Eugenio Triana, 2015) outline some of the practices that Pixar has implemented that offer 'visionary insight into the running of a "people" business and how to lead a creative organization'.[5] These practices include encouraging communication across the company by 'recognizing that the decision-making hierarchy and communication structure are two different things',[6] creating a safe environment in which to share and offer ideas, promoting innovation by publishing research and engaging in industry conferences, cross-training employees with the aid of Pixar University;[7] and, fundamentally, the merging of art and technology.[8] These set principles are key to Pixar's identity and, although they have developed as the company has grown, the foundational ideals established by Catmull and Lasseter have remained the same. *Toy Story* is the product of these established principles and, as its first feature film, is representative of Pixar. Catmull states that 'if we can constantly change and improve our models by using technology in the pursuit of art, we keep ourselves fresh. The whole history of Pixar is a testament to this dynamic interplay.'[9] As the pioneers of CG animation and a self-proclaimed artist-led studio, Pixar's reiterated mantra, 'art challenges technology, technology inspires art',[10] dictates the importance given by the studio to the concurrent development of technology and digital animation aesthetics. Established during the formation of the studio, for Pixar, it is essential that these two elements coincide. The *Toy Story* films exemplify this coherence between art and technology and the development of the studio over a fifteen-year period.

An accepted narrative has emerged in relation to the history of Pixar and the development of the studio's creative culture. This constructed studio narrative not only dictates the company's foundational principles, outlined above, but also states that Pixar is a filmmaker-led studio, and that its production practices are in direct contrast with corporate Hollywood, and Disney by extension. Based in Silicon Valley, Northern California, Pixar Animation Studios is situated among the world's largest high-tech corporations, including Apple, Facebook and Google, and thousands of start-up companies. Walt Disney Animation Studios, on the other hand, is based in Burbank, Southern California, along with some of the biggest media and entertainment companies, such as Warner Bros. Entertainment, ABC Studios, Marvel Studios and Nickelodeon. Not only has Pixar separated itself geographically from corporate Hollywood, but the studio is also explicit in having challenged traditional Hollywood studio practices by abandoning employment contracts and hiring staff full-time rather than project-to-project.[11] This narrative establishes Pixar as contemporary independent artists, committed to the pursuit of the latest technology. By aligning itself with the likes of Google and Apple, whose own corporate identities are based on 'trendiness', Pixar ultimately draws attention to corporate Hollywood as outdated and as prioritizing profit margins over content. As one of the largest media conglomerates in the world, Disney falls into this second category, and so signals an apparent friction between the two studios – Pixar as filmmakers creating art, and Disney as businessmen making money.

The well-publicized large, open design of Pixar's central atrium at its Emeryville headquarters, attributed to the company's former CEO Steve Jobs, is a testament to Pixar's own 'trendy' identity. Catmull explains that the building was 'designed to encourage people to mingle, meet, and communicate, to support our filmmaking by enhancing our ability to work together [without] perceived barriers'.[12] In fact, the design and aesthetic of this building is familiar to anyone who has watched featurettes or documentaries that take the viewer inside Pixar. As Richard McCulloch suggests, 'almost every single article, interview or DVD feature that takes audiences or readers behind the scenes at Pixar will either mention the atrium explicitly or use it as a filming location.'[13] Equally familiar is the narrative that Pixar is an animator's paradise; that employees ride around the building on scooters, have access to a 24-hour cereal bar and are encouraged to design and decorate their own workspaces,[14] resulting in an eclectic mix of tiki huts and garden sheds. While these commonly repeated studio narratives have fostered a fan culture, making the studio seemingly accessible to outsiders, ultimately it highlights Pixar's penchant for storytelling, in this case, its own studio narrative.[15] Not only do we see this reflected in the *Toy Story* narrative – the characters belong to an eclectic community, rather than a traditional nuclear family for example – but also, the industrial narrative feeds back into readings of the films themselves, thus the fictional narrative of the *Toy Story* series and the studio narrative of Pixar intertwine. McCulloch states that 'Pixar's screen narratives have frequently come to be understood in relation to the discursive representation of their production context.'[16] In this regard, anecdotal accounts discussed by the filmmakers in the aforementioned paratextual materials,[17] and articles written about the company, inform readings and critical responses to the *Toy Story* films. In exploring some of these common narratives, comparisons can be drawn between the constructed industrial narrative of Pixar and the film narrative of the *Toy Story* trilogy.

Toy Story: *Silicon Valley Meets Hollywood*

When discussing the industrial narrative of Pixar, the studio's relationship with Disney is fundamental. As a hardware company in the late 1980s, Pixar provided Disney with the Pixar Image Computer and the Computer Animation Production System software (CAPS) to digitize Disney's ink and paint and post-production processes. Following months of negotiations in 1991, this working relationship advanced when Disney and Pixar signed a contract for a three-picture deal, beginning with the development of *Toy Story*. However, as Price explains, 'the terms of the thirteen-page contract were lopsided enough that unless the film were a hit on the level of *The Little Mermaid* [Ron Clements and John Musker, 1989],[18] Pixar's earnings from it would be insignificant.'[19] Furthermore, the agreement granted Disney 'ownership of the picture and its characters, while Pixar retained the rights to its propriety technology for 3-D computer-animation'.[20] Although Disney had ultimate control, *Toy Story* was written, developed and produced by Pixar. According to Price, the contract stipulated that 'the production would be an arm's-length relationship in which [Jeffrey] Katzenberg would simply agree with Pixar on a script and a budget and then Pixar would deliver a negative for the finished film when it was done; Disney Feature Animation would have no creative role.'[21] Yet, when the film was released under the Walt Disney Pictures banner in November 1995, Disney's prominent branding confused audiences and critics who believed the film belonged to Disney, while Pixar were merely the technical effort behind the cutting-edge computer graphics. This is apparent in critical responses to *Toy Story* that refer to the film as 'Disney's 1995 animated extravaganza',[22] 'the miraculous new Disney feature',[23] and 'Disney's wondrous, computer-animated adventure [and] one of the finest Disney films ever made'.[24] The role of Pixar is generally limited to 'writer-technicians'[25] and 'computer wizards'.[26] In addition, *Cinefantastique* printed a 20-page article on the making of *Toy Story* that not only refers to the film as 'Disney's *Toy Story*',[27] but also attributes Lasseter's Oscar-winning short film *Tin Toy* (1988) to Disney and, further, introduces Pixar's animators as animation scientists.[28] As I have already indicated, in its early days, the relationship between Disney and Pixar had been tumultuous, and that this is reflected in the narrative of the first two *Toy Story* films. Although the purposeful prominent branding of *Toy Story* as a Disney film, and the film's subsequent success ultimately prompted Pixar's renegotiation of its 1991 contract terms with Disney, the common misconception that *Toy Story* was a Disney film marks the beginning of this off-screen friction.

The relationship between Woody and Buzz in *Toy Story* can be read as an allegory for the popularization of digital animation, pioneered by Pixar, and the subsequent displacement of traditional hand-drawn methods, commonly associated with Disney animation. Consequently, the film also allegorizes the relationship between the two companies. In this regard, Woody as the 'accepted alpha figure'[29] is representative of Disney's long-standing position as leaders within mainstream Hollywood animation. In contrast, Pixar's new digital aesthetic is represented by 'Buzz's technological appeal [that] immediately establishes him as a challenger to Woody's premiership.'[30] This is established during the sequence in which Buzz arrives, and is notable as the inciting incident of the narrative. At the beginning of this sequence, Andy and his friends run upstairs and burst into his bedroom to play with his new toy, a birthday present from his mother. In his excitement, Andy knocks Woody off the bed and plants Buzz's cardboard spaceship where Woody once sat, as though the space ranger toy is now staking claim to the revered top position. Further, the other toys refer to the bed as 'Woody's spot', a certainty in the toy domain. If the bed represents success and leadership, in this instance, Disney's Woody is removed from a position of authority and replaced with Pixar's Buzz. Buzz's own delusional tendencies suggest Pixar's inadvertent challenge to Disney's unrivalled success.

When Woody climbs back on to the bed, a tracking shot highlights Woody's fears and suggests Buzz's superiority over the cowboy doll. In this moment, Buzz appears as an imposing figure, although in actuality he is much smaller than Woody. This is relative to the contrast in the production sizes between Pixar's *Toy Story*, which employed just 110 people,[31] in comparison with Disney's *Pocahontas* (Mike Gabriel and Eric Goldberg, 1995), which was released in the same year and had a staff of over 600.[32] It is also representative of the disparity at this time between Pixar's independent studio and Disney's globally recognized brand. While Buzz seemingly respects Woody as 'local law enforcement', Woody's efforts to explain that the bed is, in fact, his domain goes unnoticed. When the other toys join Woody on the bed, they are immediately impressed with the shiny, new Buzz Lightyear. From the moment Rex asks, 'what does this button do?' referring to Buzz's technological exterior, the leading protagonists are continually compared with each other, highlighting Woody's inferiority. While Buzz's electronic voice box is a 'quality sound system', according to piggy-bank Hamm, Mr. Potato Head notes that Woody's pull-string voice box in comparison 'sounds like a car ran over it'. In a similar way, the success of *Toy Story* set a new standard by which subsequent animated films were measured, resulting in comparisons being drawn between Pixar's and Disney's outputs. This is particularly evident in reviews written about the two studios' releases. For example, *Time Out*'s review of Disney's *Treasure Planet* (Ron Clements and John Musker, 2002) states: 'while Pixar can do no wrong with its cutting edge CGI originals, Disney is falling back on old formulas.'[33] Seventeen years after its release, *Toy Story* was still being used as a measure of quality, with *Entertainment Weekly*'s review of *Wreck-It Ralph* (Rich Moore, 2012), stating: '[the film] doesn't quite carry the heft of *Toy Story*, but there's a lot of heart packed into these zeroes and ones'.[34] Similarly, *The Atlantic* titled its review '*Wreck-It Ralph* Aims for Pixar . . . and Misses'.[35] Furthermore, *Sight and Sound* notes that Pixar's *Brave* (Mark Andrews and Brenda Chapman), released in the same year, 'is nostalgically mindful of the Disney canon'.[36]

Throughout his introductory sequence, Buzz is continually distinguished from the other toys in Andy's room. He is the most advanced among a collection of fairly rudimentary toys. In fact, aside from the remote-controlled RC, whose sole purpose in the film is to serve Woody's agenda, Buzz is the only toy with batteries. The differences between Buzz and the other toys are repeated throughout, from his retractable helmet to his karate chop action and laser. The superficiality of these attributes all reflect early criticisms of CG animation as a novelty, and that hand-drawn animation techniques would never be replaced. As Chris Pallant suggests, up until 1995, Disney had been the 'dominant figure in traditional Western animation for a considerable time. With Pixar's breakthrough, not only was Disney's place within animation challenged, but the industry itself was forced to reconsider its blinkered faith in traditional 2-D animation.'[37] Within the film, Pixar's breakthrough is made explicit during a montage sequence that shows Woody swiftly being replaced by Buzz. Randy Newman's original song, 'Strange Things', is used as an internal emotional device to portray Woody's sensibility as he sees the cowboy-themed paraphernalia in Andy's room being taken over by images of Buzz and outer space. Further still, Andy's bed linen design, signalling who occupies the position of authority within the room, changes from cowboys to Buzz Lightyear.

By the end of the film, Buzz is in a respected leadership position, a status that he carries through into *Toy Story 2* (John Lasseter, 1999) and *Toy Story 3*. In the final sequence, Andy's new room is decorated with both Buzz Lightyear and cowboy posters and drawings, yet his bed linen primarily features Buzz. While there is an apparent partnership, Buzz is clearly the authority figure in Andy's room. This is further evidenced by his conducting of the 'Christmas present' mission from Andy's bed, just as Woody oversaw the opening of Andy's birthday presents at the start of the film, leading to him being replaced by the space ranger toy. Although the differences between old, dependable Woody and new, innovative Buzz are resolved by the end of the film, the differences between the formidable Disney and newcomer Pixar would take another eleven years to reconcile. Further, Woody and Buzz's own reconciliation and the outer space/western hybrid of Andy's bedroom décor, signals the renegotiation of Pixar's 1991 contract with Disney following the success of *Toy Story*. As part of the new contract, Pixar were to receive an equal logo credit, thereby dispelling any further confusion as to the studio's role in the making of its own films. Although this contract is discussed in more detail later, it is pertinent at this point to note that after *Toy Story* there is an effort to market subsequent Disney-Pixar films more clearly as co-productions.

Reiterating Buzz's position of leadership in the film, it is interesting to note that this role, although inadvertently, is afforded to him by Andy. Buzz is now Andy's favourite toy and is therefore given the responsibility of leader among the other toys. In this sense, Andy represents contemporary audiences' preference for Pixar's pioneering computer animation over Disney's hand-drawn aesthetic. During the mid-point of the film, Woody asks Buzz, 'Why would Andy ever want to play with me, when he's got you?' During the early 1990s CG special effects were becoming more sophisticated and more popular in mainstream cinema, and this comment reiterates Pallant's point that Disney's 2-D animation had been challenged by Pixar's digital aesthetic. *Toy Story* proved to be a phenomenal success with audiences for the fledgling studio, becoming the highest-grossing domestic film of 1995. In addition, the film was met with positive critical reviews that commented both on the film's technological accomplishments *and* its narratological achievements. *Variety* said that 'the filmmakers display and dispense with the most dazzling elements of graphics and concentrate on telling an effective story',[38] while *Sight and Sound* commented that 'there is a sweet-natured inventiveness throughout that makes *Toy Story* more than just a demo of the latest techniques.'[39] Further, the *New York Times* called it 'the sweetest and savviest film of the year.'[40] Tom Kemper notes that when the toys finally appreciate their worth, the relationship between Woody and Buzz is cemented, and thus the film 'adheres to the tropes of the buddy narrative, where the two antagonistic partners realise they need one another and have even developed a mutual respect and friendship'.[41] The partnership between Pixar and Disney, however, would take more than one movie to reach that stage.

Toy Story 2: *Merchandise Is King*

In 1997, following *Toy Story*'s phenomenal and unprecedented success, Pixar renegotiated the terms of their contract and signed a co-production agreement that stated Disney would support five more original films from the studio over a ten-year period. The new contract dictated that the two companies would 'equally share the costs, profits and logo credit'.[42] Furthermore, the profit-sharing arrangement exceeded box office revenue to include the sale of related consumer products. During contract negotiations, Disney was explicit that Pixar produce five original features, not sequels, 'thus assuring five sets of new characters for its theme parks and merchandise'.[43] Creating further tensions, the contract with Pixar stipulated that, as Disney held the rights to Pixar's characters, Disney Animation could produce sequels to Pixar's films without the input of Catmull, Lasseter and the studio. Disney proposed *Toy Story 2* as a direct-to-video sequel that 'could be made for less money [and] with lesser talent'.[44] However, fears that the subpar narrative and less-than-favourable reception towards Disney's previous direct-to-video releases would damage the studio's budding reputation, Pixar rewrote and re-pitched the film for theatrical release. The film experienced several production issues, including being rewritten and made in just seven months,[45] where the normal production period could be between three and four years. Although beset with production issues, when *Toy Story 2* was released on 13 November 1999, it was met with an enthusiastic reception with many stating that the film was better than the original. *Variety* said the film was a 'richer, more satisfying film in every respect',[46] and *The Guardian* proclaimed '*Toy Story 2* is not a sequel. It is an upgrade. It is a manufacturer's improvement of staggering ingenuity.'[47] The film surpassed *Toy Story*'s box office figures, grossing over $485 million globally.

At the beginning of *Toy Story 2*, during a sequence in which Andy is playing with his toys, he proclaims, 'You should never mess with the unstoppable duo of Woody and Buzz Lightyear.' With the success of *Toy Story* and *Toy Story 2*, added to the positive reaction to Pixar's second release, *A Bug's Life* (John Lasseter, 1998), the partnership between Disney and Pixar, too, was proving to be an indomitable force within mainstream animation. By 2004, Pixar had produced four out of the five original features stipulated by its 1997 contract with Disney.[48] Including *Toy Story 2*, 'Pixar's five hermetically crafted movies [had] grossed a staggering $2.5 billion at the box office, making it the most successful film studio, picture for picture, of all time.'[49] However, during this period the relationship between Disney and Pixar was affected by tensions surfacing behind the scenes at the Walt Disney Company, particularly between Disney's then CEO, Michael Eisner, and Jeffrey Katzenberg, then head of Walt Disney Studios. In short, following the death of Disney's president and chief operating officer, Frank Wells, in 1994, there was a disagreement between Eisner and Katzenberg concerning the position of president and COO. According to Price, Katzenberg 'understood Eisner to have promised *him* Wells's job if Wells left [but] was shocked to learn from a press release that Eisner would assume Wells's former titles'.[50] Four months after assuring him of his future at Disney, Eisner fired Katzenberg.[51] After leaving Disney, Katzenberg established DreamWorks SKG with Steven Spielberg and David Geffen. The new studio became Disney and Pixar's biggest competitors in the mainstream American animation market. This set off a sequence of events that saw the 'unstoppable duo' of corporate Disney and independent Pixar further diverge.

In many respects, *Toy Story 2* is representative of what has become the accepted narrative of the latter stage of the Eisner era, particularly in relation to the company's dealings with Pixar, and the position held by Disney Animation during this period. First, Disney's corporate identity is represented by Al's Toy Barn and Al's own pursuit of Woody and the Roundup Gang as a commodity. In the film, a great deal of value is placed on Woody – Al initially offers Andy's mother fifty dollars for him (after downplaying his worth), which impresses the other toys. When Woody meets cowgirl Jessie, she informs him he is 'valuable property', and later, we learn the Woody's Roundup collection is *only* valuable if he is included in it. After Al informs the Japanese toy museum he has acquired a Woody doll, they frantically offer to pay him whatever he asks. In addition, the film comments on the vast array of merchandise and Disney-branded products available to consumers, not only via the extensive collection of Woody's Roundup memorabilia, but also in Al's Toy Barn itself, in particular the Buzz Lightyear aisle and the 'new Buzz Lightyear' figure whose only distinguishing feature from the original Buzz is the addition of a utility belt. The negative tone towards the excessive commodification of Woody and Buzz throughout the film is underlined by Al's greed. Plainly presented as the antagonist, Al represents corporate Disney during Eisner's era, and highlights where the two companies diverge. To reiterate a previous point, this is indicative of the conflict between Disney as conglomerate and Pixar as an independent film studio that would 'let nothing – not the technology, not the merchandising possibilities – get in the way of [the] story.'[52]

Second, the film comments on the conventional attitude operating within Disney Animation Studios during this period, which is characterized by *Toy*

Story 2's central themes of nostalgia and preservation. At the beginning of the film, Woody is excited to spend time alone with Andy at cowboy camp, but after Woody's arm is ripped during play, Andy decides to leave the cowboy doll at home. In a nightmare sequence, Woody's fears that he will once again be replaced, or worse, discarded forever, are revealed. Thus, Woody spends most of the film actively resisting change, led by his desire to preserve his way of life, first as Andy's toy, and then as part of an antiquated toy collection. After Woody is stolen by toy collector Al, he discovers he is, in fact, the star of Woody's Roundup, a 1950s marionette western television show. In a sequence in which the former Roundup Gang – Woody, Jessie, horse Bullseye and the Prospector – watch taped episodes of the old TV show that nostalgically 'romanticizes low-tech, anachronistic media',[53] the Prospector explains that the show was cancelled due to public interest in America's well-publicized, and televised, space exploration in the late 1950s and the US moon landing in 1969 displacing interest in western heroes. Here, the narrative mirrors Woody's fate in the original *Toy Story*, which saw him replaced by Buzz, and substantiates the reading of the films as an allegory for the replacement of Disney's traditional animation with Pixar's digital methods. In *Toy Story 2*, however, this allegorical reading is apparent on a much larger scale – a popular, long-running television show, referred to as a 'national phenomenon', much like Disney's internationally recognized brand, is dismissed when its audiences are dazzled by the new. Thus, Woody's Roundup is consigned to a museum, a metaphor for the approach taken by Disney during this period, when the studio was accused of 'merely recycling the ideas of its past and capitalizing on its founder's fame'.[54]

In addition, the narrative is reflective of Disney's resistance to fully embrace and publicize its use of new digital animation techniques, at a time when Pixar's CG films were highly popular and successful. Instead, it opted to market its animated films as wholly traditional and in 2-D, essentially selling nostalgia for its 'classic' aesthetic. This is reflected in *Toy Story 2*'s exploration of self-preservation by living in the 'safety' of the past. Woody's fear that he will be discarded by Andy leads him to stay with the Roundup Gang where he will be 'adored by children for generations' in a museum. However, as Buzz later argues, he will be left to 'watch kids behind glass and never be loved again'. Thus, in an attempt to preserve himself, Woody is in fact resigned to a life that, albeit safe, is also halted. Similarly, Jessie's song reveals that while she 'stayed the same', her owner Emily moved on, leaving Jessie alone. In a montage sequence that reveals Jessie's past, we see her fall from Emily's bed on to the floor. As I have already indicated in my analysis of *Toy Story*, within the toys' domain the bed is a symbol of authority. In each film, Woody and then Jessie are knocked from the bed and replaced with something new. Like Woody, Jessie is led by her self-preservation, choosing a life as 'the yodelling cowgirl' that is secure and free from heartache, but one that will see her suspended in time.

Much like Woody and Jessie, by failing to fully embrace the future – in this case, the increasingly popular CG animation techniques initiated by Pixar and

Toy Story – Disney animation, too, was left behind. By 2004 most of the major Hollywood animation studios, including DreamWorks, had retooled their 2-D animation departments to focus solely on computer-animated films.[55] In addition, a number of other studios, including Blue Sky Studios and Illumination Entertainment,[56] were set up specifically to make CG animated features. Eventually, Disney dismantled its hand-drawn department and moved to concentrate exclusively on digital animation following the disappointing commercial and critical responses to its last 2-D feature *Home on the Range* (Will Finn, 2004). However, by this time, Pixar had gained prominence with a succession of box office hits, and became regarded as the 'new Disney'. In fact, a ten-page article in *Wired* in 2004 noted, 'Pixar hasn't just turned into the new Disney. It has out-Disneyed Disney, becoming the apprentice that schooled the sorcerer.'[57] Adding to the friction of the ever-diverging duo, while Pixar had become an 'animation superpower',[58] Disney struggled to replicate the success of its so-called Renaissance Period (1989–99), and released films that, while stylistically and narratologically experimental,[59] suffered from uncharacteristically low box office figures and largely negative critical reviews.

The final break between the two companies came in 2005 when Eisner announced the formation of Circle 7, 'a new division within Disney Animation . . . created to exercise the studio's right to make sequels to [Pixar's] films without [Pixar's] input'.[60] With *Toy Story 3* in production at Circle 7, direct parallels can be drawn between Al's commodification of Woody and Buzz in *Toy Story 2*, and Eisner's commodification of Pixar during this time. In contrast, Pixar's studio principle, 'story is king' (i.e., the narrative takes precedence over merchandise and franchising possibilities), is reflected in Woody's words to Jessie, 'this is what it's all about, to make a child happy', further highlighting the polarity between Disney's corporate image and Pixar's constructed idealistic, filmmaker-led brand. During contract negotiations to renew the 1997 partnership agreement, Disney and Pixar had a very public falling out. Jobs and Eisner halted contract discussions and announced that Pixar would not be renewing its contract with Disney. That same year Eisner suffered 'the highest no-confidence vote ever against a chief executive of a major company'.[61] In 2005, Eisner was removed as CEO and replaced by Robert Iger, who immediately approached Jobs with the possibility of a Disney-Pixar merge.

Toy Story 3: *'You've Got a Friend in Me'*

On 24 January 2006, Disney announced that it had 'agreed to acquire Pixar for 287.5 million shares of Disney stock, then worth roughly $7.4 billion',[62] a considerable investment, particularly when taking into account that the company later purchased Marvel Studios and Lucasfilm for approximately $4 billion each. In their newly appointed positions as President and Chief Creative Officer of Disney Animation, Catmull and Lasseter shut down the Circle 7 division, halting all non-Pixar-approved sequels. *Toy Story 3* was released four years later, developed solely by Pixar. Like its predecessors, the film, which was released on 12 June 2010, was met with commercial success and critical acclaim. It became the highest-grossing Pixar film ever, receiving over $1 billion in box office revenue. In addition, *Entertainment Weekly* deemed *Toy Story 3* 'the studio's greatest achievement since *The Incredibles* [Brad Bird, 2004], and – just maybe – since the original *Toy Story*',[63] while the *New York Times* noted, 'this film – this whole three-part, 15-year epic – about the adventures of a bunch of silly plastic junk turns out also to be a long, melancholy meditation on loss, impermanence and the noble, stubborn, foolish thing called love.'[64] Furthermore, the *Toy Story* trilogy showcases the development and refinement of Pixar's digital aesthetic across a fifteen-year period, which is particularly evident in the appearance of the series' human characters. Not only do we see Andy's character become more refined, but we also see him grow up across the series.[65] The central narrative to *Toy Story 3* is how the toys deal with Andy's imminent departure for college. In this respect, the film revisits themes of self-preservation and the fear of being replaced or discarded that were explored in the first two films. However, *Toy Story 3* offers a final resolution whereby the toys choose to move on and thus, move forward.

The final film in the trilogy, then, is reflective of the coming together of, and the reconciliation between, Disney and Pixar, and the post-acquisition period. In fact, while the film deals with issues of abandonment and separation, the narrative is driven by the toys' desire to be together. In *Toy Story*, Woody is *alone* at the top as Andy's favourite, until Buzz replaces him, and they spend the film competing with one another. Although they are allies in *Toy Story 2*, they are separated from each other for most of the film and Woody initially decides *not* to go home with Buzz and the other toys, instead choosing to live *alone* in a display cabinet. By *Toy Story 3*, Woody finally realizes that, as Andy is growing up, it is more important for the toys to stick together, whether in the attic, or at Sunnyside, or at the city dump as they face their ultimate fear – death. The narrative arc and Woody's personal journey throughout the trilogy are indicative of the relationship between Pixar and Disney. In the first instance, Disney was *alone* as the top animation studio, until Pixar disrupted the status quo. Next, while Pixar's new digital aesthetic was popularizing CG animation, Disney was hesitant to fully embrace it opting instead to continue its 2-D output. Finally, under Iger's new leadership, the two companies came together to form a Disney-Pixar alliance. In fact, Iger recounts that he considered the possibility of a merge during the opening parade of Disneyland in Hong Kong: 'I realized there wasn't a character in the parade that had come from a Disney animated film in the last ten years except for Pixar.'[66] *Toy Story 3*, then, acknowledges the enduring legacy of Pixar's characters and the amalgamation of the two studios, under the Disney banner.

The film's predominant theme of togetherness, indicative of the Disney-Pixar merger, is presented through exchanges between the characters. At the start of the film the toys begin preparing for 'attic mode' after a failed attempt to get the now grown-up Andy to play with them. Buzz says to Woody, 'we'll always have each other', to which Woody replies, 'for infinity and beyond'. Later, when Woody returns to Sunnyside to rescue his friends he says, 'it was my fault for leaving you guys. From now on, we stick together'. This statement reconciles the relationship between Pixar and Disney pre- and post-acquisition. It both acknowledges Disney's part in halting contract negotiations in 2005, during the latter period of Eisner's leadership, while also cementing the future of Pixar as part of the Disney family under Iger. By the end of the film, Woody and Buzz have once again joined forces, and adapted the rules to suit their co-existence in this new world as Bonnie's toys. *Toy Story 3* reconciles the differences between Woody and Buzz and there is a sense of harmony at the end of the film, but also a chance to move forward. In this final instalment, the original *Toy Story* characters are incorporated into Bonnie's room and her group of toys, indicative of Iger's Disney – a far more positive corporate image than Al's Toy Barn – an allegory for the Disney–Pixar merge and of Pixar as part of the larger Disney corporation. When Andy passes his toys to Bonnie, this reflects the literal exchange of the franchise from *Toy Story*'s creators, Pixar as an independent studio, to the new, larger Disney corporation, along with the possibility of new franchises and new films within the world of *Toy Story*. The final song over the closing credits, 'We Belong Together', further emphasizes the film's theme of togetherness, and underlines the Disney–Pixar merge as a positive business decision.

Conclusion

The long-established, publicized and reiterated importance that Pixar places on narrative highlights the parallels between the studio's own constructed narrative and the narrative of its films. In particular, the *Toy Story* trilogy reflects the industrial narrative of the studio and its relationship with Disney. These stories, which evolved from paratextual materials produced by the studio, extend to articles and texts exploring Pixar's creative culture and permeate critical responses to the studio's films. In this regard, Pixar's self-promoted reputation as the pioneers of CG animation and as an artist-led studio has become central to understanding and analysing the studio's films. The *Toy Story* trilogy tracks fifteen years of aesthetic and technological development, which has progressed from the clean, plastic-look, characteristic of the medium's early years, to a more expressive and textured aesthetic that is recognizable in Pixar's later films. Therefore, the *Toy Story* films exemplify the coherence between art and technology, a principle that is intrinsic to the foundations on which the company was founded. Thus, the *Toy Story* trilogy can be read as an allegory for the apparent popularization of Pixar's digital animation and the subsequent displacement of Disney's hand-drawn techniques, and further, the industrial narrative and relationship between Disney and Pixar. By the end of *Toy Story 3*, Woody, Buzz and Andy's remaining toys have become a part of a much larger universe alongside Bonnie's toys. In addition, the subsequent *Toy Story Toons* Series (2011–12) and television shorts, *Toy Story of Terror!* (Angus Maclane, 2013) and *Toy Story That Time Forgot* (Steve Purcell, 2014), portray the original cast as partners at best, and supporting characters at worst, to a new collection of toy characters. The *Toy Story* universe has been expanded, reflecting Pixar's new place in mainstream Hollywood animation as a subsidiary of the Walt Disney Company.

Notes

1 See, among others, Chris Pallant, *Demystifying Disney: A History of Disney Feature Animation.* (London: Continuum, 2011), pp. 126–27; Colleen Montgomery, 'Woody's Roundup and WALL-E's Wunderkammer: Technophilia and Nostalgia in Pixar Animation', *Animation Studies*, no. 6. (2011), pp. 7–13.

2 Linda Ruth Williams, '*Toy Story*', in Linda Ruth Williams and Michael Hammond (eds), *Contemporary American Cinema* (Berkshire: Open University Press, 2006), pp. 369–75 (p. 369).

3 Ed Catmull, *Creativity, Inc.: Overcoming the Unseen Forces That Stand in the Way of True Inspiration* (London: Bantam Press, 2014), p. 66.

4 David A. Price, *The Pixar Touch: The Making of a Company* (New York: Vintage Books, 2009), pp. 28–29; Karen Paik, *To Infinity and Beyond! The Story of Pixar Animation Studios* (London: Virgin Books, 2007), p. 19.

5 Angus Finney and Eugenio Triana, *Film Business: A Market Guide Beyond Hollywood*, 2nd ed. (London and New York: Routledge, 2015), p. 204.

6 Ibid., p. 205.

7 Pixar University is the company's in-house training department and offers free classes to Pixar staff. Since its inception in 1996, the programme has offered classes on 'sculpting, painting, acting, programming, design and colour theory [and] ballet'; see, among others, Catmull, *Creativity, Inc.*, p. 220.

8 Finney, *Film Business*, pp. 205–06.

9 Catmull, *Creativity, Inc.*, p. 204.

10 Ibid.

11 Ibid., pp. 261–62; Price, *The Pixar Touch*, p. 157.

12 Catmull, *Creativity, Inc.*, pp. 302–03.

13 Richard McCulloch, 'Whistle While You Work: Branding, Critical Reception and Pixar's Production Culture', in Roberta Pearson and Anthony N. Smith (eds), *Storytelling in the Media Convergence Age: Exploring Screen Narratives* (Hampshire: Palgrave MacMillan, 2015), pp. 174–89 (p. 181).

14 Although Pixar appears to promote and encourage this kind of individual creative expression, it is worth noting that in some cases these workspaces are only semi-permanent, as there is a staff turnover at the end of each feature film production cycle.

15 While it is my aim to highlight that these constructed studio narratives have been repeated and accepted as fact since the company formed in 1986, and particularly since the completion of the studio's Emeryville building in 2000, I note it only to

draw attention to the function of narrative and story from an industrial context. For a more in-depth analysis of Pixar's production culture and the branding of the workplace, see McCulloch, 'Whistle While You Work: Branding, Critical Reception and Pixar's Production Culture'.

16 McCulloch, 'Whistle While You Work', p. 175.

17 Paratextual materials refer to material produced or endorsed by the company, in addition to the film itself. This includes documentary films, DVD extras and bonus features, and so on.

18 *The Little Mermaid* grossed over $200 million globally and received a largely positive critical response. The film is widely credited as marking the beginning of Disney Animation's 'Renaissance' era.

19 Price, *The Pixar Touch*, p. 123.

20 Tom Kemper, *Toy Story: A Critical Reading* (London: BFI, 2015), p. 33.

21 Price, *The Pixar Touch*, p. 118.

22 Caroline Westbrook, '*Toy Story* Review'. *Empire*, 1 January 2000. http://www.empireonline.com/movies/toy-story/review/ (accessed 15 April 2016).

23 Owen Gleiberman, '*Toy Story*', *Entertainment Weekly*, 24 November 1995. http://www.ew.com/article/1995/11/24/toy-story (accessed 15 April 2016).

24 James Delingpole, '*Toy Story*, Review', *The Telegraph*, 23 December 2013. http://www.telegraph.co.uk/culture/film/filmreviews/10514520/Toy-Story-review.html (accessed 15 April 2016).

25 Gleiberman, '*Toy Story*'.

26 Westbrook, '*Toy Story* Review'.

27 Frederick Clarke, 'Contents', *Cinefantastique*, vol. 27, no. 2 (1995): p. 3.

28 Lawrence French, '*Toy Story*: Walt Disney and Pixar Team Up to Launch the First Computer-Animated Movie', *Cinefantastique*, vol. 27, no. 2 (1995): 17–37 (p. 17).

29 Pallant, *Demystifying Disney*, p. 127.

30 Ibid.

31 Price, *The Pixar Touch*, p. 133.

32 'The Making of *Pocahontas*', *Pocahontas* Special Features. Blu-ray. Walt Disney Studios Home Entertainment. 2012.

33 '*Treasure Planet*', *Time Out*, 23 June 2006. http://www.timeout.com/us/film/treasure-planet (accessed 22 May 2016).

34 Keith Staskiewicz, 'Movies: *Wreck-It Ralph*', *Entertainment Weekly*, 9 November 2012. http://www.ew.com/article/2012/11/09/wreck-it-ralph (accessed 22 May 2016).

35 Christopher Orr, '*Wreck-It Ralph* Aims for Pixar . . . and Misses', *The Atlantic*, 2 November 2012. http://www.theatlantic.com/entertainment/archive/2012/11/wreck-it-ralph-aims-for-pixar-and-misses/264439/ (accessed 22 May 2016).

36 Thirza Wakefield, 'Review: *Brave*', *Sight and Sound*, vol. 22, no. 9 (2012): p. 97.

37 Pallant, *Demystifying Disney*, p. 127.

38 Leonard Klady, 'Review: *Toy Story*', *Variety*, 20 November 1995. http://variety.com/1995/film/reviews/toy-story-2-1200443736/ (accessed 15 May 2016).

39 Leslie Felperin, '*Toy Story*', *Sight and Sound*, vol. 6, no. 3 (1996): 51–52.

40 Janet Maslin, 'Film Review: There's a New Toy in the House. Uh-Oh', *The New York Times*, 22 November 1995. http://www.nytimes.com/movie/review?res=9905EEDA1339F931A15752C1A963958260 (accessed 15 May 2016).

41 Kemper, *Toy Story*, p. 89.

42 Steve Lohr, 'Disney in 10-Year, 5-Film Deal with Pixar', *The New York Times*, 25 February 1997. http://www.nytimes.com/1997/02/25/business/disney-in-10-year-5-film-deal-with-pixar.html?_r=0 (accessed 18 May 2015).
43 Price, *The Pixar Touch*, p. 179.
44 Ibid., p. 175.
45 Catmull, *Creativity, Inc.*, p. 73.
46 Todd McCarthy, 'Review: *Toy Story 2*', *Variety*, 17 November 1999. http://variety.com/1999/film/reviews/toy-story-2-2-1117759786/ (accessed 18 May 2015).
47 Peter Bradshaw, '*Toy Story 2*', *The Guardian*, 4 February 2000. http://www.theguardian.com/film/2000/feb/04/6 (accessed 4 February 2000).
48 Pixar had released five films during this period, including *Toy Story 2*. The four original features released after the 1997 contract were *A Bug's Life*, *Monsters, Inc.* (Pete Docter, 2001), *Finding Nemo* (Andrew Stanton, 2003) and *The Incredibles* (Brad Bird, 2004).
49 Austin Bunn, 'Welcome to Planet Pixar: How the Pixel-Packing Upstart Became an Animation Superpower and Left Disney in the Dust', *Wired*, vol. 12, no. 6 (2004): 126–33 (p. 130).
50 Price, *The Pixar Touch*, p. 168.
51 Ibid., p. 169.
52 Catmull, *Creativity, Inc.*, p. 66.
53 Montgomery, 'Woody's Roundup and WALL-E's Wunderkammer', p. 9.
54 Price, *The Pixar Touch*, p. 251.
55 Montgomery, 'Woody's Roundup and WALL-E's Wunderkammer', p. 7.
56 20th Century Fox-owned Blue Sky Studios produced the likes of *Ice Age* (Mike Thurmeier, 2002), *Robots* (Chris Wedge, 2005) and *Rio* (Carlos Saldanha, 2011). Illumination Entertainment is owned by Universal Studios and is known for *Despicable Me* (Pierre Coffin and Chris Renaud, 2010), *Despicable Me 2* (Pierre Coffin and Chris Renaud, 2013) and *Minions* (Kyle Balda and Pierre Coffin, 2015).
57 Bunn, 'Welcome to Planet Pixar', p. 130.
58 Ibid., p. 126.
59 Pallant, *Demystifying Disney*, p. 111.
60 Catmull, *Creativity, Inc.*, p. 243.
61 Price, *The Pixar Touch*, p. 240.
62 Ibid., p. 253.
63 Owen Gleiberman, '*Toy Story 3*', *Entertainment Weekly*, 31 July 2012. http://ew.com/article/2012/07/31/toy-story-3-5/ (accessed 18 May 2015).
64 A. O. Scott, 'Voyage to the Bottom of the Day Care Center', *The New York Times*, 17 June 2010. http://www.nytimes.com/2010/06/18/movies/18toy.html (accessed 18 May 2015).
65 Adding further poignancy to this point, John Morris was hired to reprise his role as Andy after voicing the character in *Toy Story* and *Toy Story 2*.
66 Robert Iger quoted in Price, *The Pixar Touch*, p. 252.

Chapter 13

AN INTERVIEW WITH STEVE SEGAL

Noel Brown

Production histories of *Toy Story* tend to focus on 'big names' such as John Lasseter and Pete Docter. In this book, we also want to convey a sense of the animator's place in the making of the film and their perspective on what happened, along with their professional journey leading up to that point. Steve Segal was born in Richmond, Virginia, in 1949. He made his first animated films as a high school student before studying Art at Virginia Commonwealth University, where he continued to produce award-winning, independent animated shorts. After graduating, Segal opened a traditional animation studio in Richmond, making commercials and educational films for ten years. After completing the cult animated film *Futuropolis* (1984), which he co-directed with Phil Trumbo, Segal moved to Hollywood and became interested in computer animation. In addition to producing his own computer-generated (CG) animated short, *Dance of the Stumblers* (1987), his many professional credits include contributing special effects to *The Brave Little Toaster* (Jerry Rees, 1987), and animation for *Pee-wee's Playhouse* (1986–91) and numerous other feature films and television shows. During the 1990s, he worked at Pixar, where he produced animated shots for *Toy Story* and *A Bug's Life* (John Lasseter, 1998), and the short film *Geri's Game* (Jan Pinkava, 1997). He has taught animation at Virginia Commonwealth University, Cal Arts, the San Francisco Academy of Art University and California College of the Arts.

Noel Brown: To begin with, would you like to tell us how you became interested in animation in the first place?

Steve Segal: Well, I'm always mystified why everyone isn't interested in animation, because I don't know any kid that didn't watch cartoons. I guess the idea that you could make them – I remember in my Sabbath School class, in Fourth Grade, I made flip-books, and it was probably the most boring of all my classes. I think I saw it on the Disney show. I was five-years-old when Disney started his Sunday show, and about a year later started the Mickey Mouse Club. And they would occasionally show the process, and on Walter Lantz's show [*The Woody Woodpecker Show*, 1957–58], he would show it quite frequently – maybe every other week he would go behind the scenes on 'how do you write a story', 'how do you design a character', 'how do you animate'. I started fooling around making flip-books and animating my G.I. Joes, and whatever I had. I made a film, I guess when I was about 17 or 18, a minute-and-a-half film – it's on YouTube – called *Evolution* [1968]. It was just drawn on paper with watercolour, and it shows waves, and an amoeba morphing into a paramecium, then a fish, then an amphibian, then a reptile, and one animal kind of resembles the other. I believe in Darwin's Theory of Evolution, so I have an animal walking up, then a squirrel jumps up on two legs and becomes a chimpanzee, then becomes a human, and then his head pops off and it's a robot. I made one more film when I was still in high school. *Evolution* was silent (although a friend put sound on it, so the one on YouTube has sound), and then I decided I would try a sound film. So I got a song that was popular at the time called 'A Walk in the Black Forest' by Horst Jankowski, and I made a little guy walking. It's three minutes or so, and I think it won first place in the Super 8 Film Festival.

NB: That must've been a proud moment.

SS: It certainly was. Then my thesis project at school – I worked on it for three years – it was my first time working on 16mm. And that won first place at the International Independent Film Festival. So I had a couple of good credits early on. This was kind of avant-garde. *A Walk in the Black Forest* [1969] was kind of inspired by *Fantasia* [Samuel Armstrong et al., 1940] . . . Not so much *Fantasia* but the later Disney musicals like *Make Mine Music* [Jack Kinney et al., 1946] and *Melody Time* [Kinney et al., 1948]. I love those, because they're sort of abstract. *Pandora's Box* [1972], the 16mm film, had a lot of special effects. It was pretty much just stream of consciousness. It's 7½ minutes.

NB: And obviously you would have had very limited resources?

SS: Well, I had my own camera, and I built an animation stand out of wood. It was crude. I remember my first film: I didn't know anything, so I punched the drawings with a hand punch and put them in a loose-leaf notebook and just flipped the pages, so they kind of wiggle around, but it didn't matter. And then I learned about actual animation pegs and peg bars, so I started using that. I used cels in *A Walk in the Black Forest* and *Pandora's Box*.

NB: So even though resources were limited, you were still able to make films. I suppose at that time, it was a case of making a virtue out of necessity?

SS: It was a definite advantage. Today it's relatively easy to make this stuff – some of the effects you could do in a few minutes. But there was a lot less competition, because it took a lot of time, a lot of patience. You've got reams of paper, and you've got to punch them, and now you can just draw on a tablet. So it's a little harder to cut through the clutter now.

NB: Tell us about the films you produced while you were at Virginia.

SS: After *Pandora's Box* I did a film called *Russian Rooster* [1974], which won a prize at the Nashville Film Festival. I liked the music of Rimsky-Korsakov, so I got a recording of 'Le coq d'or', and I did a drawing on film of these hunters chasing a bird. It was a really simple story, very simple style. It was maybe a little more elaborate drawing-wise than [Norman] McLaren. McLaren would do these very simple drawings and then optically print colours in it. I was drawing on the frame – I didn't have access to an optical printer, so I just coloured it using Dr. Martin's dye. Actually, no: I used magic markers. I coloured the whole thing with permanent markers. And it looked great when I was looking at it – I would see the colour be very rich – but then when it was projected it was very washed out. I was very disappointed. So I found out, for the next film about Dr. Martin's dyes. Then I got the colour I wanted. The following year, *Red Ball Express* [1975], which was done to bluegrass music . . . I actually started a piece, the 'Little' Fugue by Bach, and I probably animated a minute. I had a recording on a synthesiser and animated these abstract shapes, and after about a minute I looked at it and thought, 'this is kind of boring', and scrapped it. And I'm still amazed that I would do that. I don't think I gave it a second thought. I didn't go, 'Oh, I worked on that for five months' – or probably two months – I just went, 'Just start over'. So the next day I just got another recording, 'Orange

Blossom Special'. At that time, the movie *Deliverance* [John Boorman, 1972] was popular, and it had duelling banjos. In Virginia, there was a lot of that music. I drew it directly on to film, and painted it with Dr. Martin's dye. I wanted to do something more abstract – *Russian Rooster* was almost strictly figurative.

NB: At this point, there was a commercial niche animating for advertisements, and this is how you made a living for a while.

SS: In film class I met Phil Trumbo, and a bunch of other people were working on a film that was inspired by Red Grooms's film, *Fat Feet* [1966]. Red Grooms is a sculptor who builds these sort of cartoon environments, but he also made pixilated films, as did McLaren. I liked that, because the environment was all a cartoon. It was a giant drawing. In one scene I remember, a real live person dressed in a cartoon suit walks up to this drawing of a revolving door, and the moment he touches the revolving door, he becomes a life-size drawing. And I went: 'That's genius!' So Phil and his team decided to do something inspired by Red Grooms, and I said, 'That's for me'. Our film was called *Monster Monster* [1972], about this monster that attacks a beauty salon. And you never see the monster, you just see these giant monster feet. It's silly nonsense, and it was great fun to do and we could let our imagination run wild. Based on that, when I graduated – that was my senior year – Phil and I started working together, and we got a commercial.

Robbin Thompson, who had done a couple of songs in Virginia, had written a jingle for Mr. Moe Subs, a sub shop, and they wanted something like *Monster Monster*. So we built a set. The recording studio that I was associated with was going to rep[resent] us, because they were already recording jingles, but they didn't have a film department. I became their film department. They had a big space on the second floor, and we built a set of this sandwich shop. Then we got our friends from college to be in the film. So it was just this silly, crazy thing of people dressed in cartoon suits in black and white except for the food. The food's in colour. So that got on the air – and how exciting is that? And the first response: Oh my god, the colour looked terrible. What have they done? They've ruined it! Then we found out,

NTSC means 'Never The Same Colour'! It didn't look good, it didn't sound good. Now, of course, everything's much better, because it's digital, and high definition is much more precise. We also lost a lot on the edges. We were learning. This is stuff that wasn't relayed to us: that you lose like 20 per cent on the edge of the picture.

But we made it, and I think on the strength of that, they had three jingles for rules of the road, so we did a group of three super-cheap, like $3,000 each. But we had a studio going, and we did cel animation, and we hired people from school. That was awesome: we had an actual cel animation studio, very unlike working in pixilation where you're just shooting live. We were animating on paper, doing a minute-and-a-half of animation. That went well: the Highway Safety Commission liked those, and then when they passed a new law that said you can do right turns on a red light we introduced that. Then we got connected with the American Forest Institute, and did a series of commercials with them. I think those are the best things we did. We did a lot of that kind of stuff. Early on we said we'll never advertise cigarettes. I was really against smoking. Luckily we were never put to the test. Even though Virginia is a big supporter of tobacco; the Philip Morris factory is right there. Nobody ever asked us to do that. 'Here's $30,000: would you like to make a cigarette commercial?!'

NB: So, to a large degree, the animation you made was dictated by the demands of your clients.

SS: Absolutely. I mean, they did allow us a lot of creativity. We didn't work through agencies. They would come to us and say: Here's the message. We rarely sold a product. So we did that for about 10 years, 15 years. Phil and I really wanted to take what we had learned and apply it to a bigger film. So we thought we'd make a longer film. I'd gotten a grant from the Nashville Film Festival – at that time, it was called the Sinking Creek Film Festival – to make another film. For *Red Ball Express* I got, I think, $5,000, something like that. And so we made a film. We always planned it to be a 20 or 30 minute film. And we did about the first eight minutes that we presented the following year. It went over very well. We hadn't done the sound yet. We created the sound live. Phil and I had microphones and we performed all the voices and the sound effects.

And even the music, because we hadn't done the sound mix yet. But we had animation on there – there was a lot of pixilation. It was similar to *Monster Monster*. This was *Futuropolis* [1984]. A lot of special effects, really going crazy with everything we could think of. After that first year, we said 'Let's finish the film'. Then we worked on it for another eight years. It took us a total of nine years. In fact, we started it before the first *Star Wars* [George Lucas, 1977] movie. We didn't finish it until after the third film in the trilogy! People say 'You must've been inspired by *Star Wars*', but no, we started it about a year before. We were really inspired by *Forbidden Planet* [Fred M. Wilcox, 1956], *The Time Machine* [George Pal, 1960], and these great old science-fiction films of the fifties, and figured it's time for a renaissance. We could see it coming; so could Steven Spielberg, so could George Lucas, James Cameron. Everyone could see it coming. They grew up on George Pal and Ray Harryhausen.

So yeah, we worked on that film between commercials. Phil and I would get together, we'd write, we'd do it on the weekends whenever we had any time. And it was also good because we had this staff. With these commercials, you'd get a commercial, and then you'd have some time off. And so I had done a bunch of animation drawings, and I would hand it to the staff and say, 'Ok, we'll pay you half of your regular rate, but, you know, you're working on an independent film'. Otherwise you'd get laid off. So they were happy to be involved in it. They knew we weren't making any money on it. I figure I put about $30,000 of my own money into it. But we got the thing finished, and showed it at the Los Angeles Animation Celebration. Actually, I sent it to every festival and got rejected. And it got rejected without anyone ever looking at it. At that time, they had a strict 30-minute limit, and our film was 38 minutes. And I said, 'Just watch the first 30 minutes and then turn it off'. And they said 'No, we can't do that'. They said, 'If your film is that long, it's going to dominate, and we've got a bunch of films that are five minutes long'. Then if you have a film that's over 30 minutes, it just kind of takes over. My plan was to do what I'd done to all my other films: send it to festivals and get accepted. I was really blasé about that. I wish I had the money to go: I got accepted at Zagreb, and I didn't go; I wish I had.

So, I was pretty frustrated and started studying computer graphics. Then people told me there's a big computer graphics conference called SIGGRAPH in Minneapolis. I knew there was a guy in Minneapolis who had a fanzine devoted to animation called *Mindrot*, so I wrote to him and said I've got this science-fiction film, and I'd like to show it. He said 'Sure, we'll set up a screening'. So he set up a screening at the Uptown Theatre in Minneapolis. Also – this is a great story – I didn't have the money to go to SIGGRAPH. So I just went in with a crowd. Well, I'd wait for like a coffee break when everyone goes back in at the same time. After about 45 minutes there'd be a coffee break and they'd go out into the lobby, and then I would get with a crowd of people and go in. That's how I attended SIGGRAPH with no money.

I remember that my friend Brad deGraf, who later formed deGraf/Wahrman, one of the pioneering computer graphic companies, was looking in the [conference] brochure and said, 'Hey, Steve, look at this: all attendees can get a projector and a room'. I said, 'I'm not an attendee!' He said, 'Well, you should try'. I went over there; they never checked to see my credentials or anything. I said, 'Can I get a projector and a room?' They said 'Sure'. So I put up these posters around SIGGRAPH. And *Futuropolis* is not a computer-animated film. It's pixilation and cel animation. The very end has some computer graphics with a programme that I wrote in BASIC, done on a Commodore 64. But, for the most part, it's traditional. So I put up these posters, and I went to a lecture by Bill Kroyer on character animation – one of the ones I snuck in on – and he mentioned John Lasseter. And I had heard of John Lasseter, and I asked, 'Do you know where I could meet him?' And he said, 'He's sitting right over there'. He was talking to Chris Wedge. I just went up and introduced myself to the two of them. Neither one of them were any better known than I was. John Lasseter, who became the king of animation, and is the current-day Walt Disney, and Chris Wedge, founder of Blue Sky [producer of the *Ice Age* and *Rio* series]. And I said, 'Hey, I've got a movie – you should come and see it'. And both came to see my movie. So my introduction to John Lasseter was him seeing my 38-minute science-fiction film, which he liked.

Then I showed it at the theatre, which was open to the public, probably a couple of days later, and not connected with SIGGRAPH. And the projectionist said, 'That's a cool film', and they contacted the chain in LA and said 'We've got this film here – it's pretty interesting'. So Terry Thoren from Landmark put together a theatrical package called '*Futuropolis* and Timeless Tales of Fantasy', with lots of science-fiction shorts, and got me interviewed with Terry Gross on *Fresh Air*. By that time I had made my first computer-animated film. I got my Amiga computer and had a programme called Aegis Animator, and made *Dance of the Stumblers* [1987]. It probably took a couple of years to get this theatrical package off the ground. Terry Thoren did another theatrical package called 'Classics of Computer Animation', and *Dance of the Stumblers* was in that package. So that was pretty cool: If I tell people I was interviewed by Terry Gross, they go 'What? Are you actually important?' The distributor gave me money upfront. But people don't make [serious] money on these films. John Lasseter didn't make money with his short films. You do it for the prestige. So, we got the film in theatres. I could actually see it in the *Variety* listings. That was pretty cool – you open up *Variety* and look at the top 50, and down there in the upper forties is *Futuropolis*. We made $30,000 this week: Wow!

NB: And it did become something of a cult success.

SS: I've run into people who've seen it . . . That's harder and harder to do these days. But yeah, I [recently] went to the Animation Festival, and nobody had heard of me, nobody had heard of any of my films. But, you know, that's from another decade. I took 20 years off to raise two kids. So yeah, *Dance of the Stumblers* – that got shown at SIGGRAPH. In 1987 it had to be one of the most low-tech films at that conference. Everything else came from universities or big studios. It was the only film from an independent. And it was four minutes long. Usually these pieces are little 15-second tests. So I had a four-minute film, done to Rimsky-Korsakov music. I think it's my best film.

I submitted it to the Ottawa Festival, which I had been regularly attending, and I know the festival director. And he said he was in a screening room when that was being screened for consideration, and one of the judges loved that piece of music – 'The Snow Queen' – so they said, 'I love this music: don't show me this film. I don't want my imagery ruined. Turn the film off!' And the other judges said, 'Oh, Ok'. And they forget that you work for a year on it, and then on a whim, 'We're gonna crush your dreams. We did that last time with your 38-minute thing, 'cause we decided [even though] it's an art form it's got to fit in a perfect box. And now we're going to crush your dreams because I like this piece of music, and I don't think you should animate to that piece of music'. And you can tell, I'm still mad about that. That still pisses me off. And again, this is pre-video. This is 1987. You had to submit on film. So you've got this $100 thing, let me make 10 prints, because there's a price break at 10. So there's $1000 invested. And then these are big, heavy things, so you put them in the mail, and you send it to Yugoslavia. Well, that's $35 right there. Then you're waiting to get it back so you can send it to the next festival. Now you post it one time to one site and it goes everywhere. But then – and again, the competition is less. You've got to invest a lot. You've got to really want to do it. Actually, *Futuropolis* was probably more like $1000 – it was a lot of money to make a 16mm print. I think I only made four prints. So I couldn't send it to very many festivals.

After *Dance of the Stumblers*, I got married and had kids, and I started working regular. Because, you know, you've got mouths to feed. So, I started teaching full-time. Then I got hired full-time at Pixar, which was a goal. I really wanted the credential of saying, you know, 'Hey, I worked in a real studio'. Because I have great admiration for the artists who work at Disney. So, I applied at Disney and didn't get in, but I did get in to Pixar.

NB: So, how did that come about?

SS: Well, I was living in LA, and I had already made contact with John Lasseter. In fact, I still remember that I had seen him at SIGGRAPH, and he had seen my film, and a month later I was at the Ottawa Festival. And he's walking down the road, by himself, and I'm walking the other way, and he says 'Steve!' and opens his arms wide. He's a very warm person. And I thought: 'John Lasseter remembers me?!' So he gave me a big hug and asks, 'How are you doing, how's your films?' So I go, 'You know, I've read that you've got a deal to make a film with Disney, and I'd really love to work on it'. He says, 'We'll keep you in mind – we're not hiring at this time, but we'll keep you in mind'. And I think I had my reel on a DVD, so I gave him the reel. Then John called me in person and said, 'Ok, we're ready to staff up, so send your latest reel'. So I went that day and sent my DVD, but then didn't hear back – didn't hear anything. I thought, 'I guess I wasn't good enough'. My reel had arrived at roughly the same time that Disney had shut down production [on *Toy Story*]. So I was taking it very personally, but it had nothing to do with me.

As it happened, I was taking part in a summer arts programme up in northern California. You can't get there directly – I was living in LA, so I flew to San Francisco and thought, as long as I'm in San Francisco, I'll go see my friend Joe Ranft. We'd worked together on *Brave Little Toaster*. So yeah, I got a job on *Brave Little Toaster* because one of the judges at the LA Celebration had seen my film and knew I made it with sort of hand-made equipment. And he said, 'We're going to be making this film in Taiwan, and the equipment's not Disney standard'. Which was true; it was pretty funky. So they put me in charge of the camera department. Basically, anything you see photographed, any camera moves, it's stuff that I did. And I did the special effects. I didn't do much animation. So that was a good credential. I met Jerry Rees, who's still doing stuff for Disney, and Kevin Lima, who directed *Tarzan* [Kevin Lima and Chris Buck, 1999] and *Enchanted* [Kevin Lima, 2007]. A lot of great people. Primarily Joe Ranft, the head of story. We were both big fans of John Lasseter, and we both wanted to work at Pixar. And so Joe got me an interview at Disney. So he was there, and I went to work on *The Little Mermaid* [Ron Clements and John Musker, 1989]. I went through seven interviews, so they were seriously considering me. This was to head up the computer animation on *Little Mermaid*. They picked someone that was already part of their staff, which makes sense to me. I knew how to do some basic stuff in computers . . . But I did write a three-page treatment on what I thought you could do using a computer, and the first thing I said was, 'You should do the whole thing on computer. Don't even use cels'. I knew that the technology was there.

NB: So did that seem to you that a fully CG-animated film was a logical evolution of the form?

SS: Yeah, and I was one film too soon. *Little Mermaid* was the last thing they did using cels. In fact, at the time, some technicians at Pixar were writing their paint system [CAPS]. I had used a paint system on the Amiga, so I knew what you could do with it, that you could do colour fills and compositing. But I was doing stuff in low-res, and I was doing individual frames. But I remember talking about rendering a ship in three-dimensions, and doing light filtering from water down, and how a computer can illuminate shapes by delineating edges, things that are hard to do in hand-drawn. So I went from there to doing this presentation for the summer arts programme, had to stop in San Francisco and went to see Joe [Ranft] at Pixar. And he showed me the army man sequence, and I thought, 'Oh man, this thing's gonna be a big hit'. I said, 'Look, I know you're not interested – I've already sent two reels and heard nothing – but here's my latest reel'. So, I gave him the reel, and taught my classes, and went back home and couple of days later I got a call from [*Toy Story* producer] Ralph [Guggenheim], and he said 'We want to hire you'. And I said, 'Ok, how much are you offering?' And he said, 'How much do you want?' I said, 'Well, here's how much I get now'. He said, 'Ok, we'll pay you that'. It was probably really low, but, you know, *Toy Story* looks good on your résumé. They paid for me to move up to Northern California.

NB: Was it the case, do you think, that your expertise in computer animation was one of the factors in getting you hired?

SS: Well, that was a small . . . They don't really care if you have computer expertise. I'm sure that was a point, [but] they were really looking for animators. I was probably more of a self-starter than most, because I had made a bunch of films, so I think they saw that as a plus.

NB: Do you think that the skills required for computer animation are markedly different from those required for cel animation?

SS: Most animators see the action in their brain, and then use whatever means to get it on the screen. Most hand animators seem to be able to make the transition. There are a few who hate the computer getting in the way and just want to put pencil to paper. It's a disconnect – especially with some stop-motion animators, since they work straight ahead [animating shot-by-shot in a linear fashion], with no chance to refine. It's sort of a Zen approach. But there are lots of those animators who made the transition well.

NB: What stage had the production reached by the time you came aboard?

SS: It was about three-quarters written, and most of the models had been built and rigged – although they did make some improvements to the two main characters. Only the army man sequence had been animated, and a few test shots with Buzz and Woody.

NB: Which scenes did you end up working on?

SS: On *Toy Story*, I animated about 30 shots. The biggest shot was all the mutant toys surrounding Sid. I got a good response when Buzz puts on his seatbelt, and a laugh when Potato Head gets smacked in the back of the truck. I also animated the only kiss in the movie: Bo Peep grabs Woody and kisses him. And some decent lines, an alien in the crane game: 'I have been chosen'; Potato Head blocked by other toys, 'I can't see a thing'; Slinky Dog after being stretched out, 'I shoulda held on longer'. You can see some shots in my reel at YouTube.[1]

NB: How was work assigned to you?

SS: Work was assigned in a piecemeal fashion. Whenever a sequence had been approved and an animator became available, work was handed out even if one shot was a continuation of an emotion or dialogue from an adjacent shot. They got better organised as the production progressed. And key moments were given to the top animators: Pete Docter, Doug Sweetland or Mark Oftedal.

NB: What was your typical day working on *Toy Story* like?

SS: A typical day at Pixar started 8am for dailies. That's when the director – John Lasseter – and the animators and producers get together, and they look at the shots as works-in-progress. John's very specific about his direction. He'll give a direction like, 'The timing's a little bit off, the staging, or maybe you have to shift the weight to the other foot'. The exact opposite of a director who says, 'I'm not sure what I want but I'll know it when I see it'. And everyone is encouraged to contribute to the dailies, which adds to the *esprit de corps*. It doesn't matter if it's the story people, or the animator, director, or even the janitor, if they have a good suggestion they will take the time to listen. When you're animating, you'll get a shot sheet, with information like the storyboard panel, description of the dialogue, description of the action. For later productions they [animators] got whole sequence sheets. When you get your shot, you'll listen to the soundtrack, and you'll analyse it, break it down, phoneme [the shape made by a mouth during speech] by phoneme, syllable by syllable. And they made a programme that prints off what you write with the phonemes. The dialogue scenes would usually have a video of the actor performing the voice, and that can be a tremendous help to study the facial expressions and the hand gestures, to get the general feel of the performance and apply that to your animation. At the end of the day, they'll go through what they call walk-through. The director – and Andrew Stanton, sometimes – would look at your shot at your desk. Then you can discuss ideas and work out problems. Once your shot was complete – was accepted for the production – John would actually bring out a box of toys – and you got a toy! I think they only did that on *Toy Story*. I think they're all Happy Meal toys that John got for his kids, but it's just a nice touch.

NB: With *Toy Story* did you feel like you were working towards a new aesthetic in animation – not simply a new technology but a new style altogether?

SS: I think John had already showed us the way. Especially with *Tin Toy* [1988]. And really, *Luxo, Jr.* [1986], even though there are no faces. Just the way that that [lamp] moves. It doesn't move in a mechanical way, it moves in a very naturalistic way. And it's very subtle. It's not robotic. And the fact that these are mechanical things that look like they could *be* robots that move in a very believable way – that was it. I mean, that's the watershed right there. There's *before Luxo, Jr.*, and everything *after*. I can't remember anything – there's a really great Bob Abel commercial with a woman talking about keeping foods for thousands of years in cans, but she's a robot. And she moves like a robot. And I remember there was a Benson and Hedges commercial that had a very mechanical-looking tiger, but then you see this little conjurer. I said, 'Oh, wow: *that's* the way it's supposed to look'. They finally got it. This is before *Luxo*. And then I later on found out that the tiger was computer generated. The conjurer was a rod puppet, moved in real time against a green screen, superimposed into the CG. *That's* why he moved in a believable way – he was filmed in real time! So, it wasn't until John figured out – and he wrote a paper on it ['Principles of Traditional Animation Applied to 3D Computer Animation', 1987] and presented it at SIGGRAPH – how to do character animation on computer, and that was the bible for a decade. People were quoting that constantly. I mean, you can still look at it today and say, 'Oh yeah, that's true'. He knew that way back. He'd just done [*The Adventures of*] *André and Wally B* [1984], which was sort of mechanical, and came up with a new technique. And that technique, which he called the 'layering' technique, is what turned the corner. It's not done all the time today, but we did a lot on *Toy Story*.

NB: So when it came to the creative vision for *Toy Story*, was John really the auteur figure?

SS: Oh, without a doubt. I mean, he relied on Andrew Stanton a lot; he relied on Pete Docter . . . Maybe not as much. Andrew Stanton was basically the co-director. But whenever there was any kind of discussion, whenever there was a disagreement, there was never any question which way it was gonna go: it was always gonna go John's way. I remember I had a scene where Potato Head's about to be hit by the RC Car. And there are all these other toys in the back of the truck. So I animated them running out of the way . . . or hopping out of the way. And he said, 'It's taking too long. Just get them out of the way in like, three frames'. And I said, 'Well, their legs aren't long enough'. He said, 'It doesn't matter'. So I did a scene and they just, whoosh! Moved out of the way. And damned if it didn't look so much better that way. It's not realistic. The same thing with the sheep – Bo Peep had these sheep, and instead of using IK [Inverse Kinematics] and planting the sheep on the ground, he said 'No, just move the body and wiggle the feet. Nobody will notice'. So that's what we did. Same thing for Potato Head. Potato Head's feet were not attached to his body. Because they didn't have IK at that time. So, you would just move a foot and leave it there, and move the other foot and leave it there, and then you waddle his body. It wasn't attached. So this is all stuff John said, 'Yeah, let's do this'.

NB: At the time, what was the atmosphere at Pixar? Was there a feeling that the film would play such a significant role in changing the face of animation?

SS: I think there was. I can even remember one specific incident, which is when Steve Jobs came and said, 'We're gonna go public, and we're gonna be issuing Pixar stock'. And I said: 'Are you going to go public before the film's release, or after?' Which I think was a pretty good question. And Steve Jobs said: 'One or the other'. So, he hadn't actually decided at that time. And the whole thing is, if word of mouth is good, but you don't know how the film's gonna do, then you go public *before* the film's release. But he had a pretty good indication that the film was gonna be a big hit. And so he waited till after. And the film became the highest-grossing film of the year [in North America], and he went public, and the stock – I think they thought it was gonna go like 30, and it went to like 70. Then it came back down to normal. So yeah, there was a general sense. I mean, I looked at the film and I thought, even before the score was in it, this is gonna be a huge hit. I thought that even with the army man sequence, because it was so smart. I thought: 'this isn't really a kids' film'. There are these war movie references that kids aren't gonna get, adults are going to get them. And they have a scene where Potato Head takes his lips off and puts it on his butt! And I said, 'That's a great gag!' And most of the kids in the audience aren't gonna get that. So this is a really smart film. It's about toys and kids are gonna love it, adults are gonna like it, it's got Randy Newman music, it's got Tom Hanks: it can't miss. I didn't feel the same way about *A Bug's Life* [Lasseter, 1998]. I thought there were too many characters. And I still feel like *A Bug's Life* is not one of their better films. They didn't make a sequel to that one. That's one of the few they didn't make a sequel to.

NB: Did any of the creative decisions that were made on voice casting have an impact on your work process?

SS: Oh, sure. Well, you listen to the [audio] track, so you're listening to the intonation, and Tom Hanks has a certain way that he speaks, way that he enunciates. He puts emphasis on certain words and syllables. I did some [animation] to Annie Potts, and she had a certain timbre to her speech, and you try to match. Same thing for Don Rickles, I did a couple of those. I think I did every character. You can't help it. If you do good casting, that person will bring something to the performance. Tom Hanks especially.

NB: How do you think Randy Newman's score added to the finished product?

SS: Newman's music serves the same purpose as just about any other composer; he has the added advantage of being a popular music songwriter and his songs – especially 'You've Got a Friend in Me' – have become part of our culture. I love his work, especially his sardonic songs. But I think there are dozens of able composers who would have done a great job: Danny Elfman would have been good, or Hans Zimmer or Howard Shore. And I always knew that Paul McCartney was a big supporter of animation and had written some beautiful scores – what a coup to get *him* to write. *Toy Story* is sort of an American sensibility, but how could you turn down Sir Paul? For a long time John Lasseter wouldn't use any other composer but Randy Newman, but now Michael Giacchino has become the house composer.

NB: Finally, when the film was eventually released, and it was a massive hit, how was it?

SS: Well, it was very cool to be able to say, 'I worked on *Toy Story*'. I went to do a presentation at this local place at the beach and the guy who ran it would say, 'Here's the guy who made *Toy Story*!' Actually, I was [also] just at a magic show and the guy [who] called me out of the audience said 'This is Steve Segal. Have you ever seen *Toy Story*? He made that!' Just this past weekend. This is 20 years later. There aren't that many movies that have that kind of resonance. *Toy Story* created a whole industry. Almost all animation in America is CG. That was like turning the switch, closing the door. I [still] think we'll see some more hand-drawn [features]. Brad Bird says he wants to do it again. And I think the new technology will probably make it financially feasible, because you can build three-dimension backgrounds but still do the character animation by hand. And you don't need to use paper. You can draw it on a tablet. I remember thinking, 'Wouldn't it have been great to work on *Snow White*?' To be there for the first feature – the first American feature, anyway. I really wished I could have worked on that. I know I did the next best thing.

Note

1 To view Steve's animation reel, visit https://www.youtube.com/watch?v=iVNrEZDUBMM.

A GUIDE TO FURTHER RESEARCH

Toy Story: How Pixar Reinvented the Animated Feature

Toy Story

Ackerman, Alan. *Seeing Things: From Shakespeare to Pixar* (Toronto: University of Toronto Press, 2011). [Especially ch. 4, 'The Spirit of Toys: Resurrection, Redemption and Consumption in *Toy Story, Toy Story 2* and Beyond', pp. 97–120.]

In an interdisciplinary study that traverses an impressively broad history of literature, theatre, painting and film, Ackerman's fourth chapter considers *Toy Story* and its sequels in the context of storytelling media's long-standing fascination with vision (or the problem of visualizing that which may lie beyond the concrete bounds of reason and experience) and in relation to changing modes of representation and the impact of technology.

Garwood, Ian. *The Sense of Film Narration* (Edinburgh: Edinburgh University Press, 2015). [Specifically ch. 3, 'Storytelling through the Imperfect Image', pp. 63–98.]

In this insightful study of the sensory properties of cinema and their relationship to narrative understanding, Garwood examines Pixar's films specifically in terms of debates about digital aesthetics, examining what happens when the plastic cohesion of this studio's animated features is disrupted by the introduction of materially different image formats. While he refers to a broad range of Pixar films, Garwood includes detailed discussion of key moments in *Toy Story 2* and *3*, examining instances of digital excess in the former and low-resolution home video in the latter.

Gurevitch, Leon. 'Computer Generated Animation as Product Design Engineered Culture, or Buzz Lightyear to the Sales Floor, to the Checkout and Beyond!' *animation: an interdisciplinary journal*, no. 7 (2012): 131–49.

In an article concerned with the relationship between cinematic image and contemporary consumer culture, Gurevitch addresses the impact of computer generated (CG) animation. In particular, he argues that features created using this digital technology and which employ characters that are mainly manufactured objects indicative of product placement prompt a significant reevaluation of such a relationship.

Herbrechter, Stefan. 'Toying with the Postmodern "To Infinity and Beyond"', in Ivan Callus and Stefan Hebrechter (eds), *Post-theory, Culture and Criticism* (Amsterdam: Rodopi, 2004), 141–66.

In line with the book's overall aims, Herbrechter's chapter argues that *Toy Story* provides a productive way of understanding the postmodern and considers the series' shifting concerns as emblematic of the move from theory to post-theory.

Kemper, Tom. *Toy Story: A Critical Reading* (London: BFI, 2015).

This short book provides an academic analysis of *Toy Story* from its production to its reception. In particular, Kemper foregrounds a reading of the film in the context of the pop art movement, referring to Pixar's postmodern take on consumer culture and their stylistic break from Disney's familiar fine-art aesthetic.

Lanier, Clinton, Scott Rader and Aubrey Fowler. 'Anthropomorphism, Marketing Relationships, and Consumption Worth in the *Toy Story* Trilogy', *Journal of Marketing Management*, no. 29 (2013): 26–47.

This co-authored article finds significance in the *Toy Story* trilogy's portrayal of the human–toy friendship from the vantage point of the toys, arguing that this anthropomorphized, reverse point of view prompts reconsideration of the nature of this relationship and the perceived value of the objects involved.

Maloney, Marcus. *The Search for Meaning in Film and Television* (New York: Palgrave Macmillan, 2015). [Specifically ch. 2, 'Just a Toy', pp. 22–24.]

This study addresses what the author considers to be the central dilemma of our age: the search for meaning in contemporary Western life. He does so by exploring the ways in which popular texts engage with this problem and uses *Toy Story* as one of his four main case studies. Overall, he considers how the film reinterprets a Disney narrative founded on the idea of self-fulfilment, exploring modern-day themes through the lens of the toys' experience.

Solomon, Charles. *The Toy Story Films: An Animated Journey* (New York: Disney Editions, 2012).

With a foreword from Hayao Miyazaki and an afterword from John Lasseter, this Disney-approved coffee table book presents the official version of the 'making of' the *Toy Story* trilogy. It tells its story through exclusive concept artwork and interviews with the cast and crew, making it a useful resource for scholars.

Wells, Paul. 'To Affinity and Beyond: Woody, Buzz and the New Authenticity', in Thomas Austin and Martin Barker (eds), *Contemporary Hollywood Stardom* (London: Arnold, 2003), pp. 90–102.

Woody and Buzz are measured against traditional paradigms of film stardom, taking into account the unique ways in which audiences typically conceive of animated characters. Considering the textual and extratextual contributions of Tom Hanks and Tim Allen, as well as the characters' status as 'toys' both on and off-screen, Wells assesses the notion of 'post-human' stars.

Pixar

Clarke, James. *The Films of Pixar Animation Studio* (Harpenden: Kamera Books, 2013).

One of the first lengthy critical studies of Pixar's output, Clarke's book includes in-depth analyses of each of the studio's films – including *Toy Story*. It relates them to wider developments in animation and includes useful background information on their incubation processes.

Goldmark, Daniel. 'Pixar and the Animated Soundtrack', in John Richardson, Claudia Gorbman and Carol Vernallis (eds), *The Oxford Handbook of New Audiovisual Aesthetics* (New York: Oxford University Press, 2013), pp. 213–26.

Offering a welcome focus on Pixar's approach to music and soundtrack, Goldmark argues that this studio is distinctive in granting each of these elements considerable priority during the filmmaking process and for challenging the dominant format of the Disney animated musical. Through detailed analyses of *Up* and *WALL-E* in the second part of the chapter, he explores the ways in which music and sound design are central to the construction of space and the emotional landscapes in and of these films.

Haswell, Helen. 'To Infinity and Back Again: Hand-drawn Aesthetic and Affection for the Past in Pixar's Pioneering Animation', *Alphaville: Journal of Film and Screen Media*, no. 8 (2014): 1–17.

Chiefly focusing on Pixar's 2011 short, *La Luna*, but incorporating analyses of many of their films, including the *Toy Story* series, Haswell argues that the studio's more recent experiments with 2-D animation – facilitated by their own history of advancements in 3-D – reflect a thematic preoccupation with nostalgia traceable throughout their oeuvre.

Holian, Heather L. 'Animators as Professional Masqueraders: Thoughts on Pixar', in Deborah Bell (ed.), *Masquerade: Essays on Tradition and Innovation Worldwide* (Jefferson, North Carolina: McFarland, 2015), pp. 231–40.

In this influential article, Holian argues that digital animators are 'professional masqueraders'; that is, actors who manipulate images and characters by briefly inhabiting them (putting on 'masks'). Holian explores this conceit with reference to animators at Pixar, drawing both on detailed accounts of the animation process and interviews with animators.

McCulloch, Richard. 'Whistle While You Work: Branding, Critical Reception and Pixar's Production Culture', in Roberta Pearson and Anthony N. Smith (eds), *Storytelling in the Media Convergence Age: Exploring Screen Narratives* (Hampshire: Palgrave MacMillan, 2015), pp. 174–89.

This article explores the synergy between Pixar's perceived creative identity (advanced popularly in a multitude of paratextual materials) and its culture of production, particularly focusing on the associations of Pixar's Emeryville headquarters as a place of fun, community and creativity. Emeryville, McCulloch argues, functions as a reification of Pixar's central brand identifications.

Meinel, Deitmar. *Pixar's America: The Re-Animation of American Myths and Symbols* (Basingstoke and New York: Palgrave Macmillan, 2016).

A broad-ranging examination of Pixar within the cultural and political context of North American society. Through close analysis of each of the studio's films in turn, Meinel situates these productions within foundational mythologies of freedom and individualism, as well as more contemporary concerns such as gender politics and neoliberal ideologies.

Montgomery, Coleen. 'Woody's Roundup and *WALL-E*'s Wunderkammer: Technophilia and Nostalgia in Pixar Animation', *Animation Studies*, no. 6 (2011): 7–13.

Elaborating on the theme of nostalgia in Pixar's work, Montgomery suggests that the affinity for analogue and obsolete technologies expressed in films like *Toy Story* and its sequels is reflective of anxieties surrounding the studio's significant technological innovations and their industry-wide impact, as well as of marketing concerns and the filmmakers' own proclivities.

Munk Rösing, Lilian. *Pixar with Lacan: The Hysteric's Guide to Animation* (London and New York: Bloomsbury Academic, 2016).

A Freudian/Lacanian psychoanalytic interpretation of Pixar's output. Rösing argues for the universalism of Pixar films, noting that many of their tropes can be related to fundamental concepts in Lacanian psychoanalysis. There are chapters on each of the *Toy Story* films.

Neupert, Richard. *John Lasseter: Contemporary Film Directors* (Urbana: University of Illinois Press, 2016).

An auteurist account of the *Toy Story* director and his 'signature' as a filmmaker, analysing both the aesthetic and the narrative dimensions of his films. As well as discussing each of Lasseter's films in turns, Neupert suggests a necessary synergy between his creative vision and the collegial structure at Pixar, which promoted a collaborative form of authorship which has informed subsequent works at the studio.

Paik, Karen. *To Infinity and Beyond: The Story of Pixar Animation Studios* (San Francisco: Chronicle Books, 2007).

An in-house account of Pixar's development from its origins in the 1970s up to *Ratatouille* and taking in *Toy Story* and its sequels. The book combines a narrative history of the studio – drawing on interviews with many of the key participants – with high-quality artwork and original sketches

Pallant, Chris. *Demystifying Disney* (New York: Bloomsbury Academic, 2011). [Especially ch. 8, 'Digital Disney', pp. 226–42.]

This chapter places *Toy Story* and the rise of Pixar in the context of Disney's aesthetic history, comprehensively delineated by Pallant over the course of the book. As well as examining the artistic and commercial interplay between the two studios, he also addresses Pixar's pioneering three-dimensional realist aesthetic and the influence of live-action film on their digital cinematography.

Price, David A. *The Pixar Touch: The Making of a Company* (New York: Vintage Books, 2008).

A valuable narrative history of Pixar for the popular market, drawing on extensive interview material with leading figures in the company, including Ed Catmull, Alvy Ray Smith and John Lasseter. Price documents the beginnings of computer animation in the 1970s and goes on to explore the origins of Pixar, its development from a computer software company to an animation studio, and the creative ethos underpinning the company.

Scott, Ellen. 'Agony and Avoidance: Pixar, Deniability and the Adult Spectator', *Journal of Popular Film and Television*, no. 42 (2014): 150–62.

Using the *Toy Story* films and *WALL-E* as her examples, Scott illustrates how Pixar, using a 'principle of deniability', has broadened its audience to include adults by addressing inherently 'grown-up' themes beneath a colourful, cartoonal veneer. In doing so, she places the texts in the tradition of classical Hollywood and film noir.

BIBLIOGRAPHY

Ackerman, Alan, *Seeing Things: From Shakespeare to Pixar* (Toronto: University of Toronto Press, 2011).

Adamson, Glen and Victoria Kelley (eds). *Surface Tensions: Writings on Popular Design and Material Culture* (Manchester: Manchester University Press, 2013).

Akers, Chelsie Lynn. 'The Rise of Humour: Hollywood Increases Adult Centred Humour in Animated Children's Films' (unpublished Master's thesis submitted to Brigham Young University, July 2013).

Allison, Tanine. 'Blackface, *Happy Feet*: The Politics of Race in Motion Picture Animation', in Dan North et al. (eds), *Special Effects: New Histories, Theories, Contexts* (London: BFI/Palgrave Macmillan, 2015), pp. 114–26.

Altman, Rick. *Film/Genre* (London: BFI, 1999).

Amidi, Amid. *The Art of Pixar: The Complete Colorscripts and Select Art from 25 Years of Animation* (San Francisco: Chronicle Books, 2011).

Ansen, David. 'Disney's Digital Delight', *Newsweek*, 27 November 1995, p. 89.

Balcerzak, Scott. 'Andy Serkis as Actor, Body and Gorilla: Motion Capture and the Presence of Performance', in Jason Sperb and Scott Balcerzak (eds), *Cinephilia in the Age of Digital Reproduction, Vol. 1: Film, Pleasure and Digital Culture* (London: Wallflower Press, 2009), pp. 195–213.

Balio, Tino. 'Hollywood Production Trends in the Era of Globalisation, 1990–1999', in Steve Neale (ed.), *Genre and Contemporary Hollywood* (London: BFI, 2002), pp. 165–84.

Barber, Benjamin. *Consumed: How Markets Corrupt Children, Infantilise Adults and Swallow Citizens Whole* (London and New York: W. W. Norton, 2007).

Barker, Jennifer M. *The Tactile Eye: Touch and the Cinematic Experience* (Berkeley, CA; London: University of California Press, 2009).

Barrier, Michael. *Hollywood Cartoons: American Animation in Its Golden Age* (Oxford: Oxford University Press, 1999).

Barthes, Roland. *Mythologies*, trans. Annette Lavers (London: Vintage, 2000).

Beale, Lewis. 'At Long Last, Disney Is Shooting for the Hip', *New York Daily News*, 20 November 1995, p. 36.

Bell, John. *American Puppet Modernism: Essays on the Material World in Performance* (New York: Palgrave Macmillan, 2008).

Benjamin, Walter. 'On the Concept of History' (1940), trans. Dennis Redmond, 2005. https://www.marxists.org/reference/archive/benjamin/1940/history.htm (accessed 24 March 2017).

Berger, John, *Ways of Seeing* (London: Penguin Modern Classics, 2008).

Bestor, Nicholas. 'The Technologically Determined Decade: Robert Zemeckis, Andy Serkis, and the Promotion of Performance Capture', *animation: an interdisciplinary journal*, vol. 11, no. 2 (July 2016): 169–88.

Bianchi, Suzanne, John Robinson and Melissa Milke. *The Changing Rhythms of American Family Life* (New York: Russell Sage Foundation, 2006).

Bird, Michael. 'The Perception of Symmetry', *Tate Etc.*, 1 May 2004. http://www.tate.org.uk/context-comment/articles/perception-symmetry (accessed 20 October 2016).

Blackford, Holly. '"Luke, I Am Your Father": Toys, Play Space and Detached Fathers in Post-1970s Hollywood Family Films', in Noel Brown and Bruce Babington (eds), *Family Films in Global Cinema: The World Beyond Disney* (London and New York: I.B. Tauris, 2015), pp. 137–51.

Bode, Lisa. 'From Shadow Citizens to Teflon Stars: Reception of the Transfiguring Effects of New Moving Image Technologies', *animation: an interdisciplinary journal*, vol. 1, no. 2 (2006): 173–89.

Bode, Lisa. '"Grave Robbing" or "Career Comeback"? On the Digital Resurrection of Dead Screen Stars', in Kari Kallioniemi, Kimi Kärki, Janne Mäkelä and Hannu Slami (eds), *History of Stardom Reconsidered* (Turku: International Institute for Popular Culture, 2007), pp. 36–40.

Bode, Lisa. 'No Longer Themselves? Framing Digitally Enabled Posthumous "Performance"', *Cinema Journal*, vol. 49, no. 4 (2010): 46–70.

Bode, Lisa. 'Fleshing It Out: Prosthetic Makeup Effects, Motion Capture and the Reception of Performance', in Dan North, Bob Rehak and Michael S. Duffy (eds), *Special Effects: New Histories/Theories/Contexts* (London: BFI/Palgrave, 2010), pp. 32–44.

Bonifer, Mike. 'Rule #23', *GameChangers*, 7 October 2013. http://www.gamechangers.com/rule-23/ (accessed 29 August 2016).

Botwinick, Stacy. 'Power Rangers Deliver Knockout Punch', *Playthings*, 1 December 1994. https://www.highbeam.com/doc/1G1-16540112.html (accessed 4 September 2016).

Bouldin, Joanna. 'Cadaver of the Real: Animation, Rotoscoping, and the Politics of the Body', *Animation Journal*, no. 12 (2004): 7–31.

Bowie, Malcolm. *Lacan* (Cambridge, MA: Harvard University Press, 1993).

Bradbury, Ray. *Something Wicked This Way Comes* (New York: Simon and Schuster, 1962).

Bradshaw, Peter. '*Toy Story 2*', *The Guardian*, 4 February 2000. http://www.theguardian.com/film/2000/feb/04/6 (accessed 21 June 2017).

Bradshaw, Peter. 'The Pirates! In an Adventure with Scientists', *The Guardian*, 29 March 2012, p. 15.

Brennan, Judy. 'Summer School Lessons', *The Los Angeles Times*, 12 September 1996, p. F1.

Brodie, John. 'Disney Wannabes Play Copycat-and-Mouse', *Variety*, 2 January 1995, p. 3.

Brodie, John and Jay Greene. 'Dwarfs Tell Disney: Draw! – Rival Studios Get Serious about Animation', *Variety*, 11 July 1994, p. 1.

Brown, Bill. 'How to Do Things with Things (A *Toy Story*)', *Critical Inquiry*, vol. 24, no. 4 (1998): 935–64.

Brown, Noel. *The Hollywood Family Film: A History, from Shirley Temple to Harry Potter* (London and New York: I.B. Tauris, 2012).

Brown, Noel '"Family" Entertainment and Contemporary Hollywood Cinema', *Scope: An Online Journal of Film and Television Studies*, no. 25 (2013): 1–22.

Brown, Noel. *British Children's Cinema: From The Thief of Bagdad to Wallace and Gromit* (London and New York: I.B. Tauris, 2016).

Brown, Noel. *The Children's Film: Genre, Nation and Narrative* (New York: Columbia University Press, 2017).

Brown, Noel. *Contemporary Hollywood Animation* (Edinburgh: Edinburgh University Press, forthcoming).

Brown, Noel and Bruce Babington (eds). *Family Films in Global Cinema: The World Beyond Disney* (London and New York: I.B. Tauris, 2015).

Bruno, Giuliani. *Surface: Matters of Aesthetics, Materiality, and Media* (Chicago: University of Chicago Press, 2014).

Bryant, Jacob. 'John Lasseter, Ed Catmull and "*Toy Story*" Team Celebrate 20th Anniversary', *Variety*, 2 October 2015. http://variety.com/2015/scene/vpage/toy-story-20th-anniversary-john-lasseter-ed-catmull-1201608613/ (accessed 18 April 2017).

Buchan, Suzanne. *The Quay Brothers: Into a Metaphysical Playroom* (Minneapolis and London: University of Minnesota Press, 2011).

Bunn, Austin. 'Welcome to Planet Pixar: How the Pixel-Packing Upstart Became an Animation Superpower and Left Disney in the Dust', *Wired*, vol. 12, no. 6 (2004): 126–33.

Carnicke, Sharon. 'Emotional Expressivity in Motion Capture Technology', in Joerg Sternagel, Deborah Levitt and Dieter Mersch (eds), *Acting and Performance in Moving Image Culture: Bodies, Screens, Renderings* (Piscataway, NJ: Transaction, 2012), pp. 321–38.

'Cars 2', *Rotten Tomatoes* https://www.rottentomatoes.com/m/cars_2/ (accessed 28 August 2016).

Casement, Ann. 'Encountering the shadow in rites of passage: a study in activations', *Journal of Analytical Psychology*, vol. 48, no. 1 (2003): 29–46.

Cassar, Ignaz. 'Viewed from Behind: The Projected Image and Its Doppelgänger', *Parallax*, vol. 14, no. 2 (2008): 115–25.

Catmull, Ed. *Creativity, Inc.: Overcoming the Unseen Forces that Stand in the Way of True Inspiration* (New York: Random House, 2014).

Chion, Michel. 'On a Sequence from *The Birds*: Sound Film as Palimpsestic Art', in *Film, A Sound Art*, translated by Claudia Gorbman (New York and Chichester, West Sussex: Columbia University Press, 2009 [2003]), pp. 162–85.

Chion, Michel. 'The Sensory Aspects of Contemporary Cinema', in John Richardson, Claudia Gorbman and Carol Vernallis (eds), *The Oxford Handbook of New Audiovisual Aesthetics* (Oxford: Oxford University Press, 2013), pp. 325–30.

Chow, Kenny. *Animation, Embodiment, and Digital Media: Human Experience of Technological Liveliness* (Basingstoke: Palgrave Macmillan 2013).

Clarke, James. *The Films of Pixar Animation Studio* (Harpenden: Kamera Books, 2013).

Clarke, Frederick. 'Contents', *Cinefantastique*, vol. 27, no. 2 (1995): 3.

Clayton, Alex. 'Performance, With Strings Attached: *Team America*'s Snub to the Actor', in Tom Brown and James Bennett (eds), *Film Moments: Criticism, History, Theory* (London: BFI, 2010), pp. 127–30.

Collings, Matthew. *This Is Modern Art* (London: Weidenfeld & Nicolson, 1999), p. 248.

Courrier, Kevin. *Randy Newman's American Dreams* (Toronto, Ontario: ECW Press, 2005).

Crafton, Donald. *Shadow of a Mouse: Performance, Belief, and World-Making in Animation* (Berkeley: University of California Press, 2013).

Cunningham, Jennifer. 'Children's Humour', in W. George Scarlett et al. (eds), *Children's Play* (London and New Delhi: Sage, 2005), pp. 93–109.

Darley, Andrew. *Visual Digital Culture: Surface Play and Spectacle in New Media Genres* (London and New York: Routledge, 2000).

Day, Aubrey. 'Interview: John Lasseter', *Gamesradar+*, 3 June 2009. http://www.gamesradar.com/interview-john-lasseter/ (accessed 30 August 2016).

De Guzman, René. *Pixar: 25 Years of Animation* (San Francisco: Chronicle Books, 2010).

Decoster, Pieter-Jan and Nancy Vansieleghem. 'Cinema Education as an Exercise in "Thinking through Not-Thinking"', *Educational Philosophy & Theory*, vol. 46, no. 7 (2014): 789–804 (p. 793).

Delingpole, James. '*Toy Story*, Review', *The Telegraph*, 23 December 2013. http://www.telegraph.co.uk/culture/film/filmreviews/10514520/Toy-Story-review.html (accessed 15 April 2016).

Denby, David. 'This Toy's Life', *New York*, November 1995, pp. 126–29.

Dirks, Tim. 'Pixar-Disney Animations', *AMC: Filmsite*. http://www.filmsite.org/pixaranimations.html (accessed 28 August 2016).

Docter, Pete and Richard Crouse. 'Pete Docter | In Conversation With . . . | TIFF 2015', *YouTube*, 19 June 2015. https://www.youtube.com/watch?v=iml_slMLBUs (accessed 30 August 2016).

Douglas, Nathan E. and Harold Jacob Smith. 'The Defiant Ones Script', in George P. Garrett, O. B. Hardison, Jr. and Jane R. Gelfman (eds), *Film Scripts Two*, The Film Scripts Series (Milwaukee: Applause Theatre & Cinema Books, 2013).

Dunne, Sara. 'Randy Newman and the Extraordinary Moral Position', *Popular Music and Society*, vol. 16, no. 3 (1992): 53–61.

Eberle, Scott G. 'Exploring the Uncanny Valley to Find the Edge of Play', *American Journal of Play*, vol. 2, no. 2 (2009): 167–94.

Elsaesser, Thomas and Malte Hagener. *Film Theory: An Introduction Through the Senses* (London: Routledge, 2010).

Featherstone, Mike. *Consumer Culture and Postmodernism*, 2nd edn (London: Sage, 2007).

Felperin, Leslie. '*Toy Story*', *Sight and Sound*, vol. 6, no. 3 (1996): 51–52.

Finney, Angus and Eugenio Triana. *Film Business: A Market Guide Beyond Hollywood*, 2nd edn (London and New York: Routledge, 2015).

Fleming, Dan. *Powerplay: Toys as Popular Culture* (Manchester: Manchester University Press, 1996).

Freedman, Yacov. 'Is It Real . . . or Is It Motion Capture?: The Battle to Redefine Animation in the Age of Digital Performance', *The Velvet Light Trap*, no. 69 (2012): 38–49.

French, Lawrence. '*Toy Story* Beginnings: An Animation Brain Trust Devised the Toys' Story', *Cinefantastique*, November 1995, p. 36.

French, Lawrence. '*Toy Story*: Walt Disney and Pixar Team Up to Launch the First Computer-Animated Movie', *Cinefantastique*, November (1995): 20–22.

Friend, Tad. 'Second Act Twist: Andrew Stanton, the Director of "Finding Nemo" and "WALL-E", Faces the Complications of Live Action', *The New Yorker*, 17 October 2011. http://www.newyorker.com/magazine/2011/10/17/second-act-twist (accessed 20 October 2016).

Freud, Sigmund. *The Uncanny* (London: Penguin Classics, 2003).

Gaines, Jason M. *Composing for Moving Pictures: The Essential Guide* (New York: Oxford University Press, 2015).

Gallo, George. Midnight Run Shooting Script (USA: Universal n.d.), unpublished screenplay. http://www.weeklyscript.com/Midnight+Run.html (accessed 30 August 2016).

Gans, Andrew. '*Toy Story – The Musical*, by GrooveLily and Dickstein, Will Debut on Disney Cruise Line', *Playbill* (7 March 2008). http://www.playbill.com/article/toy-storythe-musical-by-groovelily-and-dickstein-will-debut-on-disney-cruise-line-com-148213 (accessed 21 April 2017).

Garwood, Ian. *The Sense of Film Narration* (Edinburgh: Edinburgh University Press, 2013).

Gaut, Berys. *A Philosophy of Cinematic Art* (Cambridge: Cambridge University Press, 2010), p. 140.

Gerstal, Judy. 'Animated Toy Dazzler Lights Up the Season', *The Toronto Star*, 24 November 1995, p. D3.

Giroux, Henry A. and Grace Pollock. *The Mouse That Roared: Disney and the End of Innocence* (New York: Rowman & Littlefield, 2001).

Glieberman, Owen. 'Plastic Fantastic', *Entertainment Weekly*, 14 November 1995, p. 74.

Gleiberman, Owen. '*Toy Story*', *Entertainment Weekly*, 24 November 1995. http://www.ew.com/article/1995/11/24/toy-story (accessed 15 April 2016).

Gleiberman, Owen. '*Toy Story 3*', *Entertainment Weekly*, 31 July 2012. http://ew.com/article/2012/07/31/toy-story-3–5/ (accessed 18 May 2015).

Goldin, Daniel. 'Inside Screenwriting: Script Gurus in 21st Century Hollywood', originally in *Premiere Magazine Online*, n.d., republished with author's permission at Screenplayology.*com*, ed. Andrew Kenneth Gay. http://www.screenplayology.com/PremiereScriptGurus.pdf, 3 (accessed 30 August 2016).

Goldmark, Daniel. *Tunes for 'Toons: Music and the Hollywood Cartoon* (Berkeley and Los Angeles: University of California Press, 2005).

Goldmark, Daniel. 'Pixar and the Animated Soundtrack', in John Richardson, Claudia Gorbman and Carol Vernallis (eds), *The Oxford Handbook of New Audiovisual Aesthetics* (New York: Oxford University Press, 2013), pp. 213–26.

Goldmark, Daniel, Lawrence Kramer and Richard Leppert. 'Introduction. Phonoplay: Recasting Film Music', in Daniel Goldmark et al. (eds), *Beyond the Soundtrack: Representing Music in Cinema* (Berkeley and Los Angeles: University of California Press, 2007), pp. 1–12.

Goldstein, Jeffrey, David Buckingham and Gilles Brougère. 'Introduction', in Jeffrey Goldstein, David Buckingham and Gilles Brougère (eds), *Toys, Games, and Media* (London: Routledge, 2004), pp. 1–10.

Graser, Marc. 'Pixar Run by a Focused Group', *Variety*, 20 December 1999, p. 76.

Gray, Jonathan. *Show Sold Separately: Promos, Spoilers, and Other Media Paratexts* (Chesham: Combined Academic, 2010).

Gunning, Tom. 'Animating the Instant: The Secret Symmetry between Animation and Photography', in Karen Beckman (ed.), *Animating Film Theory* (North Carolina: Duke University Press, 2014), pp. 37–53.

Gurevitch, Leon. 'Computer Generated Animation as Product Design Engineered Culture, or Buzz Lightyear to the Sales Floor, to the Checkout and Beyond!' *animation: an interdisciplinary journal*, vol. 7, no. 2 (2012): 131–49.

Halberstam, Judith. *The Queer Art of Failure* (Durham: Duke University Press, 2011).

Harari, Yuval Noah. *Homo Deus: A Brief History of Tomorrow* (London: Harvill Secker, 2016).

Haring, Bruce. 'Computer Animation No Longer Just a "Toy"', *USA Today*, 15 August 1995, p. 1D.

Harris, Kathryn and Claudia Eller. 'Studio Chief Katzenberg to Leave Disney', Los Angeles Times, 25 August 1994. http://articles.latimes.com/1994-08-25/news/mn-31054_1_jeffrey-katzenberg (accessed 30 August 2016).

Haswell, Helen. 'To Infinity and Back Again: Hand-drawn Aesthetic and Affection for the Past in Pixar's Pioneering Animation', *Alphaville: Journal of Film and Screen Media*, no. 8 (2014): 1–17.

Henderson, Joseph. 'Ancient Myths and Modern Man', in Carl Jung (ed.), *Man and His Symbols* (London: Penguin, 1978), pp. 95–156 (p. 156).

Henne Mark, Hal Hickel, Ewan Johnson and Sonoko Konishi. 'The Making of *Toy Story*', *COMPCON '96: Proceedings of the 41st IEEE International Computer Conference* (Santa Clara, CA: IEEE, 1996), pp. 463–68 (p. 466).

Herbrechter, Stefan. 'Toying with the Postmodern "To Infinity and Beyond"', in Ivan Callus and Stefan Herbrechter (eds), *Post-Theory, Culture and Criticism* (Amsterdam: Rodopi, 2004).

Herhuth, Eric. *Pixar and the Aesthetic Imagination: Animation, Storytelling, and Digital Culture* (California: University of California Press, 2017).

Hobsbawm, Eric. *Fractured Times: Culture and Society in the Twentieth Century* (London: Little, Brown, 2013).

Holian, Heather L. 'Animators as Professional Masqueraders: Thoughts on Pixar', in Deborah Bell (ed.), *Masquerade: Essays on Tradition and Innovation Worldwide* (Jefferson, North Carolina: McFarland, 2015).

Holland, Patricia. *What Is a Child? Popular Images of Childhood* (London: Virago, 1992).

Honeycutt, Kirk. 'Review of *Toy Story 2*', *The Hollywood Reporter*, 18 November 1999, pp. 7, 21.

Horwitz, Jane. 'Ode to "Toy": An Animation Sensation', *The Washington Post*, 23 November 1995, p. D7.

Hughes, Robert. *Culture of Complaint* (Oxford & New York: Oxford University Press, 1998).

Isaacson, Walter. *Steve Jobs* (New York: Simon & Schuster, 2011).

Jackson, Kathy Merlock (ed.). *Walt Disney: Conversations* (Jackson: University Press of Mississippi, 2006).

Jaffé, Aniela. 'Symbolism in the Visual Arts', in Carl Jung (ed.), *Man and His Symbols* (London: Penguin, 1978), pp. 255–332.

Jameson, Fredric. 'Postmodernism and Consumer Society', in Hal Foster (ed.), *The Anti-Aesthetic: Essays on Postmodern Culture* (Port Townsend: Bay Press, 1983), pp. 111–25.

Jurkowski, Henryk. 'Transcodification of the Signs Systems of Puppets', *Semiotica: Journal of the International Association for Semiotic Studies*, no. 47 (1983): 123–46.

Kalinak, Kathryn. *Film Music: A Very Short Introduction* (Oxford and New York: Oxford University Press, 2010).

Kaplin, Stephen. 'A Puppet Tree: A Model for the Field of Puppet Theatre', *TDR: The Drama Review*, vol. 43, no. 3 (1999): 28–35.

Kashani, Tim and Robert McKee. 'ShowbizU: When Pixar Met Robert McKee', *YouTube*, 22 July 2014. https://www.youtube.com/watch?v=kpN7KeWfbmE (accessed 30 August 2016).

Kemper, Tom. *Toy Story: A Critical Reading* (London: BFI, 2015).

Khouri, Callie. Thelma & Louise Final Shooting Script (USA: Metro Goldwyn Mayer, 1990), unpublished screenplay. http://www.dailyscript.com/scripts/thelmaandlouise.html (accessed 30 August 2016).

Kirby, Alan. *Digimodernism: How New Technologies Dismantle Postmodernism and Reconfigure Our Culture* (London: Continuum, 2009).

Klady, Leonard. 'Review: *Toy Story*', *Variety*, 20 November 1995, p. 2.

Klein, Melanie. *Envy and Gratitude* (London: Vintage, 1997).

Klein, Melanie. *Love, Guilt and Reparation* (London: Vintage, 1998).

Klein, Norman. *The Vatican to Vegas: A History of Special Effects* (New York and London: New Press, 2004).

Klein, Sheri. *Art & Laughter* (London and New York: I.B. Tauris, 2007).

Koons, Jeff and Norman Rosenthal. *Jeff Koons: Conversations with Norman Rosenthal* (London and New York: Thames & Hudson, 2014).

Krämer, Peter. 'Would You Take Your Child to See This Film? The Cultural and Social Work of the Family-Adventure Movie', in Steve Neale and Murray Smith (eds), *Contemporary Hollywood Cinema* (London: Routledge, 1998), pp. 294–311.

Krämer, Peter. '"The Best Disney Film Disney Never Made": Children's Films and The Family Audience in American Cinema since the 1960s', in Steve Neale (ed.), *Genre and Contemporary Hollywood* (London: British Film Institute, 2002), pp. 185–200.

Krämer, Peter. '"It's Aimed at Kids – The Kid in Everybody": George Lucas, *Star Wars* and Children's Entertainment', in Yvonne Tasker (ed.), *Action and Adventure Cinema* (London and New York: Routledge, 2004), pp. 358–70.

Krämer, Peter. *The New Hollywood: From Bonnie and Clyde to Star Wars* (London: Wallflower Press, 2005).

Krämer, Peter. 'Welterfolg und Apokalypse: Überlegungen zur Transnationalität des zeitgenössischen Hollywood', in Ricarda Strobel and Andreas Jahn-Sudmann (eds), *Film transnational und transkulturell. Europäische und amerikanische Perspektiven* (Paderborn: Wilhelm Fink Verlag, 2009), pp. 171–84.

Krämer, Peter. 'Hollywood and Its Global Audiences: A Comparative Study of the Biggest Box Office Hits in the United States and Outside the United States since the 1970s', in Richard Maltby, Daniel Biltereyst and Philippe Meers (eds), *Explorations in New Cinema History: Approaches and Case Studies* (Oxford: Wiley-Blackwell, 2011), pp. 171–84.

Krämer, Peter. 'Steven Spielberg', in Yvonne Tasker (ed.), *Fifty Contemporary Film Directors*, 2nd edn (London: Routledge, 2011), pp. 372–80.

Krämer, Peter. 'Disney, George Lucas und Pixar: Animation und die US-amerikanische Filmindustrie seit den 1970er Jahren', *Film-Konzepte*, no. 33 (February 2014): 6–21.

Krämer, Peter. 'The Rise of Animation', *Pure Movies*, 7 October 2014. http://www.puremovies.co.uk/columns/the-rise-of-animation/.

Krämer, Peter. '"I'll Be Right Here!" Dealing with Emotional Trauma in and through *E.T. The Extra-Terrestrial*', in Adrian Schober and Debbie Olson (eds), *Children in the Films of Steven Spielberg* (Lanham: Lexington Books, 2016), pp. 91–121.

Kristeva, Julia. *Desire in Language: A Semiotic Approach to Literature and Art* (Oxford: Blackwell, 1980).
Kristeva, Julia. 'Revolution in Poetic Language', in Toril Moi (ed.), *The Kristeva Reader* (Oxford: Blackwell, 1986), pp. 89–136.
Kristeva, Julia. *Melanie Klein* (New York: Columbia University Press, 2001).
Lanier, Clinton, Scott Rader and Aubrey Fowler. 'Anthropomorphism, Marketing Relationships, and Consumption Worth in the *Toy Story* Trilogy', *Journal of Marketing Management*, vol. 29, nos. 1–2 (2013): 26–47.
Lasseter, John and Steve Daly. *Toy Story: The Art and Making of the Animated Film* (New York: Disney Editions, 1995).
Levine, Ken. '"Beware of This Man" . . . by Ken Levine: The World As Seen by a TV Comedy Writer', 1 March 2007. http://kenlevine.blogspot.com/2007/03/beware-of-this-man.html (accessed 30 August 2016).
LoBrutto, Vincent. *By Design: Interviews with Production Designers* (Westport, Connecticut: Praeger, 1992), p. 85.
Lohr, Steve. 'Disney in 10-Year, 5-Film Deal with Pixar', *The New York Times*, 25 February 1997. http://www.nytimes.com/1997/02/25/business/disney-in-10-year-5-film-deal-with-pixar.html?_r=0 (accessed 18 May 2015).
Lussier, Germain. 'Pixar's Rejected "*Toy Story*" Titles Revealed', *Film*, 24 August 2011. http://www.slashfilm.com/pixars-rejected-toy-story-titles-revealed/ (accessed 30 August 2016).
Lynch, R. A. 'The Alienating Mirror: Toward a Hegelian Critique of Lacan on Ego-Formation', *Human Studies*, vol. 31, no. 2 (2008): 209–21.
McCarthy, Todd. 'Review: *Toy Story 2*', *Variety*, 17 November 1999. http://variety.com/1999/film/reviews/toy-story-2-2-1117759786/ (accessed 18 May 2015).
McCulloch, Richard. *Towards Infinity and Beyond: Branding, Reputation, and the Critical Reception of Pixar Animated Studios* (PhD thesis submitted to the University of East Anglia, 2013).
McCulloch, Richard. 'Whistle While You Work: Branding, Critical Reception and Pixar's Production Culture', in Roberta Pearson and Anthony N. Smith (eds), *Storytelling in the Media Convergence Age: Exploring Screen Narratives* (Hampshire: Palgrave MacMillan, 2015), pp. 174–89.
McKee, Robert. *Story: Substance, Structure, Style, and the Principles of Screenwriting* (New York: Harper-Collins, 1997).
McKee, Robert. 'Q&A: If "Buddy Salvation" Is a Sub Genre of the Love Story Genre, Which of the Love Story Conventions Apply to It?' *Robert McKee's Storylogue: The Education of a Writer*, 5 November 2013. http://www.storylogue.com/docs/question-answer.html?documentId=1544 (accessed 30 August 2016).
McManus, Kevin. '"Toy": Animation Sensation', *The Washington Post*, 24 November 1995, p. N54.
Mahari, A. J. *The Shadows and Echoes of Self – The False Self Born out of the Core Wound of Abandonment in Borderline Personality Disorder* (Ontario: Phoenix Rising, 2007).
Maloney, Marcus. *The Search for Meaning in Film and Television: Disenchantment at the Turn of the Millennium* (Basingstoke: Palgrave Macmillan, 2015), pp. 25–30.
Markham, Laurie and Jane Chiu. 'Toy Story 3', *Journal of Feminist Family Therapy*, vol. 24, no. 2 (2012): 182–89.
Marks, Laura U. *The Skin of the Film: Intercultural Cinema, Embodiment and the Senses* (Durham: Duke University Press, 2000).

Mars-Jones, Adam. 'A Film, Not a Plaything', *The Independent*, 21 March 1996, p. 8.

Martin, Adrian. 'Bopping Toys Have Dual Appeal', *The Age*, 7 December 1995, p. 14.

Maslin, Janet. 'There's a New Toy in the House. Uh Oh', *The New York Times*, 22 November 1995, p. C9.

Meinel, Deitmar. *Pixar's America: The Re-Animation of American Myths and Symbols* (Basingstoke and New York: Palgrave Macmillan, 2016).

Merlock Jackson, Kathy (ed.). *Walt Disney: Conversations* (Jackson: University Press of Mississippi, 2006), pp. 89–103.

Mihailova, Misha. 'Collaboration without Representation: Labor Issues in Motion and Performance Capture', *animation: an interdisciplinary journal*, vol. 11, no. 1 (February 2016): 40–58.

Montgomery, Colleen. 'Woody's Roundup and WALL-E's Wunderkammer: Technophilia and Nostalgia in Pixar Animation', *Animation Studies Online Journal*, no. 6, 2011. https://journal.animationstudies.org/colleen-montgomery-woodys-roundup-and-walles-wunderkammer/ (accessed 20 April 2017).

Murphy, Ryan. 'The Kids Are All Right', *Entertainment Weekly*, 16 April 1993, unpaginated.

Myers, Scott. 'GITS Q&A Part 3: Mary Coleman (Pixar)', *Go into the Story: Official Screenwriting Blog of the Black List*, 29 February 2012. http://gointothestory.blcklst.com/2012/02/gits-qa-part-3-mary-coleman-pixar.html (accessed 29 August 2016).

Neupert, Richard, *John Lasseter: Contemporary Film Directors* (Urbana: University of Illinois Press, 2016).

'New Plan to Put Warners in Family Way', *Variety*, 9 December 1991, pp. 1, 3.

Niffenegger, Audrey. *The Time Traveller's Wife* (New York: Scribner, 2003).

Oglesby, Les. *C. G. Jung and Hans Urs Von Balthasar: God and Evil – A Critical Comparison* (Routledge, East Sussex, 2014).

Orr, Christopher. '*Wreck-It Ralph* Aims for Pixar . . .. and Misses', *The Atlantic*, 2 November 2012. http://www.theatlantic.com/entertainment/archive/2012/11/wreck-it-ralph-aims-for-pixar-and-misses/264439/ (accessed 22 May 2016).

'Overview: Preparing to Apply', *Disney Cruise Line/Disney Careers*. http://dcl.disneycareers.com/en/prepare-to-apply/overview/ (accessed 20 April 2017).

Paik, Karen. *To Infinity and Beyond: The Story of Pixar Animation Studios* (San Francisco: Chronicle Books, 2007).

Pallant, Chris. *Demystifying Disney: A History of Disney Feature Animation* (London: Continuum, 2011).

Pallant, Chris. 'Digital Dimensions in Actorly Performance: The Aesthetic Potential of Performance Capture', *Film International*, no. 57 (2012): 37–49.

Pallant, Chris and Steven Price. *Storyboarding: A Critical History* (New York: Palgrave Macmillan, 2015).

Pascale, Amy. *Joss Whedon: The Biography* (Chicago: Chicago Review Press, 2014).

Perkins, Victor. 'Film Authorship: The Premature Burial', *CineAction* no. 21/22 (November, 1990): 57–64.

Persall, Steve. 'A True Treasure from the Toy Box', *The St Petersburg Times*, 24 November 1995, p. 3.

Pessoa, Fernando. *The Book of Disquiet* (London: Penguin Modern Classics, 2015).

'Pixar Movies at the Box Office', *Box Office Mojo*. http://www.boxofficemojo.com/franchises/chart/?id=pixar.htm (accessed 28 August 2016).

Plantinga, Carl. *Moving Viewers: American Film and the Spectator's Experience* (Berkeley: University of California Press, 2009), pp. 21–25.

Porter, Tom. 'Creating Lifelike Characters in *Toy Story*', *ACM SIGART Bulletin*, vol. 8, nos. 1–4 (1997): 10–14 (p. 14).

Portman, Jamie. '*Toy Story* Is Success Story for Disney', *The Gazette*, 21 December 1995, p. D5.

Price, David A. *The Pixar Touch: The Making of a Company* (New York: Vintage, 2009).

Prince, Stephen. *Digital Visual Effects in Cinema: The Seduction of Reality* (New Jersey: Rutgers University Press, 2012).

Proschan, Frank. 'The Semiotic Study of Puppets, Masks, and Performing Objects', *Semiotica*, no. 47 (1981): 1–4.

Proschan, Frank. 'Puppet Voices and Interlocutors: Language in Folk Puppetry', *The Journal of American Folklore*, vol. 94, no. 374 (October–December 1981): 527–55.

Purse, Lisa. 'Digital Heroes in Contemporary Hollywood: Exertion, Identification, and the Virtual Action Body', *Film Criticism*, vol. 31, no. 1 (2007): 5–25.

Rea, Steven. 'An Adventure in Animation That's Dazzling', *The Philadelphia Enquirer*, 22 November 1995, p. C1.

Riffaterre, Michael. 'Compulsory Reader Response: The Intertextual Drive', in Michael Worton and Judith Still (eds), *Intertextuality: Theories and Practices* (Manchester: Manchester University Press, 1990), pp. 56–78.

Riva, Massimo. 'Beyond the Mechanical Body: Digital Pinochio', in Katia Pizzi (ed.), *Pinocchio, Puppets, and Modernity: The Mechanical Body* (New York and London: Routledge, 2012), pp. 201–14.

Rose, Simon. 'Talk of the Toon', *The Daily Mirror*, 21 March 1996, p. 3.

Rösing, Lilian Munk. *Pixar with Lacan: The Hysteric's Guide to Animation* (London and New York: Bloomsbury Academic, 2016).

Royle, Nicholas. *The Uncanny* (Manchester: Manchester University Press, 2003).

Rubin, Michael. *Droidmaker: George Lucas and the Digital Revolution* (Gainesville, FL: Triad, 2006).

Ryzik, Melena. 'Animation Advocacy, Pixar Style', *The New York Times*, 9 February 2011). http://www.nytimes.com/2011/02/10/movies/awardsseason/10bagger.html?_r=0 (accessed 18 March 2017).

Schaffer, William. 'The Importance of Being Plastic: The Feel of Pixar', *Animation Journal*, no. 12 (2004): 72–95.

Schickel, Richard. Review of *Toy Story 2*, *Time*, 29 November 1999, unpaginated.

Schweitzer, Marlis and Joanne Zerdy. *Performing Objects and Theatrical Things* (London: Palgrave Macmillan, 2014).

Scott, A. O. 'Voyage to the Bottom of the Day Care Center', *The New York Times*, 17 June 2010. http://www.nytimes.com/2010/06/18/movies/18toy.html (accessed 18 May 2015).

Scott, Ellen. 'Agony and Avoidance: Pixar, Deniability and the Adult Spectator', *Journal of Popular Film and Television* vol. 42, no. 3 (2014): 150–62.

Scott, Sanders, 'Disney Cruise Line's *Toy Story* – The Musical Aboard the Disney Wonder Closing in 2016 [Updated]' (posted 24 November 2015), *Disney Cruise Line Blog*. http://disneycruiselineblog.com/2015/11/disney-cruise-lines-toy-story-musical-aboard-disney-wonder-closing-2016/ (accessed 20 April 2017).

Searls, Colette. 'Unholy Alliances and Harmonious Hybrids: New Fusions in Puppetry and Animation', in Dassia N. Posner, Claudia Orenstein and John Bell (eds), *The Routledge Companion to Puppetry and Material Performance* (New York and London: Routledge, 2014), pp. 294–307.

Seiter, Ellen. *Sold Separately: Children and Parents in Consumer Culture* (New Brunswick: Rutgers University Press, 1995), pp. 130–31.

Smith, Alvy Ray. 'Digital Humans Wait in the Wings', *Scientific American*, vol. 1, no. 13 (2000): 72–76.

Smith, Susan. 'The Animated Film Musical', in Raymond Knapp, Mitchell Morris and Stacy Wolf (eds), *The Oxford Handbook of the American Musical* (Oxford and New York: Oxford University Press, 2011), pp. 167–78.

Sobchack, Vivian. *Carnal Thoughts: Embodiment and Moving Image Culture* (Berkeley: University of California Press, 2004).

Sodaro, Robert J. and Alex G. Malloy. *Kiddie Meal Collectibles* (Iola, Wisconsin: Krause, 2001).

Sokolow, Alec and Tony Camin. 'The God of Story: An Interview with Robert McKee', *VICE*, 1 July 2014. http://www.vice.com/read/the-god-of-story-0000339-v21n6 (accessed 29 August 2016).

Solomon, Charles. *The Art of Toy Story 3* (San Francisco: Chronicle Books, 2010).

Solomon, Charles. *The Toy Story Films: An Animated Journey* (New York: Disney Editions, 2012).

Sperb, Jason. *Flickers of Film: Nostalgia in the Time of Digital Cinema* (New Jersey: Rutgers University Press, 2016).

Spottiswoode, Roger et al. *48 Hrs*. Undated Script (USA: Paramount, n.d.), unpublished screenplay. http://www.dailyscript.com/scripts/48hours.html (accessed 30 August 2016).

Stafford, David and Caroline Stafford. *Maybe I'm Doing It Wrong: The Life & Music of Randy Newman* (London: Omnibus Press, 2016).

Stanton, Andrew. 'The Clues to a Great Story', TED: Ideas worth Spreading, 2012. https://www.ted.com/talks/andrew_stanton_the_clues_to_a_great_story?language=en (accessed 28 August 2016).

Staskiewicz, Keith. 'Movies: *Wreck-It Ralph*', *Entertainment Weekly*, 9 November 2012. http://www.ew.com/article/2012/11/09/wreck-it-ralph (accessed 22 May 2016).

Stewart, James B. *Disneywar: The Battle for the Magic Kingdom* (New York: Simon & Schuster, 2005).

Stilwell, Robynn J. 'The Fantastical Gap between Diegetic and Nondiegetic', in Daniel Goldmark et al. (eds), *Beyond the Soundtrack: Representing Music in Cinema* (Berkeley and Los Angeles: University of California Press, 2007), pp. 184–204.

Tankersley, Holley. '"What Is Family?" Defining the Terms of the U.S. Welfare State', in Dennis Wiseman (ed.), *The American Family – Understanding Its Changing Dynamics and Place in Society* (Illinois: Charles C Thomas, 2008), pp. 21–38.

Tillis, Steve. *Toward an Aesthetics of the Puppet: Puppetry as a Theatrical Art* (New York: Greenwood Press, 1992).

Tillis, Steve. 'The Art of Puppetry in the Age of Media Production', in John Bell (ed.), *Puppets, Masks and Performing Objects* (New York: New York University and Massachusetts Institute of Technology, 2001), pp. 172–85.

'The *Toy Story* Effect: How the Film Franchise Has Increased Toy Sales', *Hollywood Branded*, 17 November 2014. https://www.hollywoodbranded.com/toy-story-effect-how-film-franchise-increased-toy-sales/ (accessed 4 September 2016).

Toy Story press book (Disney: 1995), p. 13; in the press clippings collection of the Deutsche Filminstitut, housed at the Deutsche Nationalbibliothek, Frankfurt am Main, Germany.

'*Toy Story* – The Musical', *DIS* website. https://www.wdwinfo.com/wdwinfo/cruise-new/ToyStoryMusical.htm (accessed 20 April 2017).

'*Treasure Planet*', *Time Out*, 23 June 2006. http://www.timeout.com/us/film/treasure-planet (accessed 22 May 2016).
Turkle, Sherry (ed.). *Evocative Objects: Things We Think with* (Cambridge, Massachusetts and London: MIT Press, 2007).
von Frantz, Marie Louise, 'The Process of Individuation', in Carl Jung (ed.), *Man and His Symbols* (London: Penguin, 1978), pp. 157–254.
Wakefield, Thirza, 'Review: *Brave*', *Sight and Sound*, vol. 22, no. 9 (2012).
Wasko, Janet. *Understanding Disney: The Manufacture of Fantasy* (Oxford: Polity, 2001).
Watts, Steven. *The Magic Kingdom: Walt Disney and the American Way of Life* (Columbia: University of Missouri Press, 1997).
Waxman, Sharon. 'Study Finds Film Ratings Are Growing More Lenient', *The New York Times*, 14 July 2004, p. E1.
Weinraub, Bernard. 'Fun for the Family Is No Longer "Pollyanna"', *The New York Times*, 22 July 1997, pp. C9.
Weinstein, David. 'Of Mice and Bart: *The Simpsons* and the Postmodern', in Cristina Degli-Esposti (ed.), *Postmodernism in the Cinema* (New York and Oxford: Bergahn, 1998), pp. 61–72.
Wells, Paul. *Understanding Animation* (London and New York: Routledge, 1998).
Wells, Paul. *Animation and America* (Edinburgh: Edinburgh University Press, 2002).
Wells, Paul. *Animation: Genre and Authorship* (London: Wallflower Press, 2002).
Wells, Paul. *The Fundamentals of Animation* (Lausanne: AVA, 2006).
Wells, Paul. 'To Sonicity and Beyond! Gary Rydstrom and Quilting the Pixar Sound', *Animation Journal* (2009): 23–35.
Wells, Paul. 'From "Sunnyside" to "Soccer": Reading upon Animation . . .', *Animation in Practice, Process and Production*, vol. 1, no. 1 (2011): 3–9.
Wells, Paul. 'Chairy Tales: Object and Materiality in Animation', *Alphaville: Journal of Film and Screen Media*, vol. 8 (2014). http://www.alphavillejournal.com/Issue8/HTML/ArticleWells.html (accessed 18 April 2017).
Westbrook, Caroline. '*Toy Story* Review', *Empire*, 1 January 2000. http://www.empireonline.com/movies/toy-story/review/ (accessed 15 April 2016).
Wetmore Jr., Kevin J. '"Great Reckonings in Little Rooms", or Children's Playtime: Shakespeare and Performing Object Theatre of Toys', in Jennifer Hulbert, Kevin J. Wetmore Jr. and Robert L. York (eds), *Shakespeare and Youth Culture* (New York: Palgrave Macmillan, 2006), pp. 43–56.
Whedon, Joss et al. *Toy Story* Final Draft Script (Pixar Animation Studios/Walt Disney Animation, 1995) http://www.pages.drexel.edu/~ina22/splaylib/Screenplay-Toy_Story.pdf.
Wilkie-Stibbs, Christine. 'Intertextuality and the Child Reader', in Peter Hunt (ed.), *Understanding Children's Literature* (London: Taylor & Francis, 2005), pp. 168–79.
Williams, Linda Ruth. '*Toy Story*', in Linda Ruth Williams and Michael Hammond (eds), *Contemporary American Cinema* (Berkshire: Open University Press, 2006), pp. 369–75.
Willis, Susan. 'Imagining Dinosaurs', in Beverly Clark (ed.), *Girls, Boys, Books, Toys: Gender in Children's Literature and Culture* (Baltimore: John Hopkins University Press, 2000), pp. 183–95.
Winkler, Peter. 'Randy Newman's Americana', *Popular Music* vol. 7, no. 1 (1987): 1–26, reprinted in Richard Middleton (ed.), *Reading Pop: Approaches to Textual*

Analysis in Popular Music (Oxford and New York: Oxford University Press, 2000), pp. 27–57.

Winnicott, D. W. *Playing and Reality* (London: Routledge, 2005).

Wise, Damon. 'Buzz, Woody . . . and Barbie Plays Too', *The Observer*, 5 December 1999. https://www.theguardian.com/film/1999/dec/05/2 (accessed 4 September 2016).

Witchel, Alex. 'Talking Toys With: Betty James; Persevering for Family and Slinky', *The New York Times*, 21 February 1996. http://www.nytimes.com/1996/02/21/garden/talking-toys-with-betty-james-persevering-for-family-and-slinky.html (accessed 4 September 2016).

Wood, Aylish. *Software, Animation and the Moving Image: What's in the Box* (Basingstoke: Palgrave Macmillan, 2015).

Wooden, Shannon R. and Ken Gillam, *Pixar's Boy Stories: Masculinity in a Postmodern Age* (Lanham: Rowman and Littlefield, 2014).

Yates, Christopher S. 'A Phenomenological Aesthetic of Cinematic "Worlds"', *Contemporary Aesthetics*, no. 4 (2006). http://www.contempaesthetics.org/newvolume/pages/article.php?articleID=394 (accessed 08 January 2013).

Zaretsky, Natasha. *No Direction Home: The American Family and the Fear of National Decline, 1968–1980* (North Carolina: University of North Carolina Press, 2007).

Zinoman, Jason. 'Robert Mckee's Unconvincing Story', *Vanity Fair: The Hive*, December 2009. http://www.vanityfair.com/news/2009/11/robert-mckee-200911 (accessed 30 August 2016).

Zipes, Jack. 'Once upon a Time beyond Disney: Contemporary Fairy-Tale Films for Children', in Cary Bazalgette and David Buckingham (eds), *In Front of the Children: Screen Entertainment and Young Audiences* (London: British Film Institute, 1995), pp. 109–26

Zipes, Jack. *The Enchanted Screen: The Unknown History of Fairy-Tale Films* (New York: Routledge, 2011).

FILMOGRAPHY

48 Hrs. (1982), [Film] Dir. Walter Hill, USA: Paramount Pictures.
A Bug's Life (1998), [Film] Dir. John Lasseter, USA: Walt Disney Pictures.
A Walk in the Black Forest (1969), [Film] Dir. Steve Segal, USA: Independent.
Adaptation (2002), [Film] Dir. Spike Jonze, USA: Columbia Pictures.
Adventures of André and Wally B., The (1984), [Film] Dir. Alvy Ray Smith, USA: Lucasfilm.
Aladdin (1992), [Film] Dirs. Ron Clements and John Musker, USA: Walt Disney Pictures.
Avatar (2009), [Film] Dir. James Cameron, USA: 20th Century Fox.
Back to the Future (1985), [Film] Dir. Robert Zemeckis, USA: Universal Pictures.
Bambi (1942), [Film] Dirs. David Hand et al., USA: Walt Disney Pictures.
Beauty and the Beast (1991), [Film] Dirs. Gary Trousdale and Kirk Wise, USA: Walt Disney Pictures.
BFG, The (2016), [Film] Dir. Steven Spielberg, USA: Walt Disney Pictures.
Brave (2012), [Film] Dirs. Mark Andrews and Brenda Chapman, USA: Walt Disney Pictures.
Brave Little Toaster, The (1987), [Film] Dir. Jerry Rees, USA: Hyperion Pictures.
Cars (2006), [Film] Dir. John Lasseter, USA: Walt Disney Pictures.
Cars 2 (2011), [Film] Dir. John Lasseter and Brad Lewis, USA: Walt Disney Pictures.
Close Encounters of the Third Kind (1977), [Film] Dir. Steven Spielberg, USA: Columbia Pictures.
Crow, The (1994), [Film] Dir. Alex Proyas, USA: Miramax Films.
Curious Case of Benjamin Button, The (2008), [Film] Dir. David Fincher, USA: Paramount Pictures.
Dance of the Stumblers (1987), [Film] Dir. Steve Segal, USA; Independent.
David Copperfield (1935), [Film] Dir. George Cuko, USA. Metro-Goldwyn Mayer.
Dawn of the Planet of the Apes (2014), [Film] Dir. Matt Reeves, USA: 20th Century Fox.
Day & Night (2010), [Film] Dir. Teddy Newton, USA: Walt Disney Pictures.
Defiant Ones, The (1958), [Film] Dir. Stanley Kramer, USA: United Artists.
Deliverance (1972), [Film] Dir. John Boorman, USA: Warner Bros.
Despicable Me (2010), [Film] Dirs. Pierre Coffin and Chris Renaud, USA: Universal Pictures
Despicable Me 2 (2013), [Film] Dirs. Pierre Coffin and Chris Renaud, USA: Universal Pictures.
Dumbo (1941), [Film] Dirs. Ben Sharpsteen et al., USA: Walt Disney Pictures.
Enchanted (2007), [Film] Dir. Kevin Lima, USA: Walt Disney Pictures.
E.T. The Extra-Terrestrial (1982), [Film] Dir. Steven Spielberg, USA: Universal Pictures.
Evolution (1968), [Film] Dir. Steve Segal, USA: Independent.
Exorcist, The (1973, [Film] Dir. William Friedkin, USA: Warner Bros.
Fantasia (1940), [Film] Dirs. Samuel Armstrong et al., USA: Walt Disney Pictures.

Fat Feet (1966), [Film] Dir. Red Grooms, USA: Independent.
Finding Dory (2016), [Film] Dir. Andrew Stanton, USA: Walt Disney Pictures.
Finding Nemo (2003), [Film] Dir. Andrew Stanton, USA: Walt Disney Pictures.
Forbidden Planet (1956), [Film] Dir. Fred M. Wilcox, USA: Metro-Goldwyn-Mayer.
Freaks (1932), [Film] Dir. Tod Browning, USA: Metro-Goldwyn-Mayer.
Frozen (2013), [Film] Dirs. Chris Buck and Jennifer Lee, USA: Walt Disney Pictures.
Futuropolis (1984), [Film] Dirs. Steve Segal and Phil Trumbo, USA: Independent.
Geri's Game (1997), [Film] Dir. Jan Pinkava, USA: Walt Disney Pictures.
Gladiator (2000), [Film] Dir. Ridley Scott, USA: DreamWorks Pictures.
Good Dinosaur, The (2015), [Film] Dir. Peter Sohn, USA: Walt Disney Pictures.
Grease (1978), [Film] Dir. Randal Kleiser, USA: Paramount Pictures.
Happy Feet (2006), [Film] Dir. George Miller, Australia/USA: Warner Bros.
His Girl Friday (1940), [Film] Dir. Howard Hawks, USA: Columbia Pictures.
Hobbit: The Battle of the Five Armies, The (2014), [Film] Dir. Peter Jackson, USA: Warner Bros.
Hobbit: The Desolation of Smaug, The (2013), [Film] Dir. Peter Jackson, USA: Warner Bros.
Hobbit: An Unexpected Journey, The (2012), [Film] Dir. Peter Jackson, USA: Warner Bros.
Home on the Range (2004), [Film] Dir. Will Finn, USA: Walt Disney Pictures.
Hunchback of Notre Dame, The (1996), [Film] Dirs. Gary Trousdale and Kirk Wise, USA: Walt Disney Pictures.
Ice Age (2002), [Film] Dir. Mike Thurmeier, USA: 20th Century Fox.
Incredibles, The (2004), [Film] Dir. Brad Bird, USA: Walt Disney Pictures.
Independence Day (1996), [Film] Dir. Roland Emmerich, USA: 20th Century Fox.
Indiana Jones and the Temple of Doom (1984), [Film] Dir. Steven Spielberg, USA: Paramount Pictures.
Inside Out (2015), [Film] Dir. Pete Docter, USA: Walt Disney Pictures.
Jurassic Park (1993), [Film] Dir. Steven Spielberg, USA: Universal Pictures.
Jurassic World (2015), [Film] Dir. Colin Trevorrow, USA: Universal Pictures.
King Kong (2005), [Film] Dir. Peter Jackson, USA: Universal Pictures.
La Luna (2011), [Film] Dir. Enrico Casarosa, USA: Walt Disney Pictures.
Life in the Freezer (1993), [TV] Presented by David Attenborough, UK: BBC.
Lion King, The (1994), [Film] Dirs. Roger Allers and Rob Minkoff, USA: Walt Disney Pictures.
Little Mermaid, The (1989), [Film] Dir. Ron Clements and John Musker, USA: Walt Disney Pictures.
Little Princess, The (1939), [Film] Dir. Walter Lang, USA: 20th Century Fox.
Little Women (1933), [Film] Dir. George Cukor, USA: RKO Radio Pictures.
Lord of the Rings: The Fellowship of the Ring, The (2001), [Film] Dir. Peter Jackson, USA: New Line Cinema.
Lord of the Rings: The Two Towers, The (2002), [Film] Dir. Peter Jackson, USA: New Line Cinema.
Lord of the Rings: The Return of the King, The (2003), [Film] Dir. Peter Jackson, USA: New Line Cinema.
Luxo, Jr. (1986), [Film] Dir. John Lasseter, USA: Pixar.
Make Mine Music (1946), [Film] Dir. Jack Kinney et al., USA: Walt Disney Pictures.
Maleficent (2014), [Film] Dir. Robert Stromberg, USA: Walt Disney Pictures.

March of the Penguins (2005), [Film] Dir. Luc Jacquet, France: Buena Vista International.
Mary Poppins (1964), [Film] Dir. Robert Stevenson, USA: Walt Disney Pictures.
Melody Time (1948), [Film] Dirs. Jack Kinney et al., USA: Walt Disney Pictures.
Men in Black (1997), [Film] Dir. Barry Sonnenfeld, USA: Columbia Pictures.
Midnight Run (1988), [Film] Dir. Martin Brest, USA: Universal Pictures.
Minions (2015), [Film] Dirs. Kyle Balda and Pierre Coffin, USA: Universal Pictures.
Moana (2016), [Film] Dirs. Ron Clements and John Musker, USA: Walt Disney Pictures.
Monster Monster (1972), [Film] Dir. Steve Segal and Phil Trumbo, USA: Independent.
Monsters University (2013), [Film] Dir. Dan Scanlon, USA: Walt Disney Pictures.
Monsters, Inc. (2001), [Film] Dir. Pete Docter, USA: Walt Disney Pictures.
Mrs. Doubtfire (1993), [Film] Dir. Chris Columbus, USA: 20th Century Fox.
Neon Genesis Evangelion (1995–96), [TV] Dir. Hideaki Anno, Japan: Gainax.
Nutty Professor, The (1996), [Film] Dir. Tom Shadyac, USA: Universal Pictures.
Odd Couple, The (1968), [Film] Dir. Gene Saks, USA: Paramount Pictures.
Pagemaster, The (1994), [Film] Dirs. Joe Johnston and Maurice Hunt, USA: 20th Century Fox.
Pandora's Box (1972), [Film] Dir. Steve Segal, USA: Independent.
Pee-wee's Playhouse (1986–91), [TV] USA: CBS.
Pirates! In an Adventure with Scientists, The (2012), [Film] Dir. Peter Lord, UK/USA: Columbia Pictures.
Pinocchio (1940), [Film] Dirs. Ben Sharpsteen et al., USA: Walt Disney Pictures.
Pocahontas (1995), [Film] Dirs. Mike Gabriel and Eric Goldberg, USA: Walt Disney Pictures.
Princess and the Frog, The (2009), [Film] Dirs. Ron Clements and John Musker, USA: Walt Disney Pictures.
Raiders of the Lost Ark (1981), [Film] Dir. Steven Spielberg, USA: Paramount Pictures.
Ratatouille (2007), [Film] Dir. Brad Bird, USA: Walt Disney Pictures.
Real Steel (2011), [Film] Dir. Shawn Levy, USA: DreamWorks Pictures.
Red Ball Express (1975), [Film] Dir. Steve Segal, USA: Independent.
Return of Jafar, The (1994), [Film] Dir. Tad Stones, USA: Walt Disney Pictures.
Rise of the Planet of the Apes (2011), [Film] Dir. Rupert Wyatt, USA: 20th Century Fox.
Rio (2011) [Film] Dir. Carlos Saldanha, USA: 20th Century Fox.
Robots (2005) [Film] Dir. Chris Wedge, USA: 20th Century Fox.
Russian Rooster (1974), [Film] Dir. Steve Segal, USA: Independent.
Saturday Night Fever (1977), [Film] Dir. John Badham, USA: Paramount Pictures.
Seinfeld (1989–98), [TV] USA: Columbia TriStar Television.
Short Circuit (1986), [Film] Dir. John Badham, USA: TriStar Pictures.
Shining, The (1980), [Film] Dir. Stanley Kubrick, USA: Warner Bros.
Shrek (2001), [Film] Dirs. Andrew Adamson and Vicky Jenson, USA: DreamWorks Pictures.
Simpsons, The (1989–), [TV] USA: 20th Century Fox Television.
Sixth Sense, The (1999), [Film] Dir. M. Night Shyamalan, USA: Buena Vista Pictures.
Snow White and the Seven Dwarfs (1937), [Film] Dirs. David Hand et al., USA: Walt Disney Pictures.
Spider-Man 3 (2007), [Film] Dir. Sam Raimi, USA: Columbia Pictures.
Star Trek II: The Wrath of Khan (1982), [Film] Dir. Nicholas Meyer, USA: Paramount Pictures.

Star Wars (1977), [Film] Dir. George Lucas, USA: 20th Century Fox.
Star Wars: The Empire Strikes Back (1980), [Film] Dir. Irvin Kershner, USA: 20th Century Fox.
Star Wars: The Force Awakens (2015), [Film] Dir. J. J. Abrams, USA: Walt Disney Pictures.
Star Wars: Return of the Jedi (1983), [Film] Dir. Richard Marquand, USA: 20th Century Fox.
Superman (1978), [Film] Dir. Richard Donner, USA: Warner Bros.
Superman II (1980), [Film] Dir. Richard Lester, USA: Warner Bros.
Swan Princess, The (1994), [Film] Dir. Richard Rich, USA: New Line Cinema.
Tarzan (1999), [Film] Dirs. Kevin Lima and Chris Buck, USA: Walt Disney Pictures.
Terminator 2: Judgment Day (1991), [Film] Dir. James Cameron, USA: TriStar Pictures.
Thelma & Louise (1991), [Film] Dir. Ridley Scott, USA: Metro-Goldwyn-Mayer.
Time Machine, The (1960), [Film] Dir. George Pal, USA: Metro-Goldwyn-Mayer.
Tin Toy (1988), [Film] Dir. John Lasseter, USA: Pixar.
Transformers, The (1984–87), [TV] USA: Hasbro Studios.
Toy Story (1995), [Film] Dir. John Lasseter, USA: Walt Disney Pictures.
Toy Story 2 (1999), [Film] Dir. John Lasseter, USA: Walt Disney Pictures.
Toy Story 3 (2010), [Film] Dir. Lee Unkrich, USA: Walt Disney Pictures.
Toy Story of Terror (2013), [TV] Dir. Angus Maclane, USA: Disney-ABC.
Toy Story That Time Forgot (2014), [TV] Dir. Steve Purcell, USA: Disney-ABC.
Treasure Planet (2002), [Film] Dir. Ron Clements and John Musker, USA: Walt Disney Pictures.
Tron (1982), [Film] Dir. Steven Lisberger, USA: Walt Disney Pictures.
Tron: Legacy (2010), [Film] Dir. Joseph Kosinksi, USA: Walt Disney Pictures.
Up (2009), [Film] Dir. Pete Docter, USA: Walt Disney Pictures.
WALL-E (2008), [Film] Dir. Andrew Stanton, USA: Walt Disney Pictures.
WarGames (1983), [Film] Dir. John Badham, USA: Metro-Goldwyn-Mayer.
Who Framed Roger Rabbit (1988), [Film] Dir. Robert Zemeckis, USA: Touchstone Pictures.
Wizard of Oz, The (1939), [Film] Dir. Victor Fleming, USA: Metro-Goldwin-Mayer.
Woody Woodpecker Show, The (1957–58), [TV] USA: NBCUniversal.
Wreck It Ralph (2012), [Film] Dir. Rich Moore, USA: Walt Disney Pictures.
Zootopia (2016), [Film] Dirs. Byron Howard and Rich Moore, USA: Walt Disney Pictures.

CONTRIBUTORS

Jane Batkin is a Senior Lecturer and joint programme leader of the BA (Hons) Animation programme at the University of Lincoln, where she tutors on the dissertation and critical studies modules on animation and media. Her book *Identity in Animation: A Journey into Self, Difference, Culture and the Body* was published in February 2017 and she has had a paper published in the Society for Animation Studies journal on Looney Tunes and culture, titled 'Rethinking the Rabbit'.

Noel Brown is a Lecturer in Media and Communication at Liverpool Hope University. He has published widely on British and Hollywood cinema history, particularly in relation to children's films, family entertainment and animation. He is the author of the forthcoming *Contemporary Hollywood Animation*; his previous books include *The Children's Film: Genre, Nation and Narrative* (2017), *British Children's Cinema: From The Thief of Bagdad to Wallace and Gromit* (2016) and *The Hollywood Family Film: A History, from Shirley Temple to Harry Potter* (2012), and, as co-editor (with Bruce Babington), *Family Films in Global Cinema: The World Beyond Disney* (2015). He also co-organized the *Toy Story at 20* conference.

Karen Cross is Senior Lecturer in Media and Communications in the Department of Media Culture and Language at the University of Roehampton, UK. She writes and teaches broadly on the topics of media and memory with a special focus on photography and screen cultures. Her recent research is especially interested in the role of the past and application of psychoanalytic perspectives to transitional spaces of online and digital media.

Lucy Fife Donaldson is Lecturer at the University of St Andrews and her research focuses on the materiality of style and the body in popular film and television. She is the author of *Texture in Film* (2014), and a member of the editorial board of *Movie: A Journal of Film Criticism*.

Andrew Gay is an independent filmmaker and Associate Professor of Digital Cinema at Southern Oregon University in Ashland, Oregon, where he teaches a range of courses in screenwriting, film production and creative entrepreneurship. He is also a programmer with the Ashland Independent Film Festival, and his current research interests include entrepreneurial screenwriting techniques and 360° video production for virtual reality.

Helen Haswell is completing her PhD on the studio narrative of Pixar Animation, at Queen's University Belfast. Her research focuses on the development of digital animation technology and its contemporary aesthetic, and Pixar's relationship with the Walt Disney Company and the impact of the 2006 Disney-Pixar merger. Her article 'To Infinity and Back Again: Hand-Drawn Aesthetic and Affection for the Past in Pixar's Pioneering Animation' was published in *Alphaville: Journal of Film and Screen Media* in January 2015 and was awarded the Screen Annette Kuhn Essay Award in 2016.

Heather L. Holian is an Associate Professor of Art History, teaching classes on the art of early modern Europe, Disney and Pixar at the University of North Carolina in Greensboro. Her current research interests include the art, artists and collaborative process of Pixar, which is the subject of her forthcoming book to be published by Disney Editions, and tentatively titled, *Art and Filmmaking at Pixar: Collaboration, Inspiration and Collective Imagination.* Holian's animation scholarship has appeared in edited volumes for McFarland, Cambridge Scholars (forthcoming 2018), and the *Animation Studies* journal. Holian has also published studies on the Italian Renaissance, her doctoral field.

Christopher Holliday is a Teaching Fellow in Film Studies at King's College London specializing in film genre, international film history and contemporary digital media/animation. He has published several book chapters and articles on animation, including work that examines child voice acting in computer-animated films and representations of the animated house. More recently, he has published articles on contemporary digital animation in *Animation Practice, Process & Production* and *animation: an interdisciplinary journal.* He is currently writing a monograph on style and genre in the computer-animated film, and is co-editing a collection of essays that examines the intersection between fantasy and animation.

Peter Krämer is a Senior Lecturer in Film Studies at the University of East Anglia, Norwich, UK. He has published more than 70 essays on American film and media history, and on the relationship between Hollywood and Europe, in academic journals and edited collections. He is the author and co-editor of eight academic books, including, most recently, a BFI Film Classic on *The General* (2016) and *Stanley Kubrick: New Perspectives* (2015). He also co-wrote a book for children titled *American Film: An A-Z Guide* (2003).

Susan Smith is Reader in Film Studies at the University of Sunderland, UK. She has long-standing research interests in stardom and performance, tone and emotion in cinema, children's films, the musical and thriller genres, and has become increasingly preoccupied with animation, especially as this intersects with her other specialisms. She is author of *Elizabeth Taylor* (2012), *Voices in Film* (2007), *The Musical: Race, Gender and Performance* (2005) and

Hitchcock: Suspense, Humour and Tone (2000). In recent years, she has co-organized the *Toy Story at 20* (2015) and *Child Actors/Child Stars: Juvenile Performance on Screen* (2011) conferences. She co-edited a Child Performance Dossier for *Screen* (2012) and is co-editor of the BFI/Palgrave's 'Film Stars' series.

Sam Summers is a PhD candidate at University of Sunderland's Centre for Research in Media and Cultural Studies. His research focuses on intertextuality in contemporary animation in general and DreamWorks' animation in particular, with a view to contextualizing and historicizing the studio's role in the development of the medium. He has also produced work on star studies and transmedia storytelling, organized the *Contemporary Children's Media* symposium (2016) and co-organized the *Toy Story at 20* conference (2015).

Paul Wells is Professor of Animation and Director of the Animation Academy, Loughborough University, UK, and Chair of the Association of British Animation Collections. He has published widely in Animation Studies, including *Animation, Sport & Culture* (2014), and is an established writer and director for film, TV, theatre and radio. He is currently completing *Screenwriting for Animation*, a collection of short stories, and a gallery exhibition on 'Animation and Sport'.

INDEX

Made in the USA
Las Vegas, NV
19 September 2026

c3771a64-22c3-4658-a6f9-7203764c174aR01